D1246920

THE REAL ESTATE GAME

The Intelligent Guide to Decision-Making and Investment

William J. Poorvu
with
Jeffrey L. Cruikshank

THE FREE PRESS

THE FREE PRESS
A Division of Simon & Schuster Inc.
1230 Avenue of the Americas
New York, NY 10020

Designed by MM Design 2000, Inc.

Manufactured in the United States of America

10 9 8 7 6 5 4

Library of Congress Cataloging-in-Publication Data

Poorvu, William J., 1935–

The real estate game : the intelligent guide to decision-making and investment / William J. Poorvu with Jeffrey L. Cruikshank.

p. cm.

Includes index.

1. Real estate business. 2. Real estate investment—Decision making. I. Cruikshank, Jeffrey L. II. Title.

HD1375.P6643 1999

333.33—dc21 99-32272

CIP

ISBN 0–684–85550–X

ACKNOWLEDGMENTS

THE main direction and focus for this book came from a meeting that Jeff Cruikshank and I had with Paula Duffy and Maria Arteta of The Free Press. Paula and Maria suggested that the book summarize what I had been teaching to thousands of Harvard Business School students over the course of many years.

This turned out to be a bigger challenge than I expected. I began by reflecting on the myriad of cases that I had either written or led discussions of in the classroom. It seemed to me that, collectively, the cases provided a good background for understanding how to evaluate, develop, and operate various kinds of properties, as well as a good grounding in the workings of the financial markets that are so important to the property world.

My book would certainly have to cover these subjects. But many good books had already been written along these lines, and the world probably didn't need another one. So what else might there be to write about?

After lots more reflection, I decided that the answer was *people.* How do real estate practitioners really think, and act, and why? What prompts them to engage in what might look like illogical (even irrational!) behavior? How do they think about value creation—for themselves and for the broader society? How do they actually *manage?*

These were major themes in most of the cases that I had written and taught over the years. The cases more or less successfully captured many of the human complexities inherent in real business situations. I decided that I would let these human stories drive my book.

I also decided that I would augment stories from these cases with examples from my own career and from the careers of my friends in and around the real estate industry. For this reason, the book has become much more personal than I anticipated. The reader may decide that this is for the good or not for the good. But it was the only way I could think of to produce a manuscript that wrestled with complexity—important both for the novice to the real estate field and for the seasoned professional.

Let me move on to the formal process of acknowledgment. I was struck by a statement made last spring by Daniel Schorr, senior correspondent on National Public Radio. He said, in so many words, that when you reach a certain stage and stature in life, you are entitled to listen to what your colleagues say, turn it over in your mind, and then repeat it in your own words. I should confess here that I've been using this approach for many, many years.

For example: For more than twenty-five years, I've been engaged in a running debate with my Harvard Business School colleague Howard Stevenson about the most effective conceptual framework to use in describing the multifunctional, multidisciplinary, entrepreneurial world of real estate. I first taught with Howard, and I owe him a great deal. Subsequent coteachers, especially John Vogel, Don Brown, and now Arthur Segel, have contributed their ideas, experiences, and cases—not only to the course, but also to this book. Harvard has generously provided me with a series of skilled research assistants, of whom I'd like to mention two. The first is Elizabeth McLoughlin, who has experienced triple jeopardy by working with me three times in her career. The other is Dan Rudd, my current assistant, who contributed hugely to Appendix A, the Note on Property Types, and the glossary.

It is never easy to teach a specialized, industry-driven course like real estate. (Most other single-industry courses of study have long since left academia.) As a result, many talented individuals have gone back and forth between being practitioners and being academics, and sometimes even do both at once. Included in this talented camp are Charles Field, Dorn McGrath, Mike Miles, Richard Peiser, Joel Peterson, and Ellen Shuman. Their comments on the manuscript have been very helpful, in part because they were so unvarnished. Yes, Mike, I do think I understand capitalization rates better now, and I do realize that you have been using the game metaphor to depict the real estate industry in your books. And Dorn, I probably should have placed more emphasis in this book on the importance of good planning and design, but I would say in my defense that there's more than there would have been if you *hadn't* lectured me on the subject.

Claude Ballard, John Foy, Sam Plimpton, and Will Zeckendorf have helped me in my narrative and also in my storytelling, setting me straight not only on some of the facts but also as to how some of the players were actually thinking. There were some interesting surprises in this review process: I wrote confidently about the sale of the land under Rockefeller Center by Columbia University; Claude Ballard corrected a few key facts and casually noted that it was he who put the deal together.

When I gave my good friend Seth Klarman a copy of the manuscript, he asked (with apparent glee) if he was expected to be "a real pain." I told him I expected nothing less. The result was an amazing line-by-line, thought-by-thought edit of the manuscript. Most of his edits are included in the following pages.

No one at Investment Resource Group, the real estate management company led by my son Jonathan, escaped involvement in this project. Jonathan, in particular, had dealt very well with my eccentricities (although he has had years of practice). As for Cathy Foley and Linda Kelly-Hayes—who run my corporate and academic lives, respectively—I can only say that neither Western Civilization nor this book would have happened without them. My wife Lia, my mother May, and my daughter Alison Jaffe continue to offer comments, advice, and support, and sometimes imbue me with a becoming sense of humility. They are crucial to my life.

Jeff Cruikshank, my coauthor, is principally responsible for making close to forty years of my experiences in the classroom and in practice come together in a more or less linear way between two covers. No easy task! His willingness to challenge my use of jargon, and sometimes even my deep insights, was crucial. I should also note here how much I appreciate his wife Ann's willingness to let Jeff attend working sessions on the Vineyard during the summer of 1998. Honest, Ann; we worked around the clock. Really.

These acknowledgments began with Paula Duffy and Maria Arteta at The Free Press, and I should also acknowledge Liz Maguire, Chad Conway, and other Free Press colleagues who helped get this book done and out.

Finally, to all those colleagues, students, and practitioners whom I have not mentioned but who have shared triumphs, heartaches, irritations, coups, and insights with me over the years, thank you. My education couldn't have gone so far, or been as much fun, without you.

Bill Poorvu
Cambridge, Massachusetts
May 1999

INTRODUCTION

THIS is a book about the real estate business, and how you can increase your chances of being successful in it. The book explains, in simple terms, how you can take advantage of emerging opportunities in the property market when the capital markets—and the world in general—are going through dramatic changes. It should help you whether you're buying a small apartment house, or are involved in a large, multi-use project.

The Real Estate Game uses the analogy of a game to capture some of the complex and unpredictable interactions of the real estate field; it also lays out the "rules" that shape the game. It identifies the key players, and how they play their parts. It also follows the game through the distinct stages of a property's life cycle, from the initial conception of a project to its "harvesting." It uses a series of recurring case studies to illustrate key points—and, I hope, to make the concepts more human and interesting by placing them in a practical, real-life context.

The book also draws on my experiences as a teacher and a practitioner in the field of real estate. For the past three decades, I've taught the real estate course at the Harvard Business School. This is an elective class for second-year students, which means that since they don't *have* to be there, they must have some enthusiasm for the field.

In the initial class session, I try to do two things with their enthusiasm. First, I try to temper it a bit. I tell them that real estate is *not* for everyone. If you want to be a passive coupon-clipper, real estate is not for you. If you're not interested in paying attention to a plethora of small but important details, in getting your hands dirty, in mixing it up with a wide range of people, then real estate is almost certainly not for you.

The other, somewhat contradictory thing I try to do with their enthusiasm is to *encourage* it. I've been in real estate for four decades—I tell them—and there is no more interesting, stimulating, or exciting field in which to make your living and your career.

It's a field where you can make a difference. For example, on a local level, you can build something that is architecturally significant, that makes a neighborhood better, that creates wonderful and humane spaces in which people can work or play. You can get to know all about how your city or town works, and use that knowledge to make good things happen. You can work extremely hard to create something, and at the end of that process, you have the sheer delight of going inside that thing and *walking around* in it. This *concreteness*, this immediacy, had great appeal for me when I was a young Harvard MBA, and still does today. My sense is that today's students are equally drawn to this aspect of real estate.

Going up a few levels, from the micro to the macro, you can change the way a city or an entire region operates. You can make deserts bloom. You can create new investment vehicles, and steer huge amounts of capital in innovative new directions.

To simplify greatly, today's real estate world consists of two mostly separate universes. One is the universe of individual properties managed by local firms and financed by means of a project-specific mortgage. The other consists of the large, mostly public real estate investment and service firms operating nationally, or even globally. These firms manage dozens (or even hundreds) of properties, often in a range of property types and markets.

No matter which universe you inhabit (I tell my students), you are very likely to work with all kinds of interesting people. Often, you will work with them in unexpected, antihierarchical ways. Not long ago, I was talking on the telephone with a prominent elected official from a nearby state when an emergency call came in from my plumbing contractor on line two. I told the politician I'd have to call him back.

Real estate is also exciting because it brings together all sorts of specific activities under one roof, ready to be managed by skilled professionals. At the Harvard Business School, we refer to this as the "general management" track. If you don't think you'd relish several decades of working your way up the ladder in corporate accounting, for example—if you would rather try your hand at doing and managing a broad range of activities, or at least managing the people who are performing those tasks—then real estate may be a good choice for you.

If you are seeking financial reward, real estate can be a very good game to play. But to succeed you have to play it *well*, especially when larger trends turn against you. This requires flexibility. Entrepreneurs in real estate (as

CONTENTS

well as in other fields) are often narrowly focused on their specific opportunities. As a result, they often lose sight of the macro-environment, which can sometimes turn hostile indeed. The number of real estate moguls tends to wax and wane as larger economic trends either favor or don't favor the industry. In 1988, in a good phase of the real estate cycle, 87 members of the Forbes 400 were described as having made their money in real estate (up from 48 in 1983). But on the down side of the cycle, in 1993 there were only 32 real estate moguls. Five years later, the number had dropped to 27.

And as a last thought in this opening section: if you enjoy taking risks, real estate may not be the best game for you to choose. In my experience, real estate entrepreneurs don't perceive of themselves as great risk takers, but instead as *risk managers.* In fact, they believe (rightly or wrongly) that they can calculate and deal with the many types of risks inherent in most real estate projects. One thing I hope to do in this book—in addition to identifying opportunity—is to help you spot risks, develop strategies for coping with risks, and assess whether those strategies give you both enough protection and an adequate return.

AIMING AT USEFULNESS

Most existing real estate books don't help the professional who wants to be involved in—or at least understand—real estate. This book attempts to be different. It is designed to help you, personally, make decisions in real estate, by showing how successful practitioners actually think about and solve problems. Alternatively, it is designed to help you understand the decisions that other professionals are making at every stage of the process, and what might be motivating them. I hope this will make the book interesting and useful for people in allied professions, such as architecture, public-sector management, banking, law, and construction.

This book won't qualify you to take the real estate board examinations in any state. It won't make a technocrat out of you. Another point that I make to my students, and that I'll make in this book at regular intervals, is that real estate doesn't require a great deal of specialized education. Common sense can carry you a long way. Yes, there are concepts that one has to understand, such as the math skills that you will call upon almost every day in your professional life. But if you have mastered introductory algebra, you have all the training you need to do the kinds of "back of the envelope" calculations that are necessary for success in real estate.

But even the simplest calculations can be dangerous. Why? Because you still have to make the right *assumptions,* which is part of what this book is about. For example: Let's say you take a ten-year spreadsheet and assume that rents will go up by 5 percent per year, and at the end of ten years, you're going to sell the property at a very favorable capitalization rate and make a lot of money. Sounds good, right? Everyone should play this game!

But have you taken into account all of the problems you're going to have just getting the project going? Are you really going to end up owning that property for the full ten-year period? And what level of interest rates and inflation (or deflation) did you plug into your spreadsheet calculations?

As in most fields of business, you can make the projections come out any way you want. Most people want their projects to happen, and therefore jigger the numbers to fit—either consciously or unconsciously. Most people, too, make the assumption that whatever is true today is going to be true tomorrow. In the real estate game both of these assumptions can be fatal, and yet, they're made all the time. As my colleague John Vogel (at Dartmouth's Tuck Business School) likes to point out, real estate is an industry characterized by ten-year cycles and five-year memories.

WAR STORIES VS. CASE STUDIES

The following pages will include a lot of what might be characterized as "war stories." I prefer to think of them as case studies, used to illustrate what can go right (and what can go wrong) in real estate. Sometimes I will cite my own experiences in the real estate field, mostly to clarify a specific point. It seems more appropriate to highlight my own numerous missteps than to beat up on my colleagues and competitors.

But when the examples are particularly instructive, I will also invoke the lessons of some of the biggest players in real estate in this century. Bill Zeckendorf, for example, was one of the most creative and productive developers who ever played the real estate game. He gave us Kips Bay in New York City, Mile High City in Denver, Century City in Los Angeles, Place Ville Marie in Montreal—and eventually had most of his properties taken away from him. It's important to understand what Zeckendorf got wrong (for example, getting too far out in front of reality and overleveraging his properties), as well as what he got right (a vision of the future of our downtowns that was uncannily accurate). We've recently seen more or less the same phenomenon replayed at London's Canary Wharf, developed by the ambitious Reichmann family of Canada.

In addition, I will draw on what I've learned through teaching real estate at the Harvard Business School for more than thirty years. One reason why I chose to teach at the Harvard Business School in the first place was that HBS emphasizes the use of *cases* in the classroom—small "slice-of-life" stories about real people in real business situations (although sometimes the identifying particulars are disguised). In my experience as a teacher, the case method preserves the true complexity of business situations, including real estate deals. It prevents me and my students from reducing real estate to a simple problem set—in other words, a simplified collection of standard techniques to employ and punch lists to check off.

The case method also allows me to adapt the course quickly in response to changing conditions or emerging topics of interest. For example, we have recently added cases on projects in Mexico, Russia, and China. We have tackled new housing options. We can (and do) accommodate rapidly evolving markets, changing tax policies, and dramatic restructurings of financial institutions.

In some cases, the players are disguised to allow either more complete candor, or a gathering together of several themes into one composite story. I'll take the same approach in this book, disguising certain individuals involved in specific deals. This seems only fair. They didn't know, when they went into business with me, that they would wind up in a book one day.

I have tried to write *The Real Estate Game* less like a rule book and more like a friendly guidebook to an interesting, sometimes exotic land. I will help you spot the foreign in the familiar, and the familiar in the foreign. I will help you avoid some of the pitfalls into which some of the most prominent people in real estate have fallen—some of them more than once.

My belief is that learning to be a "value investor"—that is, buying at the right price at the right time, and finding creative ways to enhance the value of what you own—is the best long-term strategy for real estate. How to make this work in practice for you is the main theme and purpose of this book.

I will debunk some of the truisms that you may have heard about real estate. For example: It's really not just a narrow focus on "Location, location, location." Instead, I'd say your rule of thumb ought to be something like, "Learn the dynamics of how locations change, and figure out how that knowledge can help you buy and sell properties."

And yes, changes in capital markets influence the behavior of real estate players. But what is important is that you have a choice as to whether you want to follow the crowd.

I'll constantly recommend taking a broader perspective. For example, I think real estate is as much about *people* as it is about *property.* It's *people* who add value or subtract value in the real estate game—whether by design or by accident.

And people are only one of the many factors that can make the difference between success and failure in real estate. In the following pages, I'll introduce you to many more such factors.

CHAPTER 1

THE GAME

I'VE called this book *The Real Estate Game* because I think the real estate business—like all sophisticated games—is an interesting and challenging context for competition.

It's also a game that lends itself to personalization. I'm not the first person to talk about "the real estate game." But what you'll find in the following pages is my own particular slant on that game, interspersed with the perspectives of a cast of other players of the game.

In adopting the metaphor of a game, I don't mean to imply that real estate is a trivial pursuit. Far from it! The aggregate annual stakes in real estate owned for investment purposes are probably something like $4 *trillion.* Depending on how you play it, the financial gains or losses can be enormous. In addition to the personal financial stakes, of course, real estate is also an enormously important factor in the fortunes of national economies. It has huge impacts on people's lives—affecting, among other things, where we live, work, and play, how we house the sick and elderly members of our society, and how we provide jobs for millions of people.

Like most games with staying power, real estate involves big risks and big rewards. (Of course, in real estate, you're playing with real money.) It requires intellectual and emotional commitment. To invoke a biological metaphor, it involves both your left brain and your right brain.

Monopoly™, Charles Darrow's old Depression-era standby, is a very popular real estate game, but it's not a very good one. It's not contingent enough: one move doesn't affect all subsequent moves to a sufficient extent. Players don't have enough control over their fate. Luck counts for too much. Things don't change fast enough. The properties aren't different enough.

(The hotels and the houses all look the same; there aren't any shopping malls, industrial sites, or mixed-use developments.) The rules specifically forbid informal negotiations to arrive at win-win outcomes for two or more players. Many regular players of Monopoly™ wind up agreeing to additional rules that render the game more complicated and interesting, and therefore more like real life.

There really isn't a board game that is a good analogy to real estate. But if there were, it would involve all sorts of contingencies: if X happens, then Y or Z has to follow—but A, B, or C definitely couldn't happen next.

In my ideal real estate game, the pieces would have some very interesting characteristics. For example, they would change in value over time—sometimes predictably, sometimes not. Most would be more valuable to some players than to others. More often than not, they would increase in value, but only if the player was good at the real estate game and *really worked at it.* A premium would be paid for being in the right place at the right time.

My ideal real estate game would involve at least four decks of cards, none of which would bear any resemblance to ordinary playing cards. There would also be some version of a dealer, or croupier. But he or she would deal only part of the time. Sometimes you, as a player, would pull your own cards. Sometimes the croupier would hand you a card you *really* didn't want to take. Sometimes that card would propel you to the top of the game—but other times, it would knock you out of the game, either suddenly or slowly.

You could make a real fortune. Alternatively, you could lose one. As the old saying goes, "A great way to make a small fortune in the real estate business is to start out with a large one." Your game could be over quickly—or it could go on for many years.

THE RULES OF THE GAME

In this book, we will view the real estate industry through two different lenses to help you understand how the real estate game is played. The first involves the key variables—the "decks of cards" that I was referring to earlier. These are:

- properties
- capital markets
- players
- external environment

These four variables can be represented in the form of a diamond, which I'll call the *game diamond.* The game changes with the times, the nature of the project itself, the source of financing, and the structure of the real estate firms that are involved. What doesn't change is that these four dynamic forces must always be taken into account as we make our decisions in the real estate game.

As you can see, the points of this diamond are connected with double-ended arrows, underscoring the fact that all four forces affect each other more or less profoundly throughout the duration of the game. I've arranged the variables in a way that corresponds roughly to a balance-sheet configuration: assets (primarily the properties) on the left, liabilities (including mortgages) on the right. This is a useful way to think about the various elements involved in the real estate game.

The game begins when you pick a card. (Sometimes our croupier starts the game by dealing your first card to you, perhaps in the form of an inherited building, but we'll return to that later.) You can pick a card from any of the four decks. When you do so, you embark on a specific and unique path. To win the game, you must assemble matching cards from all four decks. But these "matches" are hard to make. Each card that you pull affects the others, and often you have to pick more than one card from each deck. Your job, as you make subsequent moves in the game, is to figure out how to create or preserve a competitive advantage for yourself.

Outside of the game diamond, you'll see two additional building blocks for the real estate game: the scorecard, and the game clock ("periods of play").

Let's look at each of these building blocks in turn, beginning with the *properties.* The *properties* in the real estate game are extremely diverse. There are numerous types (based, for example, on intended or unintended uses, geography, scale, and condition). They may exist today, or they may be no more than an idea in someone's head or a rough sketch on a drawing board. They may be short-lived or long-lived, mass produced or highly customized. They sit within markets that are mostly local and fragmented, and are subject to more or less intensive controls, in the larger context of a litigious society.

As I noted above, I've located the properties on the left-hand side of the game diamond. They are our opportunities and our assets, and therefore belong on the left side of the game board.

The *capital markets* are, in a sense, the backdrop against which this capital-intensive game is played. They are located on the right side of the board, corresponding to the liabilities and equity on a balance sheet. Simply

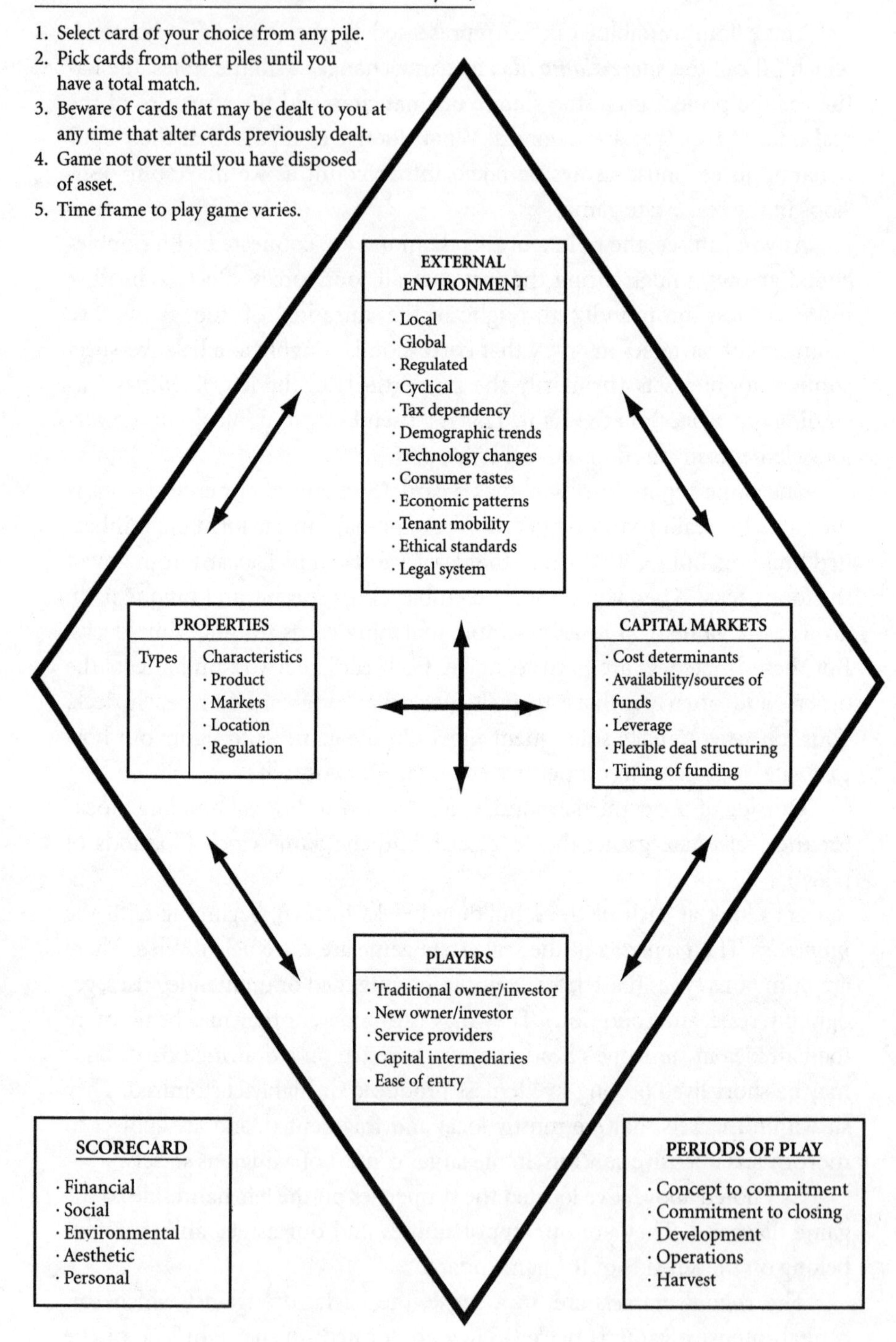
Rules of the Game (Unlimited Number of Players)
1. Select card of your choice from any pile.
2. Pick cards from other piles until you have a total match.
3. Beware of cards that may be dealt to you at any time that alter cards previously dealt.
4. Game not over until you have disposed of asset.
5. Time frame to play game varies.
EXTERNAL ENVIRONMENT
· Local
· Global
· Regulated
· Cyclical
· Tax dependency
· Demographic trends
· Technology changes
· Consumer tastes
· Economic patterns
· Tenant mobility
· Ethical standards
· Legal system
PROPERTIES
Types
Characteristics
· Product
· Markets
· Location
· Regulation
CAPITAL MARKETS
· Cost determinants
· Availability/sources of funds
· Leverage
· Flexible deal structuring
· Timing of funding
PLAYERS
· Traditional owner/investor
· New owner/investor
· Service providers
· Capital intermediaries
· Ease of entry
SCORECARD
· Financial
· Social
· Environmental
· Aesthetic
· Personal
PERIODS OF PLAY
· Concept to commitment
· Commitment to closing
· Development
· Operations
· Harvest

put, is there money to be had out there, from what sources, and how much does it cost? The increasing globalization of the capital markets, as we will see, has profound implications for the real estate game.

The capital markets often operate independently of the property world—but at the same time, the expectations of those markets can affect both what is built and how it is priced. Debt/equity rates, moreover, often determine who gets to play the real estate game. The key issue is, in other words, how much of your own cash you will have to put up. The desire or need to use other people's money, either in the form of debt or equity, is a central part of this business. This kind of "leverage" can either engender risk (by getting you out on a limb) or reduce it (by minimizing the extent to which you have to commit your own capital).

The *players* are the change agents—either directly or indirectly. It is the players who scramble to connect the properties with the capital markets. As the game diamond indicates, I differentiate here between the traditional players and the new players. The traditional players tend to be small, local, and "flat" organizations, entrepreneurial in spirit and out of necessity. They outsource much of what they do, and generally would rather use other people's money than their own. *Leverage*—making limited resources go a long way—is often the name of their game. The projects in which they are involved are separately owned, and the partnerships behind those projects are ad hoc. For these players, entry into the real estate game is fairly easy.

The other kind of player I'll call the "newer" player, although (as I'll emphasize throughout this book) there's not really that much that's new under the real estate sun. These players tend to be large, even huge, companies. Some are builder/developers, others are service providers, and still others are financial conglomerates. Some use the real estate investment trust (REIT) format; others use a more traditional corporate format. There are also interesting hybrids out there, such as the large commingled funds sponsored by some of the world's most prominent investment banks.

Many of these larger players are an outgrowth of recent industry consolidations, aimed at creating publicly held entities large enough and diversified enough to permit investment by huge financial institutions. They are often characterized by vertical and horizontal integration, aimed at incorporating a wide variety of functions. An increasing number are now concentrating on international (in addition to domestic) growth. Some have changed their format in response to trends in the capital markets. One large corporation, for example, recently went from being an operating company to being a REIT. A large hotel company did just the opposite in the same time period.

One of the key challenges that I will pose to the readers of this book is to figure out which kind of player *you* hope to be. This is a valid question both for people who are new to the field and for those who have been in it for decades. Where are you starting from? (Has a card been dealt?) What is your motivation for reading this book? What do you bring to the game?

The *external environment* comprises all of those outside-world influences that can change the calculations inherent in the real estate game. These can be shifts in tax policy, regulation, demographic or employment trends, new technologies, unexpected consumer tastes, and so on. Being human, we tend to think of these external factors as disruptive, and therefore more or less negative. The fact is, however, that change almost always creates opportunity for those who are equipped to spot it.

Buildings change; the uses of buildings change; the quality of locations changes. Thanks in large part to the power of the external environment, ownership is an *active*, not a passive, process.

The *scorecard* for the real estate game is simply a way of (1) thinking through what's important for each player, and (2) keeping track of how well each player is doing according to simple economic criteria, as well as the less quantifiable standards that he or she has set. These standards include, for example, social, environmental, aesthetic, and personal considerations. It may strike some readers as strange that someone could lose significant amounts of money in real estate and still consider himself or herself a "success." But there are many people to whom providing affordable housing, completing the faithful restoration of an historic building, or producing an exciting new building is even more important than financial reward.

My experience is that people who go into real estate just to make a lot of money usually get into trouble. They lose sight of the fact that unless they make the right decisions for the *property*, they go wrong. If they forget that short-term fixes can be disastrous over the long term, they get into trouble. They do things that look good on paper, but don't work out over time.

The scorecard, too, is dynamic, rather than static. It is not just a short-term, quantitative result. This means that unless you create and maintain a property that is able to reach a particular market over the long run—and help the community in the process—you will eventually lose the ability to make money. People who get lost in the numbers often also wind up as losers in the real estate game. In saying this, I don't mean to minimize the value of quantitative analysis, which we'll introduce in the next chapter and to which we'll return throughout this book. I simply mean to emphasize that running the numbers is not how value gets created in the real estate game.

The last component of the game diamond involves *periods of play.* Because this is the other lens through which this book will examine the real estate game, I'll introduce it separately.

PERIODS OF PLAY

One reason why the real estate game is unlike many others is that the period of play is so variable. Depending on the properties, capital markets, players, and external environment involved, a particular game can end within a few months, or can take many years to play out. In most cases, the time frame is extremely difficult to predict.

Let's say, for example, that you've spotted an undervalued residential property in your neighborhood that you'd like to fix up and "flip" (or resell as quickly as possible). If you've calculated right, if your work is good, and if the housing market doesn't collapse around you, your total involvement in the game may be measured in months.

At the other end of the time spectrum, imagine that you have purchased a cornfield adjacent to a proposed interchange for the new freeway extension. Your cornfield looks like a perfect place for a regional shopping mall, and you happen to be in the business of developing regional shopping malls (or can partner with somebody who is). You know from the outset that you'll be in the game for a very long time—maybe five years, maybe a decade—before the first customer parks in your new parking lot.

The five periods of play that we will focus on follow the "flow" from inspiration to reward:

1. Concept to commitment
2. Commitment to closing
3. Development
4. Operation
5. Harvest

Each of these phases serves as the core of a subsequent chapter, although not every real estate project involves every phase. (There may not be a "development" of an existing property, and a condominium project may not involve an "operation" phase.) Some activities of real estate, such as financing or leasing/marketing, are found in several of the phases. As we go through each phase, we will touch each corner of our game diamond—properties, capital markets, players, and external environment—to see how it affects that particular period of play. Remember that the period of play is expandable, something like an accordion: The bigger and more complicated the project, the longer the period of play. But the phases, and the activities within them, are pretty consistent, and therefore serve as a useful "spine" for this book.

Why do developers so often run out of cash toward the end of a project? Why do investors so often fail to sell when it's easy to see that the market is overheated? We can answer these questions by examining the dynamics of the real estate game, phase by phase.

FOUR LIVING, BREATHING EXAMPLES

Perhaps this sounds too structured—like wheels turning within wheels, and clocks ticking inside other clocks. I don't mean to make the real estate game sound mechanistic, because that's not how I've experienced it personally, nor how other people have described their experiences to me. What *is* important to understand, as an introduction to subsequent chapters of this book, is that there is a very real structure to the real estate game. It is never played exactly the same way twice—but that doesn't mean that there are no rules. What matters is where you begin the game, which card you pull (of the cards that are available to you), and what you do to create competitive advantage with that first card (given the options that are still open to you after picking it) and with the subsequent cards you pull.

INVESTING YOUR OWN MONEY

Let's look first at Charlie Leonard, a former student at the Harvard Business School. (This is not his real name. As is true for many of the subjects of HBS cases, the way we achieve candor and thoroughness is to disguise the protagonist.) Leonard had inherited $25,000, and was looking for a promising place to invest that money. He decided that he wanted to "get into real estate." To put this in the terminology of our game, Leonard pulled a "Player, small" card from the Player deck. The game begins.

Leonard knew that his lack of experience and relatively small amount of capital were disadvantages. Because he had a very limited amount of cash, he would have to borrow money to meet most of his costs. In real estate, high leverage translates into a higher capital risk.

He therefore picked a second card by settling on an area—Boston's historic Beacon Hill—that was well accepted by both prospective tenants and lenders ("Property, conservative"). After some careful investigation, he concluded that from a competitive standpoint, he would be better off rehabilitating an existing property than starting from scratch. But by taking this route, Leonard knew, he was venturing into an arena (rehabilitation) about which he knew very little, and in which the risk/reward ratio can quickly turn against you.

INVESTING YOUR OWN TIME

Our second example involves Ben Alexander, another former student at the Harvard Business School (also disguised). Alexander began with an inherited building on an excellent site near the State University at Collegetown. He entered the game, in other words, with a card drawn (or dealt to him) from the "Property" deck. He was an undergraduate at the university when he inherited the building—a modest frame house—from a distant relative. He rented the house to some fellow undergraduates, and put some time and money into fixing it up, and gradually educated himself on the property's potential for development.

Using free help provided by architecture students at the university, and calling upon the advice offered by others willing to talk to him, Alexander put together an ambitious plan for redeveloping the property. By definition, he was a small player, but he traded in his "Property, existing" card for a "Property, new" card. He developed plans for a multiunit apartment building, aimed at satisfying some of the high demand in the area for off-campus student housing.

Alexander's plans were persuasive, and he was able to secure preliminary financial backing ("Capital markets, availability of funding"). But a series of delays set in, and things began to look less promising. Other would-be developers had perceived the same opportunity that Alexander did, and their projects got underway sooner, driving up construction costs and threatening future rents. Meanwhile, the economy was beginning to overheat, and inflation began rising rapidly ("Capital markets, cost of money"). Eventually, Alexander's financing evaporated, and he was forced to abandon his plan. He was left with a deteriorating, underused building.

INVESTING OTHER PEOPLE'S MONEY

A different real estate game was played by Cameron Sawyer, who was the subject of a field-study report by one of my second-year students several years ago. My faculty colleagues and I got interested in his story, and wrote a case study based upon it that is used every year in our real estate course. As is true for many subjects of Harvard Business School cases, Sawyer comes to Boston every year when the case about him is taught, so I've gotten to know him in that context. His story is only thinly disguised, in the case and in this book.

In the late 1980s, Sawyer was working in the real estate department of an Atlanta-based law firm. He was struck by how many people in the booming Atlanta area were making a lot of money in real estate. They also seemed to be enjoying themselves. Drawing on his previous business connection with a Russian emigré in Germany—who argued persuasively that Russia was the next field of immense opportunities in real estate—Sawyer decided that he would go into real estate in Russia. Let's say he first pulled an "External factors, markets-in-transition" card.

Next, of course, he had to define himself creatively as a player. He went to Russia and went to work for somebody else while he learned the language. He then found a competent and well connected local partner—a move which is almost a prerequisite in international real estate deals, as I'll emphasize in later chapters—and they undertook a series of small projects for others, mostly aimed at testing the market. His first project involved a joint-venture land lease agreement, which by its nature minimized his need for capital ("Capital markets, constrained"). On that site he proposed to build an office building, which eventually was backed by Italian money ("Capital markets, less constrained"). Although this project took longer than expected, it was ultimately successful.

Now Sawyer is putting together a suburban retail project that he is trying to prelease. Sawyer is well into the real estate game. Will he survive the turbulence of the Russian economy at the turn of the century? He expects to, but that game is still being played out.

BUILDING BUSINESSES

At the other end of the real estate spectrum, far from the individual entrepreneurs just starting out, are people like Bill Sanders (not disguised). In the early 1990s, Sanders—who earlier had founded and then sold his interest in one of the premier national real estate service firms, LaSalle Partners—decided that publicly held real estate investment trusts, or REITs, were very likely once again to become a major source of funds focused on real estate investment. (As I'll explain in later chapters, REITs are a cyclical phenomenon that come to the fore about once a decade.) To be sure,

Sanders had a well established record as a player in the real estate game. But I like to think of him as pulling a "Capital markets, flush" card as he got into his current version of the game. Based on the strong demand for real estate investment opportunities from institutional and wealthy individual investors at a time when properties in general were undervalued, Sanders created a series of REITs, each designed to hold a different property type. His interests in these REITs were owned by a master corporation, which reinvested much of the distributions from the REITs into new start-up companies. These companies, in turn, became major players in their particular real estate niches.

By moving early and quickly, Sanders developed his company, Security Capital, into one of the largest real estate firms in the country. Today, he plays a new and challenging game based on his recent success—a game focused on managing the complexity of what he has already assembled, on making investors understand a very complicated business, and on satisfying the growth expectations of Wall Street. He is trying, with some difficulty, to prove that the parent company is more valuable than the sum of its component investments.

PLAYING THE GAME YOUR WAY

These four stories make two somewhat paradoxical points. First, the real estate game lends itself to endless variations. Second, the structure of that game is fundamentally consistent. If you play, sooner or later you will have to deal with our four elements:

- properties
- capital markets
- players
- external environment

Equally important, you will have to improvise to adjust your real estate game to your very specific situation. Much has been written about the rules governing properties and capital markets. You may have to rewrite some of these rules as you go along—and if you do, you'll have to be well aware of the limits on the kinds of rules you can write.

Throughout this book, I'll refer back to this game structure. My goal is not to set forth an all-encompassing set of rules for real estate. (That would be a hopeless and endless task!) Instead, I want you to practice adopting this lens, because I think it can help you make better decisions as you venture into the real estate game. I'll also be carrying forward the stories of Charlie Leonard, Ben Alexander, and a number of other players of the game. As these stories unfold, they can help remind us that behind every real estate deal—from the simplest to the most complicated—are *people:* the players of the real estate game.

CHAPTER 2

USING NUMBERS IN REAL ESTATE

LET'S assume that the game metaphor introduced in Chapter 1 was interesting and tempting enough to keep you turning the pages. Before we actually start playing the game, we need to give you some tools to make you into a skilled player.

In real estate, one of the most important skill sets consists of quantitative skills. You need to be able to work comfortably with numbers in order to spot, evaluate, and create value in the real estate game.

Let me offer some quick reassurance to the nonquantitative among my readers. I like numbers myself, but I'm far from being a born number cruncher. In this chapter, I will try to present numbers in the way that real estate professionals really use them—that is, in simple, interesting, and highly practical ways.

As we'll see in Chapter 3, one of the most important tasks in the early stages of the real estate game is managing your time effectively. This is made much easier by an approach that is referred to as *back-of-the-envelope analysis.* In many cases, back-of-the-envelope analysis (using historical and pro forma numbers) is all you need to assess a particular real estate opportunity. I'll devote most of this chapter to this approach.

There are cases in which a more detailed financial analysis is either helpful or required. These often take the form of *spreadsheets.* I'll spend some time describing spreadsheet applications toward the end of this chapter, as well as when you should use one or both of these two approaches.

Real estate is neither an art nor a science. It's a combination of intuitive and quantitative elements, and the successful player of the real estate game has to be comfortable in both realms.

BACK-OF-THE-ENVELOPE (BOE) ANALYSIS

There are many ways to think about and use quantitative analysis in real estate. In academia, where I spend about half of my time, the trend for many years has been toward more detail. (Academics love to run numbers in esoteric ways.) Sophisticated quantitative analyses also have their place in certain kinds of real-world transactions. For example, computerized spreadsheets have made it easier to analyze multiple scenarios, to calculate potential returns based on each of those scenarios, and to keep track of what has happened over the longer term.

For the most part, though, practitioners tend to rely heavily on more informal kinds of analysis to make their initial commitments. To the uninformed, these techniques can seem like an unreliable, "gut feel" approach—like Grandmother throwing together her chicken soup with no discernible recipe. But like Grandmother's soup, the BOE analyses employed by real estate professionals almost always perform as expected.

Let's work our way into BOE analysis by using a series of hypothetical (but realistic) scenarios based on my own experiences. As you'll see, it's the *underlying assumptions*—the structure behind the numbers—that turn out to be the key ingredients. It is a form of quick-and-dirty sifting that allows you to get to the heart of the matter quickly, and helps you decide how best to spend your time. Remember: your goal is not complicated. You're trying to buy a property at a price below what you expect to sell it for, some time in the future, thereby earning a reasonable time- and risk-adjusted return on your capital.

USING BOE: THE WALTHAM WAREHOUSE

Let's imagine, first, that I'm working in my office one day when a phone call gets put through to me. It's Joe Pena, a broker with whom I've dealt frequently in the past, and whose judgment I trust. After we trade a few general observations on the state of the industry, he gets right to the point. "Bill," he says, "I've got something I think you might be interested in."

Since I believe that Pena has a very good idea of my kind of property, I listen carefully. It's an 80,000-square-foot office/warehouse in an attractive section of Waltham, a midsized industrial city twenty miles northwest of Boston. The asking price is $1.5 million, Pena says, and although the price is firm, the owner might be willing to take back a second mortgage at a favorable rate. (Seller financing at better-than-market terms is good for buyers because they may be able to buy more building on a limited amount of equity invested, and it's good for sellers because it may enable them to get a higher price.) Pena thinks that it would be possible to upgrade the building to office use, but confesses that he hasn't really explored that option.

As Pena talks, I reach for my yellow pad and a sharp pencil. I ask about the condition of the building and the competitive context. After a few minutes, my notes look something like this (with the entries cleaned up to make sense to the reader):

PRO	CON
Good location	Roof needs repair
Simple construction	All four leases set to expire
Only 10 years old	Small size (may be inefficient)
Rail access	Few constraints to competitive construction
Potential for expansion	Environmental hazard status unclear
Efficient design	

All of the positives are attractive. None of the cons is bad enough, in and of itself, to turn me off to the offering, although the roof definitely gives me pause. Since roof repairs are not my specialty, maybe I could ask the owner to fix it as part of the deal. A buyer who had a good roofer—although some in the business would call this an oxymoron!—would rather add value by doing it himself. More power to him. My experience is that roof leaks are random occurrences, and that guarantees on roof repairs are more or less unenforceable.

I don't like the fact that all four current tenants will have the opportunity to leave, or perhaps demand a rent reduction, in the near future. I'm also not happy that in this part of Waltham there is plenty of available land and there are minimal constraints on potential competitors. But the offering price is below $20 per square foot, or psf ($1.5 million divided by 80,000 sf). I know that to build a comparable warehouse in eastern Massachusetts would cost about $40 psf, which gives me some protection. In making this simple calculation, I've just run my first test: comparing acquisition cost with replacement cost. Now or later, I can also check to see if $20 psf is the going market rate for properties of this type. By the way, note that the $40 psf is not just the construction cost of the bricks and mortar, but includes the raw land, development costs of the land, architectural and engineering fees, leasing, financing, and other costs that go into the creation of the final product.

Turning to a new yellow sheet, I set up and gradually fill out a grid that looks something like the following. Again, I'll stay away from the kind of personal shorthand that would confuse the reader. Don't be alarmed by the sudden appearance of a bunch of abbreviations (ROA, CFO, etc.); they are defined in the accompanying box.

Year 1 (based on $1.5 million purchase price and existing rents of $2.50 psf):

Cash flow from operations (CFO)	$162,000*
Mortgage payment (interest and principal)	106,000**
Cash flow after financing	$56,000

Return on assets (ROA): $162,000/$1,500,000 = 10.8%
Financing cost (FC): $106,000/$1,200,000 = 8.9%
Return on equity (ROE): $56,000/$300,000 = 18.7%

*I.e., gross rents of 80,000 × $2.50 or $200,000 less vacancy allowance, operating expenses, and capital reserves.

**80% of purchase price, or $1.2 million, financed at 8% over 30 years, results in an annual mortgage payment of $106,000.

This is what's known as a "setup"—in other words, a snapshot of a property's financial performance at a given point in time. The setup focuses entirely on cash flow (rather than financial accounting). Why? Because most real estate investors are very interested in cash flow issues, and are only secondarily interested in net income that deducts depreciation as an expense. (Cash flow not only reflects what they can actually spend, but ultimately will determine what they can borrow or sell properties for.) The setup is often used to monitor the performance or near-term prospects of a property that one already owns, or to assess the financial feasibility of a proposed improvement. I also use it to do a quick assessment of a potential acquisition.

"Cash flow from operations" (CFO) is the figure most often used by investors and brokers to describe the operating income of a property, because it represents the amount of cash flow that is available for distribution to debt and equity holders. It represents the net operating income of a property, less a reserve or allowance for normal capital expenditures, and after costs associated with obtaining new tenants have been deducted. It does not reflect an allowance determined by the IRS for depreciation or amortization. "Depreciation" is a formal way of representing the wear and tear on the building and its systems. "Amortization" generally refers to the write-off of other prescribed expenditures, such as leasing commissions.

CFO is also of great interest to lenders, as well as owners, since it represents the amount of cash flow that is available to make loan payments. And finally, because it's property-specific, it's very useful for the kinds of com-

○ GLOSSARY OF BOE TERMS ○

net operating income (NOI): net property revenues less building operating expenses

cash flow from operations (CFO): NOI less capital expenditures or reserves for such items as tenant improvements (TIs), leasing commissions, and structural reserves

financing costs (FC): debt or mortgage payments of principal and interest, often in the form of a constant payment that amortizes the loan over a given time period

cash flow after financing (CFAF): CFO – FC

return on assets (ROA): CFO/purchase price

return on equity (ROE): CFAF/cash invested or cash on cash

parisons we're talking about. In the real estate game, it's very important to distinguish between the *property* and the financial structure that is put together to *purchase* the property.

When the CFO is divided by the purchase price, it yields a *return on assets* ratio, or ROA. ROA is a necessary jumping-off point for more sophisticated calculations. In essence, it represents the current yield from operating the property. It is sometimes used interchangeably with a ratio called the *capitalization rate,* or "cap rate," which generally relates to the market value of a property. It is simply the real estate professional's effort to get at a relevant yield on invested capital (much like the inverse of a P/E ratio in the stock market). These terms, though, are different in subtle but important ways. I'll return to cap rates later in this chapter.

Cash flow after financing (CFAF) is the amount available to the investor after he or she meets the financing charges. Since many real estate transactions are highly leveraged, CFAF is highly sensitive to small changes in CFO. In the case of the property that Joe Pena is bringing to my attention, a 3⅓ percent increase in the CFO ($5,000) would increase CFAF by more than 8 percent. This phenomenon is called *operating leverage.*

There are clearly great benefits to the investor from obtaining positive operating leverage. But there is another type of leverage—*financial leverage.* In the absence of debt, the ROA in the above example is 11 percent. The use of an 8 percent interest rate loan with a constant mortgage or financing cost of 8.9 percent would increase the return to the investor from 10.8 percent to 18.7 percent. (This is because the owner's return is calculated as a percent of the actual equity invested, rather than the total asset cost.) This is sometimes referred to as the *pretax ROE*, or the *cash on cash return*.

A higher mortgage (say, $1.4 million rather than $1.2 million) dramatically increases the return on the reduced cash equity—but only as long as the mortgage constant (in this case, 8.9 percent) does not rise substantially. If the ROA drops lower than the mortgage constant, the result is negative financial leverage. The greater the financial leverage, the greater the impact that operating leverage has on the bottom line (in other words, on the ROE).

In today's environment—where you can get a mortgage at 7 percent interest with an 8 percent constant payment (including principal and interest), an overall 9 or 10 percent return on assets looks pretty good in the short run. A few years ago, when interest rates were 9 percent and typical carrying costs might have been in the range of 10.5 to 11 percent, the leverage was negative, and therefore reduced your return on equity substantially.

What's a high enough pretax ROA to justify buying? Everybody answers this question differently. In my classes, I always say, "At 6 percent you sell, at 14 percent you buy, and somewhere in between you find your own break point."

So it seems that at least up to this point, having come up with an apparent 18.7 percent pretax ROE for a property that can be bought at roughly 50 percent of replacement cost, Joe Pena has done a good job. I'm tempted to look at this property. We keep talking.

If you've already asked yourself the following question, give yourself credit for staying ahead of the teacher: *Which year do you use?* In other words, which numbers do you plug into your setup to perform your BOE analysis?

Most people who've had some practice at this try and sketch out what is sometimes called a "stabilized year." I could look at Joe Pena's offering and decide that the current or upcoming year is a "stable" portrait of the building, and decide that 100 percent occupancy is the most likely future for this building. Alternatively, I could look at those ready-to-expire leases, anticipate vacancies, and conclude that my CFO should really be based on 80 percent occupancy, rather than 100 percent.

This illustrates the point that your BOE analysis (like any analysis or projection) is only as good as the assumptions that lie behind it. So let's turn over another yellow sheet and see what happens if we adjust some of our assumptions. (By the way, I'm still on the phone with Joe Pena. When you get good at these BOE techniques, you can easily pepper the broker with questions while you run these kinds of rough numbers.) Let's say that I wonder out loud what happens if an empty building across the street from my proposed acquisition is rehabbed and opened up for business, and the result is that rents are driven down from $2.50 per square foot (psf) to $2.00 psf. I start scribbling again (see table).

Year 1 (based on $1.5 million purchase price and $2.00 rent per square foot):

Cash flow from operation (CFO):	$126,000
Mortgage payment (principal and interest):	106,000
Cash flow after financing (CFAF):	$20,000

Return on assets (ROA): $126,000/$1,500,000 = 8.4%
Financing cost (FC): $106,000/$1,200,000 = 8.9%
Return on equity (ROE): $20,000/$300,000 = 6.7%

What happened here? Operating leverage went in the wrong direction. Even though I only dropped rents by 20 percent—testing the possible impact of competition across the street—the pretax ROE dropped by almost two-thirds, to dismal levels.

Later, we'll look again at issues like the size of the relevant market, the vacancy situation, and the potential for new competition. But at this point, knowing that Pena knows I wouldn't be interested in a pretax ROE of under 7 percent, I might ask Pena if I'm missing something here. "While we've been talking, Joe," I say, "I've been running through some back-of-the-envelope numbers, and they don't hold up very well, especially if the rental market starts to soften. Is there anything else I should know about this property?"

Let's imagine that Joe at this point starts to make a case that my organization has strong enough rental skills that we could rent into a weaker market. He probably knows that I think this is true about my organization, so it's not a bad argument for him to try. But even as he's talking, I'm going in a different direction. I'm turning to a fresh sheet of yellow paper, leaving the rent at the reduced rate, and lowering the assumed price by $200,000, and the loan to a proportionate degree by $160,000. The resulting BOE analysis looks better.

Year 1 (based on $1.3 million purchase price and $2.00 rent per square foot):

Cash flow from operations (CFO):	$126,000
Mortgage payment (principal and interest):	$92,000
Cash flow after financing (CFAF):	$34,000

Return on assets (ROA): $126,000/$1,300,000 = 9.7%
Financing cost (FC): $92,000/$1,040,000 = 8.9%
Return on equity (ROE): $34,000/$260,000 = 13.3%

The lower price in effect boosts the return on equity, and overcomes most of the difficulties that a soft rental market would create. When pressed, the broker admits there might be some flexibility in the price. The 13.3 percent pretax ROE is enough to motivate me to drive out to Waltham for a site visit. Someone who was just starting out, liked this kind of property, and was trying to start developing a reputation among the local brokers as a player would be well advised to go take a look.

This sequence of setups was designed to illustrate the usefulness of a BOE analysis, which lies mainly in sifting through properties before you commit the time to go and look at them. Most of the time, I run the numbers first, and go see buildings that make sense. But not always. And the BOE screen is also helpful *after* you've seen a property—and particularly if you've had a positive emotional response to that property.

In my experience, there is very often a surprising amount of emotion involved in looking at buildings. Architecture and landscape and neighborhoods are very personal issues, and we invest a lot of ourselves in them. Sometimes you see a building that you *just really want to own. You have a good feeling about it. It feels right in your gut.* If and when you hear yourself saying these things, and if you haven't yet run your BOE numbers, remind yourself that this is probably a very good time to do so.

And by the way: If it doesn't wind up feeling right in your gut, don't push it. This will not be the last opportunity that will come your way.

USING BOE: THE CONCORD OFFICE BUILDING

I laid out the preceding example in a pretty ponderous way to give you a sense of the important variables that can be involved in a BOE analysis. In real life, I would never wind up with a series of sheets that looked like the setups described above. Watching me would be less like watching an accountant at work, and more like watching Grandmother make her famous chicken soup: Eventually, you'd see the soup, but you wouldn't be sure about how it came into being.

Let's take another example, this time tracking a little more closely how I would actually think about a prospective deal. A few years ago, my son Jonathan and I received a call from a local real estate player whom I'll call Charlie McCarthy. (Jonathan runs our real estate property company, and has worked with me since he graduated from business school in 1990.) McCarthy was trying to sell a vacant office building in Concord, Massachusetts, about fifteen miles due west of Boston. McCarthy told us that the owner was a financial institution that was anxious to liquidate its Boston portfolio of foreclosed properties. So we had an anxious seller, selling into what was then a weak market. For countercyclical investors like us, this had a strong initial appeal.

The size of the building (McCarthy went on to say) was 75,000 square feet and the asking price was $2,225,000. This gave us enough information to do our first calculation. The price per square foot was under $30 ($2,225,000 divided by 75,000). Again, as in the Joe Pena/Waltham example, a square-foot approach is most useful, permitting more apples-to-apples comparisons than other approaches.

It always makes sense to do a competitive analysis. You may or may not decide that you want to play the game, given the larger economic cycle, but you should always be prepared to figure out what others in a given market are paying at any given point in time.

Although Jonathan and I weren't very familiar with Concord, we knew from recent experience in nearby communities that the likely replacement cost—that is, the price of putting equivalent new office space on line—was more than $100 psf. (This is in contrast, for example, to the $40 psf cost of creating new warehouse space in Waltham.) This meant that no one was likely to put competitive space into the market anytime soon. We also used the $30 psf cost to compare the sales price of this property with others that were then on the market. As it turned out, the psf price was low, reflecting the seller's determination to unload this building.

Our next step was to compare the net operating income with the price, in order to develop a rough sense of a return on assets (ROA). McCarthy thought we could get rents of $15 *per square foot gross*—meaning total rent before either a vacancy allowance or the building's operating expenses (including real estate taxes) are taken into account.

The *vacancy allowance* is simply a deduction from the projected income on the building based on an expected rate of vacancy. Vacancy allowances will vary both with market conditions and with the type of property. (Large retail centers often experience 10 percent vacancy rates in the small mall stores, whereas a 10 percent vacancy rate in an apartment complex would be uncomfortably high.) We settled on a 6.66 percent projected vacancy rate, or $1 off of the $15 psf gross rent.

Operating expenses can be derived from your own experience or from the experience of banks, appraisers, and property managers in the area. No two properties are the same, of course; but comparable experience is the best guide. We estimated that this property would cost $5 psf to operate on an annual basis.

So: from a $15 psf gross, we are down to a *net operating income* of $9 psf (gross minus the vacancy allowance and operating expenses). This meant that we'd make a $9 annual return on our $30 psf investment, or an ROA (return on assets) of 30 percent. This was the kind of potential return that investors dream of—almost three times the ROA in the rosiest scenario that I ran on Joe Pena's office/warehouse in Waltham.

But we had some more thinking and calculating to do. The office building, McCarthy informed us, had been used by a single tenant, and as a result the space was largely open floor space without offices. Jonathan had in mind a target market of the kinds of software and hardware start-ups which were blossoming in that area as a result of downsizing by local high-tech giants. Appealing to this market would mean reorganizing the base building systems (heat, utilities, etc.) and subdividing and customizing spaces, all of which would be costly. We would probably end up with a number of smaller, minimally capitalized tenants, each of whom would want a customized layout.

We therefore added another $30 psf to our proposed acquisition costs to allow tenant improvements (TIs), and another $5 psf for "soft" costs such as interest, legal and leasing services, and interim building operating costs while we renovated and rented up the property. The ROA was now $9 on a $65 psf asset base ($30 + $30 + $5), which came out to slightly under 14 percent psf, which was still attractive.

The property was attractive from another perspective, as well. Judging from other comparable properties in the Concord area, we guessed that when the building was fixed up and leased out, it would probably sell for about $100 psf—in other words, well above the $65 psf that would have been invested in it up to that point.

This initial discussion of the "harvesting" phase leads us back to the notion of capitalization rates, introduced in the Joe Pena example. Let's look again at that net operating income (NOI) of $9 psf. If Jonathan and I pay

$100 psf for that $9 of NOI, that constitutes a "cap rate" of 9 percent. This 9 percent cap rate doesn't imply that the potential buyers are expecting only a 9 percent return. The 9 percent is only the current expected yield. In fact, we may have an expectation of future growth—perhaps resulting from higher rental rates when leases roll over, or through positive financial leverage—that would increase the return to more than 12 percent, over time.

Is that a reasonable expectation, and if so, is 12 percent "good"? Beauty is in the eye of the beholder, both for humans and cap rates. One person might look at a 9 percent cap rate and see a 12 percent return over time, based on his or her assumptions. Another might look at 9 and see 18—or, conversely, 6. They would all begin at the same starting point, and then make different assumptions about the future. At this point, let's simply define the *current yield* to mean a derived product of the relationship between value and income at a given point in time, and one which we can use as a starting point for additional analysis. (It is our initial ROA.) When we use the 9 percent not only as a derivative of the current yield, but also as a reflection of what we would pay for that current yield plus the future growth in that yield, we call that the *capitalization rate.* It reflects the present worth of future payments, which is the market value to us at this point in time.

We have to add another wrinkle to the story, at this point. The $9 psf NOI mentioned above does not take into account Jonathan's and my need to set up a reserve for future capital expenditures and lease-up costs. Just as we should plan to spend between $30 and $35 psf to reconfigure the building for our initial tenants, future tenants may demand similar kinds of investments from us. Even continuing tenants who renew their leases may want some changes, and it's a rare lease, indeed, that pays for roof and structural repairs!

How should we think about such a far-off, future obligation? The amount of this allowance depends on the type of property and its condition. Office buildings need larger allowances than warehouses and apartments, where the tenant needs are more generic. (In the case of Joe Pena's property, for example, the allowance would be minor.) But for the sake of argument, let's deduct $1 per square foot per year, thereby reducing our $9 net operating income to $8. This resulting number is often called the *cash flow from operations,* or CFO—a number we encountered in the Joe Pena example, but which we're now defining a little more sharply. Taking the $1 psf allowance into consideration, our ROA would still be $8 on $65, or 12.3 percent—still in the acceptable range. If we base our calculations on the $8 CFO, rather than the $9 psf NOI, we have an 8 percent cap rate, rather than a 9 percent cap rate.

There is some debate in the industry as to whether NOI or CFO should be used. The important point is for you to know which approach others are using, and make your own adjustments.

Now we have to look at the potential impact on our returns of *leverage*—that is, of borrowing some of the purchase price. If the total cost of the financing is less than the ROA, the result is positive leverage, which increases our return on equity (ROE) above the ROA. At the time that Charlie McCarthy called us, interest rates were at about 8.5 percent, and the annual carrying cost of the interest and amortization payments was about 10 percent. Lenders were reasonably conservative then, and wouldn't give us a mortgage of more than $45 psf of our $65 costs. Back in the glory days of the mid 1980s, lenders might have advanced as much as $60 or even $70 on a $65 psf project—an extension of credit that left them greatly exposed in the event of a downturn. Now they wanted us to have substantial cash equity in the deal.

In this case, happily, our leverage looks to be positive—the 10 percent cost of borrowing on the $45 is less than the 12.3 percent ROA, thus increasing the return on our $20 of equity from 12.3 percent to 17.5 percent ($8 – $4.50 = $3.50, divided by $20 equity = 17.5%). As in buying a property, closing the loan will involve some other out-of-pocket costs, which are often amortized for tax purposes over the term of the loan, but are not included in the 10 percent constant payment to the lender.

The lender's mortgage-interest-coverage ratio at the $45 psf level provides a considerable margin of safety. (This is relevant because you never want to assume the availability of financing based on unrealistic numbers.) The $8 cash flow still shows a 1.8-times coverage over the $4.50 debt service (CFO of $8 divided by $4.50 of debt service). In the future lenders might be willing to lend at a 1.3 coverage ratio, but only after the property is developed and leased.

This sequence of steps raises another question about the cost of financing. Shouldn't the true cost of financing in the above example be 8.5 percent—the interest charge—rather than the full 10 percent, which includes payments against principal? Aren't Jonathan and I building equity as we pay down our debt?

Well, yes, like a homeowner, we *are* building equity as we retire our debt. But one might ask, "So what?" We only will get the *benefit* of that equity buildup years in the (possibly distant) future, when we either sell or refinance the building. And the other stark reality in real estate is that a property can truly depreciate over time—whether for physical, functional, or economic reasons. Our BOE calculation in this case (as in most others) is therefore *meant* to be conservative.

So what did Jonathan and I learn, in those twenty minutes of thinking out loud on the phone with Charlie McCarthy? We determined at least four key facts:

- a cost-per-square foot of $65
- a ROA of 12.3 percent
- a cost of financing of 10 percent
- a ROE of 17.5 percent.

We were also reminded of the value of positive leverage. Through positive leverage, our prospective ROE (the return on our cash invested) went up well above our prospective ROA (see table).

	Income	Capital	Return
Cash flow from operations	$8.00	$65	12.3% ROA
Financing costs	$4.50	$45	10.0% FC
Cash flow after financing	$3.50	$20	17.5% ROE

It's important to remember that although these calculations appear to be deeply rooted in "facts," this appearance is more than a little deceiving. In truth, we made all kinds of assumptions based on what we knew about the surrounding area, and also on what the brokers told us about the rental and financial markets, in order to arrive at most of these numbers. For example, we made assumptions about:

- local rental market rates
- local brokerage costs
- target tenants for space
- cost of renovations
- capitalization rate upon resale
- mortgage interest rates
- loan to value ratio
- total carrying cost of a loan based on its amortization period.

All of this goes to say that our Concord BOE analysis would benefit from any kind of reality check that we can apply to it. In that spirit, what other questions can we ask to help us decide whether to pursue this potential property further?

One good reality check would be a quick assessment of our company's actual capabilities at this specific point in time. In other words, would the project be within our:

- financial capability?
- ability to evaluate, develop, and lease this property?
- time availability to do the necessary work?
- return expectations, in light of known risks?

In this case, we estimated that the total project would cost $65 psf, or slightly under $5 million for the 75,000 square feet, with an equity need after a $3.5 million mortgage of $1.5 million. That cash requirement was similar to other suburban office projects we were doing at the time. Even though this particular project looked like it might be time-intensive, we were then concluding another project, and Jonathan had staff available to put on this new job.

We were also in the process of paying off our bank loan on the nearly completed project, which meant that the bank was very likely to be willing to roll over its existing loan into a loan on the new project. And finally, the 17.5 percent pretax ROE was slightly lower than we would have liked—given that this building needed a lot of work, the cost of which is always difficult to estimate—but we were within striking distance. Rental rates seemed to be taking a positive turn. And from what McCarthy had said at the very outset, there was a motivated seller in the picture, too.

For all of these reasons, we were more than willing to investigate further, see the property firsthand, check out the local leasing scene, and generally explore what our most likely downside might be.

USING BOE: THE MADRID RETAIL CENTER

Let me cite another recent case in which I used BOE analysis to think through a suburban real estate opportunity. This time the suburb—outside of the Spanish city of Madrid—was a little farther from home. But the same general BOE rules were very helpful.

I visited the site to see what Scott Malkin was up to. Malkin is a U.S.-born, London-based developer whom I've known for a long time. In my dealings with Malkin over the years, I've always been impressed by his integrity and competence. Since my wife and I were planning to be in Madrid, and since I knew he had projects under development there, I had called him in London to let him know that we would be in Spain the following week. He phoned ahead to Madrid and made the necessary introductions.

Malkin's new project was a "value retail" center of 185,000 square feet. ("Value retail" is a term used to describe outlet centers in which local and international higher-end tenants, such as Polo/Ralph Lauren, Donna Karan, and Brooks Brothers, sell their own merchandise at substantial discounts.) I was escorted around the site by Michael Goldenberg, the head of Malkin's Spanish operations.

An interesting challenge that Malkin faced arose out of the fact that there was another retail center already in operation only five minutes down the road. Goldenberg and I had stopped at that competing site first, which consisted of about 50,000 square feet (or, in the metric system that is used in most of the world, some 5,000 square meters). Nike was the "anchor" tenant at this nearby competitor, with a long-term lease on a 20,000-square-foot store with its own entrance. In addition, there was a 10,000-square-foot discount food operator, also with its own entrance. The remaining space was occupied by medium-quality discount stores with a shared entrance.

The construction in the competing center might be called "Modern Factory." It consisted of concrete block walls, exposed steel beams, and few amenities. Overall, the center seemed poorly built and inadequately maintained. Parking was tight, even on the off-peak Monday morning hour of our visit. (I wondered what the parking situation would be like at lunch time on a Saturday.) The word on the street was that the center wasn't doing well financially, and its physical appearance seemed to confirm that assessment.

Of course, Malkin and Goldenberg were well aware of the existence of this center. But recently, word had gotten around that its owners were looking to sell it for $8 million. Its operating cash flow, Goldenberg had learned, was $600,000, or $12 per square foot.

The question that Malkin and Goldenberg were trying to answer was whether or not to buy the struggling retail center as a defensive move. For all of its problems, the Modern Factory mall had better access and higher visibility than Malkin's own location. If Malkin and Goldenberg didn't buy it, there was always the chance that a competitor would buy and upgrade the property, and significantly hurt their new value center.

Goldenberg and I retreated to a nearby coffee shop to do a quick BOE analysis. First, we computed the price per square foot to be $160 ($8 million divided by 50,000 square feet). This psf cost was well below the $220 psf cost of Malkin's project. This wasn't a mortal threat, in and of itself, because Malkin's product would be superior and his target market different. But the threat of an upgrade was still lurking out there—which was why we were huddling in the coffee shop.

Next, we looked at the return on assets. If the property went at the full $8 million asking price, the ROA would be only 7.5 percent ($600,000 divided by $8 million).

The interest rate on loans at that time, Goldenberg told me, was likely to be 7 percent, with a constant payment (including amortization) of 8 percent. In this case, the leverage would be negative to their return on equity, since the 8 percent cost of financing would exceed the 7.5 percent ROA. Their ROE after financing would most likely be even lower than 6 percent. So far, we agreed, this was a deal they could walk away from.

But we then looked at another BOE scenario. What would happen if Malkin bought the property and then spent some money to upgrade it? He might then be able to double the rents on the smaller tenants who collectively occupied 40 percent of the floor space, bringing those rents up to $30 per square foot—still below the $40 psf that Malkin was planning to charge in his new center. The rent on the Nike store would be fixed for some time, but Nike's percentage rents (a percentage of sales in excess of the base rent paid by the retail tenant to the landlord) would mostly likely go up if the whole facility started doing better. Even without any added income from Nike, doubling the rents to $30 psf for the smaller tenants would increase overall net operating cash flow from $600,000 to $960,000.

Of course, to do that, Malkin would have to spend money. Goldenberg and I talked through what the Modern Factory center needed, and concluded that $2 million would accomplish the job. This would raise the overall cost of the project (purchase and upgrade) to $10 million, or $200 psf. But at the same time, under this scenario, ROA increased to 9.6 percent, and now the mortgage cost of 8 percent (including interest and principal) was yielding positive leverage, and was increasing the ROE to more than 10 percent.

What about that parking problem? Perhaps they could tear down the discount food store when its lease expired in two years. Although providing additional parking would make the property more appealing to shoppers—and might enhance the resale value of the property—such a demolition would reduce income by $120,000 and the overall net operating cash flow to $840,000, yielding an 8.4 percent ROA. Their financial leverage would still be positive, but just barely.

After ten minutes of this kind of informal back-and-forth, with occasional scribbles by each of us on our respective yellow pads, we reached our verdict: *pass.* The Modern Factory mall could not be made into a great success either from a retail or a financial standpoint. If it were larger, it would represent a more credible threat to control the leasing market. Under present circumstances, though, we decided that Modern Factory posed no serious threat to Malkin's new project. Based on our numbers, only if the asking price were dropped substantially should Malkin (or anyone else) be interested.

USING BOE: SELLING IN PHOENIX

In a later chapter, I'll discuss the many challenges and opportunities of the "harvesting" phase of the real estate game—that is, taking your money back out of real estate. At this point, though, I'll use a disguised harvesting opportunity to illustrate another application of BOE analysis.

A New York–based friend of mine, whom we'll call Stephanie Hanson, was the managing partner of a garden apartment project in a fairly new section of Phoenix. She had hired local management to run the property, and they were doing a good job. Hanson's confidence in her local management team was high, and she rarely visited the project.

Hanson had bought the 125-unit property for $4.8 million in the late 1980s. The Phoenix market had collapsed shortly afterward, but had gradually come back. Now the property, which had a cash flow from operations (CFO) of around $450,000, was attracting interest from local investors. An offer arrived on Hanson's desk: $5 million in cash.

Working with her local managers, who knew the Phoenix market intimately, Hanson thought through her options. The proposed $40,000-per-unit sales price was consistent with recent sales in the area, as was the proposed 9 percent ROA ($450,000 divided by $5 million). (Note that in residential projects, "price per unit" is often used, as well as price psf.) Because interest rates were then at 8 percent with carrying (or mortgage) costs of 9 percent, increased leverage would not raise the buyer's short-term return, but instead would only reduce the required equity.

On the other hand, Hanson's local managers told her that the rental market was very strong, and that they anticipated raising rents by 10 percent in the near future. This would add about $60,000, and increase Hanson's CFO from $450,000 to $510,000. Based on these preliminary calculations, Hanson called the prospective buyer and told him that the price would have to be $5.7 million. This reflected the higher CFO at a 9 percent capitalization rate. In this case, the current yield of 9 percent was the equivalent of the market capitalization rate.

The would-be buyer had anticipated this counteroffer. He agreed that there was a good potential to raise rents, but argued that it would take three years to phase in all of the increases needed to get the full $60,000 increase in CFO. He shouldn't have to pay today—he argued—for increases in net operating income that wouldn't arrive for several years.

Hanson agreed that this was a valid objection, and proposed a new approach. Let's project the CFO over a four-year period, she suggested, and assume that the anticipated rent increases will be phased in as follows:

Year 1	$450,000
Year 2	470,000
Year 3	490,000
Year 4	510,000

This meant that the "lost revenue" (the difference between today's CFO and the CFO at the point when all the rent increases were in place) would be $60,000 in year 1, $40,000 in year 2, and $20,000 in year 3, for a total of $120,000. Based on this reasoning, Hanson offered to reduce her $5.7 million asking price by $100,000. (The $20,000 difference reflected the fact that the buyer would be getting the reduction up front, and that Hanson should be compensated for the time value of the money.)

The two sides were now close. The prospective buyer asked for a further $100,000 reduction to cover the cost of some deferred maintenance, to which Hanson agreed. The deal was closed for $5.5 million.

Again, I'll return to harvesting issues later in this book. In the property management section, I'll also emphasize the importance to the managing partner of having a strong operating team with a good grasp on the local market. My point in using the Phoenix example here is simply to demonstrate that BOE analysis can be a helpful tool both in understanding value and in bringing two sides together to close a deal. In this case, because rentals were below market, it made perfect sense to base a sale price in part on a projected increase in rentals. The assumptions were few, and the necessary calculations were simple.

USING BOE: THE WATERTOWN ARSENAL

I've laid out this series of examples of BOE analyses to illustrate a *mindset*—a way a real estate professional tends to think about opportunity in the real estate game. As these examples demonstrate, BOE analysis tends to focus on a consistent set of numbers and ratios, but it is *not* a cast-in-concrete formula for pushing a particular set of numbers around.

BOE analysis is a lens, and a language. In many cases—as in the Phoenix example, above—it is the shorthand that real estate professionals use to communicate and negotiate with one another. It's the framework that we use to assess value, and to understand how our competitors are assessing value.

I'll include one more case study to make my point. One of the big stories in Boston-area real estate in the late 1990s involved the historic Watertown Arsenal. This former Army arsenal sits on a choice 25-acre site alongside the Charles River in Watertown, Massachusetts, several miles upriver from downtown Boston. All told, there were around 650,000 square feet of space available for redevelopment. The city of Watertown—which had taken over the facility when the federal government vacated the premises—decided to sell the site, and was understandably interested in getting the very best deal possible.

A local developer helped in the planning for the project, and was thought by many local observers to have the inside track. When the developer's proposal came in, it had some interesting features. For example, their proposed partner was a local firm that was going to occupy about 30 percent of the space for use by its medical-devices operation, which would combine R&D facilities, warehousing, and some light manufacturing. As a result of this arrangement, the company would not have to move out of the city to meet its expansion needs. The total price offered was about $8 million.

But what happened next was surprising. A Philadelphia-based development company, the O'Neill Company, came in with a higher bid. This led to negotiations over several months, which culminated in a bid by O'Neill of $24 million, counting all the direct and indirect payments (e.g., to local community groups). It was an astounding price. The local player eventually sweetened its offer to something like $16 million, but they were still far below O'Neill. The O'Neill proposal was accepted, the property was sold, and the redevelopment is now well underway.

Some members of the local business community were convinced that O'Neill overpaid wildly for the property. Two causes were suggested: the generally overheated state of the local real estate market, and the relative ignorance of an "outsider" (O'Neill) about the true value of the property. I disagree. I think O'Neill hit a home run.

My rationale (my BOE analysis) goes something like this: O'Neill paid $24 million for 650,000 square feet, or about $35 a square foot. It will cost them approximately $100 per square foot to rehab the existing spaces and build any new spaces. So in terms of a total capital investment, O'Neill will be in for $135 a foot.

During the last year, rents have gone up substantially in the Boston area. Rentals that were between $18 and $20 in good suburban locations when the Arsenal bidding started are now up around $25 to $26. If you subtract $8 or $9 for operating expenses from the $26, you get $17 or $18 per square foot in annual income. When $18 rents are compared with the $135 per square foot investment, this is a very good return on assets—something over 13 percent.

What made the difference? I believe that the extra $5 a foot in rents—the amount that good locations in the suburban market went up in the intervening year—was worth $50 a foot (if we capitalize the extra $5 at 10 percent), or more than $30 million for the property as a whole. O'Neill may have perceived that even though the Watertown market in general might not have warranted such an increase, this particular location on the river—blessed with enough acreage to allow for a self-contained and much improved environment—should be able to command the higher rents.

In my first BOE example, Joe Pena's building in Waltham, I indicated that one of my first calculations was to compare the price per square foot with the replacement cost. The O'Neills surely did the same, and were convinced that even at the relatively high $135 psf price they paid, the replacement cost to build the equivalent property new was still well above that price. As I noted earlier, a significant gap between the purchase price of your property and the cost of building an equivalent new structure is the best possible protection for your own investment. If it costs twice as much for someone else to build something that competes on an otherwise equal footing with your building—well, they're not very likely to build that something.

USING BOE TO PASS MY EXAM

One last angle on BOE analysis: Last spring, I gave a final exam to the 104 students in my real estate course at the Harvard Business School. It was a case involving a single-family homebuilder. I asked my students to think out loud (on paper) about how this developer should assess his new project, which was then in the planning and negotiation stage.

Assuming I had done my job as a teacher, all the students taking the test knew that there are three basic issues in homebuilding:

- how much it will cost to buy the land, build the homes, and put in the infrastructure
- what price the homes will command
- how quickly the homes will sell

With those three numbers in hand, you can pretty easily work out the profitability of a proposed project assuming a two-year, three-year, or four-year sellout. And by focusing on those variables, you can determine the present value of those income streams.

What happened? Some of my students used their examination time to construct truly elaborate models, building in all the cost and income elements with every possible subset, and finally running a net present value of a particular scenario. This earned a passing grade—but no better.

Other students—the ones who got the *good* grades—focused only on the three factors or variables listed above, ran a number of simple scenarios, and gradually teased out the key sensitivities. What would happen if the homes sold for $260,000, rather than the anticipated $250,000? What if the average price dropped to $240,000?

In this particular case, the builder is in the middle of a protracted negotiation with the community about payments he may be asked to make. There's certainly going to be a school assessment, a drainage fee, and other costs, which are likely to add up to around $2.6 million. But now there's talk about an assessment for access roads outside the development—in theory the community's responsibility, but in fact likely to wind up at the developer's doorstep. (After all, the town wouldn't need to build these roads if the development weren't built.) So how high can this additional assessment go before the developer gives up on his project? A million dollars? Two million?

Does it hurt more to give up the additional money in year 1? (Yes!) How much more than in, say, year 3 or year 4?

Many of my students got to reasonable answers in a limited amount of time, using some version of BOE analysis. Based on that performance, and with a certain amount of seasoning, many of them have great potential to win at the real estate game.

SPREADSHEETS

Although I'm a great proponent of BOE analysis, there are many situations in which a more detailed analysis is helpful—or is required by one of the players in the game.

Such a detailed analysis often takes the form of a *spreadsheet,* which is a simple business tool that I'll assume the reader understands and is more or less familiar with. In their simplest forms, spreadsheets display information so that it can be easily grasped. Very often, they display information over a time period, which shows the impact, say, ten years from now of a decision you might make today. In more complicated forms, spreadsheets structure information in sophisticated ways that allow that information to be manipulated.

Spreadsheets today are almost inseparable from computers, but that was not always the case. (During most of my professional career, in fact, spreadsheets were done laboriously, by hand.) What computers have done is to make spreadsheets, and the information contained within them, easily and endlessly manipulable. It's so easy to run multiple scenarios today, testing variables one at a time to spot sensitivities. What if we needed a new roof in year 5? What would happen if vacancies went up? If rents went up? What would happen in a high-inflation context?

What capitalization rate are you assuming for your income at the time you project you're going to sell the property and exit from the deal? Suppose you're planning to buy at a 9 percent cap rate and sell at an 8 percent rate. What would happen if, when the time came, the exit rate was in fact 9 percent rather than 8 percent? These are important questions, and you'd be foolish not to take advantage of this very useful tool to try and answer them.

On the other hand, spreadsheets (and other computer-based models) have to be kept in their place. What bad things might happen when your computer does all the drudge work instantly, without complaining or costing you very much, and leaves you lots of time to think creatively? Well, for one thing, you can lose sight of the assumptions that lie behind your calculations. Once this happens, your calculations are worth a lot less.

In addition, you might be tempted to keep running the numbers until you finally find a way to make them work. At that point, you might even forget about all the scenarios that *didn't* work. Knowingly or unknowingly, you might start to accentuate the positive. I've seen it happen.

You've already seen a simple spreadsheet in this chapter, although I didn't identify it as such. Remember the multiyear analysis that my friend Stephanie Hanson put together, as she was negotiating with a prospective buyer of her garden-apartment complex in Phoenix? Hanson projected the net operating income (NOI) for her property based on rent increases phased in over a four-year period, and the result was as follows:

Year 1	$450,000
Year 2	470,000
Year 3	490,000
Year 4	510,000

Obviously, no one had to take out a portable computer to do this kind

THE USES OF SPREADSHEET ANALYSES

There are at least ten ways that spreadsheets can be used effectively in the real estate game. They include:

1. For *income properties*, to see the impact of changes in:
   - income levels
   - vacancy and rent-up assumptions
   - operating expenses
   - capital expenditures
2. For *sale properties*, to see the impact of changes in:
   - project costs (including land)
   - timing of costs (especially infrastructure)
   - unit sales price
   - timing of sales
3. To incorporate financing costs related to changes in:
   - amount
   - rate
   - terms
4. On the sale or refinancing of a property, to determine:
   - the impact of different prices and timing of receipt of funds
   - potential benefits from recouping loan amortization previously taken
5. To calculate income tax consequences
6. To calculate overall return on investment (IRR and NPV)
7. To break out return by component parts:
   - cash flow from operations
   - tax benefits
   - future sale
8. To differentiate returns to various parties, such as general and limited partners
9. To establish cash needs over time (sources and uses of funds statements)
10. To provide information to prospective lenders or investors

of math. But what if the inputs were more complicated? What if, for example, the 125 apartments in the complex weren't similar, and generated many different rents? Or what if Hanson had wanted to run multiple scenarios—

for example, testing different levels of rent increases in an effort to hit a desired NOI? In that case, she surely would have turned to a spreadsheet.

In real estate, a typical spreadsheet shows the revenue, operating expenses, debt service, and capital costs over a multiyear period. It may also show a projected sale price at the end of that period. Depending on the intended use of the spreadsheet and the tax situation of the property owner, the spreadsheet may also include the tax consequences that would result from various actions.

Let's look at some specifics.

FINANCING IMPLICATIONS

Spreadsheets can be invaluable in enhancing your understanding of the impact of financing on a proposed deal. We saw in Charlie Leonard's example how much the amount of financing (or the "coverage") can affect returns. We also can vary the cost of the financing and the amortization period of the mortgage.

Earlier in this chapter, in going through BOE analyses, we assumed that financing costs included both the interest and principal on a mortgage, and that the principal payment did not create a current value. This was a deliberate oversimplification, introduced in order to make the back-of-the-envelope approach possible.

In real life, of course, principal payments do build up equity, which obviously complicates the cost-of-financing calculations. But when will the value of that built-up equity be realized, and what will it be worth? You'll need a spreadsheet to get to this answer.

Built-up equity is realized under two circumstances: when the loan is refinanced (a nontaxable event), or when the property is sold (a taxable event). By assuming a point in the future when one of those two events will occur, you can calculate the value of this equity in terms of today's dollars. In either of these scenarios, you can quantify the value of what you've done to upgrade your property—turning dollars of optimism into real dollars—increase your income, and reduce your risk. All of these scenarios can be evaluated through the use of spreadsheets.

In the case of the Concord office building described above, for example, it became clear that Jonathan and I could sell the property at a more favorable capitalization rate in the future, after it was fixed up and rented. In fact, as the spreadsheet made clear, the earlier the sale occurred after that, the better the return, given that the assumed capitalization rate on sale of 9 percent was lower than the 12.5 percent capitalization rate at purchase. As buyers who were willing to take the risk and do the work needed to get the building leased, we expected to earn an annual cash return closer to 12 percent, versus the investor who might later buy our fully leased building at 9 percent.

Again, using spreadsheets, we could run multiple scenarios varying both the sales price and the timing of the sale.

INCOME TAX IMPLICATIONS

Up to this point, we have been ignoring the income-tax implications of our various deals. There is some logic to this pattern of omission. Lenders, for their part, are only interested in pretax cash flow. Many of the buyers in today's markets, moreover, are non-taxpaying institutions such as pension funds. And finally, real estate investment trusts (on which we'll spend some time in the next chapter) are not usually judged on the specific basis of their tax efficiencies.

But for most private investors, Uncle Sam's participation in our deals—both during the operating period and upon sale—is substantial, and therefore needs to be understood in advance. To perform our calculations, we have to keep two sets of books: one for income-tax and one for cash purposes. Consider the diagram.

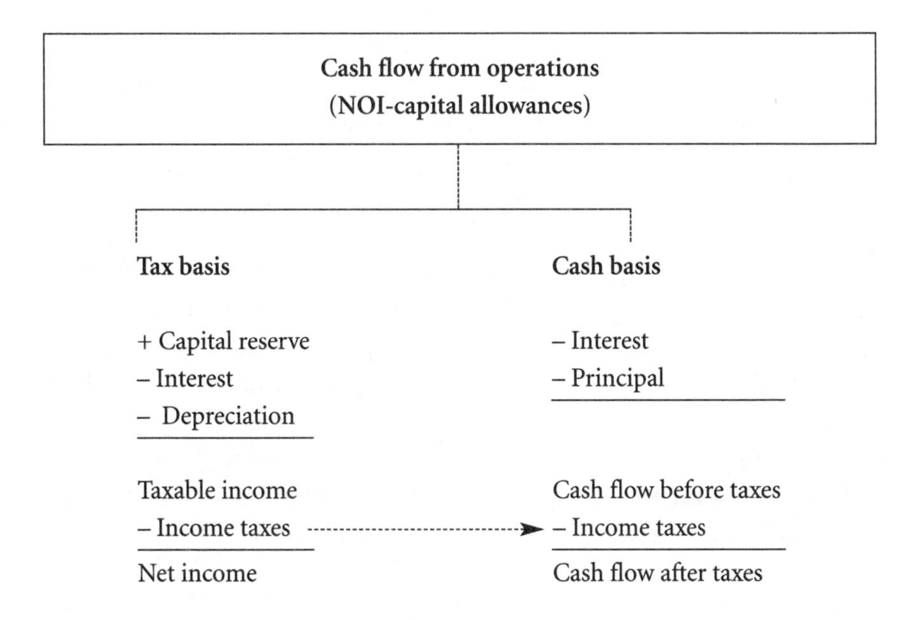

In the calculations, we've had to calculate the income taxes using general accounting principles, and then move the tax payment over to the cash side. Obviously, what we hope is that our depreciation is greater than our principal payments and our reserves. (Otherwise, we'll have to pay taxes on cash that we don't have—a bad outcome!) But one problem we face is that Congress, in recent years, has been reducing the amount of depreciation that can be taken. The revised legislation has lengthened the useful life of properties for tax purposes. In the early 1980s, the allowable useful life for commercial properties was 15 years, which translated into an annual write-off of 6⅔ percent of the cost of a property (less its land value). Now, thanks to more recent legislation, depreciation must be taken over 39 years (or 27.5 years for residential), reducing the annual write-off to slightly over 2.5 percent.

Another key variable that affects tax levels is the total amount of interest payable, which depends not only on the interest rate but also on the amount of the loan. The larger the loan as a percentage of value, moreover, the greater the benefit in an "up market." This (as we've seen in our BOE analyses) is called financial leverage. As an example, in the case of a loan for two-thirds of the value of the property, a 1 percent increase in cash flow from operations will lead to a 3 percent increase in ROE.

The tax consequences are not only of personal significance to the investor, but also affect the ability of taxpayers to compete with non-taxpayers. In the past, during periods of more favorable tax treatment, properties were often cash-flow positive, as they generated taxable losses that could be used to offset other income. This is far less common today, in light of the longer depreciation schedules and other changes in the law restricting such offsets. Today, as a result, the nontaxable investors have the advantage.

NPV VS. IRR

I've gone through these digressions to illustrate some of the more complex valuation and financing questions that can only be answered through the use of a spreadsheet. As part of preparing a typical real estate spreadsheet, it is common to calculate the result of the sale of the property (generally at the end of the tenth year) at a number that capitalizes that final (or the coming) year's cash flow. It is then possible to determine the *net present value* (NPV) or *internal rate of return* (IRR) for the proposed investment.

What's the difference? To calculate the NPV of an investment, you choose a discount rate that you believe is appropriate to the risk level inherent in the investment and discount back from your spreadsheet all after-tax cash flows at that rate (or pretax flows for nontaxable investors). This enables you to see how much profit you might expect to earn above your cost of capital, and to ascertain whether the aggregate profit is high enough to warrant both the risk and the work involved. The IRR, on the other hand, shows you what the actual rate of return on your investment is, takes into account all cash inflows and outflows, and assumes all interim cash flows can be reinvested at that same rate. Again, we use the bottom-line numbers from our spreadsheet.

Both NPV and IRR allow you to take into account *how long* your money is invested and *when* it is invested. Obviously, there's a difference between putting up all the money at once and investing it more gradually.

OVERVIEW OF FEDERAL TAX POLICY TOWARD REAL ESTATE

1. Depreciation enables cash flow from real estate investments to be partially tax-deferred.
2. The six key levers used by the federal government that impact real estate investments specifically—either positively or negatively—are:
   - the number of years over which different kinds of real property can be depreciated
   - the rate of depreciation permitted
   - tax credits for certain activities (i.e., historic preservation, subsidized housing, etc.)
   - rules regarding the use of tax losses to offset other income ("passive loss" rules)
   - the definition of what can be expensed versus what can be capitalized
   - conditions for the issuance of lower-cost, tax-exempt financing for certain real estate classes
3. The tax rate on ordinary income and the differential rate for capital gains affect *all* investments—real estate or otherwise. The federal tax rate for recapture of depreciation (currently 25 percent) is between the 20 percent rate for capital gains and the 39.6 percent highest bracket for ordinary income. In practice, of course, state income taxes should not be ignored.

The timing of the cash outflows can affect your return—although when people are holding money to put into an investment, they tend to hold it in short-term (and therefore lower-yielding) investments. This means that the opportunity to delay putting in the money is often not as helpful as promoters would lead you to believe.

So which should you use—NPV or IRR? My suggestion is to run both calculations (which your spreadsheet program will be happy to do for you) and see which makes the most sense for you. Sometimes the IRR may be very high, but if the payback period is very short, the aggregate dollars you stand to make may not be worth the effort. Similarly, you might be happier with a 20 percent IRR over a longer period of time than a 30 percent IRR of short duration if there's a strong possibility that you'd have trouble reinvesting your money at a 30 percent rate of return. On the other hand, it's difficult to compare several alternative investments if you only have the NPV of each investment in dollar terms. One useful approach is to look at the ratio of the NPV to the total investment. This creates what I call a *profitability index.* For example: a $400,000 NPV (which is the net profit after you've gotten back your initial investment) is 80 percent of a $500,000 investment—but only 50 percent of an $800,000 investment.

The crucial thing to understand, in either case, is what *drives* the returns. Is it cash flow from operating the property over time? (If so, is it from raising rents, reducing vacancy, or lowering expenses?) Or is it the tax benefits? Or is it the future benefits that will accrue either from selling or refinancing the property? Are you predicting a change in the cap rate at the time of the sale? What is your bet?

OTHER USES OF SPREADSHEETS

So far, I've talked about spreadsheets as a tool that is useful to you, as an investor or developer, in circumstances where you have to look forward and try out different "what if" scenarios. But even if you could find a way to live without them, other players in the real estate game would require them.

Prospective lenders, for example, usually expect ten-year projections. (The use of a ten-year period, rather than an eight- or twelve-year period, is only a convention, and doesn't commit you to a particular time frame.) In our Concord example, above, we calculated a loan-to-value ratio to assess the opportunity. Lenders, too, have policies about the percentage of the value of a property that they're willing to loan. (It generally ranges from 60 percent to 80 percent of appraised value.) In most cases, the lender hires an independent appraiser who evaluates the cash flows over the upcoming ten-year period, projects the cash from a sale at the end of the period, and arrives at a valuation. In such cases, your role will be to provide accurate information to the appraiser. (Be cooperative, and don't hesitate to make sure the appraiser takes into account any new sources of revenue or operating savings that you project.) Obviously, an understanding of spreadsheets is a prerequisite to serving this support role.

Investors, too, often demand ten-year projections. In my experience, though, less sophisticated investors (of whom there are many!) don't understand spreadsheets. They pay either too little attention to them, or too much. I hope this book helps address this problem in two ways: by making investors more adept at understanding spreadsheets, and by making direct players of the real estate game better at explaining them. Looking at the longer term, if an investor really understands the assumptions behind the spreadsheets, he or she tends to be a much more tolerant and cooperative partner when you hit a bump in the road.

Spreadsheets are especially useful for projects that are designed for sale, such as single-family home developments, residential or commercial condominium projects, or land developments. These spreadsheets tend to differ from those prepared for income properties, since they spread project costs and sales only until the project is sold out. The key variables are not only the total costs and sales proceeds, but also the *timing* of the flow of funds. This, in turn, determines not only profitability, but also the need for cash. In designed-for-sale projects, it's important to do sensitivity analyses to see what happens if sales are slower than expected. Are your pockets deep enough?

Take a concrete example. A major decision in such projects is what percentage of the infrastructure (e.g., roads, utilities, clubhouses, parks, and so on) has to be put in up front to promote sales. If you plan on selling two hundred homes and wind up selling only one hundred, you'll have to amortize all these costs over only half the anticipated number of units—and you will need considerably more equity in the deal. A spreadsheet lets you look at the consequences of coming up short on the sales side.

In many parts of the world, lenders and investors have much shorter time horizons than are typical in the United States. One reason may be that there is no functioning mortgage market, and investors may want a quick payback to compensate them for the substantial risks involved in real estate.

But a countervailing pressure arises from the fact that longer-term buyers in these circumstances may also fear inflation, and may want to own (rather than lease) real estate. For them, real estate provides a hedge against high inflation. As a result, projects in these countries are often built for condominium, rather than rental, use. Spreadsheets are extremely important in such cases to quantify the plan, and to test the assumptions that lie behind it.

SPREADSHEETS, CAP RATES, AND REALITY

As noted earlier, the use of capitalization rates based on a single year's return can create two kinds of serious definitional problems. First: how should we define the income of the target year? Is it, as suggested earlier, the net operating income (NOI), or is it the cash flow from operations (CFO), that is, before financing and after reserves?

And second, which time period should be used?

- last year (audited or unaudited)
- current leases projected
- the upcoming year
- a "stabilized" year

Some make this decision based on whether they're in a buyer's or a seller's market. My preference is generally to use either the upcoming year, or—if I'm making major changes to the property—a stabilized year. But as we've already seen, if achieving stabilization requires many years, then we need to perform either a multiyear BOE, or a more detailed spreadsheet.

And my answer to the first question, above—NOI vs. CFO—is to use CFO when buying and NOI when selling. (Rest assured that the other side will do its own analysis, anyway, and will only use your number if it reinforces their bargaining position.) But it's worth reiterating, at this point, that both NOI and CFO are subject to a number of operating assumptions. In fact, even "stabilized income" is really only a reflection of current conditions.

Over time, for example, spreadsheets normally assume an increase in rents and expenses. But as we in the business know all too well, rents don't only rise; they also fall. (In the late 1980s, scenarios were often run at inflation rates of 4 percent, zero percent, and –4 percent.) Operating expenses do not always increase at constant rates—as owners found out in the 1970s when heating and electricity costs skyrocketed. Most commercial leases today have operating escalation clauses that pass increases on to the tenants, but in the last analysis—that is, at the time of lease renewal—these higher expenses influence the total amount that a tenant is willing to pay.

The next-to-bottom line, therefore, is to keep a close eye on your assumptions, whether you're engaged in a simple BOE analysis or a sophisticated spreadsheet exercise. Looking at multiple assumptions is a good idea. Growth rates are not always positive. See *clearly* what you're betting on.

And the very bottom line is to do whatever kind of analysis that you're inclined toward—BOE, spreadsheet, or whatever—on a *before-financing* basis first. That's the way that lenders and institutional investors will look at your cash flow. Yes, you should calculate how the amount and cost of financing (and if appropriate, the income-tax consequences) will affect value, but the ability to generate cash flow before financing is what will produce long-term returns.

INTO THE GAME

If you take nothing else away from this book, I hope that you take away a level of comfort and familiarity with back-of-the-envelope (BOE) analysis.

Why? Because that is how the world really works, most of the time. At a recent panel discussion that I moderated, for example, I took an informal survey of the 150 attendees, most of whom were real estate professionals.

"How many of you," I asked them, "use a back-of-the-envelope approach to exploring opportunities, and how many of you use some more sophisticated form of computer modeling?" One person indicated that he relied on computer modeling, and *everyone else* voted for their own version of BOE analysis. Maybe they were all defining "BOE" differently in their own minds, but they all were comfortable with the concept.

A few months later, Sam Zell—head of Equity Office Properties, the largest of all the office REITs—gave a speech to Harvard Business School students. Among his many other observations, he made a point of swearing allegiance to his own version of the BOE approach. *Don't get carried away with number crunching,* he warned the participants.

From my standpoint, BOE helps me allocate my time, as I decide which projects to investigate. It also forces me to isolate and better monitor the key assumptions over time.

In the next chapter, you'll be diving into the first phase of the real estate game: from concept to commitment. In that and subsequent chapters, I'll make regular reference to BOE analysis, and I'll make occasional references to spreadsheets and other more sophisticated kinds of analysis. If these references don't make sense after one or two readings, I'd suggest you take a quick refresher course in the relevant section(s) of this chapter.

CHAPTER 3

FROM CONCEPT TO COMMITMENT

There are four basic ways to invest in real estate from the equity side (as opposed to the debt side)—and thereby to play the real estate game. Going across the spectrum from deep involvement to relative detachment, they are:

- *buying a property directly.* This is the scenario in which you alone, or you in combination with partners, buy a property and play the real estate game directly. (Although we will focus here on direct equity investments, there is always the possibility of providing a loan with both an interest return and some equity upside.)
- *investing in private syndications.* This involves a less intensive commitment on your part. In most cases, you look at a prospectus and decide whether or not you want to become a partner (general or limited) in a particular property or properties.
- *investing in multiproperty funds.* These funds are normally sponsored by a financial advisor or intermediary, and specific properties held by the funds may or may not have been identified in advance.
- *investing in public securities.* As is true for almost any other industry, you can get into real estate through the stock market. REITs (real estate investment trusts) are one of the important financial innovations of the twentieth century.

I assume that you, as a reader of this book, are at least tempted to be an active participant in the real estate game—or that for professional reasons, you have a vested interest in understanding how an active participant looks at the real estate game. If so, the next two chapters should be helpful to you.

They describe how direct investments are made in real estate. They summarize how deals are carried from concept to commitment (Chapter 3) and from commitment to closing (Chapter 4).

Another group of readers may be more interested in what I call "indirect" investments in real estate—single-property syndications, multiproperty pooled funds, and public real estate securities. These kinds of investments are examined in Chapter 5. Even in these cases, though, most properties are acquired by the "umbrella" entity one property at a time, and are usually held in a separate legal title. (This is because the lender wants to make sure that the owner doesn't milk Property A—in which the lender has invested—in order to benefit Property B, financed by somebody else.) So even the biggest real estate investment trust (REIT) is at its heart a collection of individual deals.

Even if you are leaning toward these indirect investments (and away from direct investment), I recommend that you try to understand how real estate professionals proceed from concept to commitment and from commitment to closing. After all, when you invest in a syndication or a REIT, you are really participating in someone else's direct investment. (In the language of Chapters 3 and 4, you are committing to someone else's closing—either impending or already concluded.) It makes sense, therefore, for you to understand how the direct players play the game.

INTRODUCTION: CONCEPT TO COMMITMENT

Concept to commitment is the first phase of the real estate game for the direct investor. In it, you pull your first card, and then—as explained in Chapter 1—you work hard to put together a successful "hand" by pulling and playing cards from that and the other three decks. In this stage, a project progresses from its initial stages—an opportunity emerging after many hours of hard work, or a lightbulb going on unexpectedly—through to a more or less binding commitment.

Let's talk first in general terms about "the real estate business." As I've emphasized in earlier chapters, real estate is not just one business. It is multiple businesses at multiple scales, involving very different kinds of properties. Just because you are "in the real estate business" does not mean that you can do any type of deal. Developing a regional mall is very different from developing a neighborhood center. Success in suburbia does not guarantee success in the city.

Real estate is a relatively easy field to enter. There are many reasons for this. For example:

- There are hundreds of thousands of individual properties out there that are all potential investments.
- Many of these potential investments are small enough that one doesn't have to be Warren Buffett to buy them.
- Virtually all of these properties are custom-designed. This means that there is no overall "pattern" to them, and that each one has to be understood on an individual basis.
- Local knowledge is important, in part because rental markets are highly fragmented and dependent on locale.
- Real estate is an industry that has traditionally financed individual properties as separate legal entities. One doesn't usually get legal title to a block or a neighborhood; one usually gets title to an individual parcel of land, with whatever buildings are on it.

These are the fundamental realities of real estate, and the industry has structured itself to accommodate these realities. By and large, it is an industry of small firms, accustomed to owning just a few properties. (This is changing, for reasons we'll consider in Chapter 5.) Because these firms are small, they tend to purchase most of their services outside, rather than keeping specialists on the payroll. For example, they use outside lawyers, architects, brokers, appraisers, and contractors.

This means that to succeed in this field as a small player, you have to be able to *manage* all these outside, function-based suppliers. You have to understand what a contractor does, what a lawyer does, and so on. The chances are good that you'll pay much more than necessary to your contractors if you can't assess their bids. If you don't understand how law applies to real estate, there's a good chance that your lawyer will negotiate—at a considerable cost!—all kinds of points that may be marginal. And in some cases, you have to know as much as the experts. If the seller's broker tells you that the market will allow you to raise the rents 20 percent, and if that is what will make the deal possible, you have to know whether the broker's assessment is accurate.

I mentioned earlier that real estate is a great field for someone who wants to act as the general manager in a business setting, but doesn't relish the prospect of spending thirty years climbing the ladder at a slow-moving, established company (in other words, the kinds of places that have ladders!). Well, the concept-to-commitment phase is where general management begins, and it requires that you understand all sorts of things.

The three key things that you're trying to accomplish, in the concept-to-commitment phase, are to (1) get information, (2) manage money, and (3) manage your time. Simultaneously, you are trying to evaluate the operating-side risks that may be involved, including, for example:

- location
- product
- marketing/leasing
- regulatory
- environmental

These are evaluations that continue in later phases, but the groundwork all has to be done now.

The concept-to-commitment phase starts with an *opportunity.* As noted earlier, there are lots of opportunities out there. I'll try to offer some suggestions below about how to find good ones.

Once the opportunity is found, it has to be evaluated. I wrote in Chapter 2 about looking at location, market forces, and the visible condition of the building; about doing an initial setup through BOE analysis; and so on. I mentioned that there are free (or at least inexpensive) resources out there to help you in this very preliminary phase—for example, local experts such as bankers and brokers, or data bases on the Internet or elsewhere. Over time, it is likely that the Internet will become an ever more important source of data, both for general contextual research and in regard to specific projects.

During the concept-to-commitment phase, this scrutiny has to become much more intense. But you have to decide how much detail you're going to get into, and when. One of the problems of this initial stage—where you haven't even decided if you're interested in a particular property—is that you really don't want to be spending a lot of your own money on a deal that you may wind up backing away from. Let me say that again in slightly different words for emphasis: During the concept-to-commitment stage, it is *your money* that you are spending. Outside financing comes only after you have tied up the deal. True, you'll probably spend lots more money at that stage, but that money very often belongs to someone else.

Up to a point, you may still get some free (or inexpensive) help in this early phase of the game. If you've already established yourself as a credible source of deals for some of the specialists we've talked about, then they may be willing to help you move a deal through its initial stages. An architect or an engineer, for example, may be willing to come out to a site, perform an informal inspection for you, and not charge you too much. If your lawyer is like most lawyers, he or she likes to charge by the hour, but may charge less when you're just having preliminary discussions about a property.

There are some hidden pitfalls in relying on these more or less informal relationships, including the danger of making forward commitments to specific professionals. In other words, in the concept-to-commitment phase, you are assembling a team. This is a team with special talents, which are appropriate for the acquisition phase, but not necessarily for later phases of the real estate game. The analogy I make is to a political campaign: Those without jobs are often the ones who have the time to give their all to the campaign. Then, when the election is over, they tend to expect important managerial jobs—for which they weren't qualified before the campaign, and for which they aren't qualified now.

Expediency can be costly, over the long term. You'll recall Ben Alexander: one of our four examples from the end of Chapter 1. Alexander began with an inherited building on an excellent site near the State University at Collegetown, and gradually educated himself on the property's potential for development. Early on, he started working with architecture students from the university. Things went well with his development plans—that is, until he ran into an unanticipated soil problem on the property. Solving this problem added substantially to his construction costs. If he had done soil tests earlier, he would have discovered this problem in advance—but to do so would have required money that he was loathe to spend.

Similarly, he used student architects mainly because they were free. When the project got more complicated, inexperienced help became costly help. It's easy to fall into this trap.

Assuming that your deal keeps moving forward, you also begin several sets of parallel discussions in the concept-to-commitment stage. These include exploratory talks with potential partners and potential lenders, as well as very specific negotiations with the seller.

If these negotiations are successful, they lead to a letter of commitment. This is a document that, although usually not binding, leads to formal commitments in subsequent phases.

I'll look at each of these activities in turn. Toward the end of this chapter, I'll present five short case studies, and draw out their concept-to-commitment lessons.

FINDING OPPORTUNITIES

Let's assume that larger market conditions and your personal financial circumstances favor an investment in real estate. How and where does a would-be player find good opportunities?

Well, they say that good writers write about what they know. Generally, I advocate the same thing in real estate. Work with the familiar when possible, and branch out into the unknown only when necessary (or when you can make the risks manageable). If you grew up in Larchmont and have stayed in touch with Larchmont ever since, then Larchmont may be a very good place for you to deal in residential real estate. If you've spent the past five years making loans on commercial properties in Wichita, you've already got the Wichita equivalent of the education that our friend Charlie Leonard was looking for on Beacon Hill. Leonard, you'll recall from Chapter 1, got into the real estate game as a relatively small player, and decided to concentrate on properties on Boston's historic Beacon Hill. In other words, he set out to develop an expertise.

Work with the familiar. It's efficient. It helps you estimate the inherent value of a given property accurately. It keeps you out of trouble by minimizing the element of surprise.

Similarly, *work with people that you know and trust.* I'm now investing in Scott Malkin, the young London-based developer we met in the last chapter. When he went to England to develop his off-price mall concept, I already knew he was thoughtful, committed, and honest. He spent two years studying the best way to get into his chosen niche. By the time he was ready to invest in his first project, I was ready to invest in him. I asked as many questions as I thought would be helpful, and then told him I'd be happy to be involved. Given the results of his initial project, I'm very happy I decided to make that investment.

My approach is to get involved in a market or markets where I have (or a trusted associate has) strong local knowledge and connections. Let me give an example of what I *don't* mean. At the time of this writing, some of the "best" real estate deals for "bottom-fishers" were thought to be in Indonesia. The market had collapsed; properties were being dumped. The concurrent collapse of the local currency made the U.S. dollar powerful. In some ways, this was a perfect moment to jump in and scoop up bargains.

But even while I was thinking in the most preliminary way about venturing into this opportunity-rich environment, I received a phone call from a former student. This student is an Indonesian of Chinese descent. For many years, the ethnic Chinese minority has controlled a disproportionate amount of the wealth and power in Indonesia. Now, in the midst of economic chaos and steep declines in the standard of living, a backlash against the ethnic Chinese community was beginning to gather force. My student told me that his wife—fearing for the family's physical safety—was pleading with him to move the family to Singapore. Since *he* didn't want to play in this market, it certainly made no sense for me, as a complete outsider, to try to establish myself there.

To cite a less extreme example: Several years ago, I received a very handsome mailing offering a position in a very attractive-looking upscale shopping mall in Raleigh, North Carolina. I don't know a lot of people in the North Carolina real estate game, but I did know one person who was intimately familiar with this particular part of the state. "Forget it," he said. "There's a new mall going in two miles up the road with much better anchors. The one they're trying to pitch to you is in for hard times." Frankly, this conversation only confirmed my gut instinct. Why was someone trying so hard to find a buyer a thousand miles from home? What did the locals know that I didn't?

One more example in this vein: About twenty-five years ago, a friend of mine told me he was going to look at a series of adjacent buildings that had come up for sale in a predominantly Italian section of Boston. The area had survived the destructive waves of urban renewal during the 1960s. Situated on the very fringes of the downtown financial district, cut off only by an elevated highway that might someday be removed, this looked like prime real estate.

We started our tour at one end of a row of picturesque brownstones. We went up four flights to the top of the building, and back down to the ground floor. Then we went to the top of the next building, and back down to the ground floor. We toured four or five buildings in a row in this fashion. At the last building, I told the broker, "I really think we should see the basement in one of these buildings."

I was only attempting to be prudent. You learn a lot in basements. We were a few blocks from the ocean. Maybe the basements were under water. "No, no," said the broker with obvious alarm. "You really don't want to see the basement!"

His reaction only heightened my interest in the basement. I pushed the door open and went down the gloomy staircase. When I got to the bottom of the steps, I was astonished to see that large pieces of the walls separating all the basements of the row houses had been knocked down, creating one extremely long, low-ceilinged room. This room was filled with dozens of people busily engaged in bottling gallon jugs of home-made wine. They looked every bit as surprised to see me as I was to see them.

What happened here? My friend and I had strayed far from our home turf (even though we weren't more than a few miles from home). Our excursion into unfamiliar territory wasn't a very productive one. My friend didn't purchase any real estate there. We made several dozen people uncomfortable, and wasted everybody's time.

I want to digress for a few paragraphs on the subject of time management. When you run your own real estate business—in fact, when you run any kind of business—you have to put as many of your hours as possible into productive activities. This is not the same as being stingy with your time, or denying yourself the pleasures of home and family. In fact, one great thing about real estate is that your time is more or less your own. Within reason, you can read that book on Monday at lunchtime, or go to that movie with your spouse on Sunday afternoon, or play that game of tennis on Saturday morning.

In real estate, managing your time well means, first, *only seeing the properties that are useful for you to see.* The definition of "useful" varies greatly depending on where you are in your career. Charlie Leonard knew very little about Boston real estate when he started. Having determined that Beacon Hill was not only a stable neighborhood but one to which he easily related, he set out to look at just about everything he could see in that part of town. This is an inefficient way to buy one property, but it's an excellent way to learn about a given context (a street, a neighborhood, a city, a region, or whatever). To Leonard, almost every property in his chosen neighborhood was useful to look at. Each contributed to his ongoing education in the real estate game.

Later in his real estate career, it's likely that Leonard will be visiting far fewer properties, For one thing, there are only a finite number of buildings on Beacon Hill. After a while, Leonard will have seen all of the building types and many of the individual buildings within those types. More important, he will have established his reputation in the game. Brokers will know to call him when certain kinds of properties come on the market—at least as long as he confines his activities to Beacon Hill.

I don't want to miss the point that some people make a vocation (or at least an avocation) out of looking at properties. Claude Ballard, formerly the head of real estate for Prudential and a general partner at Goldman-

Sachs, has one of the most astounding minds for real estate I have ever encountered. If you name a prominent property in any medium-sized city in the United States, and even in many smaller cities and towns, Ballard can probably tell you something interesting about it, and can usually give you informed insights into the neighborhood within which it is located.

Where did Ballard acquire this deep reservoir of knowledge? In part, it was an outgrowth of his days as a lender at Prudential, where he reviewed literally thousands of potential deals. But equally important, when Ballard travels on business, he likes to rent a car and drive around looking at buildings. When he spots something unusual, he gets out and pokes around, and he remembers almost everything he learns.

My HBS colleague, Arthur Segel, who also runs a large firm investing for major pension funds, checks out most of his acquisitions himself. He wants to have a firsthand grasp on his buildings and their markets—and sees this as the best possible use of his time.

Most of us don't have that kind of time, opportunity, or encyclopedic memory. As a result, we specialize—whether by locale, property type, scale, or condition. As one of my friends used to say, "I am an expert in retail properties, but only those with more than one million square feet. I have no real experience in any other area." He used this knowledge of his own strengths and weaknesses very effectively.

It's experience that gets you to this desired state. In some cases, I know enough about a given neighborhood and building type to know immediately that I'm interested or not interested in a given property. For example: A few years back, when a building next door to one I already owned in Cambridge, Massachusetts, came on the market for a price that seemed reasonable, I knew immediately that I was going to spend a good deal of time trying to make that deal.

This is not a straight-line progression, however. As your scope of activity broadens geographically—as it often does, in the course of a successful real estate career—you may find that you're becoming interested in properties that take *more* time, not less time, to get to and investigate. I used to think twice about going out to visit a property in Worcester, an hour west of Boston. Today, I still think hard about making that trip to Worcester, which has never become familiar territory to me, and where I have no competitive advantage over the locals. In some ways, I'm more inclined to look for opportunities in London, which—although farther away than Worcester!—is more familiar territory to me, since I lived there once for a year.

One last piece of advice on finding opportunities: *make your own.* For example, I'm a firm believer in analyzing the implications of demographic trends for specific real estate markets and types of properties. The Baby Boom, the Baby Bust, and the Baby Boom Echo are certainly familiar enough trends to all of us who read newspapers or watch the evening news. But it's very unusual, in my experience, for people in the real estate business to think systematically about the implications of these and similar demographic phenomena. I'm currently very interested in pilots and prototypes for new kinds of elderly housing. Where will all these Baby Boomers be living in twenty years? Where is the real estate opportunity that lies behind the answer to a societal challenge like that?

And just as important, can I find projects that meet long-term needs and still survive economically in the short term? The real estate field is full of examples of projects whose first and second owners went under—and whose third owners made a lot of money. How can I be one of these "third owners," or at least avoid being an unhappy first or second owner? In many cases, you learn the most from the deals you *don't* do. This is a great form of education, with an attractive cost of tuition.

EVALUATING OPPORTUNITIES

Remember our game diamond, introduced in Chapter 1? One of the four corners of the diamond was labeled "external forces," and I want to open this section with a reference to that corner.

Simply put, when dealing in real estate, you always have to worry about where you are in the cycle. Nobody has a crystal ball, of course. But even as a newcomer to the business, you should be able to develop a feeling for whether you're in a period like the early 1990s—when properties were selling for 30 percent or 40 percent of replacement cost, and were therefore hard to lose money on—or a period like the late 1990s, during which properties are selling near or above replacement costs.

It is always easy in retrospect to identify these cycles. It's *not* so easy, when vacancy rates are high and forecasts call for decades of oversupply, to see the coming upside of the cycle. Down in these depths, you need strong financial partners and an even stronger stomach in order to place your bets on the future.

Periods of low interest rates, in which you may be able to lock in cheap money for long periods of time, are often good junctures to get into the market. Conversely, if interest rates are very high, you may either decide not to get in, or you may use that discontinuity to attempt to negotiate the selling price way down, on the assumption that when interest rates drop you can refinance at a lower rate. This is when you need to ask yourself, *Do I really want to incur significant interest-rate risk, or, does the lower purchase price adequately compensate me for that risk?*

I often use the pressure of external forces as a negotiating tool. "Rates are high," I'll argue, "so I can't afford to pay more." Looking at the same issue from the other side of the table, I try very hard *not* to sell when interest rates are at 15 percent. No one is going to give me top dollar for my property, in that circumstance.

If you're not sure where you are in the larger investment cycle, find out. What are your more experienced peers in the real estate business currently doing? Are they buying, selling, or sitting tight, and why? Buying a property at a 9 percent or 10 percent capitalization rate on existing rents may be quite attractive at or near the bottom of the cycle—unless, of course, the present leases reflect above-market rates.

Another good (and related) question to ask is, "Is it important to be fully invested in real estate at this point in time?" A mutual fund manager often acts on the assumption that he or she has to keep the fund's money more or less fully invested. If you've put your money in the Magellan Fund—your manager figures—you've evidently made the decision that you want to be in the market; so the manager acts on that mandate.

Real estate should be viewed differently. For one thing, direct real estate investments do not come in the small-dollar chunks that you can use to buy an interest in a mutual fund like Magellan. In real estate, you tend to be channeled into large investments. Real estate, moreover, is an illiquid investment. (You won't be able to pull your money *out* of real estate as easily as you can pull out of Magellan.) Therefore, the purchase decision in real estate should be seen as a *highly opportunistic one*, and you should not feel pressured to be fully invested at all times. Besides, prices of individual properties do not change as rapidly as individual stocks. You don't have to worry about the market running away from you so quickly.

We've already discussed (in Chapter 2) some tools for evaluating opportunities, in the context of BOE analysis. But there are other good questions to ask, when it comes to evaluating opportunities.

One of these good questions is, *Why did this deal come to me?* Why am I so lucky?

Is it because everybody who knows something about this property has turned it down? Has everyone else already decided the price is too high? Is it coming to me because I've got similar properties? Is it coming to me because they know I have money available to invest at this point in time? Is it coming to me because they can't figure out what to do with the property, and they figure I might come up with something unusual to do with it—perhaps because I've rehabbed and changed use of properties before? Is it coming to me because there's a tough zoning problem involved, and they think I have the connections to work that out? Are they bringing it to me because they think the seller is someone I might develop a rapport with?

Obviously, there are all sorts of reasons, good and bad, why a deal might be brought to you. It's important to understand these motives up front. Some of my best deals were brought to me because people knew I would include them as partners in the deal, and they wanted a chance to be on the equity side. (One of the big lures of real estate is the relative ease of becoming an equity owner, since each project has its own legal structure and is run as a separate business.) By contrast, if they took the deal to a big company, there'd be little chance of that big company allowing a small player to participate in a meaningful way in the ownership structure.

BOE analysis, combined with the answer to the *why me?* question, should help you rule properties in or rule them out. The next set of questions you should ask should be designed to give you a clear sense of the *context* of the deal. Is there a competing mall going in up the street? Are the rents below, at, or above market? How many leases are close to expiring, and what does that mean? (If your leases are below market and the market is strong, impending vacancies are a good thing; if you're likely to be overpriced in a weak market, vacancies may be poison.)

To some extent, the broker involved in the deal can help with comparative statistics. Most large brokerage firms can supply you with vacancy reports on particular submarkets, and that information (if up-to-date) tends to be fairly reliable. Remember, though, that the broker works for the other team, and is compensated only if the deal goes through. You are generally well advised to develop your own, independent sources of information, and to cross-check everything that you learn.

Marketing data bases, available for a price through the Internet, can be a useful resource, although information pertaining to individual properties at this point is often very sketchy, and tends to get out of date quickly. (The Internet is only as up to date as the latest data entry.) There are a number of specialized research firms who do nothing but track certain kinds of real estate-related data, and these firms will be happy to sell you a service. Don't forget an important resource that you've already paid for: the U.S. government's census data and other demographically based information.

If you sense that you're getting into a situation where you simply can't do the homework that's necessary—and maybe that Italian section of Boston twenty years ago was a good example of this—consider bailing out. Be appropriately skeptical when you can't get the information that you need. Make it a goal to learn what you don't know. Above all, *get into the network.* Charlie Leonard had to spend a lot of time not only getting to know his Beacon Hill market, but also establishing contacts and credibility with the local brokerage community, which eventually provided him with his first deals

IS THIS DEAL FOR ME?

A potential real estate deal can be good or bad on its own merits. (BOE analysis, as presented in the last chapter, can help you sift and sort among deals that are promising and deals that are not.) But there's a second important question to ask about an opportunity: Is this deal for me?

As I explained in Chapter 1, you get into the real estate game by pulling a card from any one of the four decks in our game: players, properties, capital markets, or external forces. (The exception, of course, is when the first card is dealt to you, as in the form of an inherited property.) This decision ought to stem from your understanding of your own goals and values. Are you trying to put a building or plot of land to more productive use? Are you looking to diversify your holdings or generate income for your children's college tuitions? Or are you trying to add some value yourself—thereby creating the possibility of making more money—by capitalizing on a particular trend, by drawing upon the personal skills of you and your associates, or by taking advantage of your knowledge of a particular area?

If you're drawn to the active role, rather than the role of the passive investor, how much time do you have? What personal experiences can you bring to bear on a project? How confident are you that once you've pulled the first card from the deck, you can put together cards from the other three decks to make a successful deal? How much money do you have available to put up? How much money can you afford to lose?

Another way to ask this question is, *What's your risk profile?* Do you want to get involved with a property in an area that you think may be risky, but will have enormous upside potential if it works? Or do you want a more secure property? Are you looking "far out" in the market, trying to anticipate trends? Or are you more comfortable working within an established market?

Does the project involve construction or extensive remodeling? If so, do you have the time and experience needed to supervise the job? Charlie

Leonard thought he did, when he bought his four-unit building on Boston's Beacon Hill. He also was willing to go farther out on the risk curve in search of greater rewards.

In addition to risk profiles, you have to think about your own personal set of values. For example: Is this a property where you'll have to evict people to change uses? Are you planning to provide assisted living units for elders, and if so, do you really feel comfortable running that kind of business? If you know a certain deal is going to be highly political, do you want to get involved? Traditionally, the landlord is portrayed by politicians, the media, and community activists as someone who is trying to change a community for the worse—and the more visible the project, the more intense the invective is likely to become.

If you don't like seeing yourself portrayed negatively in the paper, there are certain kinds of projects you don't ever want to get involved in. Suppose you're contemplating a development in the middle of a beautiful wooded area, to which everybody in town has a romantic attachment. For some developers, this is no big deal: I've got the zoning I need, so damn the torpedoes. For other developers, this is one to run from, as hard and fast as possible.

Working in foreign countries poses different kinds of challenges, many of which can lead to our same basic question: Is this deal for me? Leverage is often hard to achieve. Legal documents, including tenant leases, rarely take the same form or have the same meaning as in the United States. (For example: Under the Napoleonic Code, which governs all real estate in France, tenants can't be evicted between October and May—a rule originally formulated to protect tenant farmers from being evicted in the off-season.) What if you find yourself working in a region where nothing much gets done unless government officials are paid off? Will you be comfortable delivering the payoffs? Will you be comfortable if you're paying someone to do it for you? Will you be comfortable if you never quite know who's paying off whom?

WORKING WITH FINANCIAL INSTITUTIONS

There's another set of negotiations that begins in the concept-to-commitment phase. These are the negotiations between the prospective buyer and the financial institutions that will make the deal possible. But a basic principle to remember is that *the best opportunities in real estate tend to arise when financing is most difficult to obtain.*

When a deal presents itself to me, one of the first questions I ask myself is, "If I do this deal, how am I going to finance it?" I have ongoing relationships with a few banks, and this is a point when I'm very likely to take advantage of one of those relationships. I make an appointment with one of my favored short-term construction lenders—let's call her Sarah Smith—and I go in and describe the broad outlines of the deal to her. I share some of my BOE calculations with her, and describe what I know about the tenancy, current and prospective. "I think I'll be able to pick up this warehouse for $1.35 million," I say. "What kind of mortgage can you give me on that?"

If I've told Smith that I've got solid, long-term tenants lined up, she may suggest that a 70 percent (or $900,000) mortgage would be appropriate. If my prospective tenancy is less solid, she may tell me that the bank is unlikely to go above 60 percent.

Nothing is actually being committed at this point. Nevertheless, through this kind of back-and-forth, I'm picking up some very useful information from Smith. If her institution has an opinion about this particular property or area, for example, I'm getting a feel for that. (I was once talked out of a deal in New Hampshire by the cautionary tales of a local banker in that state. He was exactly right, for that point in time.) If the bank is skittish about the direction of the local economy, I learn more about that. I'm getting a feel for how the bank will look at this deal (and to some extent, how they're looking at me). If I'm counting on an 80 percent mortgage and Smith tells me the real number is likely to be more like 60 percent, I may have to consider bringing in more partners on the deal or putting in more of my own money. Or, of course, I can go try another bank.

But I don't do so lightly, because relationships will become more important in subsequent phases of the deal. In many cases, the deal needs to change in midstream, and the bank has to be prepared to be flexible. Let's say you and your bank agree on a loan of a certain size, based on the assumed gradual lease-up of vacant space. Then a very attractive prospective tenant arrives on your doorstep with a proposal: "I'll take all your available space on a long-term lease if you'll put up an extra $20 per square foot for tenant improvements—for which I'll be happy to pay a higher rent." Now you need more up-front money from the bank, and you need your banker to be flexible enough to adjust the deal accordingly. And to restate the obvious: they'll be *much* more likely to flex if they know you well, and trust you.

Jonathan and I once bought a small office building in a suburban office complex. The building had very good tenancy. Our bank offered us an 80 percent mortgage. A year later, a similar building came on the market, and we wanted to buy it as well. The problem was that this building was empty. The bank proposed a 60 percent mortgage. Negotiations began. The agreement that we finally reached was that the bank would indeed put up 80 percent, but that we would personally guarantee the difference between 60 percent and 80 percent until this new building was leased up to the same level as the first building—at which point we would be released from our guarantee.

So banking relationships are important. The problem is that these relationships are harder to come by today—and this isn't simply a case of me waxing nostalgic for the Good Old Days. When banks got into trouble in the early 1990s, three bad things happened. First, a lot of savings and loans (S&Ls) went belly up because they had overloaned on too many properties. These small, independent, and proudly local banks were a very important resource to people like Charlie Leonard, the would-be Beacon Hill real estate entrepreneur. They knew—or at least *thought* they knew—local real estate intimately. When a newcomer like a Charlie Leonard struck a good deal, the S&L was inclined to back him.

The second bad thing that happened as a result of the troubles of the early 1990s was that the surviving banks became much more bureaucratized. Under the stern gaze of the regulators, banks became much less willing to put real authority in the hands of their junior loan officers, who—because of their relative inexperience—might get the bank into trouble again. Because I've been at the real estate game for a while, I get to talk to someone like Smith, who is in a position to give me good guidance and can make decisions. Unfortunately, the Charlie Leonards of today are far more likely to talk to people who *sound* something like Smith, but are really only gatekeepers.

Third, there are fewer people to talk to. The wave of bank mergers (which will most likely continue) has reduced substantially the number of lenders.

When dealing with banks, remember that personal liability is a very important issue. One of the things that got real estate investors into trouble in the 1980s was signing a mortgage personally, allowing the lender to look not only to the cash flow from the property but also to all the other assets of the borrower. This is something my grandfather warned me about a long time ago, based on his personal experience in the 1930s: Don't *ever* sign for anything personally you can't pay back with ease. Lots of people lost all their assets in the 1930s when they failed to heed this rule—and two generations later, a new round of investors made the same mistake.

To some extent, the need for "recourse financing" depends on the percentage of the transaction that the bank is being asked to finance—in other words, the bank's exposure. (A "recourse" mortgage is a loan for which the borrower is personally liable. A non-recourse mortgage means that the property being financed is the sole security for the loan.) If the bank is only being asked to loan two-thirds of the property's value, it will be much less insistent on getting personal signatures than it would be if it were loaning 90 percent of value. The lesson for new players in the real estate game, therefore, is to bring in enough capital, even if you have to involve partners, to ensure that the bank's comfort level is fairly high—and then try like crazy not to put your personal guarantee behind *any* deal.

There are alternatives to going directly to a bank. One such alternative is a mortgage broker, whose job it is to put together sources of money with deals that are appropriate for that particular source. Mortgage brokers exist because there are so many different sources of potential mortgage money in the marketplace today, and not even an experienced developer can hope to keep up with the changing cast of characters. It may be, for example, that a particular insurance company is interested in putting out money in the next three to six months to back a certain kind of property. If so, I as a developer am not likely to know that—but a mortgage broker is.

Because mortgage brokers are experienced players in the real estate game, they often can lend valuable perspectives on proposed deals. And because they almost always work on commission, they are highly motivated to spot sensible deals and help them go through. Like a good banking relationship, therefore, a good relationship with one or more mortgage brokers can be a key asset.

Keep in mind that one rarely gets a formal commitment of money at this stage of the game. (If you don't control the property through an agreement with the seller, you usually can't get such a commitment.) But you can get a good feel for the market by talking with potential lenders, and this can be very useful when it comes to negotiating with the seller. Just be reasonable about how often you bother a particular banker before you actually buy a building. Recognize that the banker needs reassurance that you know what you're doing, part of which means using his or her time wisely.

NEGOTIATING WITH THE SELLER

The most important negotiations in the real estate game take place in the phase that we're currently discussing: the concept-to-commitment phase. This is the phase when the deal takes shape. Curiously, many more negotiating hours are likely to be expended in the commitment-to-closing phase.

Those conversations, though, are generally aimed at hammering out the less important details of the deal. By that point, the die is more or less cast.

A great deal has been written about negotiations. Some of my academic colleagues specialize in what one calls the "art and science of negotiation." Students at the Harvard Business School (and at other business schools) take courses in negotiation strategies and techniques. If you want a sense of the vitality of the negotiation/mediation/arbitration industry, go to any bookstore and count the number of books devoted to these subjects.

I'm convinced that there's no one "right" way to negotiate. Effective negotiation depends in part on the style of the person who's doing the negotiating. Some people love to pound on tables, while others feel very uncomfortable doing that. Some people are flexible enough to adopt very different roles for different sets of negotiations (or even different stages of the same negotiation). And it may be appropriate to negotiate one way with one group of people and another way with another. I've often found that the personal rapport that develops (or doesn't develop) in a negotiation can be very important. This rapport may be with the broker—the intermediary—as well as with the seller. Prior relationships often influence outcomes.

Effective negotiation also grows out of the nature of the particular deal at hand. It's great to "get to yes," and let everybody win; but in some cases this isn't possible. Are there key issues besides the price that are very important to each side? If so, this may make trading across issues (the source of "win/win" solutions) possible. But it won't work if there's nothing to trade.

This means (to me, at least) that a good negotiator's greatest skill is in reading people and understanding what they are really looking for. For example, it may be that a *speedy* sale is very important to the seller. Or it may be that the seller wants rock-solid assurances that the buyer has the money. If this is the case, the seller may take a lower offer from that gold-plated buyer, rather than taking a chance on someone who offers a slightly higher price but may have to scramble to get the money.

Maybe this topic deserves a few more words at this point. Every seller wants to be sure that the buyer will have the capacity to close on the deal, roughly on the terms that have been agreed to in the letter of commitment. What the seller *doesn't* want is for the property to go off the market for two months—thereby slowing down its sale—and then return to the market with a "damaged goods" odor attached to it. The next round of potential buyers is very likely to ask, "What went wrong with that last buyer? What did he or she discover?"

Some buyers fail to get the financing that they committed to in their offer. In some cases, this is an honest miscalculation; in others, it's an unsavory bait-and-switch. "Gee, I *wanted* to pay you the full $5 million," says the buyer, "but that turns out to have been too much. The bank says I can't go above $4 million." Obviously, this is the kind of buyer that the seller dearly hopes to weed out, much earlier in the process. A buyer who ties up properties by offering high prices initially and then renegotiates downward eventually acquires a credibility problem, and sooner or later gets cut out of the "deal stream" by sellers and their agents.

Having asserted that all negotiations are different, I should add that there *are* certain general rules you can follow in order to increase your chances of success at the bargaining table. The most important of these is to *come prepared.* The person who knows the most about the property oftentimes will be the most creative in figuring out how to do a deal. A former labor leader was known nationally as a tough negotiator. When asked if that was the key to his success in obtaining favorable contracts for his union, he said no, but that his industry was made up of a lot of small, regional firms. As he was the only one negotiating nationally, he knew more about what they could afford than *they* did. Since he had more information at his command, he could do a better job negotiating.

Another good reason to be fully prepared: in the give-and-take of negotiation, you have to be able to think (and act!) on your feet. Suppose someone on the other side of the table makes a surprise concession, or presents a brand-new inducement, and you sense that they're ready to make a deal. If you have to spend a lot of time evaluating that offer, you may wind up losing the chance to accept (or counter) it. You can only move quickly if you've done your homework.

A second fundamental rule of negotiations in the commitment-to-closing phase is to *understand value.* You simply can't get to the right bottom line unless you know the assumptions driving your analysis. The imperative to understand value is one reason why I devoted a lot of space in the previous chapter to BOE analysis.

But remember that in real estate, as in the stock market, "value" is not a precise term. It's "value" as best you can come up with it at a given point in time, having made a lot of spoken or unspoken assumptions about the future. If you're someone who's willing to pay a terribly high multiple for Microsoft, that's because you think Bill Gates's company will continue to grow and dominate its world. Similarly, some people have gotten comfortable paying a high multiple for Coca-Cola because they truly believe that Coke can guarantee sustained growth around the world.

Keep in mind that when you're negotiating a real estate deal, you may have two parties at the table who define "value" quite differently. The sooner you know that, the better.

Many people who are new to the real estate game (or to any kind of negotiation, for that matter) assume that they have to beat down the other side to succeed. This is not always true. I recently gave an exam to my students in which I had an experienced developer pay the full asking price ($5.4 million) for a parcel of land outside Washington, D.C. This was a site with a lot of wetlands, which the town had zoned for 450 garden apartment units. Why, I asked my students, would an experienced builder pay full price for what looked like a suspect property?

I also gave them enough clues to tease out the answer. The property that sat under a garden apartment might be worth $10,000, more or less. But a slightly larger piece of the same property sitting under a single-family home might be worth $30,000 or $40,000. Because of the wetlands, the property didn't make sense as a site for 450 garden apartments, but it turned out to make a lot of sense as a site for 160 single-family attached homes. Once the developer got reassurance from the town that this revised use would be acceptable, he was more than willing to pay the full asking price. It was a fair deal, and he would have been foolish to risk losing the property over the relatively small amount he might have saved by dickering and trying to beat the other side down.

This is not to say that prospective buyers should throw money around, or fail to get the best possible deal. This is yet another fundamental rule of negotiation: *Figure out the position of the seller.* Assume the seller is as smart as you. Why is he or she walking away from the opportunity that this property represents? Is there a chance that the seller knows something you don't? To avoid this risk, I always aim to be the most prepared person at the table. (*Come prepared!*) I want to be able to represent their point of view better than they can.

Another rule of negotiation is, *Be relentlessly clear-eyed.* Value is the present worth of future benefits. You have to apply appropriate discounts for risk, even though it is not easy to quantify them. Put a price on things you know, and on things you can't know.

For example? In Japan today, American real estate "vulture firms" are bidding less than 10 percent of the face value of some nonperforming commercial mortgages. Why? To be sure, some are simply bottom-feeding. (They have in their minds the kinds of deals they got back in the States in the early 1990s, when the Resolution Trust Company unloaded thousands of unwanted properties that the government had taken over.) The discounts that U.S. investors are applying in Japan are even greater, allowing those investors to account for various uncertainties. They are not sure, for example, about the dependability of foreclosure laws in Japan, and they're not convinced that they would get very good title to the buildings if they were to foreclose. They're also worried about the long-term viability of some of their prospective Japanese tenants. They are building these and other uncertainties into their highly discounted bids.

Sometimes reducing the risks is more important than reducing the price. As my Harvard colleague Howard Stevenson likes to say—with only slight exaggeration—"If you let me name the terms, I'll let you name the price." What he means, for example, is that if the seller is willing to take back 90 percent of the purchase money at a below-market rate, the price can go up and not hurt the deal. Maybe the seller could wind up being a tenant in your building. If so, what rent are they willing to pay, and how much of the available space would they be willing to take? Again, how much risk are they willing to take off your shoulders? Will the seller give you a long-term option to attempt to change the zoning?

Certainly you should *know your alternatives to this deal* when you negotiate. Is there a time delay associated with this particular set of negotiations? If so, will that prevent you from concluding some other deal? When the other side starts making demands, know the point at which you lose interest. If you're negotiating with current or potential tenants in a soft rental market, for example, be clear in your own mind the point at which you'll stop making concessions to these tenants and start looking for new ones. Yes, it's a lot tougher playing a weak hand, but these are the times when your skills as a negotiator must come into play.

What else? *Be patient.* Too many people lose patience in the course of negotiations. As a result, they wind up negotiating with themselves—that is, making three successive offers before the other side has had a chance to respond to the first.

We're currently working with somebody on a particular parcel of land that he owns, that he would like to co-develop. One of the conditions for this to occur is that the business he's currently running on the property has to be sold to someone else, who will agree to relocate. We've figured out that it really doesn't make much sense for us to spend a lot of time negotiating the particulars of the deal with him until he negotiates such a sale. Although it's a deal we'd like to do, we've only spoken to him occasionally during the past four or five months, and it may be many more months before he's really ready to talk with us.

Leave your ego home. It has often struck me that some people are more interested in impressing their partners or their adversaries with their tough negotiating posture than in getting the deal done. You can't focus on what the seller needs if you're concentrating on your own image.

In the same spirit, it's almost never a bad idea to acknowledge that you've made a mistake. Let me give a somewhat roundabout example. A woman was offered a large parcel of land in 1960 on the Martha's Vineyard waterfront. The price was $50,000. She thought that was very high, and turned the deal down. A year later, the person who bought the land came to her and said he'd sell her *half* of it for $50,000. This time, even though nothing dramatic had changed in the market, she bought—and that $50,000 investment is probably worth $5 million today. My point is that she disengaged her ego from that second round of negotiations—she didn't get hung up on the fact that she blew it, first time around—and made an excellent investment as a result.

THE LETTER OF COMMITMENT

When real estate negotiations are successful, they lead to agreement on the major points of the deal: price, timing of purchase, the broker(s) involved, special conditions regarding financing or tenants, the amount of time allotted to do the physical inspection, and so on. This set of agreements is summarized in a document sometimes called the letter of commitment, and other times called the letter of intent.

The letter of commitment is a first draft. It is subject to revisions, both large and small, and it is not binding. No money changes hands. But it serves several useful purposes. Most important, it gets the two sides to agree to something in writing. Almost as important, it defines what remains for the lawyers to do. "We've got a deal that is based on the following price and terms," the letter of commitment says, in effect. "Go work out the details."

Let's revisit Joe Pena, the broker from Chapter 2 who was trying to interest me in a warehouse/office complex in Waltham. My BOE analysis was leading me to think that $1.3 million was the right price for this property, as opposed to the owner's asking price of $1.5 million. This is often the point in the conversation when the broker politely says that the owner is firm at his asking price, and my response is usually, "Well, O.K.; keep me in mind if and when he decides to come down a bit."

Let's assume that the broker calls back after a few weeks or months and says that he now has a more motivated seller, who might respond well to an offer of around $1.35 million. At this point, we're only separated by $50,000, more or less. I run my BOE numbers again, and I decide that I like what I see. At this point, if I'm unfamiliar with the property, I may go visit it for a visual once-over. Assuming that I get no bad surprises and am feeling even more optimistic about the market, I contact the broker and say that I'm in at $1.35 million.

Now the broker prepares a "term sheet," which both parties ultimately are expected to sign. The term sheet generally includes the price of the property, financing contingencies (if any), the term before closing (most often sixty days), the amount of the deposit (often approximately 5 percent of the price), any required actions for due diligence (described subsequently), and any other actions that need to be taken between now and the closing.

For example, as the buyer, I may insert a condition saying that during the first thirty days of the sixty-day period, I will commission a physical inspection of the building and any environmental testing that seems to be necessary. I may also stipulate that if the property comes up short—and in the environmentally conscious and litigious 1990s, this most often means environmental problems—I will get all my money back. (The term "soft money" is often used to denote a deposit that is easily returnable, while "hard money" is considered forfeitable if I don't go through with the deal.) I may stipulate that the owner cannot negotiate with any other parties during the initial thirty-day period.

The owner, too, seeks to protect his interests. He is taking his property off the market for one or two months, and deserves reassurances that I'm serious about the proposed deal. He may insert a clause stating that during the second thirty-day period, I can only get my deposit back if he fails to deliver a valid title (which is needed in order for me to own the property free and clear of any unwanted liens).

When the term sheet is signed, it becomes what is known as a "letter of commitment." The underlying reality of the letter of commitment is that it is not legally binding. In fact, most letters of commitment include a statement to that effect: "Neither the buyer nor the seller is bound by this until a formal purchase and sale agreement is signed by both parties." But it is important for the two parties to get the basic parameters of the deal on paper, and to emotionally commit to them.

FIVE DEALS, AND WHAT THEY MEAN

Now that we've walked through the key activities that occur during the concept-to-commitment phase, let's look at five specific examples of how individuals or companies went from concept to commitment. I've chosen these five stories to illustrate concept to commitment on a variety of scales, and also in a wide range of contexts. Although these examples underscore how different one real estate deal can be from the next, they do have some fundamentals in common—and collectively, they portray an early and important phase of the real estate game.

BILL ZECKENDORF BUYS THE STOCKYARDS

Between the 1950s and 1970s, William Zeckendorf, Sr., was one of the most creative players of the real estate game. He was initially responsible for projects like Kips Bay in New York, Mile High Center in Denver, Century City in Los Angeles, and Place Ville Marie in Montreal.

Zeckendorf possessed an amazingly prescient vision of the possible futures of our downtown areas, and he was also bold. This was a combination that led to both triumphs and disasters. When he brought enough people along with him in his vision, he achieved great things. But when he got too far ahead of conventional thinking, he sometimes found he had no troops behind him. Sometimes he couldn't get things built. Sometimes he got things built, only to find that the host city couldn't complete the infrastructure necessary to make his project work. And more than once, he had to sell other properties to pay down the high levels of debt on his new ventures. In his enthusiasm to do *more,* he often found himself on the financial cliff edge.

In the years immediately following World War II, Zeckendorf was starting to get active in New York City real estate. He was far from a real estate mogul at that time—in fact, he was scrambling to make a living. So when a broker approached him about a very unusual nine-acre parcel on New York's East Side, Zeckendorf had mixed reactions.

The biggest problem was the property itself. The parcel was the site of the last working slaughterhouse on the island of Manhattan. Owned by members of the Chicago-based Swift meat-packing empire, the slaughterhouse was a blight on the entire neighborhood. It generated terrible smells, was an eyesore, and created unnecessary congestion in an already crowded part of the city. For all these reasons, it dragged down property values for blocks in every direction. Was this a good proposition for a young and relatively inexperienced developer? Zeckendorf was then concentrating on midtown office properties. This parcel—a working slaughterhouse in a grimy industrial section—seemed to be about as far from his own area of expertise as he could get and still stay on the island of Manhattan.

A second problem was the credibility of the broker. At first, it wasn't clear whether this broker really spoke for the Swift family. Maybe, Zeckendorf speculated, the broker was freelancing—trying to line up an eager buyer as a way to strengthen an unsolicited approach to the owner. If that was the case, Zeckendorf didn't want to waste his own time.

Zeckendorf was soon persuaded that the broker was authorized to represent the seller. (It soon emerged that the broker's wife was related to the Swifts, and therefore he really did have an exclusive on it.) But the proposed price was a sticking point. Zeckendorf knew that land prices in the area of the slaughterhouse were then between $3 and $5 a square foot. The broker was asking $17. Zeckendorf offered $5 a foot, and got turned down cold.

As negotiations progressed, Zeckendorf gradually began to rethink his position. Why was he only bidding $5 a square foot, when land only a few blocks away was going for between ten and twenty times as much? What was depressing the slaughterhouse area was the *slaughterhouse*—which the buyer of the property could simply tear down.

Here's one of the simplest back-of-the-envelope analyses imaginable: I'm going to engage in a total tear-down, so the conditions of the buildings is irrelevant. I know the overall area, and have good sources of information. If I buy a depressed property and remove the eyesore that sits in the middle of it, my investment is likely to triple or quadruple in value, almost overnight.

Zeckendorf offered the full asking price: $17 per square foot. He put some interesting conditions on the purchase, however. The first was financing: Zeckendorf needed time to assemble the necessary $6.5 million. Getting a mortgage for a large percentage of the $6.5 million would have been difficult. He proposed that he put $1 million down—$1 million that he didn't actually have in cash, at that point—and hand over another $5.5 million at the end of a year, at which point the property would change hands. The Swifts agreed, in part because it would give them a year to shut down their operations in an orderly way. The search for money began.

Meanwhile, Zeckendorf put another condition on the sale: that it should be kept confidential during the one-year waiting period. Again, this suited the needs of the sellers—who were in no hurry to announce large-scale layoffs—and they agreed. What Zeckendorf had in mind was to buy up as much property as possible in the immediate vicinity of the slaughterhouse at the then-depressed price levels. How would he use this ever-growing site? He didn't know.

We'll leave Bill Zeckendorf much as he was in the spring of 1946, at the end of his concept-to-commitment phase: on the hook to hand over an additional $5.5 million for a site which he didn't know exactly how he would develop. In the next chapter, we'll finish his story. For now, I'll offer two observations on Zeckendorf.

First, I'll put him in the context of the real estate game described in Chapter 1. The first card, in his case, was a *property* card, dealt to Zeckendorf by the broker representing the Swift family. What Zeckendorf first had to do was define himself as a player in this particular game: Do I want to get involved in this? Can I add value?

Next, he had to buy time so that he could assemble backing from the *capital markets,* which turned out to be a substantial challenge. And finally, he had to grapple with an unexpected turn of events in the "real world"—to which we'll return in Chapter 4.

I also want to draw out some of the concept-to-commitment lessons inherent in the Zeckendorf story. First, we see how important it is to have knowledge of a particular area. We see how important creativity is—the ability to see things in new ways. Specifically, in the case just described, Zeckendorf saw the irrelevance of "comparable prices" when the proposed deal could change the rules of the game. I mentioned earlier that deals sometimes come to you because people think you're imaginative, and you may be able to see potential that others may not. Zeckendorf was viewed as someone who might see potential resulting from removal of the slaughterhouses, and so the deal came to him.

We also saw how important the terms of the letter of commitment were, in Zeckendorf's case. First, they gave him a long time frame in which to close. They also assured him secrecy, which gave him the chance to buy numerous adjacent parcels of land. These were the key variables that affected the ultimate outcome of the deal.

AVA BERGMAN MOVES TO NEW YORK

For our second story, we'll stay in New York City, but go quite a few blocks uptown to a very different setting. We'll also move forward about a half century to the very recent past.

About a year ago, a friend of my wife and me, whom we'll call Ava

Bergman, decided for personal reasons that she needed to move from Philadelphia to New York City. She knew New York slightly, but had only a rudimentary sense of New York property values. She was being told by her financial advisors that both the real estate and stock markets were then very high, and she was determined not to overpay at what looked like it might be the height of the market. Or, put more positively, she wanted to make sure she got good value, so that when the downturn came, she would not be hurt too badly.

Like Charlie Leonard (introduced in Chapters 1 and 2), she began doing her homework. She met with a lot of brokers, and looked at a lot of apartments. Finally, she found one that she really liked: a co-op on the Upper East Side. It was a medium-sized co-op apartment with lots of attractive features—high ceilings, nice finishes, the right number of rooms, and so on. It was in a middle-sized building: small enough to be homey, and large enough to have good security.

At this point, Bergman gave me a call, and we had the first of several discussions that went on over the next several weeks. I listened to her enthusiasm for the property, and also to her anxiety about overpaying. (In addition to worrying about her potential investment, she didn't want to seem "amateurish" as she moved into a new city.) I told her that her calculation should be different from that of a real estate professional. Unlike Charlie Leonard, for example—the Beacon Hill real estate novice described in Chapter 2—she planned to *live* in the property she would be acquiring, and live there for a long time. She had other assets, and didn't really need to make a quick or substantial return on this investment. She hoped to get much of the money needed for the purchase from the sale of her existing home in Philadelphia.

"If I were you," I said, "I think I'd ask myself four questions. First, am I willing to wait an unspecified period of time—maybe several years—for the next real estate recession to knock down prices? If the answer is 'no,' then I need to buy something. This is how corporations needing space look at their real estate purchases: sometimes you have to buy, even though it might be the top of the market.

"Next, how much is the quality of life that this particular apartment would give me *worth* to me? If the answer is 'a lot,' then this looks like a good choice from that perspective.

"Third, what's the market like for the sale of my current home? Is it correlated to New York? If my present house sells slowly, can I arrange interim or 'bridge' financing?

"And finally, how much can I afford to lose, and over what time frame will I be measuring this loss? If the value of the property goes down 50 percent in year 2 and recoups that loss in years 3 and 4, I don't lose anything—as long as I keep living there.

"Your home is a liability," I concluded, "until the day you decide to sell it. Then it becomes an asset."

Based on these conversations and on her previous investigations, Bergman was inclined to offer the sellers their full asking price. At this point, the broker told Bergman that it looked as if at least three other buyers were getting ready to offer the full asking price for the co-op, and at least one of those might offer more than the asking price. Bergman and I talked again on the phone, and we agreed that she should do a little more homework about this particular deal.

Through the broker and other sources, she was able to determine that the seller was a divorcée who was moving to California. The seller was well known in a certain segment of New York society. She was liked and admired as a principled, thoughtful person. She was giving up her Upper East Side lifestyle with great reluctance, and was moving to San Francisco only because she wanted to be closer to her children.

Bergman and I agreed that it made sense for her to set up a meeting with the California-bound seller. From what I could tell, Bergman and the seller were likely to hit it off—and there would be no negative consequences if they didn't. As it turned out, the two women met, became friends, and the seller ultimately turned down at least one higher bid to sell her property to Bergman. (Apart from friendship, I'm guessing that the seller felt that Bergman was very likely to pass muster with a picky co-op board!)

Bergman's situation was very similar to that of students of mine at Harvard, who often ask me for help thinking through their first home purchase. I usually tell them that buying a home can be an intensely personal experience. (For many people, real estate and architecture define a lot of what they're about, in their own eyes.) But it's also a fairly straightforward financial question: *What can you afford?*

The "Game" Lessons. Bergman entered the real estate game as a *player* in search of a *property.* She was very concerned, early in her search, about the possible negative impacts of the *capital markets* (as they were then, and as they might be in the near future). It seemed to her, and to many of the professionals with whom she was consulting, that *external factors* beyond her control might push the real estate market off the table, and transform her investment from a good one to a bad one. As of this writing, however, her investment is holding up well—and she is living in a place she loves.

The Concept-to-Commitment Lessons. Through Bergman's example, we learn important things about how to go about finding information in a market. We learn again—as in Zeckendorf's case—that a relatively long closing period was crucial to the success of the deal. This long closing period served the interests of both parties. The seller didn't want to move to California until the fall; meanwhile, Bergman had to try to sell her existing house in Philadelphia in order to get cash to move. She needed a longer time frame; therefore, it was worth paying a little more to have time to close. Finally, we learn that relationships and rapport can be important in a real estate transaction. Bergman's relationship with the seller played a major part in her closing the deal.

SAM AND DAN BUY INTO LOWELL

This is a story of a building in Lowell, Massachusetts, that my friends Sam Plimpton and Dan Prigmore didn't want to buy.

Plimpton and Prigmore were out looking for properties to buy in the early 1990s. They represented a group of strategic value investors who were convinced that because banks and other financial institutions were then selling lots of unwanted properties, there were deals to be had. (The group was also interested in non-real estate investments, as well, and in fact only included real estate in their portfolio after the early 1990s turndown.)

One day, a developer named David Winstanley called Plimpton and Prigmore and told them of an 800,000-square-foot office-and-manufacturing facility in Lowell which was being put on the market by an insurance company that had foreclosed on the property. Their reaction in this first conference call was negative. "Hey," Plimpton told Winstanley, "Lowell's full of these old, half-empty mill buildings that nobody wants; this isn't for me." Prigmore added that he himself had lost a lot of time and money fixing up an old warehouse in Lowell several years earlier, and wasn't inclined to go back there.

But Winstanley came back strong. "Gentlemen," he said, "this isn't what you think. This is a nearly brand-new building that a computer company built for itself on the edge of the Lowell city limits, out near Route 495. It has problems, but I also think it has all kinds of potential. And it's going to go for a very good price. I know the kinds of places you're interested in, and I really think you should take a look at this one."

Plimpton and Prigmore did a quick BOE analysis. A large electronics manufacturer had recently occupied a little less than half of the building, and was in the early stages of a ten-year lease. That rent would provide a 7 percent return on the purchase price, even if not another square foot was leased. If the rest of the building were rented at the same rates, the owner might realize a 14 percent return or better. Equally important, the property was being offered at $16 psf, which was well below reproduction costs, meaning that at that price, new competitors in the market were unlikely.

Winstanley then added another interesting wrinkle. It was such a great deal, he said, that he himself wanted to be a partner in it, and help run the building, rather than take a commission. Plimpton had worked with this individual before, and was confident that the two of them could work together on this basis. It was also clear to Plimpton that he had been offered this deal in part because Winstanley thought Plimpton would cut him in on the equity side.

On the strength of this BOE analysis and Winstanley's strong recommendation and interest, Plimpton and Prigmore decided to drive the thirty-five miles from Boston to Lowell to take a firsthand look. Very quickly, they saw both the problems and the potential to which Winstanley had referred. On the negative side, this was a three-story facility, which would present "flow" problems to most kinds of manufacturers. (Most manufacturers want only horizontal, not vertical, flows of materials.) Second, the building had limited parking, which meant a conversion to offices would be either difficult or impossible. And third, the computer company, which had built the facility for its own use, had only installed one main entrance. This would make subdivision of this large property difficult.

On the other hand, this was a very attractive corner of Lowell—farther up the Merrimac River, very green, with much lower density. And as they went through the building, Plimpton and Prigmore saw that it had a very high quality of tenant finish for a manufacturing building. For example, the HVAC and other mechanical systems were nearly new and quite sophisticated, and could be operated for about a third of the cost of most comparably sized systems. Clearly, the original owner had lavished money on the building, which might translate into an extra $20 psf of original cost. The facility's high ceilings and 30-on-30 column spacing—not typical of older mill buildings—were very appealing for certain kinds of manufacturing operations.

Plimpton and Prigmore also saw that there was a warehouse at the far end of the property—that is, the end away from the existing entrance—that could be demolished in order to make room for an entrance at the other end of the huge manufacturing facility. This would begin to make subdivision feasible by allowing the installation of new elevators and stairways. The existing tenant, moreover, was using its space fairly intensively. It didn't appear that the tenant would be retrenching, any time soon. In fact, the electronics firm might be needing more space in the near future.

The pluses were beginning to outweigh the minuses, as the two investors continued their investigation. But a large question remained: could they count on renting out some or all of the remaining space?

Neither was familiar with this particular geographic market, nor were they well acquainted with manufacturing companies that needed large amounts of floor space. They knew they had some homework to do. The first thing they did was to sketch out on a map the territory that was within a thirty-minute drive from the facility. They next asked several local brokers to tell them how many large manufacturing spaces were available within this geographic area. The answer: there were very few vacancies in modern facilities (although there were plenty of old, half-empty mills in the Lowell area). Yes, there were lots of 20,000 to 40,000 square foot spaces; but a manufacturer who wanted 200,000 square feet in a well appointed, well equipped building might be out of luck.

They also asked for a list of all the local lease transactions that had taken place in the previous few years. This was the best way they could think of to get a handle on the market, and it proved to be very effective. They were reassured that the rent being paid by the electronics manufacturer was in line with the market.

Plimpton and Prigmore made the commitment to buy the building. But meanwhile the electronics firm—which had a considerable sum invested in its half of the building, and didn't want to lose any future options for expansion—began to discuss the possibility of taking a "master lease" on the whole building. If this happened, the electronics firm would be responsible for renting the entire facility, which would take most of the remaining risk out of the deal.

The "Game" Lessons. I think you could argue that this game started with the *capital markets,* which had entrusted Plimpton and Prigmore with a substantial sum of money to invest. (This was a time, I should point out, that most investors were interested in almost anything *but* real estate.) Obviously, this game had at least two motivated sets of *players:* Plimpton and Prigmore, on the one hand, and Winstanley on the other. The *property* was what brought the capital markets and the players together—to the mutual benefit of the direct players and the investors. The key *external factor* that influenced this particular game was the "overhang" of properties constructed in the boom times of the 1980s, and depressing real estate values in Massachusetts and across the country. Whatever deal these players came up with had to be structured in the context of this overhang, which (when combined with the depressed local economy) was creating vacancy rates of 25 percent and higher in certain markets. What the buyers did was to look *behind* these dismal aggregate numbers and spot an opportunity in a niche market, backstopped by an existing lease that minimized their risk.

The Concept-to-Commitment Lessons. What Plimpton and Prigmore did was to move at a time in the cycle when prices were relatively low. They were consciously looking for particular market niches where they would be able to find something that other people weren't focusing on, and the Lowell property fit nicely with that. And finally, I can't overemphasize the importance of their decision to let Winstanley in as a partner in the deal. In fact, that's one reason why Plimpton and Prigmore got the deal in the first place, rather than one of many other competing funds: they had a reputation for being willing to do joint ventures with good people, as well as the proven ability to add value in the planning and conceptualization of projects.

JBG MEETS EQUITABLE

Also in the early 1990s, the JBG Companies—a large Washington-area property company—was in the business of buying and syndicating individual properties for a group of wealthy investors in that area. Like Bill Zeckendorf (but unlike Sam Plimpton), JBG would first tie up a property, and then go raise the money needed to buy it.

JBG, under the leadership of Ben Jacobs and Don Brown (a former colleague of mine at HBS), had sold much of their property before the bust of the early 1990s, and earned a reputation for being savvy about the real estate cycle. The investors in previous JBG partnerships, therefore, were for the most part receptive to the idea of going into new JBG ventures.

In 1990, JBG was offered the opportunity to bid on a property being sold by Equitable Life. Twinbrook Metro, in Montgomery County, Maryland, was a substantial property: almost thirty acres of land, with nineteen buildings containing more than 554,000 square feet of office and R&D space. It was well located, being near the main Food and Drug Administration (FDA) office building and adjacent to a metro stop.

On the negative side, many of the nineteen buildings were worn out. They housed a large number of tenants on short leases, making it very management-intensive. For JBG, as for most people in the industry, this was not a good time to secure mortgage financing. This particular problem was greatly offset, however, by the fact that Equitable had announced that it would be willing to take back 80 percent of the eventual purchase price in the form of a note for ten years at an interest rate of 9 percent.

Equitable was asking $40 million for the property, which was then only throwing off $3.5 million fully leased, or less than 9 percent. It seemed that a lot of capital improvements would be needed, which would reduce the yield still further. (Remember the caution I put forward in Chapter 2: There's an important difference between net operating income and the cash flow that is actually available for distribution.) It also appeared that the depreciation on the property wouldn't cover all the income—which if true would have unfavorable tax implications for the kinds of wealthy investors who tended to buy into JBG's partnerships.

The first thing JBG had to do was figure out the state of the market, starting with tenancy. (This effort was led by another partner, Michael Glosserman.) Twinbrook Metro was already fully rented, but because many of the tenants had FDA contracts, JBG engaged the services of a Washington consulting firm that specialized in assessing how secure a particular government contract was likely to be, looking forward. In other words, would the contractor's services be renewed or cut out, at the end of the contract period?

There was also some development potential at the site: some buildings could be expanded, and others might be torn down and replaced. This necessitated further investigation into the physical condition of the existing buildings. JBG's own construction and management teams were qualified to perform this first-stage analysis.

The upshot of these investigations was that Twinbrook Metro looked attractive—but not at $40 million. JBG calculated that a $40 million purchase price, when combined with the cost of anticipated capital investments, would lead to a return of between 6 and 8 percent. (Here, BOE analysis was not enough, given the sheer numbers of buildings and leases involved. Spreadsheets were an important tool, especially in calculating the timing and cost of tenant improvements and other capital expenditures that might be looming down the road.) The prospect of picking up 80 percent financing was appealing—but not beyond a certain point. In fact, it looked as if the facility was worth less than $30 million. Based on conversations with the seller's broker, however, it appeared that Equitable would accept nothing less than $30 million.

But JBG now faced the strategic issue of *bidding*. Equitable had already announced that it would take the two or three best offers it received and negotiate with all parties to strike the best possible deal. So did JBG want to come in with a low price, and risk being cut out of the deal entirely? Or did it want to come in high, which probably meant paying more than absolutely necessary for the property?

There was likely to be some competition in the bidding process. But JBG was convinced that the management-intensity of Twinbrook Metro was likely to scare away most potential bidders—or at least drive down the prices that they were willing to pay. JBG felt that its experience managing similar properties in the Washington area was a competitive strength.

JBG also learned as much as it could about Equitable's position in Twinbrook Metro. Like many insurance companies at that time, Equitable was under pressure to reduce its real estate exposure. It appeared that the insurance giant actually had invested something like $40 million in the property, but did not really expect to get all of that back. JBG decided to come in at $30 million—but also to make it clear that they were a strong bidder with the financial resources to go to closing quickly. JBG said it was willing to pay 9 percent interest on the purchase-money mortgage, but made it a condition that only 6.5 percent would be paid during the first five years of the loan, and that the remaining 2.5 percent would accrue and be due at the end of the term.

The strategy worked. Based on the offer and a brief round of negotiations, JBG and Equitable signed a letter of commitment for $30 million, based on the financial structure JBG had proposed. The deferral of the 2.5 percent interest on the $24 million loan was worth $600,000 per year—or $3 million over the first five years—which was sufficient to return half of the $6 million in equity that JBG had put up.

More on the Twinbrook Metro story in Chapter 4. For now, I'll summarize the "game" and concept-to-commitment lessons of the JBG/Equitable story.

The "Game" Lessons. This was a game driven by *external factors* and a *property*. (Without getting into the intricacies of the insurance business, Equitable wanted to stop carrying reserves against a building that was overvalued.) The key player, JBG, went to great lengths to understand the property, the market, the competition, and the seller—who sidestepped the *capital markets* by offering to take back an 80 percent mortgage, at a time when most lenders were unwilling to go beyond 60 percent. Equitable, for its part, apparently had concluded that pension fund investors—who were less concerned about financing—wouldn't be interested in this management-intensive property, especially at a time when those managers were taking losses on their existing real estate portfolios.

The Concept-to-Commitment Lessons. We saw that one reason why JBG was brought the deal—and may have had an edge in negotiations—was their reputation. They were seen as savvy and well-heeled: two nice results of having sold a lot of properties before the crash. Equitable clearly thought that JBG would be able to get the necessary equity financing when it came time to close the deal.

We also saw how JBG drew on its local knowledge to size up and appraise a complex property. We saw how JBG drew on its experience in handling messy situations—such as would be presented by multiple tenants in each of nineteen buildings!—to structure a sensible deal. And finally, we saw how JBG negotiated in a tough-but-fair fashion. They made the judgment that Equitable was not really serious about the $40 million asking price—a sum that probably represented book value at that time—and would not be insulted at a $30 million offer. They decided that the property's $30 million price tag, as well as the larger market cycle, were both so favorable that it would be foolish to try to drive down the price even further—a tactic that might have brought a lot of other bidders into the process. Yes, they were determined to pay less than the seller was asking; but they weren't going to go so low that the seller would be tempted to throw up its hands and stop dealing with JBG.

THE ALISON CORPORATION SCARES OFF THE COMPETITION

My last example comes from very early in my own career. In 1959, the federal government was auctioning off garden apartment complexes that had fallen into financial problems, in many cases due to developer greed and other antics. The feds had taken over the mortgages, and—in the course of auctioning them off—were giving FHA mortgages for 90 percent of the purchase price.

A fellow I was working with at the time, Ted Shoolman, heard about a 140-unit apartment complex in Groton, Connecticut. We knew very little about Groton, so I called a friend of mine who practiced law in the area. He told us the nuclear submarine business—with production headquartered in Groton at G.E.'s Electric Boat subsidiary—was prospering, and that the Coast Guard Academy was a major presence there. Pfizer, the pharmaceutical giant, was also growing a research lab there.

Based on this sketchy information, we visited the site. We were immediately pleased to discover, when we got there, that this particular complex—unlike many then controlled by the FHA—was not in a blighted downtown area, but in a pleasant residential neighborhood. The FHA had spruced it up and painted the clapboards and trim, in anticipation of putting it on the market.

We soon decided that this was the best of the available garden apartment complexes. They were two-story apartments, each with its own ground-floor entrance. (One-over-one apartments in frame construction can get noisy, creating angry tenants.) We also decided that Groton was a good place to buy such a complex. Career military families in Groton for a short tour of duty weren't inclined to buy single-family homes, which buoyed the rental market. Electric Boat and the pharmaceutical giant Pfizer also provided local employment and helped sustain the local economy.

The property was set to be auctioned in Hartford the following week. This meant that we would either send in a sealed bid, or drive to the federal office building in Hartford and make our bid in person. The terms were 10 percent down.

The hitch was that we didn't have any money, which meant that we had to persuade potential investors to go to Groton with us. This was hard to do, in part because we had no track record with this type of property, and in part because it was just far enough from our home base—Boston—to discourage such a trip. But we knew we needed 10 percent of the $1.5 million we were willing to bid for the property. Eventually, we scrounged together the $150,000 that we thought we'd need, but no more.

We drove down to Hartford with our certified check, and found the auditorium where the auction was to take place. We were asked what the name of the bidding company was, and—it's embarrassing to recall—we hadn't anticipated this. My first child, Alison, had just been born, so I said that we were the "Alison Corporation."

As we sat down, we then faced a strategic decision: should we bid early in the process, or hold off until late in the game? We decided to wait. The bidding started low, but got higher and higher, finally getting to $1.4 million and just two remaining bidders. We then jumped in with our $1.5 million bid, the other two bidders dropped out, and we won it.

Needless to say, we were pretty pleased with ourselves. As we were getting ready to leave, one of the other two final bidders approached us. "You know," he said affably, "I think that property is worth more than $1.5 million. In fact, I would have gone quite a bit higher. But when the Allison division of General Motors wants something, I know I can't compete!"

The "Game" Lessons. I guess the point of that story is that at the end of the day, and at the end of the auction, a lucky *external factor* may inject itself into the most rational process. We had done our homework, investigated the *property,* figured out the tax implications of the deal for our investors, done our pro formas and spreadsheets, rounded up our backers, prepared ourselves to take advantage of positive financial leverage in the *capital markets* (as represented by the FHA), and otherwise covered every base we could think of. But what won the day for us was my daughter's name. I like to say that Alison paid for her college education in advance.

The Concept-to-Commitment Lessons. As noted, we were determined to take advantage of very favorable FHA financing. Without this below-market money, there certainly would not have been a deal. In addition, after being down in Groton and touring the property and the city, we became convinced that the FHA's income-and-expense numbers were quite conservative. The FHA had actually run the property itself for several years, and thought it had a good handle on the property's potential. We disagreed—among ourselves, of course. We thought we could both raise the rents and operate the property more efficiently.

And just so we don't end on too celebratory a note, let's also remember that in this chapter we reviewed some deals that *didn't* come together—in Indonesia, Raleigh, and Boston. Without going back into all the embarrassing particulars, let's just say that my partners and I made the determination that we didn't know enough about those markets to effectively judge these properties. The best we could do was to figure out why the locals were staying away from them.

I'll recount a few more memorable Poorvu nonstarters (or at least not-so-profitable ventures) in the next chapter. And even when I discuss "winners," keep in mind that luck may play as big a role as smarts, in many cases.

ON TO THE NEXT PHASE

This brings us to the end of the concept-to-commitment phase—which as you've seen blends almost imperceptibly into the next phase (commitment to closing). The negotiations that you begin in the former phase continue into the latter phase. The details of the deal get sketched out. And although the deal can still come undone, there are two parties who are more or less committed to making it go forward. There are also a number of professionals who will only be compensated if and when the deal closes—which creates its own kind of momentum.

CHAPTER 4

FROM COMMITMENT TO CLOSING

THIS is the phase of the real estate game in which the buyer's exposure, especially his or her financial exposure, increases dramatically. It begins early in the "commitment" process—for the purposes of this chapter, after the letter of commitment has been signed—and continues through to the closing, when title is conveyed to the new owner.

A first challenge is to work out the purchase-and-sale (P&S) agreement. This is largely the domain of the lawyers, but both the buyer and seller have to make sure that the deal that was outlined in the letter of commitment is reasonably well captured in this much more formal document.

Starting with the signing of the P&S, the formal "due diligence" process begins. Here, the prospective buyer looks as hard as he or she can at the property, trying to determine whether there is sufficient reason (perhaps related to building condition or environmental problems) either to renegotiate or back out of the deal. The buyer may even begin preliminary negotiations with potential tenants, insurers, contractors, engineers, and architects.

Meanwhile, the buyer often has to line up the money needed to complete the purchase. This can be a hair-raising process. In most cases, two very complex sets of negotiations are going on: one with a bank or other financial institution (for debt money), and another with one or more potential investors (for equity money). Both sets of negotiations have to succeed.

Both as a result of the hunt for financing and the due-diligence process, the prospective buyer is now putting up (or at least committing to put up) significant chunks of his or her own money to meet a number of critical requirements. He or she must do so knowing that this particular deal may come unglued very late in the process, which is likely to mean that the investments that he or she has made up to that point will be forfeited.

After all this drama, the closing itself often comes as an anticlimax. It is a punctuation point at the end of what can a very complicated story. I'll continue some of the real-life stories begun in Chapter 3 to show how the closing marks the end of a challenging phase in the real estate game—and of course, the beginning of another.

THE PURCHASE AND SALE AGREEMENT

The purchase and sale agreement (P&S) is when the Money Bell sounds: that is, when the buyer starts to spend real money in an effort to make sure the deal is a good one, and—in most cases—to make that deal succeed.

If you're a homeowner, you've already encountered the residential version of the P&S agreement. You'll remember it (if you remember it at all) as an oversized, preprinted form written in legalese, with the blanks filled in to reflect the specifics of your particular home purchase. The residential P&S sets forth the terms and conditions that have to be met before the closing can occur. When the P&S is signed, the buyer hands over a deposit, and the seller takes the property off the market.

The commercial P&S is similar in its fundamentals. As I explained in Chapter 3, the letter of commitment is the tool that the buyer and seller employ to hammer out the outline and some of the particulars of the deal. In my experience, many buyers and sellers also use the letter of commitment to put some limits on the lawyers (on both sides of the deal). The letter of commitment signals the end of the first round of negotiations, and also signals that the two sides have defined the broad outlines of the deal. At this point, the lawyers' job is to translate the relatively informal, nonbinding letter of commitment into a binding legal document, which generally takes a week or two to complete. In most cases, you don't want the lawyers finding new things to negotiate about.

Having said that, I will stress that you definitely want a lawyer defining and defending your interests as the P&S is drawn up. But make sure that your lawyer understands the scope of his or her assignment. Since you (and the seller) very likely know more about this property than the lawyers do, it makes sense to restrict their work to the legal aspects of the deal, and not the business aspects.

The P&S normally includes the following kinds of information:

- *the parties.* Who's involved in this deal?
- *the property.* What's being sold? What rights are assumed, particularly if development is contemplated either now or in the future?
- *the title.* As with residential real estate, the buyer wants assurance that he or she will be getting a "clear title" to the property, meaning that no one can successfully step up with a claim to impede ownership or use of the property. If some third party has an easement on the property—for example, to maintain access to an adjoining property, or to maintain underground pipes or cables—this needs to be represented in the title, and therefore in the P&S.

  There are more variations on "titles" in commercial real estate than in the residential equivalent. In commercial real estate, for example, it is not unusual for the seller to retain title to the land, but to convey title for the building(s) on that land. Title may also be conveyed on a time-limited basis with agreed-upon encumbrances.
- *the status of existing leases.* If there are already tenants in the building(s), how will the change in ownership affect them? (I'll return to this question later in this chapter.)
- *the condition of the property.* Is the property being sold "as is," or have both parties agreed that the seller will make certain improvements before the closing? What happens if there is a fire or a structural collapse in the interim? Who gets the insurance proceeds? Under what conditions must the buyer go forward?
- *the terms of the deposit.* How much will the buyer have to put down to take the property off the market? (Five percent is standard.) Who will hold the deposit? (Often it's the attorney for the seller, or—if known at this early juncture—the title company.) Who will get the interest on the deposit? (This is sometimes split between the two parties, or may be assigned entirely to one party.)
- *the time for performance.* As we'll see throughout this chapter, this is the most exciting (read "scary") aspect of the deal from the buyer's perspective. This is the time frame that the seller allows the buyer to get everything done that needs to get done: inspections, title searches, financing, and so on. A sixty-day time frame between the P&S and the closing is common, and from the buyer's perspective, is often tight. From the seller's standpoint, of course, sixty days is a long time to keep a valuable asset off the market. In some cases, the P&S defines the conditions under which one side or the other can extend the 60-day period.

- *adjustments.* Are there any kinds of financial adjustments that both parties have agreed to, involving items like rents, operating expenses, real estate taxes, brokerage fees? If so, these are detailed in the P&S.

  In some cases, both sides use brokers, and the P&S would state either that the seller is responsible for all brokerage fees, or that each side is responsible for its own brokerage fees. (The P&S might refer to separate letters of agreement between the parties.) What the seller wants to have clearly stated in the P&S, however, is that brokerage commissions will only be paid if the deal goes through—and if for any reason the deal *doesn't* go through, the broker agrees (in writing, in advance) not to sue the seller for a commission.
- *contingencies.* As is the case with home-buying, the buyer wants to protect himself or herself from bad developments that couldn't have been anticipated. If the building has serious structural problems, or if the site holds a concealed environmental disaster, the buyer wants (and usually gets) the right to bail out without financial consequences. The buyer *absolutely* wants to limit his or her personal liability to the deposit—meaning that the seller can't look for additional compensation beyond the deposit, if the deal comes undone late in the game. Sometimes the seller will want an additional escrow put up midway during the process to ensure that the buyer is still committed. The seller, of course, wants to have as few contingencies as possible. As for those contingencies that *do* make it into the P&S, the seller makes every effort to have them expire in the first thirty days of the agreement. In other words, the seller wants to structure the agreement in such a way that the buyer can bail out and get his or her deposit back only early in the game—and that if the buyer bails out late in the game without cause, the deposit is forfeited to the seller. In the lingo of the trade, the deposit money has "gone hard"—i.e., has become nonrefundable.

The P&S is obviously an important step in the process. It transforms the deal from nonbinding to binding. It requires the buyer to put real money on the table, which he or she stands to lose if the deal comes undone. It takes the property off the market, which limits the seller's options.

If the agreement is disclosed, moreover, it also puts the real estate community on notice that this property is "in play." This creates a general awareness that can hurt the seller if the property subsequently comes back on the market. Inevitably, the next round of potential buyers will be very curious to know why the previous deal did not go through. Did the first buyer find out something we should know about?

But from the perspective of the experienced real estate professional, not many commercial real estate deals come undone because the seller fails to fulfill his or her obligations. (It's relatively rare, for example, for a cloudy title to sink a deal.) It's the *other* things that are going on, beginning in this same time period, that therefore get the most attention from the buyer.

ASSEMBLING THE TEAM

I've introduced the idea of *team building* in previous chapters. Team building is important to all business start-ups, of course; but the team building issue is especially important in real estate. This is because the real estate business is intensely project-based, and so many of its functions have to be outsourced by most real estate companies.

In Chapter 3, I cited the example of Ben Alexander's small project at Collegetown, and introduced the idea that teams created for a specific purpose may not be appropriate for all subsequent purposes. Alexander worked out an arrangement whereby architecture students at State University did his design for free as part of a studio course. This was fine in the early, brainstorming phase of his project. The students did a good job, and Alexander felt an obligation to keep them on the team in the later phases of the project.

As it turned out, the students *weren't* the right people to do the work in the next round. Their lack of practical, real-world experience only exaggerated Alexander's own lack of experience in the real estate game. Alexander's project cost more than anticipated, partly because of changes in the market, but also because the building was overdesigned for that market. "Edifice complexes" are very common in the real estate game, and have to be guarded against.

This scenario is something like the problems faced by start-ups in other industries. The people who are most helpful in getting the deal going—those who have the time, and are willing to work for free or cheap—often aren't the best people to do the work once you've got the deal. Is the broker who spent the most time with you in the early stages (maybe because he didn't have too many other clients at the time) the right one to help you lease the building, once you acquire it?

No one should be above this kind of scrutiny. Even the visionary who thought up the deal in the first place may get left behind by events. Think how often you've heard about the brilliant entrepreneur who turns out to be a terrible manager of day-to-day operations. I've seen it happen in real estate many times.

I raise this issue again to emphasize the point that the *acquisition team* and the *operating team* often need to be distinguished from each other. The acquisition team, by definition, should be skilled at acquiring properties; the operating team should be skilled at managing properties. Without foreclosing options prematurely, it makes sense to get these issues on the table while the acquisition team (which necessarily comes first) is being assembled. It makes sense, even in this preliminary stage, to ask good questions. For example: If this deal goes through, exactly who is going to manage this property?

There is always the question of what level of professionals to use. Even though more experienced and more highly skilled professionals cost more on an hourly basis, I don't usually economize in this area. The best advisors give better advice, work more efficiently, and save money over the long run. No, it's not easy to find the extra money when you're just starting out, and it may even be hard to get the attention of the top professionals. I maintain that it's usually worth the effort.

We'll return to this question later in this chapter, when we explore the issues of signing up equity partners.

DOING DUE DILIGENCE

A great deal has been written about the process of due diligence, and I won't restate that large body of work here. Much of what applies when it comes to home buying also applies to assessing commercial real estate. For example, much of what you learned from your first home inspection is good training for your first commercial purchase.

But let me provide some overview-level comments. "Due diligence" is a series of activities that both you (as the prospective buyer) and the bank (as the prospective lender) do, after you've made your respective commitments, to make sure that the deal is what it's supposed to be. You need assurances that this property doesn't have any hidden defects: physical, environmental, legal, or whatever. The bank needs similar assurances, and if it finds problems, it may set higher (i.e., more conservative) hurdles for you and the building to leap over.

In an entirely rational universe, you (as a buyer of a property) would begin all aspects of "due diligence" the moment your signature began to dry on the P&S agreement. After all, the P&S is likely to specify that you only have thirty days to get out of the deal whole if you find something you don't like. After that, in most cases, you can lose both your deposit and your sunk costs of time and money spent on due diligence.

But the commitment-to-closing universe is not an entirely rational one. For example: In many cases, you find you have to delay commissioning your own expert studies until *after* you've got your loan commitment from a bank. Why? Because many banks only accept the work of certain experts. You want to make sure that you don't hire an environmental testing firm that's not on the bank's approved list, because you may find that you have to waste money commissioning a second one. Similarly with the building inspector, and the appraiser: You have to make sure the bank will accept their work.

I've developed very good relationships with the environmental testing firms that I consider to be the best in the Boston and New England region. But I was recently reminded not to take anything for granted in this realm. We secured a loan from a national lender, which then informed us that they had hired one national firm to prepare all of their environmental reports. Well, this environmental testing company had a minimal Boston presence, and I had never done any work with them. They wouldn't have been my choice, had I gone ahead and hired an environmental testing outfit—and the upshot probably would have been that I would have wound up buying *two* such studies.

Remember, the outlay of money accelerates greatly during this phase, and if you're the would-be buyer, it's your money that's being spent. If the deal goes through, you'll get this cash back, in a sense, as part of the financial package put together to fund the overall project cost. If the deal falls apart, you won't, so spend wisely.

What problems do you have to look out for? I'd cite a few basic categories and themes:

ENVIRONMENTAL CONSIDERATIONS

What's the environmental legacy of this site? Are there any time bombs (e.g., underground storage tanks) ticking? Take a look at your loan agreement, where you're likely to read that you're personally responsible for fixing any environmental problems that emerge on the site. Are you prepared for this? What are the seller's responsibilities under the P&S? Can any of these risks be insured against affordably?

Who's next door? What do they do (or, what did they do twenty years ago)? What if the neighbor's gasoline storage tank leaks into the brook that separates your two properties? Look at *all* your prospective neighbors. Who has the deepest pockets? That's where the courts and regulators are likely to go for money, if environmental mitigation is needed.

Is this an older residential building with lead paint? If so, the paint must be removed before you can rent to families with young children. Deleading can be extremely expensive.

These examples may make environmental considerations sound black and white, but unfortunately, that's not the case. The law in this area is still evolving. As a result, reports will often come back inconclusive, leaving you (and your attorneys) to make the final judgment call.

CODE COMPLIANCE

A huge topic! Is there asbestos on the site? (Will the asbestos insulation on the pipes have to come off, or can the pipes be encapsulated?) Are the bathrooms (or enough of them) handicapped accessible? Does the building otherwise meet the codes laid out by the Americans with Disabilities Act (ADA) and the Fair Housing Accessibility Guidelines for new multifamily housing? What's the status of the sprinklers, smoke alarms, central alarm systems, and so on? What records do the local authorities have concerning the building or the site?

Be aware that when the time comes, your local fire marshals will want you to make it *very easy* for them to deal with trouble in your buildings. They will have strong opinions (often backed up by code) as to where your alarm "annunciator" should be, and what functions it should perform. In many cases, they will also want a master key that will give them access to the entire property, and will strongly encourage you to master-key the property if it is not so equipped already. (And when the fire department "strongly encourages," most people listen!)

STRUCTURAL, SYSTEMS, AND SITE ISSUES

This is the first thing that most people think of when they imagine what goes on between the P&S and the closing. It's certainly important (but note that I didn't put it first). What shape is the building in? How old are the critical systems and subsystems? I tend to focus on roofs (including insulation in the roofs), and HVAC (heating, ventilation, and air-conditioning) systems, because (1) they're expensive, (2) one or the other of these Unholy Two always seems to be on the verge of failing, and (3) changing technologies (even in roofing) can change your payback calculations from year to year.

Structures are full of surprises. It was not until well after I purchased the historic Brattle Theater in Harvard Square that I discovered that the great cross beams in the theater—which appeared to be holding up the roof—were actually being held up by the roof (!). The barn builders who had come down from New Hampshire a century earlier to throw up the building had left out some absolutely critical columns that I—and everybody else—had assumed were enclosed in the walls. I'll admit that this was not an inexpensive problem to fix, and use it as an argument for *checking out that building thoroughly.*

Looking beyond the building itself: If there's property attached, what shape is *it* in? Is the parking lot big enough? (If not, is there room to expand, and will the host city permit such an expansion?) What shape is the blacktop in? Are the lots lined for the maximum number of spaces? (By designating certain areas for compact cars, you can sometimes increase the overall number of spaces.)

Is the site subject to flooding, mud slides, or earthquakes? Are there access issues?

LEGAL ISSUES

Title is the most obvious legal issue to be dealt with. Titles can be clouded in all kinds of ways, all of which should be taken seriously. But as noted earlier, in my experience, title problems don't usually kill deals, especially if the property has changed hands in the recent past. Unpaid taxes or other legal liabilities *can* kill deals, and your lawyers have to protect your interests here. The survey will help you understand easements, boundaries, and other legal issues pertaining to the site itself.

Your lawyers will most likely be involved with one or more issues relating to existing tenants in the building (if any). Normally, both the lender and the buyer want what is known as "estoppel agreements" from the owner and from any existing tenants in the building. These state that through a certain specified date, (1) the lease and the amendments are as specified, (2) the tenant has paid all rents and other payments that are due, and (3) the landlord has not defaulted on any of his or her responsibilities. As the buyer, you're of course interested in confirming that your prospective tenants meet their financial obligations. But equally, you need reassurance that the seller hasn't done things (or failed to do things) that give your prime tenant legal cause to break the lease, or to come after you to spend money that you didn't anticipate spending.

Be aware that a lender may want estoppel agreements in a specific form, which—again—means that the buyer may not be able to initiate this process until the loan comes through. Meanwhile, of course, it may be difficult to track down the right person in the tenant's organization to sign the necessary forms. (In one case, a tenant in a building I was trying to buy had delegated the estoppel job to a particular employee—who was out of the country on vacation until well after the specified closing date. Briefly, it appeared as if the deal might be derailed.) The tenant's lease should obligate the tenant to furnish an estoppel within a specified time frame, but this can be difficult to enforce.

Meanwhile, you need to read the leases for yourself to look for unusual clauses. There may have been special arrangements made, for example, in how and when the rent is paid. Were there rent concessions in the early months that make the current rent above market? Was extra work done that increased the tenant's rent but is of no benefit to future tenants?

ZONING ISSUES

Sooner or later, almost every serious player of the real estate game gets tripped up in a zoning problem. Beware of someone who assures you that getting a particular property rezoned will be a slam-dunk; it's rarely that easy.

At one point in the 1970s, I had a former colleague who was going back to Fairfax County, Virginia, to participate in the great development boom that was then going on there. He located a parcel of land that was then being used for farming, which he assured me could be rezoned for housing. I called a couple of sophisticated friends, one of whom was a top executive with a major shopping-center development company, and the other of whom was working at a land-development company for another successful group.

We all agreed that this was a sure deal, and we formed a syndication together with our local partner to buy the property. To make a painful story slightly less painful, many years later we sold the property, still un-rezoned, at the price we had originally paid for it—meaning that we lost the carrying costs for those many years, plus the opportunity costs on our money.

At the same time, this same triumvirate of hotshot investors also purchased a large chunk of land on Moriches Bay, on the south shore of Long Island. This property had a half-mile of beachfront on the bay, as well as a river that abutted one side of the land. Once again, the land was being farmed, and once again, our local land-development partner (who found us the deal) was in charge of getting the necessary zoning changes. And once again, after several years of paying interest on the purchase-money mortgage (that is, the mortgage taken back by the seller as part of the purchase price), attending endless hearings, and keeping several teams of lawyers happily compensated, we were able to arrange a sale at our original purchase price we had paid all those years earlier. Again, we lost the carrying charges for the property, which in this case were much greater, since we had to hire fancy architects and lawyers to present our case, and because the purchase-money mortgage was a considerable portion of the price.

In this case, however, we did receive some special compensation: a percentage of the bean harvest from the farmer who was taking care of the property while the zoning battles raged. But this bonus was largely offset by the two feet of duck manure we discovered at the bottom of our river: the result of an adjacent property once having been used as a duck farm. My partners and I have avoided Long Island roast duckling in restaurants ever since.

The lesson? We didn't do our due diligence well enough. In both cases, it was local opposition to the zoning change that stopped us. The planning boards, spurred on by local preservationists, concluded that these pristine and bucolic sites should be preserved forever. I've concluded that in most cases, outsiders are more or less unable to come into a community and attempt to reshape it to serve their own financial interests. Your due-diligence process should be designed to prove me wrong—or confirm what I consider to be hard-won wisdom.

TENANT-RELATED ISSUES

It's vitally important to examine the lease documents that are already in place. These define the relationship between the landlord (who may soon be you) and the tenant that you may be "inheriting." Is there any work required in future years, such as repainting or recarpeting? Who pays for capital replacements in the HVAC systems? What services are provided? Are there renewal rights to the lease, or option rights on other spaces in the building? Beware of tenant expansion options that force you to carve up existing spaces or create new ones, especially if the options are at fixed prices or have unknown exercise dates.

In other words, as in the acquisition phase, the *terms* of an agreement are often more important than the *price.* By talking with tenants at this point, moreover, you can often learn about their future plans, which is very important information to have. And incidentally, they may tell you interesting things about the HVAC systems or elevators that don't work, or the windows that don't open, or the roof that leaks.

Many leases include a "nondisturbance" clause, meaning that a tenant who is paying his or her rent and meeting any other lease-related obligations can't be forced out by a new owner. This usually makes sense for both parties.

This is only a partial checklist. For a more complete list, please consult the "Commercial Real Estate Due Diligence Checklist" that's included as an appendix at the end of this book. Your own list (like mine) will vary from project to project, and relative weights will change. Building from scratch (as we tried to do on Long Island, and in Fairfax County) puts more weight on zoning issues and less weight on tenant issues.

In all cases, however, due diligence involves hard and careful work. (My computer lists "assiduousness," "perseverance," and "persistence" as synonyms for diligence.) This is your best and last chance to learn relatively inexpensively all the key facts about the property you propose to acquire. And since you may be about to use other people's money for this acquisition, you are legally—and I would say morally—obligated to do a good job at learning about that property.

So *don't rush.* Don't get so caught up in the momentum that you close on a deal that ought to be dropped.

GETTING THE DEBT MONEY: THE BANKS

In my experience, what the buyer is *most* worried about during the commitment-to-closing phase is, "Will I have enough money to close?"

Of course, there are exceptions. My friends Sam Plimpton and Dan Prigmore—whom we met in Chapter 3, and who purchased the huge mill building in Lowell—are two of them. Because they represent a substantial pool of money more or less ready to go in the direction they steer it, they don't normally have to ask, "Will I have enough money to close?"

Lucky them! For those of us who *do* have to ask this question, the answer can only come from three places: financial institutions, which provide money in the form of debt; the seller, who may take back a mortgage; and investors, who provide money in the form of equity. (Throughout this book, for simplicity's sake, I assume that the lender is a bank. Of course, it could just as easily be an S&L, a life insurance company, or another type of financial institution.)

As noted at the beginning of this chapter, most deals that get into trouble get into trouble on the financing side. This is because the would-be buyer is trying to do two negotiations at once: one with the bank, and the other with the potential equity partners.

A word about balancing these two sources of financial backing: Generally speaking, buyers want to obtain the maximum loan possible from a financial institution. This is *leverage,* which allows a buyer to minimize the cash he or she has to put up personally or gets others to put up. In theory, with a 100 percent loan, the buyer would have no need for partners, and therefore could retain 100 percent of the equity. And if this 100 percent loan were non-recourse (secured only by the property), this would represent an almost risk-free investment.

This sounds good. Unfortunately, however, real life doesn't work like this. Even in a case where a property is up, fully rented, and "seasoned," lenders want adequate coverage for their loan, which means that you, as the buyer, will be required to have an equity exposure. The problem is that in a rational universe, you'd have the bank's commitment first—as big a commitment as possible, for the reasons outlined above—and *then* you'd go out hunting for equity money. Again, this almost never happens, and you wind up engaged in concurrent negotiations. Besides, in a downturn, you may be much better off with lower debt payments.

In Chapter 3, I described a not-so-imaginary meeting with a mortgage lender, Sarah Smith, during the concept-to-commitment phase of a hypothetical deal. At that early stage of the process, Smith and I were exchanging only preliminary kinds of information, and weren't making commitments. Perhaps I learned something new about the neighborhood in which I was proposing to invest. Perhaps she gave me a rough idea—based on what I told her about the building and its tenancy—about what percentage of the purchase price she might loan.

Now I need to go back to Smith for real. (Now I need the money.) I show her the letter of commitment—or the P&S, if it's ready—and tell her where things stand in terms of physical inspection of the building and other aspects of the due-diligence process.

Here we reach a crucial fork in the road. I mentioned in Chapter 3 that banks and other financial institutions, under increased regulatory scrutiny as a result of the S&L debacle of the 1980s, have tightened up their internal lending practices considerably. A parallel process has occurred, one which also makes it tougher to get bank financing. Today, more and more banks are simply "conduit" lenders, which means that they (only) originate loans, warehouse them, and put them into packages that can be sold to other people. What this means for me, as a loan applicant, is that my loan has to meet certain criteria established by the people who ultimately will buy my loan from Smith's bank, and my deal must fit within their framework. It is therefore more and more difficult to create a custom loan.

Let's imagine that I propose to buy a building on Route 495, thirty miles outside of Boston, in January. I go to Smith; she processes the loan; it's approved; the deal goes through. In February, I decide to buy an identical building next door to the one I've just purchased—same physical condition, more or less the same tenancy, and so on. I go back to Smith; she smiles politely and says her institution is not interested in this particular property. "We've already filled our New England office quota this month," she explains.

Remember the Real Estate Game diamond? Here's a case where the players, the properties, and the external factors stay about as constant as real life permits, but a change in the capital markets prevents me from putting together a deal unless I can find a new lender.

This is a good time to have relationships with more than one financial institution. I've already mentioned mortgage brokers. They generally have good information about who's in the market to loan against particular kinds of properties at a given point in time. You'll pay their fee—of between one-half to 1 percent of the loan amount—and it probably will be well worth it.

But let's assume that Smith expresses interest in this new deal I'm bringing to her. Together, she and I fill out the easy parts of the loan application; then I take the application home and use my records to complete the paperwork. In some cases, the bank demands a comprehensive personal financial disclosure, despite the fact that—at least as *I* see it—this proposed deal is supposed to stand on its own two feet. Especially in the wake of the troubles of the late 1980s and early 1990s, banks want some evidence that the individuals taking out their mortgages are solid, and have assets that are in something other than real estate. (That way, the borrower will still have places to go for money if the real estate market collapses.) The bank believes, with good reason, that borrowers with diversified assets and deep pockets are more likely to maintain the property that's being borrowed against. The larger the loan, of course, the more interested the bank is going to be in the overall financial condition of the borrowers.

I return to the bank the following day, and the real negotiations begin.

I'm asking for a loan of 80 percent of the purchase price. Smith (and perhaps her supervisor) tell me that 70 percent is likely to be the upper limit. I push on this in several ways, but it becomes clear that this is not a point on which the bank intends to compromise. Realistically speaking, my ability to negotiate interest rates is limited. Rates are generally determined in relation to the rate on Treasury securities of a similar duration, and the risk premium is generally between 1 and 2 percent.

Smith asks for my personal guarantee of the loan. This means that my personal assets can be seized by the bank if the loan payments aren't met. Personal guarantees are less important to lenders than they used to be, simply because, as noted above, the bank is required to meet the more stringent criteria established by the institution that ultimately will repurchase my loan as part of a bigger package. This institution would have no economical way of assessing the value of individual guarantees associated with the larger package, so my guarantee is of less interest to them than to the local lender. But my personal guarantee, net worth, and reputation are still important in securing loans in the development phase. (See Chapter 6.)

In any case, I decline to guarantee the loan, telling her that it seems to me that the property itself ought to be the sole security for the bank's interest—especially in light of the fact that they're only proposing to lend me 70 percent. She nods, makes a few notes, and doesn't argue the point again. What will wind up in the loan agreement is a clause saying that the bank won't look to the individual general partners for money except in cases of fraud, misrepresentation, or environmental problems. These are standard exceptions. Since I don't intend to engage either in fraud or misrepresentation, I'm always willing to sign against those two, but the environmental exception is tougher. Sometimes the lender will agree to strike this clause. For my part, I only agree to it when I'm absolutely sure that my site, and the sites of all my neighbors, are clean—and it's very difficult to get to this level of certainty about your own site, let alone those of your neighbors.

The bank now asks for its processing fee, which can range anywhere from .5 percent to a full 2 percent of the loan amount. This is a fee that usually gets returned to the buyer at the closing—assuming of course, that the deal goes through to closing. It's the bank's way of making sure I pay a substantial penalty for tying up their money if I ultimately don't go through with the deal. If the bank backs out, I get this fee back. Banks generally don't back out of deals without a reason, but if it happens to you, don't bother arguing in court with them. The agreement almost always says they don't have to have a reason.

The bank also asks me to escrow a sum of money that the bank will use to pay for an array of reports that it will commission on the property. These include the appraisal (which gives the bank an independent assessment as to what the property is worth), an environmental study, perhaps a leasing analysis, all legal fees incurred by the bank, and other services that the bank feels it needs. (On a $3 million to $5 million loan amount, the escrow might amount to between $15,000 and $25,000.) Since these are fees spent for professional services rendered, they represent an out-of-pocket cost to the lender, and are not returned under any circumstance. It is prudent to ask the bank for an upper limit—or at least an estimate—of these fees in advance.

What do I leave the meeting with? Not much. In some cases, the bank may be willing to produce its version of a term sheet, in which the bank says, in effect, "If after we've done all the due diligence that we want to do, we still like what we see, then we'll go ahead with the loan." In other words, even though the bank in good faith wants to (and normally will) make the loan, it is a full step behind me and the seller, in terms of level of commitment. The bank and its agents will most likely use almost all of the sixty days specified in the P&S to conduct its approval and due-diligence processes. (The bank's appraisal of the property, in particular, is likely to come in at the last minute.) This means that as a buyer, I'm in a hole. By the time that Smith's bank tells me they're not interested in my deal, if that's their conclusion, it's far too late for me to find another bank under the terms of the existing P&S. If the bank wants changes in the deal, my short-term options are very limited. I can only hope that they will be flexible because they value their long-term relationship with me more than they value the short-term benefits of beating me on relatively unimportant details.

If I haven't yet made the point clearly enough, let me simply state that the whole process of dealing with a lender—*any* lender—is a complicated one.

The borrower has to deal with two sets of lawyers (his own and the bank's), and in many cases, three or more sets of consultants (appraisers, construction and code compliance, and environmental). The bank, which may appear hard-nosed and unyielding, mostly acts that way because they don't have very much discretion. They aren't likely to keep the loan, as explained above; therefore, they can't violate the covenants that the master lenders (the people ultimately issuing the loans) will insist upon.

This same unyielding reality can lead to other kinds of problems. If and when a potentially expensive surprise turns up in the commitment-to-closing phase, for example, you only have three choices: back out (preferably within the first thirty days, when you can get your deposit back!), get the seller to agree to fix the problem, or fix it yourself. The bank is usually reluctant to rewrite its deal, at this point.

I explained about the secondary financial institution that's likely to buy your loan as part of a bigger package, somewhere down the road. That looming third-party presence also explains why, unlike with a residential mortgage, your bank is likely to impose severe penalties for (or even prohibit) the prepayment of a long-term commercial real estate loan. The reason is because when your lender sells a loan with a term of ten years to someone else, they are effectively selling "ten-year paper" (financial jargon for a note that will return a certain sum on a predictable basis over the next ten years). Even though your loan probably will specify a twenty- to thirty-year amortization schedule, the note itself may be due after only ten years (at which point you'll pay it off, or negotiate a new rate on the "balloon" or remaining principal still due). As a borrower, you might be tempted to refinance the property if interest rates declined from, say, 9 percent to 7 percent. But your loan agreement is likely to specify that in that event, you will pay the bank the present value of the difference between 9 percent and 7 percent for the remaining term of the loan, thereby fully negating the benefit of refinancing to take advantage of such a decline.

To summarize, your bank's goal is to create a mortgage loan that is easily salable to third parties, whose goal is to lock up an interest-rate return for a given period. In other words, they have good reason—and they have the tools—to make amendments, prepayments, and refinancings unattractive. You can expect that they'll use those tools.

GETTING THE EQUITY MONEY: YOUR PARTNERS

In a rational universe, as noted above, you'd figure out who your partners were likely to be in a given deal, get commitments of equity money from them, and then go find a bank to loan you the balance of the money in the form of debt.

Of course, it often works the other way around. You, as the buyer, go ask the bank for money to be loaned against a certain property, and (eventually) the bank tells you how much it's willing to lend. Not until that point do you know exactly how much equity money—and, depending on your own financial circumstances, how many partners—you're going to need.

Finding partners is easier for some people than for others. Sam Plimpton has his capital partners before he goes looking for properties. The JBG Companies—introduced in Chapter 3 and revisited later in this chapter—

had a pretty easy time finding investors for their Twinbrook Metro property. (I was one of them.) Many who had benefited from JBG's skill and foresight in the past were quick to invest with them again.

At the other end of the spectrum are people who are just starting out in the real estate game. These players—who have no track record or reputation to attract potential partners—often have to call upon friends, family members, or clients of their professional advisors to put together their first deals. Here's where salesmanship is critically important. You are not only selling a deal involving garden apartments in Groton, Connecticut, most likely to people who wouldn't ordinarily be interested; you are also selling *yourself.*

One of the most important selling points, of course, is the *structure* of the deal that you're proposing to put together. You may succeed in working out this structure and selling it "as is" to investors; but more likely—especially if you're just starting out—the structure is hammered out among the partners. Like the money chase, this process can be nerve-wracking. It can take the kinds of last-minute swoops and dives that cause insomnia in the coolest of people. Let's say that through hard work, you come up with three partners who agree to your terms, and you've got a fourth just about into the fold. Then the lawyers for the fourth party call up and demand changes in the structure of the deal.

"But I've already got three other partners who've agreed to things the way they *are,*" you protest. "I can't go back and renegotiate this deal with all of them."

"Well, fine," the lawyers respond. "But if you don't, our client is out." In my experience, this tends to happen when a lawyer feels that he or she has to protect an unsophisticated client from these fast-talking real estate guys. (And obviously, an unsophisticated lawyer greatly complicates these discussions.) Lawyers generally see their job as offering conservative advice, which often translates into either "don't do this deal," or, "don't do this deal unless I can take all the risk out of it for you."

But real estate (like most other investments) is never risk free. When you get this kind of call from a lawyer, you have to calculate whether it's smarter to give up on this prospect, or go back to Square One with other investors.

The deal that you ultimately strike is represented in a document called the *partnership agreement.* This document spells out all of the relationships among the partners to the deal. It commonly identifies a *general partner,* who will be responsible for actively managing the partnership and the property, and *limited partners,* who play the role of (more or less) passive investors. A general partner may be either an individual or a corporation. (The corporate approach helps limit personal liability.) An individual or corporation can be both a general and limited partner in the same deal. Many deals are done today using a *limited liability corporation,* or LLC, which accomplishes roughly the same purpose. The LLC provides a better liability shield, more flexible capitalization opportunities, and more latitude for control being exerted by the managing partner.

In most cases, *lots* of questions need to be answered in the partnership agreement or the LLC trust indenture. This can be a straightforward process, or—if the partners are new to each other or the deal is particularly venturesome—it can be very complicated. Use both your attorney and your accountant to help you think through these issues as they arise.

The first question usually involves payments to the partners. Who will get paid how much, for what, and when? For example: Is the general partner going to receive some sort of "override," or special benefit, to which the limited partners are not entitled? Will there be a sequence in which partners get income, and if so, what are the percentages and the thresholds? For example: Are we going to agree that the limited partners who put up the $1 million are entitled to the first $80,000, or 8 percent, from the property's annual income stream, and that the general partner will get 20 percent of anything over that?

The distribution of cash flow should be addressed specifically. When I play the role of general partner, I try to write the partnership agreement in such a way that my limited partners understand that I'm *not* going to be distributing all the money that the property generates. Banks require capital reserves, and our partnership is responsible for assembling them. But in many cases, I feel the need to build additional reserves. These will allow me to make improvements and keep the property up over the longer term. My partners need to understand that in advance. A problem that plagues many deals is that the general partner overpromises cash distributions in order to attract investors, and then either can't deliver, or delivers by "cheating" on investments needed to keep up the property.

Language governing possible changes in the debt and equity structure of the deal is also extremely important. What happens if more money is needed? Does the general partner have the right to borrow it, which would place a bigger debt burden on the property? Does he or she have the right to bring in more partners, which would dilute the interest of the existing partners? Can the general partner sell the property without the approval of the limited partners?

Do the limited partners get the tax and depreciation benefits, or do they go to the general partner? Generally speaking, the limited partners get 99 percent of the tax benefits. As the tax benefits of investing in real estate have diminished, the general partner has increasingly tended to get a proportionate share of the depreciation.

What happens at the end of the deal? How is the timing of the sale determined? When the property is sold, do the limited partners get their capital back first, or does the general partner get fees or some kind of guaranteed return first?

I'll return to the subject of structuring deals, and reflecting those deals in partnership agreements, when I discuss syndications in Chapter 5.

CLOSING THE DEAL

Fairly late in the game, Smith and my bank come through with the confirmation of the loan, which is written up in the form of a draft note and mortgage. Not much has changed since our last discussion, in which the bank produced a term sheet outlining the rough conditions of the loan. But now I learn exactly how much the bank is going to require from me in terms of escrows: capital reserves, real estate taxes, insurance, possibly water and sewer costs, and so on.

My partnership agreement emerges somewhere in this same process. Its t's are crossed and its i's are dotted after the particulars from the bank are known. Ideally, no lawyers call and tell me that a partner wants a better deal for himself or herself.

Meanwhile, the bank's lawyers and my lawyers are doing their version of due diligence. They are making sure that the proposed use (or reuse) conforms to local zoning regulations. They are working out title-related issues. They are ensuring that there are no outstanding liens on the property. They are extracting all the necessary estoppel and due-diligence letters. They are checking and rechecking the lease agreements that are already in place. They are surfacing any sorts of obscure existing agreements with the owners of contiguous properties: easements, restrictions on what I can't do without an abutter's permission, and so on. I've been known to say unkind things about some lawyers, sometimes; but this is a phase when lawyers definitely earn their keep. Don't scrimp on the legal budget in this phase.

At the same time, remember that you, as the buyer, are the general manager in every phase of the deal, including this one. If some critical piece of paper doesn't show up at the closing, it's not much good to blame the lawyers. Keep copies of all relevant lists—for example, a copy of your attorney's closing list. As the general manager, *you* are responsible for what goes on.

I've been to an awful lot of closings that were held up by one individual. For example, maybe the surveyor doesn't get his or her job done by the appointed date. I recently was involved in one deal in a period when our surveyor was very busy. The deadline was approaching, and he hadn't completed the survey. Without that survey, I would surely lose the loan. The only way I got the surveyor's attention was to ask him to do the job at double-time rates over the weekend. No, I did not feel good about paying twice what I should have for that survey. Yes, I think paying $10,000 instead of $5,000 was a smart thing to do to protect a multimillion-dollar closing. No, I didn't use that surveyor again.

The safest generalization to make about closings is that if something is going to come unstuck, you can't predict what that thing is going to be. There's a good chance that someone is going to get worried or unhappy about something. What's it going to be?

We once sold a post office terminal we owned to a Western Massachusetts city, which planned to use the complex for municipal maintenance. At the eleventh hour—maybe a week before the closing, which was sometime just after Thanksgiving—the city's environmental report came in. It suggested that there was some chance that a gasoline storage tank on the site had leaked. To our knowledge, it hadn't, and we told the city property manager that. "No," said the property manager, "you've got to take 'em out. And while you're at it, take out the old heating-oil tanks, too." Again, we protested, to no avail. To keep the deal alive, we paid $25,000 to get every tank of every sort off that property.

The following week, we were all at the closing at City Hall. The agreement was inked, hands were being shaken all around, and unexpectedly the mayor walked in. He said to us, beaming, "Well, I'm glad we got this wrapped up. After all, they're predicting a cold snap for this weekend, and if there's one thing I know about buildings, it's that you want to get that heat on before the pipes start to freeze up!"

As far as I could tell, this was just small talk from the top pol—no hidden agenda. I started to smile, and looked over at the property manager, who looked like he had just been shot. "Uhm, well, Mr. Mayor," he said, looking down at the floor, "we can't exactly do that right away. There aren't any oil tanks in that building."

In cases where it looks as if a closing might get complicated, there is sometimes what's called "a pre-closing." It's what the name implies: the lawyers for both sides, plus the bank's lawyer, sit down and run through every document, line by line, to make sure they've got everything they need. In my experience, there's almost always something that the bank's lawyer decides he has to go back and check with the bank.

But even the best planning and dry-running can't head off clashes of ego. I remember being at one closing for a multimillion-dollar deal—in fact, one of the biggest deals I've ever been involved with. Both the principal buyer and the seller were prominent, very sophisticated New York real estate people. Halfway through what should have been a more or less routine closing, there was a fight over who was responsible for paying a $2,500 commission. The closing was delayed for six hours while these two titans of the real estate business screamed and yelled at each other. My best guess is that the legal bills went up by $20,000 while their egos were raging out of control.

One good way to keep your ego out of the room—if you admit that in your case, this might be a good idea—is not to attend the closing. In most cases, you can sign all the necessary documents in advance, and your lawyer can represent you. There may be some symbolic value to your being in attendance at certain closings, but if not, you might as well pass. But stay in phone contact, and be available to sign a revised or new document in a crisis. I'm beginning to worry about the dark side of office automation—and specifically, voice mail. I attended a recent closing that was delayed because we literally couldn't get anyone at the bank to pick up a phone. We bounced from office to office, and from voice mail to voice mail, until we raised somebody in a far-distant corner of the bank—who then walked over to the commercial lending area and interrupted a staff meeting.

Baron Rothschild was once quoted as saying, "You have two choices in life: eat well, or sleep well." These are the kinds of adventures that bring the Baron's point home to players in the real estate game.

FROM COMMITMENT TO CLOSING: REAL-WORLD STORIES

In Chapter 3, I related a half-dozen stories (some large-scale, some local) to convey the reality of the concept-to-commitment phase. Let me carry several of those stories through to their separate conclusions to illustrate the main themes of this chapter.

When we last looked at Bill Zeckendorf, for example, he was committed to paying $6.5 million to the Swift family to purchase their slaughterhouse on the eastern side of Manhattan. In the letter of commitment, he asked for and got a one-year delay in the closing, and also a pledge of confidentiality. His goal was twofold: to raise the necessary money, which he certainly didn't have in hand, and to buy up surrounding properties at prices depressed by the presence of the slaughterhouse.

Both efforts were successful. Zeckendorf got commitments for the necessary funds, and (through multiple third-party buyers, who served as nominees for separate corporations he established for each purchase) he assembled almost another eight acres of land, giving him a total of seventeen acres at an average price of well below $17 psf. Now the question was, what was Zeckendorf going to *do* with all this soon-to-be-prime real estate, on the periphery of downtown Manhattan, bounded by the East River?

At this stage, he hired Wallace Harrison, an architect who had done a lot of work for the Rockefeller family, to help answer this daunting question. With Zeckendorf's encouragement, Harrison came up with a truly monumental plan: to build a "city within a city." He proposed to create office buildings toward the south end of the site, and a new opera house, a hotel, and apartments toward the north end of the site. The scheme was so audacious that it earned Zeckendorf and Harrison a prominent feature article in *Life* magazine.

But in addition to being a high-visibility phase of the project, this was also an expensive period for Zeckendorf. (As I've tried to emphasize, this is very often typical of the commitment-to-closing phase.) Hiring Harrison, commissioning handsome renderings and detailed architectural models, and engaging in other activities intended to begin the daunting task of marketing the novel concept consumed real money, and this meant expending real dollars out of Zeckendorf's still-limited pocketbook.

Unfortunately, as it turned out, public-relations coups and substantial investments didn't combine to win Zeckendorf the kind of backing he needed to pull off his grand "city within a city" scheme. In retrospect, it's easy to see that key players—in the financial community, in the investment community, and in political circles—were simply not ready for a proposal of this magnitude. At that point in time, people were not yet accustomed to the grand gesture in real estate. Zeckendorf was simply too far out in front of the industry and the investment community, and Harrison's visionary plan was fated to go nowhere.

Remember that Zeckendorf has already pledged $1 million, mostly of other people's money, to bind himself to a deal with the Swift family that might not go through. Maybe it would be too much to say that he faced ruin—but certainly a substantial percentage of his net worth, as well as his reputation as a savvy professional in the real estate game, were in deep peril.

At about this time, however, it became clear that the United Nations was about to relocate to Philadelphia because there wasn't a suitable site for it to make a permanent home in New York City. To Zeckendorf, this smelled like an opportunity and a potential salvation. He called the then-mayor of New York, Tom Dwyer, and told him to tell the U.N. that the city had guaranteed access to seventeen acres on the river, available at whatever price the U.N. thought was reasonable. The U.N. quickly agreed to this unexpected gesture of generosity, and the Rockefellers purchased most of Zeckendorf's seventeen acres (at the cost of his investment) to donate to the U.N.

Why did Bill Zeckendorf change his concept so dramatically? In part, it was because Harrison's city-within-a-city wasn't finding backers, and he had to scramble to make sure he wouldn't lose his $1 million. But it was also because Zeckendorf—like many other players in the real estate game—got caught up in the image of what he might be able to create. Here was the United Nations, going into the site that he had assembled, for the benefit of New York (and at the expense of Philadelphia!). Zeckendorf also had held back some properties on the periphery of the site, which he was able to develop profitably. The condominiums he built on the northern perimeter of the U.N. site are still some of the premier residential properties in New York City. And finally, his reputation as a major player in the New York real estate game was firmly established.

Another story from Chapter 3 concerned the JBG Companies, which offered to buy the Twinbrook Metro complex from Equitable Life for $30 million—an offer that Equitable accepted by signing a letter of commitment to that effect. JBG used the ensuing weeks to do due diligence on the property. This was a major task, involving multiple tenants in each of nineteen buildings. Some minor environmental problems cropped up, as well as some tenant problems, which entitled JBG to a $1.5 million reduction in the purchase price.

Meanwhile, JBG was negotiating another interesting wrinkle to the deal. As noted in Chapter 3, there were a total of nineteen properties on the site. JBG anticipated the possibility that certain tenants might someday want to purchase their buildings. JBG therefore worked out release clauses on the mortgage from Equitable. These said, in effect, that JBG would pay down its loan from Equitable by paying Equitable X dollars to release

Building A, Y dollars to release Building B, and so forth. This was a good way for JBG to recover some or all of its investors' money in the foreseeable future. The deal went forward, and JBG wound up owning and operating profitably the Twinbrook Metro complex.

On a more modest level, you'll recall the great business coup that was pulled off when The Alison Corporation beat out or scared off all other bidders in a 1959 auction of a garden-apartment complex in Groton, Connecticut. What I didn't mention in Chapter 3 was that shortly after that auction, our potential investors pulled out of the deal. I don't recall the details, but I suspect that when the deal started to become real, these investors started making inquiries, and didn't like what they heard about some aspect of it: me, my partner, Groton, garden apartments, or whatever. What they told me was that they wanted to use the funds in their core, non-real estate business.

What ensued was a mad scramble to find replacement investors. Naturally, potential new investors came with a heightened level of suspicion about it. "Why did the other guys back out?" they all wanted to know. They were also more focused on a particular line of argument that was especially embarrassing to me. "O.K., Poorvu," one of the saltier old characters said to me. "Bring your *tuchas* up to *tisch*." (Let's just say that "tisch" is Yiddish for "table.") "How much cash are *you* going to put into this great opportunity you're pitching?"

It was a fair question. An investor should have some confidence that the person who's putting together and managing the deal has more or less the same incentives as the investor. My problem was that I and my associate simply didn't *have* much cash, for this deal or any other. With a great deal of effort, we managed to put a group together, and in the long run did well by them.

This raises an important point, and one that I'll use to close this chapter. For obvious reasons, I've tended to focus on ways to keep the ball rolling and get a deal done. This is the right juncture to admit that sometimes it's an excellent idea *not* to close on a deal. Sometimes you can do better by rolling your eyes toward the heavens, making one or two very unpleasant phone calls, and forfeiting your deposit.

Why? In most deals, the momentum is in the direction of making the deal close. The lawyer wants to close, because in most cases, his or her fee will be bigger. The brokers will get their commissions only if the deal closes. In fact, all of the professionals involved are pushing in that direction. Sometimes even a bank will squint a little bit at a deal to make it look O.K.

But this can be a slippery slope. For example: Let's assume that I've put together $500,000 in equity financing from ten equal partners, including myself. I've sought and secured this amount in the hopes of holding reserves of $100,000 after the deal closes, so that I can make tenant improvements for leases soon to roll over. Now, at the last minute, one of my nine partners bails out—as most of them did, in fact, in the Groton deal. What's my response? Scramble to find a replacement investor? Tell myself that I didn't really need $100,000 in reserves, and that $50,000 will be adequate? (Why did I think I needed $100,000 in the first place?) Or pull the plug on the deal?

When a player jiggers the numbers to justify a particular price and obtain a disproportionately high level of financing, the result can be a structure that ultimately becomes that player's downfall. What happens if the rental market starts to soften? The property owner may cut back on necessary maintenance or capital investments, or may rob Peter to pay Paul by thinning out reserves on other properties.

There's no right answer for all cases. But my guess is that if you were to compare the pile of good deals that don't get funded with the pile of bad deals that *do* get funded, the latter pile would be bigger. My advice would be: Try not to add to the latter pile.

THE JOYS OF OWNERSHIP

This brings us to the end of the acquisition phase of the direct-investment story, which I sometimes refer to as "betting on yourself." We'll pick up the direct-investment approach again in Chapters 6 and 7, when we explore the development and operation of various kinds of properties.

For the moment, though, we need to put on hold our small universe of direct investors—myself, Charlie Leonard, Ben Alexander, and others in our cast of characters—so that we can examine how other kinds of investors play the real estate game indirectly, using syndicates and REITs.

These players are rarely involved in the wide range of activities that I've described in these "concept to closing" chapters. In fact, these indirect investors are almost entirely focused on a limited version of *commitment:* Do I invest, or not?

Nevertheless, for reasons that will become clear in the next chapter, indirect players have an enormous impact on how the real estate game is played.

CHAPTER 5

SYNDICATIONS AND REITS

IN the last two chapters, we've looked at the process of direct investment in real estate, whereby an individual or group purchases a specific property using money assembled for that specific deal.

As we saw, most of the protagonists in the direct-investment version of the real estate game consist of small organizations that outsource many of their functions, and operate in particular niches that give them a competitive advantage. They engage in a challenging set of activities performed in a more or less specific sequence, including:

- investigating the property's location, condition, and market
- measuring and evaluating the property's potential returns
- looking at whether the deal makes sense, given the resource commitments, skills, available time, and personal values of the protagonist
- putting together the capital structure (including both the debt and equity financing)

What does this list of activities, summarized in this condensed way, say about the real estate game? One thing it says is that most people in the world are not going to be active players of the real estate game. The effort required is simply too great, and the necessary skills are not developed. Real estate is a complicated, resource-intensive, sometimes stomach-churning way to make a living. As I noted in the introduction to this book, real estate is fun, but it's not for everybody.

But there are other, indirect ways to participate in the real estate game.

These more passive approaches to real estate are open to both individuals and institutions that want to be in the game, but don't have the time, skills, or inclination to do all the work themselves. Is the game worth being in, as a passive investor? That's for you to answer, based on the following fact: Despite the industry's celebrated peaks and valleys, real estate over time has been an excellent way to make a 10 to 12 percent return on your capital. If the property is leveraged with a mortgage that has fixed payments over time and the cash flow from operations increases, the percentage return on equity will rise by an even greater amount. Of course, as we saw earlier, the operating leverage could work in reverse during bad times.

I suggested in Chapter 2 that even those people who didn't intend to get involved in real estate directly should read Chapters 3 and 4 to get a feel for how the direct-investment end of the game is played. My point was to encourage potential investors, as well as members of allied professions, to understand the game better. We will continue that theme in this chapter, as I try to help you understand how to be an effective indirect investor in real estate. Suppose a promoter comes to you with a proposal that you put money into a particular syndication. What questions should you ask, and what indicators of potential success should you be looking for? How do you distinguish a good syndication from a bad one?

Or suppose your financial advisor, your accountant, or your savvy friend who always seems to be a step ahead on personal financial issues tells you that this is the time to plunge into REITs (real estate investment trusts). How do you assess those kinds of opportunities?

REITs have tended to gain popularity in waves, which have crested roughly once a decade. (The most recent wave, it should be noted, has dwarfed all previous ones.) Without spending too much time on what might seem like ancient history, I'll sketch out the characteristics of those several waves, and suggest the lessons that potential investors can carry forward from each of them. I'll also describe where REITs are today (that is, in early 1999), and where they may be going tomorrow.

In the middle of the indirect investment spectrum, located somewhere between syndications and REITs, are several kinds of hybrids. Pooled funds are generally put together by private groups or institutions to make real estate investments; some are for specific properties, some are "commingled," some are "open-ended," and some are "closed-ended." I'll devote some time to defining these terms, and explaining how these vehicles are different from, and complement, syndications and REITs.

SYNDICATIONS: WHAT THEY ARE, AND WHY

Simply put, a syndication is a group of people organized to carry out a defined business purpose. People syndicate horses, for example: You buy a "piece" of a racehorse that you think is going to win the Kentucky Derby someday.

Syndications are often partnerships (in the legal sense of the term), and may have only active partners or a mix of active and passive partners. In a limited partnership or limited liability corporation (LLC)—which are the forms that all but the smallest real estate syndications take—most limited partners have little voting power, and have neither management responsibilities nor personal liability for the syndication's actions. The general partner is insulated from personal liability through the creation of a separate corporation to exercise that responsibility. The corporate form is rarely used to hold the investment real estate itself, because of the double tax involved. The exception would be an operating or development company that intends to reinvest its earnings in other projects.

Real estate syndications, like racehorse syndications, can be either public or private. In a public syndication, shares in the venture are offered to the public at large. A private syndication involves a group of investors, often with some kind of preexisting ties or common acquaintances, who have come together to back a particular real estate transaction. The level of involvement ranges from very high (for the general partner) to very low (for the limited partners).

A syndication permits the key players to tackle something that is beyond their individual financial means. It may also appeal to sophisticated investors who (for cash-flow or other reasons) want to take advantage of the real estate cycle, but want to limit their financial involvement in a particular project; or who want to diversify by making smaller investments in several properties. And finally, it can be attractive to relatively inexperienced investors who simply want to get into the real estate game.

SYNDICATIONS: GETTING INTO THE GAME

My first deal in the real estate game came together in Cambridge, Massachusetts, in 1958. It involved a six-unit building on Garden Street, a few blocks outside of Harvard Square. Although this deal seemed exciting and unprecedented at the time—and it *was*, for me!—it was a fairly typical example of a group of people investing in real estate on a relatively small scale.

A friend of mine was a graduate of the Harvard Law School, and he had a group of classmates in Baltimore who were already familiar with the Garden Street location from their law school days. He evidently gave them the assurances they needed that I was reputable and could handle the project. Maybe this is a result of forty years elapsing between then and now, but I don't remember putting together any elaborate financial projections for the proposed deal. Nor do I remember anyone spending much time on the partnership agreement that we signed. We moved forward mostly on a handshake—although we certainly captured the essentials of the deal in some kind of document—and bought the property.

We sold it several years later at a very good profit to a friend of mine in the business, who sold it many years later for a much greater profit. Lesson: Unless you've got a *really* good reason, don't sell that property in Harvard Square (or the equivalent real estate elsewhere). There are very few areas that have maintained their viability over three centuries; the area surrounding Harvard University is one of them.

But let's look at this deal from the perspective of those attorneys down in Baltimore. How carefully should they have checked out this proposed deal? Should they have done more than they did—which as I recall was next to nothing? The ultimate outcome of the deal suggests that their faith in their classmate (and by extension, in me) was well placed. So is that the moral of the Garden Street story: Invest in the friend of a friend? And how do you assess whether your friend's friend is currently stretching to do deals at the top of the cycle? And what do you do if you *don't* have a friend who has a friend in the business?

Can you "spot" a great real estate deal? If so, how? The legendary stock investor Peter Lynch once suggested that people could get good ideas for investments by looking for interesting new products on the shelves of their neighborhood supermarkets. This is an appealing story—we can all relate to that—but unfortunately the grocery store and the stock market are not good analogies to the real estate market.

For one thing, unlike groceries or shares of stock in a given company, most properties are not for sale at any given time. Their prices are not fixed, or listed on a centralized exchange. In many cases, moreover, you aren't buying an interest in an ongoing business, but are part of a start-up designed to effect a change in ownership of this particular property. It's one thing to buy a block of stock in the Ford Motor Company, which is approaching its hundredth year of making cars; it's quite another thing to acquire a substantial interest in a start-up that is unlikely to be liquid for years. Or if you like Wheaties and want to buy stock in the company, you can be sure that all boxes of Wheaties contain the same product. Looking at the outside envelope of a building does not tell you what is inside.

Let's go back to our game of cards. We'll pull a property card, since an indirect investment in real estate often begins with an approach to an investor by a promoter of a specific deal. O.K., here's the property—the potential investment. Is this something you'd like to own a piece of? If the deal calls for changing the current use of the property, how comfortable are you with those plans?

Most potential investments fall into one of two categories:

- relatively stabilized operating properties
- opportunity investments, in which the goal is to develop, substantially renovate, or change usage.

This initial categorization compels you to look at your own tolerance for risk. Why are you interested in a real estate deal—to receive a stable annual cash flow, or to reap a large capital gain if all goes well? If it's the latter, are the prerequisites for success in place? What can go wrong?

Let's assume that you like the property card you've pulled. You've decided that, all else being equal, you'd like to go ahead and invest. But first you have to pull your second card—the external-forces card. Is this really a good point in the real estate cycle to invest, either in real estate as an asset class or in a specific real estate market? Are you likely to find bargains at the top of the cycle? How does the sales price of the property compare with its replacement cost? Is there a lot of speculative building going on that may destabilize the existing supply/demand balance?

These questions should sound familiar. They're more or less the same questions we asked in Chapters 3 and 4, when we were looking at ways of doing our direct-investment deals. With indirect investments, though, we have a different kind of problem. It would be nice to be thoroughly familiar with the location of a proposed investment, or at least to visit the property and neighborhood—and I'd recommend it, if at all convenient—but in reality, we are very unlikely to do any kind of intensive research into the specifics of the deal. Like my long-ago partners from Baltimore, we are directed by circumstance to focus mainly on the *individuals* involved in the deal, especially if the amount of money that we're putting into the deal is not especially significant.

Again, one of the first questions I ask myself when looking at a seemingly attractive but unsolicited opportunity is, "Given all of the potential investors in the world, why has this fabulous opportunity fallen into *my* lap?" If I'm not the first to see this deal—and past experience suggests that I'm not—than why has everyone else before me passed on it? Perhaps they're less talented at spotting opportunity than I am. Alternatively, they may know something I don't. If so, I'm determined to learn what that might be.

In most cases, I rely heavily on the opinions and advice of other people I've worked with in the past. Real estate is not really *that* big a universe. If I can't find anybody in my circle of business acquaintances who has done business with this particular seller, or with this intermediary, I tend to step aside.

And finally, if the deal gets by these initial hurdles, I'll certainly run the proposed partnership agreement by my lawyer. As a potential limited partner, I'm not expected to do my own due diligence on the property itself. On the other hand, I'm certainly obligated to do my own version of legal due diligence, and to protect my financial interests. That's when I call my lawyer.

SYNDICATIONS: DIVIDING THE SPOILS

Another way to assess a deal is to examine how much the prime mover is committed to the deal, and how he or she proposes to divide up the spoils.

There was a cartoon in the *New Yorker* a while back, depicting two affluent-looking types standing on a dock and looking at an immense yacht. One is saying to the other, "But where are the *customers'* yachts?" Real estate is one of those fields in which the agent can arrange things so that he or she does well—even when the investors he or she is representing (and whose money the agent is using) don't do so well. I've seen the occasional adulatory article about Donald Trump, and I'm happy to acknowledge his profound impact on certain types of commercial real estate in New York and New Jersey in the last few decades. At the same time, I'd feel better about Donald Trump's accomplishments if I knew of more cases in which his lenders or investors—who after all took virtually all of the risk—made some money, too.

Trump's history is not all that unusual. I've seen many projects in which the upside potential to the investors was extremely limited. The investors take nearly all of the risk—and yet, their position is often more analogous to that of a participating preferred shareholder than a full equity partner.

Because a general partner has very limited personal exposure in a transaction, it is crucial for you as an investor to understand the deal structure, and to satisfy yourself that the interests of the various parties are more or less in alignment. Simply put, you want to make sure that when a decision regarding your investment presents itself, your agent on the scene—the general partner—has more or less the same motivations as you do, and is likely to act as you would in that same situation.

What's needed is an examination of the deal structure, aimed at determining whether the split between the promoter and the investors is appropriate. Let's look again at the case of Twinbrook Metro. I described in Chapters 3 and 4 how JBG Properties had capitalized on its knowledge of the metropolitan Washington market—as well as their strong reputation for savvy dealing, which arose in part out of a timely sell-off before the crash of the late 1980s—to buy a complex of nineteen buildings from Equitable. As you'll recall, this was a juncture at which very few investors were willing to enter the market.

As noted previously, I was one of the investors they approached. My perspective on the context of the deal was quite positive: I liked Don Brown and Ben Jacobs, partners at JBG, and trusted their judgment, and I was also convinced (as they were) that it was a good time to buy back into real estate.

What was the deal offered to me (and my fellow prospective limited partners) by JBG? Think of it as dividing up successive piles of increasingly hypothetical chips:

- In total, the company offered a 75 percent share of the profits to the "limiteds," and a 25 percent share to the "general." (Note the shorthand.) These proceeds were sequenced as follows:
- First, the limiteds would receive an annual cash preference of 10 percent on their net investment. Assuming each limited put in $120,000, each would receive $12,000 a year.
- After that payment was made, the general would receive a cash allocation equal to one-third of the limiteds' distribution. In our example, the general would receive one-third of $12,000, or $4,000. This reflects the 75/25 structure of the deal.
- The limiteds would then receive any remaining annual cash flow until their original investment was fully recouped. This would mean in this case that the limiteds could expect to receive an annual 10 percent return on the unpaid balance of their investment, and also recover their capital in full in fewer than ten years.
- After the limiteds were paid back in full, all further splits would be on a 75/25 (limited/general) basis.

- When the property was sold, the same 75/25 split would apply, but only after any limiteds' capital or income preference that had not yet been returned (see the fourth bullet point in this list) had been paid to them.

What I've just taken you through is an exercise that I like to call *Follow the cash.* Learn exactly who gets what, in what order, for assuming what level of risk.

In this particular case, this was an unusual opportunity, for which I felt JBG deserved credit. It also promised to be a management-intensive deal, to which their firm could add considerable value. Furthermore, JBG had arranged for the seller to lend us 80 percent of the purchase price at favorable rates and on good terms. In light of this effort, it was appropriate for JBG to receive an "override," or disproportionate share of the profits. JBG felt they deserved such an override, and—once they put a proposal on the table—I and other potential investors accepted that proposal.

What was especially appealing about the package that JBG proposed was they were willing to subordinate their return to a 10 percent preference, substantially higher than the 6 to 8 percent preference return that characterizes many deals. The investors would also get all their capital back after the initial 75/25 split of the first 13 1/3 percent cash return. This very beneficial setup for the investors probably reflected the skittishness of the market, following the major declines in property values of the late 1980s and early 1990s. The promoter's return in the proposed deal was essentially "back-ended," which put the promoter in the position of doing well only if the limited partners also did well.

In addition, the fees proposed to be taken by JBG in this deal were very reasonable. Their acquisition fee for putting the deal together was set at under 1 percent, and their ongoing property management fee was pegged at a market rate. Finally, there would be no overall "asset-management fee." In the heyday of speculative real estate syndications, when the public's view of real estate was overly optimistic, such fees often ran to 8 to 10 percent of the income, and the promoters often took a 50 percent override (!). This is why, in the words of the *New Yorker* cartoon, the customers didn't own very many yachts. They made the mistake of being "momentum investors," rather than value investors.

In this situation, the general partners did not have much financial downside. As the property was reasonably stabilized, it wasn't necessary for them to fund construction overruns or operating deficits. We will explore the implications of these problems when we look at development in the next chapter.

SYNDICATIONS: FITTING INTO A BIGGER PICTURE

A major part of the problem in the 1970s and 1980s—until the passage of the Tax Reform Act of 1986—was that real estate deals were being done for their tax benefits, as opposed to their underlying cash flow. It is unfortunate that many investors were hurt by the tax law changes, which lengthened the useful life over which properties could be depreciated, and prohibited (in most cases) investors from writing off real estate losses against non–real estate generated income. In the long run, however, I think the changes have proven to be beneficial to the industry (and ultimately to the investor). Why? Because in the long run, the real estate industry is far better off when new construction activity and the pricing of existing properties are founded on, and driven by, tenant or owner/user demand for space.

One of the by-products of the cutback in benefits to taxpaying owners of real estate has been a growth in real estate investments on the part of non-taxpaying entities, such as pension and endowment funds. The combination of vast increases in assets held in these entities, as well as federal ERISA regulations encouraging diversification of their assets, has also fueled this growth.

The example presented on the next page shows why. What's gone on with this office property? The return on the $400,000 cash was reduced from a cash flow after financing (CFAF) of $34,000 (or 8.5 percent, pretax) to $25,406 (or 6.4 percent, posttax). The nontaxable investor did not have this disadvantage, of course; but this is only part of the story.

Note the thirty-nine-year depreciation schedule. As you'll recall from Chapter 2, depreciation is a noncash expense deduction allowed by the federal government to recognize the gradual deterioration of buildings and improvements to buildings (but not land). Suffice it to say here that at various points in time, the government jiggers the depreciation schedules and other aspects of the tax code in order to raise more or less revenue, or to discourage or encourage development.

For the real estate community, the implications of these adjustments can be enormous. Before the 1986 tax reforms, the property described here would have been depreciated *over fifteen years,* rather than thirty-nine years. This would have increased the annual depreciation allowance from $20,513 to $53,333—a difference more than big enough to cover the $42,000 in taxable income in our example. As a matter of fact, there would have been a taxable *loss* of $11,333, which at that point in time could have been used to offset other non–real estate income of the taxpayer. True, depreciation allowances only defer taxation to the time of sale, but at that time the gain is calculated using the depreciated property value, and the tax is calculated using a capital-gains rate that was recently lowered from 28 percent to 20 percent, or 25 percent for prior depreciation deductions. (I'll return to the impact of this capital-gains change shortly.)

Assumptions

Price	$1 million
Mortgage	$600,000
Cash investment	$400,000
Interest rate	8 percent
Amortization period	25 years
Cash flow from operations (CFO)	$90,000
Land value	$200,000
Building value	$800,000
Depreciation	39 years
Tax rate	40 percent

Taxable Income		Cash Flow	
CFO	$90,000	CFO	$90,000
Interest (first year, approx.)	48,000	Interest	48,000
Depreciation (800,000/39)	20,153	Principal (approx.)	8,000
Taxable income	21,487	CFAF	34,000
Tax @ 40 percent	8,594 →	Income tax	8,594
		CF after taxes	$25,406

So one key factor is the term of depreciation. When the federal government dramatically increased that term in 1986, it also dramatically *decreased* the tax advantages of investing in real estate for all except non-taxpaying entities. In other words, it made relatively more sense for my pension fund or my college to buy certain properties than for me to buy them personally.

The tax disadvantage of private owners can be partially offset by higher loan-to-value mortgages. If in the preceding example our $600,000 (60 percent) loan were increased to $800,000 (80 percent), in the first year the added mortgage interest of $16,000 would be deductible, with a corresponding decrease in taxable income.

The size of the relative advantage depends entirely on the availability and cost of mortgage money. Here's where we have to remind ourselves that the underlying principle of the real estate game is that you have to bring all the separate pieces of the puzzle together. One key piece of the puzzle is capital. Throughout the mid and late 1980s, mortgage funds were plentiful. Simply put, commercial banks, insurance companies, and savings and loan institutions were falling all over themselves to lend. Developers rushed to take advantage of the situation. They borrowed heavily and built heavily—creating a massive oversupply, that led in turn to a collapse of values to levels well below replacement costs. They got hurt, and the institutions that loaned them the easy money also suffered greatly. The predictable result? The few lenders remaining in the market grew more conservative, appraising properties at lower prices and requiring more cash equity from buyers.

This created a void, which (as we'll see in subsequent sections of this chapter) new players came forward to fill. But one more word here about the change in the capital-gains tax rate, which went into effect in 1997. Not long after my college gained its relative advantage in the real estate marketplace due to the change in the depreciation schedules, the federal government gave me an inducement to sell, in the form of an 8 percent reduction in the capital-gains tax (that is, from 28 percent to 20 percent) on investments I had held for more than one year.

In other words, at roughly the same time that my college (along with other institutional buyers) was becoming relatively stronger in the marketplace, individual property holders—some of whom were in dire financial straits—were getting a new incentive to sell. Not surprisingly, a lot of properties changed hands.

A global point of comparison: This was less true in Europe, where high transfer taxes on the overall sales price inhibit selling and encourage corporate ownership. When properties are sold in places like Europe, it's often shares in a holding company—rather than the properties themselves—that actually are sold. And some places are even tougher than Europe. On St. Kitts in the Caribbean, for example, where my family likes to vacation, there is not only a 12 percent transfer tax, but an additional 10 percent tax imposed on foreign buyers.

Did institutions become significant property holders? Yes and no. Most institutional buyers dabbled with the role of (absentee) landlord, in part because there were plenty of investment advisors who were willing (for a fee) to help institutional buyers purchase and operate individual properties. Besides the headaches of management, ERISA regulations effectively mandated third-party intermediaries for pension funds investing in real estate in order to limit their liability. Remember, too, that common stocks were a great lure during most of the 1980s and 1990s. (Institutional investors had a tax advantage over individual investors in the stock market, too, although that advantage narrowed as a result of the lowering of long-term capital gains rates; depreciation is obviously not a consideration with common stocks.) Stocks were producing unprecedented returns, they were liquid, and they presented none of the operating complexities of individual real estate properties.

But few institutional buyers were willing to put all their eggs in the stock-market basket—which over time began to look increasingly overvalued—and many still wanted ways to diversify and put at least some of their assets into real estate. This demand led to the rise of new kinds of real estate investment opportunities, in which institutions did not have to worry about individual properties.

POOLED AND COMMINGLED FUNDS

As noted at the beginning of this chapter, there is a broad spectrum of indirect investments in real estate, with syndications on one end and publicly held real estate investment trusts (REITs) on the other. Much of the territory in the intervening space is occupied by multiproperty funds, also known as "pooled funds."

Pooled funds are most often sponsored by a financial advisor or intermediary. (The initial sponsors were banks and insurance companies, but after these institutions got themselves into trouble in the late 1980s, independent firms—many of which were around in the late 1970s or early 1980s—grew dramatically in order to fill this role.) As the name implies, individual or institutional investors pool their cash resources. The fund invests these resources in a variety of properties, usually (but not always) according to some general statement of direction or intent. Specific properties held by the funds may or may not have been identified in advance.

Investors split the profits of the fund proportionate to their investment. (The definition of "profits" itself can be an interesting negotiation.) The manager of the pooled fund receives an asset-based fee, an acquisition fee, and sometimes also a percentage of the profits upon sale.

Pooled funds can be either "open-ended" or "closed-ended." In an open-ended fund, investors theoretically can redeem their interest after giving a prescribed notice to the sponsor. In theory, this minimizes the traditionally high transaction costs associated with real estate, and provides liquidity to what traditionally has been a less liquid investment.

You'll note that I used the phrase "in theory" in relation to the redeemability and liquidity of open-ended funds. In some cases, such funds are neither easily redeemable nor fully liquid. Appraisals commonly occur no more than once a year, and in some cases, occur only once every several years; so valuation can lag behind reality (in either direction).

I had a personal experience in this arena. In the 1980s, I was an advisor to an open-ended fund managed by a large commercial bank. With a weakening in the real estate market in the late 1980s, a few participating pension funds requested redemptions. Unfortunately, at that point, only the best of our properties were readily salable, and this was at a time when they could command only depressed prices. If we had gone ahead with the requested redemptions, the remaining investors would have been left in an even worse position, with an interest only in a less desirable collection of properties. The only fair solution we could think of—and it was the one we ultimately adopted—was to close the fund to redemptions. We then liquidated the fund in an orderly fashion, and the resulting proceeds were distributed to all the investors proportionately.

In fact, *lots* of open-ended funds got in trouble in this period, following basically this same scenario: Investors requested redemptions at precisely the wrong point in the cycle. Concurrently, as noted above, numerous institutional investors were deciding that they didn't want to be in the real estate management business. A common lament began to be heard: "We're spending 50 percent of our management time on 5 percent of our assets."

The convergence of these two trends led to a surge of interest during the 1990s in closed-ended, "commingled" funds. ("Closed-ended" simply means that a fixed number of investors are in for a specified duration, with no opportunity for early redemption.) These were pooled funds, but were closed to new investors after a one-time enrollment period. Small and medium-sized pension funds, in particular, were fans of commingled funds. These funds normally had a predetermined lifespan—most often ten years—which embodied a "buy-and-hold" strategy while ensuring dissolution within a given time period.

"Hold" was good because it allowed time for appreciation of the properties. "Sell" also had appeal for investors, since it meant that the fund manager couldn't extract fees indefinitely. But "buy-and-hold" also presented two disadvantages, both tied to the real estate industry's cyclicality. First, managers might not be counted upon to argue vigorously for disbanding the fund and selling off its assets in year 5, even though year 5 might be the best year in memory to sell off these particular properties. (Why forego five more years of management fees?) In a similar vein, since it is impossible to predict where the real estate cycle will be at the end of almost *any* reasonably long prescribed time period, it was possible that a closed-ended fund's specified end-date would arrive during an unfavorable juncture for selling real estate.

For this reason, the sponsor was very often given the option to extend the life of the fund for a year or two. In some cases, this was enough to outlast a down phase of the cycle; in others, it was not.

These funds normally had high equity levels and very little leverage. Sellers soon learned to love them. They represented non-taxpaying institutions, for the most part, which meant that they often were willing to bid against each other and pay higher prices. And because they had (1) cash on hand and (2) only one level of approval to deal with (the advisor level), they often were able to move more quickly than institutional buyers in search of individual properties.

Advisors such as San Francisco-based AMB Realty and Boston-based T.A. Realty moved aggressively in this field. Each has since accumulated several billion dollars of assets in its commingled and other funds. With this kind of scale came new advantages: not only economies of scale, but also the ability to hire and retain better managers. It was in many ways a virtuous circle.

While I'm focusing on new financial inventions here, it's useful to remember that (with the notable exception of the near-total demise of the open-ended funds in the 1980s) none of these vehicles has ever been displaced entirely by its successors. The sheer volume of properties has prevented that outcome. The building boom of the 1980s created a vastly increased supply of new office, warehouse, apartment, hotel, and retail properties; these were ideally suited for purchase by institutional buyers, through the mechanisms I've just described. (It's startling to realize that *half* of the present stock of commercial office space in the United States was built in the 1980s!) But at the same time, there were many existing, older, smaller buildings coming on the market (as well as better buildings in what were perceived to be less desirable locations) that did not meet institutional criteria. During this period, private syndications (for example) were still a part of the scene. But the swings of the capital markets made them less important than they had once been—or than they may be again in the future.

In the 1990s, commingled funds largely became the province of institutions, investment banks, and their entrepreneurial intermediaries, which formed pools to acquire real estate that would return profits that exceeded historical norms. As opportunistic (or "vulture") funds, they looked for undervalued assets in a wide variety of contexts. There was no one preferred approach. Harvard, to take one example close to home, continued to buy individual properties, whereas Yale sought out younger, creative entrepreneurs and helped them establish their own pooled funds in which Yale would be the lead investor. Both of these approaches did well, mainly because they hit the investment cycle almost perfectly. On the other coast, Stanford did very well in the same period, in part because of highly successful real estate investments in nearby Silicon Valley. (I tried to persuade Stanford to trade a partial interest in its shopping center in Palo Alto for an interest in some of Yale's properties in downtown New Haven, but never got a strong nibble. Perhaps Stanford felt that the two locales weren't comparable.)

By the late 1990s, many of these same institutions were targeting international markets. This shift reflected their conviction that domestic U.S. real estate was already peaking in value. This aggressive search for opportunity continues today, and is likely to carry forward into the near-term future. There's a significant challenge built into the structure of many of these pooled funds, which is that they've projected profits at levels that history would suggest are unsustainable. Meanwhile, the real estate market in general has risen around them, which means that these pooled funds have had to go farther and farther out on the risk curve of property types, development cycles, or geography if they wanted to achieve their projected profit levels. In this context, deal-making and capital-market skills become more important than real estate skills.

I hope that by now one of my major themes in this chapter has become self-evident: that the players in the capital-markets corner of our game are very, very flexible. Their vehicles are ephemeral, and their interests transitory. (I've often felt that the New York Stock Exchange could fit in comfortably on 34th Street in Manhattan, alongside the other fashion industries.) The next few sections introduce several more interesting funding pipelines either invented, or purposefully tailored, by the creative denizens of Wall Street.

A NECESSARY INVENTION: THE CMBS

With the downturn of the late 1980s and early 1990s, there was a shortage of lenders. Commercial banks and insurance companies were shrinking their real estate exposures. The government's Resolution Trust Company had seized the assets of numerous insolvent thrifts, and these were assets that the government wanted to dispose of rapidly.

The commercial real estate sector was in an uncomfortable bind. Much of the financing available in the 1980s for the purchase of existing commercial properties was short-term. The general assumption in the industry was that when the time came, this short-term borrowing could be converted into longer-term borrowing, just as it always had. Now, unexpectedly, the lenders were saying, "Hey, just pay us back. We have to get these loans off our books!" The rules were changing quickly, and the commercial real estate community was getting squeezed as a result.

In an effort to get much-needed mortgage money into the commercial arena, Wall Street came up with a creative innovation called the "commercial mortgage-backed security," or CMBS. This was an attempt to mirror what was already happening in the residential, single-family market, where the government-sponsored Fannie Mae and Freddie Mac were providing new sources of mortgage money by making it possible for financial intermediaries to package loans and sell them to the public. The goal was to try to accomplish something similar in the commercial area, but in a way that did not necessitate government involvement.

Simply put, the idea was to package a group of mortgages and finance them as bonds. These bonds were divided into different "tranches," or bundles defined by risk. The most secure tranche might involve the top 60 or 70 percent of the loan portfolio, which very often was sold to relatively conservative insurance companies. More junior tranches had a subordinated claim to the first tranches; the most junior tranche could be wiped out by the first losses on the underlying mortgage pool.

Maybe a down-to-earth example would help here. Suppose you take out a loan of $100,000 on your $150,000 house. Someone agrees to make a new loan of $60,000 against your $100,000 loan, an amount so safe that it would almost certainly be whole in the event of a default. Since this loan is obviously safer than the entire $100,000 loan, it commands a relatively low rate. If you are forced to sell your house for $60,000, then that first person gets paid, and no one else does.

A second person—one who takes, for example, the risk from the $60,000-to-$80,000 tranche—wants a higher return to reflect that higher risk; a third person who takes the $80,000-to-$100,000 tranche demands a still higher rate, and so on. Meanwhile, you as the borrower send in one check and pay one interest rate, which represents a composite of the three interest rates paid to the three parties.

In Chapter 4, our commitment-to-closing chapter, we talked about how commercial real estate mortgages are becoming more standardized because, increasingly, the traditional lenders are serving only as intermediaries—packaging loans and selling them to others. The CMBSs are the place where a lot of that "structured" money comes from. They were at first an ad hoc, conservative response to the damaging pullback of financing institutions in the late 1980s and early 1990s. The CMBS market has since grown into a $150 billion industry, and has become an extremely important financing mechanism for commercial real estate.

Here's a case, as implied above, where Wall Street deserves credit for its creativity. But we haven't yet lived through a down market that could put CMBSs to the test. Were the tranches appropriately priced? How will the foreclosure mechanisms work? Price volatility for commercial properties has historically been much greater than for single-family residences. I, for one, think there's cause for concern.

OPPORTUNITY FUNDS (TO PUT IT POLITELY)

The rise of "opportunity funds" (also known, less generously, as "vulture funds") was also fueled by the government takeover of many of the savings and loans, through the mechanism of the Resolution Trust Company (RTC). Remember the context: Values had dropped by 30 to 40 percent. Traditional sources of funding were in full retreat. The RTC decided that the best way to liquidate the loans of these insolvent institutions was to sell groups of properties.

New breeds of cat, sensing opportunity in the chaos, began appearing on the scene. Individuals such as Sam Zell—as well as venerable investment banks like Goldman Sachs and Morgan Stanley—launched what became known as opportunity funds, created for the express purpose of buying bundles of properties at distressed price levels. Initially, most of the investors in these funds were wealthy individuals in search of large capital gains.

Where were the large pension funds and other institutional investors during this period of discombobulation? For the most part, they were sitting on the sidelines. Some put money in CMBSs. Others continued to struggle with managing their own properties. Still others tried to live with the shortcomings of commingled funds and separate accounts. Meanwhile, of course, huge amounts of money were pouring into pension funds and mutual funds, all in search of smart and reasonably safe investment opportunities.

It was in this context that an old idea, several times discredited, began to be revived.

REITS: WHAT THEY ARE, AND WHY

As we've made our way through the sequence of indirect real estate investments described in this chapter, we've traced two types of progressions in the structure of real estate investments: from relatively small to relatively large, and from illiquid to more liquid. There are notable exceptions, of course, especially in the former case. Syndications, for example, weren't always the domain of smaller transactions. The Empire State Building was syndicated at one point in its history: by no means a "small" transaction.

But in general, the trend has been toward *bigger* and *more liquid.* (This is common in the advanced stages of real estate cycles.) The reasons are clear. First, Wall Street entrepreneurs were determined to find ways to increase liquidity in the real estate industry—and thereby to earn commissions for themselves—and their efforts have been increasingly successful. Second, the massive influx of money into pension funds and mutual funds in the 1980s and 1990s created an almost insatiable demand for sound investments. Pension funds alone controlled some *$5 trillion* in assets by the late 1990s, of which some $300 billion was invested in real estate stocks and bonds. As a group, institutions (including pension funds) owned more than 40 percent of the prime commercial real estate in the United States.

When the huge pension funds expressed their unhappiness with existing investment vehicles, Wall Street scrambled to find new ones. When the head of the General Motors employees' pension fund, for example, stated that the auto giant didn't want its money commingled with that of other investors, fund sponsors established "separate accounts," which would own and operate properties for a single very large investor. But separate accounts, too, had their disadvantages—for one thing, the reporting function was unexpectedly complicated—and many of these customers (and their smaller counterparts) again demanded a simpler solution.

To provide this solution, Wall Street dusted off an old and somewhat discredited vehicle: the real estate investment trust, or REIT.

Where did REITs come from? REITs were born in 1960 as a result of the Real Estate Investment Trust Act. They were authorized by Congress as a way of making it possible for small investors to own "shares" in a large number of properties. This would provide the small investor with the same low investment thresholds and diversification that were beginning to make mutual funds attractive to a broad base of investors.

Although the definition of REITs has evolved in the intervening decades, certain characteristics of REITs have remained more or less constant. Technically a "trust," a REIT combines aspects of a corporation and a partnership. Like a corporation, it has centralized management and limited liability, and its shares can be either privately held or publicly traded. But like a partnership, the overwhelming majority of the corporation's taxable income must be paid out to the shareholders each year.

What does this mean? With REITs, a large percentage of the investor's return comes in the form of the distribution of ongoing cash flows. A traditional industrial company today commonly pays only a modest dividend. (The dividend yield on the S&P 500 averages around 1.5 percent, and the investor normally expects to make most of his or her gain on the anticipated appreciation of the share price. A REIT, by contrast, pays an annual yield of 5 to 8 percent or more. In an environment in which long-term U.S. Treasuries pay 5 percent, this is an attractive and reasonably predictable income stream—at least under certain circumstances, which we'll cover in the following section.

Like a partnership, taxes on REIT income are paid only at the individual-investor level. This is an especially attractive feature for the institutional investor that isn't required to pay taxes at all. In marked contrast, a corporation pays tax on its income, and any dividends that are paid out are taxed again at the shareholder level.

At the same time, depreciation is deducted from the earnings of the REIT, which effectively shelters at least some of the distribution from taxation. So if an investor is sophisticated enough to compare the after-tax return on a REIT to the after-tax return on (for example) a utility stock in today's market, he or she is very likely to discover that the REIT is a more attractive proposition. Most REITs have leveraged their assets to a 40–50 percent level. The interest on the loans is deductible for tax purposes, and the leveraging has the potential for increasing (or decreasing) the return on equity disproportionately.

REITs have other advantages, as well. Most REITs specialize in terms of property type, so as an investor, you can pick the kind of property (office, residential, retail, etc.) that you're interested in. Some REITs specialize by geography. If you're bullish about the future of one area of the country, you may be able to find a REIT that will allow you to concentrate on that locale.

REITs must be widely held, which the IRS defines as having at least one hundred shareholders. No more than 50 percent of a REIT's shares, moreover, can be owned by five or fewer shareholders, although a pension fund is judged by the number of its plan participants or beneficiaries. These restrictions tend to preclude takeovers by an individual or a small group of investors.

The opportunity for multiple shareholders also allows for ever-bigger REITs. (Unless it is cash-rich or willing to take on leverage, an acquisitive REIT has to offer equity to the sellers of new properties it acquires.) At least in theory, a larger REIT has more liquidity, which means that as an individual investor, you are less likely to hurt the price of the stock by selling your small share-holdings. And seen from the other end of the investor spectrum, size is also good. Today's large mutual funds can't even consider a stock if they can't buy or sell many millions of dollars' worth of that stock easily. Moderate-sized REITs have trouble passing this test. A "huge" REIT used to be one with a market value of $500 million; today, a $1 billion REIT is not considered particularly big.

By investing in a REIT, you normally get a higher-quality portfolio than would be available to most individual investors. In many cases, REITs use their economies of scale to obtain debt at a lower cost. Most have the advantage of being run by professional managers, whose track records you can examine.

REITs are not without their disadvantages, of course. Since the trust's income is being distributed annually to shareholders, this limits reinvestment in the business itself. Since the amount of leverage the trust can take on is also limited by guidelines established by Wall Street analysts, the stock itself is less likely to show large price increases. (Except under unusual historical circumstances, as we'll discuss below, REITs are not rapid-growth stocks.) One side effect of this is that REITs sometimes find it difficult to attract good managers. Because REIT shares don't appreciate dramatically, management stock options aren't as valuable in the REIT context as they are in other corporate contexts.

But these disadvantages pale beside the much longer list of advantages. When a REIT is structured correctly and when external circumstances are favorable, it can provide income, liquidity, diversification, access to higher-quality properties and a wider range of choices, and (in some cases) tax breaks.

As a result of all these advantages, REITs were one of the truly important financial stories of the 1990s. A longer-term perspective is necessary to gauge the truly astonishing growth of REITs during the 1990s. Between 1970 and 1980, the total market capitalization of REITs grew from about $1 billion to about $2 billion. Between 1980 and 1989—a peak year—REIT market capitalization grew from $2 billion to $12 billion. Between 1990 and 1998, REIT market value increased from about $8 billion to more than *$170 billion.* This increase, primarily the result of new share issuances, represents about 4 percent of the total market value of investment-grade real estate.

Let me digress for a few pages and tell three stories about my own personal involvement in REITs, putting each in its historical context. Collectively, these stories—which include both happy and unhappy endings—will help you understand the changes that have occurred in the REIT industry, and prepare you to make your own assessment of REITs as potential investments.

REITS: OUR CHECKERED PAST

As noted above, REITs were created decades ago by a well-meaning Congress that wanted to help the small investor get into the real estate game. To adopt Charlie Merrill's distinction, the legislation of 1960 was intended to help Main Street, not Wall Street.

In short order, though, the REIT became a favored tool of huge financial institutions in search of large management fees. One of the largest New York money-center banks—to cite an example of a reputable institution that got caught up in this activity—fielded one of the biggest REITs of the 1960s, which wound up also being one of the industry's biggest failures. Its managers, often compensated for growth of assets under management, were extremely aggressive in search of opportunity. They went far out on the risk curve, investing in raw land and speculative development deals. Borrowing short and investing long, they loaded up their REIT with a mountain of debt. In the 1970s, this prominent REIT got caught in an interest-rate squeeze and, along with a number of other equally venturesome REITs, was effectively wiped out.

This meant that their investors lost their money. The disastrous performance of these speculative REITs gave what should have been a very solid investment vehicle an extremely unsavory reputation. Wary investors concluded, correctly, that the REIT format was subject to abuse. They also learned—too late, in most cases!—that REITs are sorely tempted to add leverage when interest rates are low.

REITs come in waves, and I missed the chance to participate in the first wave of REITs. (Early in my career, back when the Alison Corporation was bidding for garden apartments in Groton, no REITs were looking for my help as a board member or advisor.) But I served on the board of a REIT during each of the next three waves: one each in the 1970s, 1980s, and 1990s. The lessons I learned in those contexts have some enduring value, so I'll retell those stories here.

My first REIT tour of duty came in the late 1970s, when I served on the board of the Connecticut General REIT. As with all REITs, the majority of the board of directors must be outside directors, and I was serving as one of those outside directors. The REIT was sponsored by the Connecticut General Insurance Company (CG), which was then one of the leading lenders in the real estate field. This was a REIT that CG itself managed, and to which the insurance company charged a fee for its management services.

Many of the REITs launched during that time period adopted the kinds of highly speculative investment policies that their 1960s counterparts had followed—investing in raw land and development deals, and trying to earn spread income by taking on a maturity mismatch between assets and liabilities. (Many of the 1960s-era REITs were still in operation at this point, as well, since the shake-out had yet to come.) But the CG REIT was conservatively run. It held a large number of very good income properties around the country, including many very stable apartment buildings, and it had refrained from overleveraging itself.

When the REIT industry started to get in trouble in the 1970s, the CG REIT's stock plummeted along with the industry. The best I can say in retrospect is that we didn't do as badly as some other REITs, which lost up to 90 percent of their value. Nevertheless, our share price sank to a level that was, at least in the board's opinion, below asset value. During the late 1970s the stock increased in price, but we felt the price still didn't reflect the REIT's true underlying value.

In 1981, we found that others shared this opinion. The British Coal Board Pension Trust, which managed pension assets for thousands of British coal miners, surprised us by putting in an unsolicited tender offer for our stock at approximately a 20 percent premium over its market price. The Coal Board's managers, it seemed, had recognized the difference between our market price and our asset value, and had decided to make a run at the company by offering a premium over the then-current share price.

In the eyes of our board, however, this was still a price that was well below asset value. Briefly, it appeared as if we would turn this offer down and go about our business as usual. One day during this quiet interlude, I got a call from a former student who was then working on an arbitrage desk at one of the big investment banks. He was very interested in learning about the company. I informed him that for obvious reasons, I couldn't tell him anything that wasn't public information. "I didn't think you'd be able to talk to me about the CG situation," he replied. "But in any case, your company's in play now, and you won't be on that board for much longer." He was simply doing his job, which (among other things) involved seeing what he could find out about the deal.

Naively, I shrugged off his implication—only to discover shortly thereafter that he was absolutely right. The arbitrageurs on Wall Street had bought up a very large portion of the CG REIT's stock, and they wanted the company sold. At that point, we (as independent directors) separated ourselves entirely from the CG's management. (They had a vested interest in receiving fees from the continuation of the REIT, and this would present a potential conflict of interest if the board was inclined to sell.) We hired our own lawyers and selected an investment banker, who then went out and found us a bidder that was willing to bid a considerable premium over the British Coal Board offer. That bidder was the Prudential Insurance Company, which wanted our assets for some of their separate accounts. We agreed to their price, and the deal was done.

Was this good for the REIT shareholders? Yes and no. Along with my fellow board members, I thought the purchase price was fair at that particular point in time. And I have to admit that the chess game set in motion by the arbitrageurs forced a clean separation between CG and its REIT. (In fact, we had been planning to take over management of the REIT from CG, to eliminate potential conflicts of interest between the insurance company and the REIT.) So this was more or less beneficial. But the assets that had been assembled by CG had excellent long-term value, and one could have argued that our REIT had ongoing value as a company. (We'll return to this concept of "enterprise value" shortly.) In my own opinion, the shareholders would have been better served if we could have taken a longer-term perspective. Wall Street, however, was having none of that.

Another story: From 1985 to 1992, I was on the board of a new REIT put together by Dallas-based Trammell Crow. Trammell Crow (TCC) was one of the largest developer/owner/property-management companies in the country. I was familiar with TCC in part because they had a nationwide reputation, and in part because they had hired some of my Harvard Business School students. (Incidentally, TCC started all its employees as sales agents, responsible for making cold calls on prospective tenants. This was and still is a wonderful way to get into that end of the real estate business.)

TCC was then in the process of packaging a large number of commercial and industrial properties, most of which were in the Texas area, for sale to a REIT that it was organizing. TCC would then receive a management fee for advising the REIT and running the properties. Obviously, this presented the potential for a number of conflicts. But TCC made sure that there were independent appraisals to establish the sale prices, which in turn validated that the transactions were arm's-length.

The packaging process was far from easy. Most of these properties had different ownership structures, which had to be made to fit into the new REIT structure. Some of the properties were owned by TCC employees; others were not. To put it mildly, TCC pulled off a very complicated set of "internal" negotiations, arriving at purchase prices which, in retrospect, were probably not bargains.

Meanwhile, another set of negotiations was going on. The underwriter for the deal let it be known that many of the REITs being put together at that time had a certain percentage of "zero-coupon" bonds in their financial structure. These are bonds on which neither principal nor interest is due in the early years. Instead, interest accumulates at a given rate, and comes due in a lump sum at a pre-specified maturity date. The bankers recommended strongly that approximately 20 percent of the new TCC REIT capital structure should consist of zero-coupon bonds. And because these would be highly subordinated bonds—meaning that the investors who held them wouldn't be first in line for repayment—they would carry an unusually high 12 percent interest rate. All the projections, of course, showed that the income of the trust would rise sufficiently over time to cover this high rate of interest, and allow the company to refinance these "junk bonds" when they came due.

The proposal containing the zero-coupon bonds came at the eleventh hour. My impression was (and still is) that a few prominent deals—including the Rockefeller Center REIT—had just gone through using zero-coupon bonds, and this fact was influencing lot of financial people at that time. I infer, too, that the parties liked zero-coupon bonds for a very practical reason: When a company is not paying its interest on a current basis, its annual cash distribution rate obviously can be goosed a lot higher. In retrospect, TCC should have scrutinized this scheme more thoroughly, and run some less optimistic scenarios. But it appeared that in buying into these zero-coupon bonds—which in any case represented only a small part of the financing package—we were in good and sophisticated company. The deal went through. Again, you can see how the momentum to complete a deal can overwhelm a lot of people's good judgment.

If you've read the previous chapters, you can guess what happened next. In the late 1980s, the real estate market—entering one of its periodic down cycles—started to tank, and rents began to fall. Our operating income began to go down, instead of up. It was quickly apparent that these zero-coupon bonds were a huge sword dangling over the head of our REIT. When the Rockefeller Center REIT, with a structure similar to ours, got into financial trouble, we could see clearly what was ahead for us.

We aggressively pursued every opportunity to buy back the zero-coupon bonds at substantial discounts. By cutting down on what would come due in the future, we were attempting to stabilize the REIT; also, we were making what amounted to a 16 or 17 percent return by buying back the discounted bonds. Of course, in order to buy back the bonds we had to sell off properties that we didn't want to sell, especially in a tough market, but we felt that the survival of the REIT had to be our first priority. We internalized the management of the REIT to eliminate TCC's advisory fee—although we retained TCC to perform on-site leasing and management, which was their special expertise—and took other steps to restructure the company. Rather than liquidate, the company decided to stay in business on a much smaller scale. (By the way, it wasn't until the laws changed that REITs were able to self-manage effectively. The earlier nonalignment of interests between the promoter, who was fee-driven, and the return-driven investor led to all kinds of difficulties.)

What lessons did I take away from this? First, I was reminded again of the general fact that real estate people are normally much better at managing the asset side of their balance sheet than the liability side. On the liability side, they mostly want to create as much fixed-rate debt as possible—an approach that can be appropriate in private deals, but only if the property is not overleveraged.

In the case of the TCC REIT, we had a prominent Wall Street firm proposing a last-minute structural change that ultimately proved very destructive. If our company had simply issued more stock at the outset, our projected return (and presumably our share price) would have been lower, but we would have been in a much better position to ride out the inevitable downturn. If the debt had been paid as we went along, rather than zero-coupon, it still would have been a problem, but might not have been a fatal problem.

My second realization was that a REIT is two things at once: a *real estate deal*, and a *Wall Street offering*. These are not the same thing. What's good for one is not necessarily good for the other. Since that time, I've always tried to figure out in which of those directions a particular REIT is leaning—and what will happen if, for whatever reason, it starts to lean the other way.

One more tale, this time with what is so far a happier ending: In 1993, I joined the board of a REIT formed by CBL, a Chattanooga-based middle-sized shopping center development company with a record of strong implementation of an excellent strategy. CBL's approach was to develop the largest malls in middle-sized cities in southern states, including Tennessee, Mississippi, and the Carolinas. The company was family-run, with individual projects owned in a series of partnerships, many carrying a lot of debt as a result of the company's most recent round of mall building. The family wanted to take the enterprise public in order to raise equity to pay down debt, and to continue the development of the new malls that were already in the company's pipeline.

Like Trammell Crow, CBL had to go through an intensive series of negotiations to get the various owners (inside the family and out) to contribute their properties to the REIT. What was different in this case was that instead of taking cash, the family was taking shares in the REIT. Another distinction was that this deal involved the creation of what's called an "UPREIT." The UPREIT format permits an owner of a property to receive operating units in the new REIT that are ultimately convertible into REIT shares; but until that conversion takes place, no tax is due. The creation of an UPREIT allowed the family to postpone a substantial capital gain while still receiving its share of the distributions, and also to effectively retain control of the operation.

With about 40 percent of the shares, the family is able to avoid the fate of the Connecticut General REIT, where outsiders came in and accumulated enough shares to put the company in play. The investors holding the other 60 percent of the shares can take reassurance from the fact that the family is deeply committed to the success of the REIT, and its financial interests are aligned with those of other shareholders.

And finally, the resulting REIT has no external advisor, and therefore is internally managed. Both operating expenses and the potential for conflicts of interest are minimized by this arrangement. All of the profits go into the same pot. As of this writing, the CBL REIT remains a successful, publicly traded, and stable entity. The company is trying to expand its base through the acquisition of existing centers that it can upgrade, as well as the selective development of new ones. It is attempting to grow while still managing its debt level—not easy, since the market for new stock issuances is limited.

To summarize, we've seen REITs created in four separate waves. In the first wave—in the 1960s and early 1970s—institutions took advantage of a new good vehicle for investment, and wound up misusing it. They invested badly, and managed themselves badly.

In the second and third waves, roughly corresponding to the mid and late 1970s and the 1980s, REITs featured higher-quality properties, but still suffered from some inherent conflicts between management and the investors. Many REIT promoters were simply taking fees for services rendered, and didn't necessarily have the best interest of shareholders in the fronts of their minds. Some of the REITs in these waves also were hurt by misaligned financing, resulting from mistiming of the economic cycle.

The current REITs comprise the fourth wave, and, as indicated above, they are designed in a way that better aligns the interests of management and the investors. Let me make it clear that I don't mean to imply that something noble or selfless is going on in this fourth wave. This latest wave of REIT issuance came about when a group of shopping-center developers came under pressure from their lenders in the early 1990s to pay off their loans, and there wasn't any debt capital available to replace them. The shopping-mall magnates in essence had to deleverage by coming up with considerable equity capital. The only way they could do this was to form REITs. More or less by force of circumstance, they were required to put their own personal interests into these new REITs to make them viable. They issued equity to the public; they then used the proceeds to pay down their debt levels.

Think of it as a series of enforced marriages between struggling property managers and the REITs they were forced to create. For a shotgun wedding, the results have been quite good, overall. These REITs consisted of good properties, by and large, with very experienced management teams. They started out with very comfortable debt levels, mainly because the new funds were used to pay down existing debts. (Under the stern gaze of Wall Street, the new REITs tried to limit their debt to 40 percent of their total market capitalization, although recently this began climbing toward 50 percent and higher.) This lower level of indebtedness gave more protection to the investors. But the temptation to take advantage of positive financial leverage—buying properties at an 8 to 9 percent cap rate and borrowing half the price at 7 percent interest—can be irresistible.

Nevertheless, after more than thirty years, REITs were finally beginning to take the form that Congress had originally intended. They were becoming a good way for the average investor to participate in a reasonably safe, income-producing instrument, and to diversify his or her holdings—both in terms of real estate investments, and in terms of an overall portfolio. Mutual funds, which are the favored investment vehicle of individual investors, have become major shareholders in REITs. (In fact, some funds have been formed that invest almost entirely in REITs.) The merger of REITs into larger entities to facilitate public investment may not result in the substantial cost savings that some predict.

But on the fourth try, it seems that REITs are getting themselves right.

REITS: UNDERSTANDING WHAT YOU'RE BUYING

So at the end of the day, should you buy shares in a REIT (or in a fund that specializes in REIT shares)? If so, how can you differentiate between a good REIT investment and a bad one?

Let me summarize the most important things that you, as an individual investor, should consider. These include both quantitative and qualitative aspects.

As REITs have evolved over the years, so have the techniques that analysts use to assess them. Throughout the following discussion, remember that what Wall Street is *really* trying to do is to create the functional equivalent of the price/earnings ratio for real estate. Ideally—because Wall Street doesn't like things to get too complicated—this equivalent ratio would be based on some simple formula.

When REITs first emerged—and this is still true today—analysts needed to find ways to value them. For other stocks, *net income* was the most important yardstick. But the traditional price-earnings ratio that is used to assess other stocks is an *after-tax* measure, and therefore is not really reflective of real estate returns, which report on a pretax basis. The other problem with the net-income measure was that it counted historical-cost-based depreciation as an expense. This works reasonably well for a piece of industrial equipment, which definitely decreases in value over time. By contrast, a well maintained building in a good neighborhood can *appreciate* significantly over time.

The REIT industry, aided by Wall Street, therefore proposed a measure called "funds from operations" (FFO). To calculate FFO, analysts would start with net income, add back real estate-related depreciation and amortization, and adjust for nonrecurring items and for gains or losses on asset sales. With this calculation in hand, analysts could compare the REIT share price to FFO.

But in the eyes of many, FFO was a less than adequate measure, because it failed to take into account the nature of the capital structure, the degree of leverage, or the amount of capital expenditures, leasing commissions, build-out allowances, and other real (if somewhat less predictable) expenses. Since the early buyers of the 1990s-era REIT shares were mainly mutual funds and pension funds, they were more sophisticated buyers, and they insisted on coming up with more realistic measures.

In response to these pressures, the industry proposed a new standard: "adjusted funds from operations" (AFFO). This new measure gained wide currency, and analysts and industry observers began comparing REITs in terms of both FFO and AFFO multiples.

The relationship between FFO, AFFO, and net operating income (NOI, which we first encountered in Chapter 2) is summarized here. Note that NOI is calculated *before* interest expenses, while FFO and AFFO include deductions for interest expenses, but not debt principal payments.

Getting from NOI to FFO and AFFO

Private Market	Public Market
Gross property revenue	Gross property revenue
– property expenses	– property expenses
= net operating income (NOI)	= NOI
÷ capitalization rate	-overhead expenses
= gross asset value	– overhead expenses
– debt	= EBITDA*
= net asset value	– interest
	= FFO
	– capital and leasing expenditures
	= AFFO
	× multiple
	= market value

*"earnings before interest, taxes, depreciation, and amortization"

It turned out, however, that even AFFO was an inadequate measure of the dividend-paying capacity of a given REIT. It became clear that both the capital structure of the REIT, as well as the characteristics of its assets, were important factors in assessing whether a REIT could sustain its dividend payments.

Firms such as Green Street Advisors (GSA), which specialize in the valuation of REITs, have developed their own ways to value REIT stocks. GSA, for example, first focuses on the underlying value of the properties, and then adjusts the price to reflect the apparent ability of management to create value.

To get to the value of the REIT's properties, GSA applies an appropriate capitalization rate (see Chapter 2) to the real estate FFO or AFFO generated by the portfolio. In choosing a cap rate, Green Street takes into account all the factors that it considers relevant: the type of property; its quality, age, and location; and local demographic supply/demand trends. GSA combines these factors across the REIT's holdings to arrive at a net asset value (NAV).

After calculating NAV, Green Street evaluates seven factors to determine if a given REIT should trade at a premium above (or a discount below) its NAV, and if so, how great a premium (or discount):

1. *Enterprise value.* I alluded to this concept earlier. This is the perceived ability of a management team to add value and generate growth in FFO. Does this company have untapped borrowing capacity? Or conversely, is it overleveraged? Does it have a considerable amount of land available for development? Has it demonstrated great negotiating skills?

This was a sensible enough notion. In some cases, though, the enterprise valuations assigned by Wall Street were clearly outlandish. In the most extreme cases, they were adding a 30 to 50 percent "enterprise value" to the REIT, above and beyond the underlying property values.

To a certain extent, these assessments may have been honest mistakes, based upon the REIT's track record in the early 1990s. At that point in time, when REITs were buying at 60 or 70 percent of replacement cost, they were "creating" values above the cost of their holdings. But this is clearly not sustainable. More recently, "enterprise value" premiums have rarely risen above the 10 to 15 percent range, and in the not-so-distant past, REITs traded at a discount.

The key is whether the public perceives that the REIT, which has added administrative expenses, can produce more value through its property management skills, its ability to access lower-cost capital, and its development and acquisition strategies than one could obtain by buying individual projects directly.

2. *Focus.* Focused REITs are expected to perform better than widely diversified REITs, since management will play to its strengths.
3. *Insider ownership.* This relates to the "alignment of interest" issue to which I referred earlier. Substantial insider owners can be expected to take a longer-term view of the enterprise. On the flip side, entrepreneurs accustomed to running their own show can get buried in the details of running a public company, and may want to sell out or step back after going public.
4. *Potential conflicts of interest.* This is the flip side of aligned interests. Fee structures and incentives need to be carefully considered.
5. *Liquidity.* The larger the REIT, generally speaking, the more liquid its shares become.
6. *Balance-sheet strength.* Low debt levels give a REIT the financial flexibility to take advantage of future opportunities at favorable rates. Higher leverage may signify greater risk. Assets (such as developable land) that can be turned into income-producers can be either pluses or minuses, depending on the cost of the land and the potential for reuse.

The basic paradox remains, however: The biggest incentive for firms to increase their overall leverage comes when their stock prices are high, encouraging more borrowing while the property markets may also be high, thereby making it difficult to find good deals based on the return from the property alone.

7. *Overhead costs.* As in other industries, high overhead leads investors to place a discount on a REIT stock. Green Street calculates 0.7 percent of assets to be an average. It is unclear whether the present value of excessive overhead should be deducted to arrive at NAV, since potential buyers may or may not be factoring it into account.

As of the late 1990s, nearly 70 percent of REIT stocks were trading at a premium to NAV. But as recently as the late 1980s, most REIT market prices incorporated a substantial discount to NAV—in many cases, as high as 30 percent. I believe this volatility in investors' moods reflects not a future forecast, but simply their immediate psychological state. REITs seem to trade at premiums when market conditions are good, and at discounts when conditions are depressed.

I've included this GSA-derived analysis to give you a sense of how the professionals look at REITs. Green Street, Penobscot, and other firms sell their services for a fee. If you plan to involve yourself heavily in REITs, you should determine the point at which such professional services would become a sensible expense for you.

In the final analysis, when you're buying into a REIT stock, you're really buying the *properties* in the REIT, even though the current price may correlate more to the overall condition of the stock market. Therefore, you have to understand how back-of-the-envelope analysis can be applied to a public REIT stock. Simply put, you have to be able to take the AFFO, compare it with the market value of the total company, and draw the appropriate conclusions.

To set up a hypothetical example: Assume the AFFO, compared to the total market value of the company, is about 8 percent. The market is expecting 15 percent return on its money; therefore, there must be a 7 percent growth factor built into the AFFO. Therefore, they've got to be able to pay out the dividends *and* increase the AFFO to make it work.

Let's assume they're going to be 50 percent leveraged. Can they get their operating returns up 3.5 percent per year, which would drop 7 percent to the bottom line? Does the company have a lot of properties under construction that are going to add to earnings fairly soon? Is the company banking on being able to sustain a past record of great success? If it's Richard Rainwater and Crescent Realty, do I believe that he'll be able to keep pulling off spectacular deals others wouldn't have had the imagination to conceive and execute, thereby deserving and earning a high premium?

The market said "yes" to this last question—at least initially. Then it changed its mind as to Crescent and others. By the end of 1998, many REITs had lost a third of their value from their fifty-two-week highs, despite strong real estate markets and falling interest rates.

This suggests the next BOE-type question I'd ask about a given REIT: How much information are you getting from it, and how *good* is it? You may learn from a prospectus, for example, that a given office building is throwing off a lot of cash, which presents an attractive gross return. But if you deduct from that gross return the cost of amortizing the leasehold improvements and the brokers' commissions, the numbers may not look so good over any reasonable time period. The conclusion? Make sure you really understand where the numbers come from.

The Wall Street prospectus doesn't make it easy for you. The numbers are historical, and—for obvious reasons—projections for more than the upcoming year are discouraged. It is sometimes difficult to see which statements are for income-tax purposes, and which are for cash flow. The trick, as I've said earlier in another context, is to *follow the cash.*

And finally, use your common sense. Recently, I was offered the opportunity to be a board member in a private REIT that was being formed with the ultimate goal of going public. A packager was trying to get the best property manager, the best custodian, a prestigious board of directors, and so on. But there was no integrated company there; there was no experience of working together. To me, this didn't make sense, and I turned down the opportunity.

In retrospect, I can see this venture as a case in which someone was trying to design a company to fit the latest Wall Street model. Remember, though, that this is a *changing* model. REIT fads in zero-coupon bonds, a heavy emphasis on development, excessive leverage, and premiums and discounts come and go; the properties have a life of their own.

REITS: A BRIGHT FUTURE?

What's ahead for REITs? I see both opportunities and dangers.

One challenge is that Wall Street is now demanding larger and larger REITs. Originally, it was felt that a REIT with a few hundred million dollars of equity was a big REIT. The pressure today is to create multi*billion*-dollar REITs. Why? Primarily because the pension funds and mutual funds are demanding it. For a giant like Fidelity's Magellan Fund, buying 5 percent of a $100 million REIT is hardly worth the trouble of performing fundamental analysis. And illiquidity could make it difficult to accumulate or dispose of even a $5 million position.

A secondary selling point is the alleged economies of scale that result from bigness. Admittedly, it doesn't cost twice as much to administer a $1 billion REIT vs. a $500 million REIT. Operating and capital costs are sure to go down somewhat, but my guess is that they won't amount to huge dollars as a percentage of overall rents.

So at least today—that is, at this point in the cycle—REITs are getting bigger, often through the acquisition of more properties. Unfortunately, they can't do this by retaining a high percentage of their earnings, because the enforced distribution of much of these earnings prevents capital from accumulating. And they can't just keep borrowing the money, because that would throw their debt-to-market-cap ratios out of whack. So If they want to grow, they will have to keep returning to the capital markets. (This is

O.K. with Wall Street, of course, because it means more fees.) When a REIT raises $300 million from the equity markets, it can also borrow another $200 million and still maintain its 40 percent debt-to-total-market-cap ratio. (An alternative, explained earlier, is to acquire existing properties in exchange for UPREIT shares.) These two approaches, plus the tactic of merging with other REITs, are how REITs will grow big enough to continue to attract the largest institutional investors.

Hopefully, REITs will resist the ever-present temptation to increase their leverage. Hopefully, they'll take a longer-term view, deciding against strategies that would have short-term appeal but would endanger the company in a downturn. But as I've explained earlier, the temptation to add leverage is great, and the pressure to satisfy the Wall Street analysts' desire for short-term profit growth can be overwhelming.

I also foresee some tensions in the management of REITs, and especially of the "fourth wave" REITs described above, in which long-term real estate developers and promoters have taken ownership positions in the REITs they helped to create. Dealing with Wall Street imposes a new kind of discipline on these individuals, who traditionally have been, well, *resistant* to discipline. Will the traditional, entrepreneurially oriented real estate developers have the patience for endless meetings with analysts? If not, what will the new managers who replace them have as their first priority? Will they still have an alignment of interest with the shareholders, like today's owners? Or will they push for growth, in part because their own financial prospects are tied to growth?

Perhaps the most serious risk lies in the *pricing* of some REITs. One reason why so many properties today are being sold to REITs is that REITs are paying higher prices than the seller could get in the private market. If these REITs hold the line on price (and therefore on expected return), that will be well and good. But what happened in the bullish stock market of the 1990s has had a powerful impact on the REIT industry. REIT managers, trying to stay competitive with growth stocks in other industries, have been buying real estate that traditionally has returned 10 percent or so per year, and pricing it as if it will return considerably more. But the property return is independent of the expectations of the owner. If those return expectations are not met, the REITs that overpaid can be expected to drop in price.

In other words, two bad trends are occurring. First, in cases where the price of shares in a REIT is set based on an excessive multiple, investors are overpaying. Second, this psychology puts pressure on the people running these REITs to continue to push for growth. Within the healthy constraints imposed by banks, they are more likely to buy on slimmer margins, or to go further out the risk curve in the type and quality of properties they buy. In an effort to satisfy the current Wall Street appetites and fads, they are more likely to take the short-run view.

As more and more of the better properties go into these REITs, new kinds of questions will arise. For example, will there be merger activity, and is it realistic to think that REIT investors will profit from stock mergers? The answer is "probably in the short term," and there's nothing inherently wrong with this particular outcome, as long as businesses and managements are compatible (an assumption that is not a given, especially in this entrepreneurial field!). People tolerate all kinds of unexpected change, as long as it continues to bring with it good financial news.

But what we *don't* know yet is how the REITs are going to perform either during a building boom or in a bad market. A new construction boom was the major problem that arose in the late 1980s, when the real estate industry built more than the economy could absorb. Rents plummeted, income streams dried up, and REITs suffered accordingly. Today, while the overall atmosphere for real estate is more rational, there has been speculative building in some markets and asset classes, a situation that might affect the pricing of real estate securities. In many cases, there already has been considerable price correction. Few stocks have much of a premium for enterprise value.

Another scenario involves a rapid softening of the economy, either locally or nationally. If oil prices plummet, as they have recently, so may the value of a REIT located in an area dependent on that industry. If the overall economy contracts sharply, the first industries to take on water will be airlines and hotels. Hotel occupancy rates track very closely the health of the economy, and a large percentage of hotel operating costs are fixed. A hotel REIT would therefore suffer significantly.

In yet a third scenario, interest rates start to rise, and investors become drawn to higher-yielding alternatives. Investors currently are happy with a 6 percent dividend yield, plus some growth, in part because they know they're really not going to get any more than that by buying a bond (which has no growth potential). But if interest rates go up, and the same bonds yield 8 or 9 percent, will these investors hold? Or will they say, "O.K., time to sell all my real estate stocks and switch to bonds"? And what happens when they do?

I recently examined what happened to the pricing of REIT stocks on August 31, 1998, when the various overall market indices dropped between

6 and 10 percent. Almost all the larger REITs dropped by equal percentages. So much for the theory that real estate stocks are disconnected from the stock market! I also looked at the performance of the publicly traded property companies listed as of mid-October 1998. Most were off between 25 and 50 percent from their recent highs—in other words, more than the overall averages, but consistent with the performance of small-cap stocks. By the end of the year, many had recovered some of that value, but were still well off their former highs.

As I see it, "bricks and mortar" are important psychological bulwarks for at least some sectors of the real estate industry. What do I mean by this? If you own a property privately, any decline in value is somewhat masked, because you haven't put it up for sale. If it's your house—for example—you're still *living* in your house, and any loss is only a paper loss unless and until you need to sell. I've watched the "value" of my buildings fluctuate with larger economic trends, and (except early on) haven't lost too much sleep over those fluctuations. They don't have much of an impact on how I think about bricks and mortar.

But REITs, by design, are *liquid.* They don't engender attachments. If you move out of your house, or give up a commercial building with which you (and possibly your family) have been closely identified for many years, you lose something that's intangible but still very real. (You may also incur a large tax gain on this long-held, low-basis property.) With a REIT, by contrast, there may be few negatives associated with bailing out—except a loss which would be only likely to grow if you held.

My optimistic prediction is that the better REITs, and their Wall Street advisors, will begin to effect an overall shift: from *growth* investors to *value* investors, who will enjoy the limited risk, steady cash flow, and periodic undervaluation of REIT shares. These investors will recognize that REITs are not really growth vehicles, except at times when the overall markets are depressed and can be predicted to recover. REITs, in other words, will have to change the expectations of the people and institutions that invest in them. REITs that are founded on good properties will do pretty well. REITs that have gone out on the risk curve, overpaying for more dubious properties, will struggle. REITs with high operating leverage and those concentrating on the most cyclical assets, such as hotels, will remain the riskiest vehicles. And the potential for "fad abuse" seems a perennial threat in the REIT world. A fairly recent example—a Wall Street favorite—was the "paper clip REIT," in which a company could own both an operating and a real estate holding company under the same umbrella. This was used to purchase hotels. When

Congress passed legislation forbidding this vehicle, companies like Patriot American lost as much as 80 percent of the value of their stock, once again throwing REITs into disrepute.

Meanwhile, REIT investors may exert their own kind of moderating influence on the real estate game, by responding earlier to overbuilding or cyclical change in the industry. Part of the reason for the real estate cycle is that projects are often built at the wrong point in the larger cycle, as positive trends are (mistakenly) projected indefinitely into a rosy future. It's possible that REIT investors—knowingly or unknowingly—could provide a healthy restraint on capital in the up cycles, when the shares become overvalued compared to underlying asset values. At the same time, the issuance of new shares could be curtailed. Time will tell whether the rapid response will result in overreaction or healthy moderation.

ON TO THE NEXT PHASE

In this chapter, we've discussed some of the many ways in which people and institutions can make indirect investments in real estate. I hope that prospective indirect investors will read the chapters that precede and follow this one, because I'm convinced that these less active players can benefit greatly from "getting into the heads" of direct investors. Somewhere behind every syndicate and every REIT, after all, is a direct investor. Why is that person proposing to make this specific investment with your money? Is that a smart plan?

In the next chapter, we enter a new phase: development. We will once again adopt the perspective of the active player, and examine how that player plays the riskiest—and potentially most rewarding—phase of the real estate game.

CHAPTER 6

DEVELOPMENT

IN previous chapters, we've described two forks in the road which are faced by would-be players of the real estate game. The first is whether to be an active versus a passive investor. The active player buys or builds. The passive investor (one who puts money into syndications or REITs, for example) is essentially betting on someone else, who is playing the game on the investor's behalf.

The other fork in the road, faced by all active players, is whether to purchase and operate an existing facility—the main focus of Chapters 3 and 4—or to build something from scratch. (In this chapter, I'll include significant renovations and rehabbings in the category of "starting from scratch" ventures.) Much of the material that was presented in those chapters relates to life as a from-the-ground-up developer. Many of the same skills that a Charlie Leonard needs to purchase and substantially rehabilitate an existing building on Boston's Beacon Hill are also essential to developers of entirely new buildings. We will revisit some familiar territory in the early sections of this chapter, as we think about environmental and approvals-related issues.

But even players of the real estate game who intend to focus solely on buying and operating existing facilities should familiarize themselves with the ideas presented in this chapter. Why? Because one of your challenges, as you assess the merits of a particular building, is to figure out how likely it is that someone else will decide to throw up a competitive building. You need to have a good sense of what's involved in the development process—the challenges, as well as the economics—in order to make that assessment. Is this building you're looking at on Route 128, or in Silicon Valley, or in North

Carolina's Golden Triangle, likely to be the last one of its kind, or can several more just like it (only more up-to-date) be built in response to market demand? At what cost could those new competing buildings be built? What would be the impact on your property?

Another thing to keep in mind: Some day, your building (or the land under it) may well become a development opportunity. At that point, you may want to be the person who takes advantage of that opportunity, either directly or through a sale to someone who will.

Building a new facility is very often *orders of magnitude* tougher than taking over an existing property. Getting permission to change the status quo is usually a challenging assignment. Raising money to create something that has no proven ability to generate income is tougher than arranging financing for an existing money-maker. Working intensively with many additional kinds of skilled professionals—architects, contractors, and so on—puts demands on the developer that the owner-operator only occasionally faces.

So why do people take on this task? The answer should be self-evident: With higher risks may come higher rewards. For many involved in the real estate game, there is also great excitement in creating a physical structure, and in affecting in such a fundamental way how people live and work.

In this chapter, I will place the development process in the context of the larger real estate game. I'll follow development through a more-or-less logical sequence of steps—although in real life, as I'll note, many of these steps are iterative, or must take place at the same time. Later in the chapter, I'll make some observations about the complexities that are created when the developer tries to take his skills into the international arena. And finally, I'll summarize the lessons of development by talking about the key pitfalls involved in this phase of the real estate game, and describe the skills that are needed to avoid these pitfalls.

I won't devote much space to the challenges of specific *types* of developments as we move, in this chapter, through the various *activities* of development. Keep in the front of your mind, however, that hotels are different from warehouses are different from offices. For details on these differences and what they mean, see Appendix A at the back of this book.

Eventually you must make two decisions: (1) whether development in general is appropriate for you, and (2) whether a *particular* development makes sense for you, given the specifics of your situation. Understanding the general process of development, which is the focus of this chapter, should help you make both kinds of decisions.

THINKING ABOUT DEVELOPMENT

Many people think of "real estate" as an entrepreneurial field, and they are correct in that perception. But it is in the development phase of the real estate game in which the skills of entrepreneurship are really called into play. The development of a new property (or the substantial redevelopment of an existing property) is the phase in which the greatest number of balls have to be juggled simultaneously. It's the phase in which the management of risks—legal, financial, market-related, construction-driven, people-derived—is most challenging, and most important.

Of course, many of these risks are also encountered by entrepreneurs heading start-ups in other fields: high-tech, health care, consumer products, and so on. But real estate creates special kinds of liabilities. What's the difference between real estate and medicine (as the old joke puts it)? Answer: In real estate, you can't bury your mistakes.

Nor can you necessarily survive them. Don Brown, a managing partner of JBG Properties, once contrasted the life of a venture capitalist to that of a real estate developer. "In venture capital," he said, "it can be lose, lose, lose, lose, lose, lose, lose, and *win,* and you'll be sitting pretty. But in real estate, especially if you give a personal guarantee, it can be win, win, win, win, win, win, win, win, and *lose*—just one loss, after a whole lot of wins—and you can be done for."

Development is the phase in which the developer "buys wholesale and sells retail." This puts enormous pressure on the developer to make sure that there is actually adequate demand for the product that he or she is creating. Are there existing products already on the market that do what this proposed new product is supposed to do? Are these existing products available at a discount to the cost of this product?

In development, timing is terribly important. It's not just a question of what demand is like today. Even more critical is the answer to the question, *what will demand be like when your product finally gets to market?* It's not unusual for the development of a complex new facility to take five years or more. In the context of an industry that tends to go through ten-year cycles, "five years or more" can be just short of an eternity. Fortunately, there are ways to take risk out of development deals. I will review some of these approaches later in this chapter.

The real estate cycle directly impacts the timing of development deals. In the first quarter of 1998, new construction of commercial properties in the United States equaled approximately 2.6 percent of inventory on an annualized basis. Since net absorption of commercial space today runs at about 60 million square feet per year, or approximately 2.5 percent of inventory, one could conclude that we're currently running at just about replacement level. During the late 1980s, by contrast, new construction often ran as high as 13 percent on an annual basis. Many of the people who undertook substantial developments at that time took a beating as a result. It took years for the market to absorb that overbuilding.

Although hindsight is 20/20, I believe that many of these real estate professionals could have foreseen what was coming if they had chosen to look. Some of the variables in the "external factors" corner of our real estate game diamond are fairly easy to predict. Yes, demand was high when the banks financed all of these projects. But when new construction is running at five times the replacement rate, the good developer moves cautiously—if at all!

Many of the highest-return development projects involve *identification of an opportunity to effect change.* One kind of change is upgrading an underutilized property from a "lower" use to a higher use—from warehouse use to office use, for example—and thereby earning increased revenue from the same asset. Another kind of change involves a fundamental change in the *nature* and *intensity* of use (from a corn field to a clustered residential development, for example).

Today, most communities prefer to have their properties remain in the lowest-intensity use possible, which usually means the status quo. If it's an apple orchard today, says the typical community, it shouldn't be turned into a housing development. Loss of visual appeal, new burdens on the school system and other local infrastructure, etc., are common arguments. Similarly: If it's a warehouse today, it shouldn't be upgraded to an office building. (More cars, more traffic.) This kind of opposition may be inspired either by an honest concern for a given community's capacity, or by a pull-up-the-drawbridge mentality. In either case, the developer gets rewarded for overcoming either inertia or active opposition. The greater the opposition, the greater the risk and the potential reward are likely to be, because there are relatively few competing developers who will take on this challenge.

A third kind of change involves creating a facility that conforms with allowable uses, but succeeds at winning an exemption from one or more burdensome requirements in an existing code or regulation. For example, a proposed downtown office building may be uneconomical so long as the city continues to mandate that underground parking be provided for all tenants. If the developer persuades the city to make an exception to that rule, he creates a certain kind of "value"—or more accurately, if he enables a building to be put up on a lot that is too small to provide underground parking efficiently, he enhances a formerly constrained value, and gets rewarded for that success.

Indirectly, the developer gets rewarded for assembling and managing a successful team. As I've emphasized earlier, each property is its own legal entity, with its own set of owners. Similarly, each design team, each construction team, and each marketing team is project-specific (although many of the participating individuals may have worked together on other projects in the past). The developer has to be adept at wielding both the carrot and the stick, and thereby getting the best out of all participants in the process. He or she has to be a skilled negotiator—not only on behalf of the team vis-à-vis the "outside world," but also to keep members of the team reasonably focused and productive. He or she also has to be an effective salesperson, selling and reselling the product throughout the development process.

Most of all, the developer gets rewarded for *managing risk.* This may take many forms: preleasing, maintenance of adequate cash reserves, and so on. I can't say often enough that entrepreneurs aren't usually risk seekers; they are risk managers. They work from pro-forma development budgets that break out (on spreadsheets) land and acquisition costs, design expenditures, hard costs for land development and construction, and soft costs associated with marketing, financing, and administering the project. They monitor these budgets with great care, knowing how much has already been spent and how much still needs to be spent for completion. In other words, they ride herd on extremely dynamic processes, and managing risk—especially in the form of financial controls—is of fundamental importance, especially if the amount of money available is limited.

ASSEMBLING THE LAND

Land assembly is an art in itself. In Chapters 3 and 4, I told the story of how Bill Zeckendorf acquired the Swift slaughterhouses on the east side of Manhattan—as well as a large number of contiguous properties—in order to realize his vision of a "city within a city." (As you'll recall from Chapter 4, this plan was eventually scuttled in favor of creating a home for the United Nations.) Zeckendorf's approach to land assembly was *secrecy,* pure and simple, once he tied up the prime property. He moved as quickly as possible, using multiple brokers, to capitalize on land values that would escalate once it become known that the slaughterhouses would go.

The Rouse Corporation, when it was assembling the land for the "new city" of Columbia, Maryland, took a similar approach. Acquiring enough land for a planned city of 100,000 residents in this rural community was a monumental challenge, involving negotiations with dozens of farmers. Obviously, Rouse moved as quickly as possible, in an effort to stave off possible competitors and to keep acquisition prices down.

Harvard University recently came under a lot of criticism for employing roughly the same tactic, in the Allston and Brighton neighborhoods of Boston which are closest to the University's main campus in Cambridge. Harvard announced that, using a respected commercial developer as an intermediary, it had successfully completed the purchase of a number of commercial properties in these neighborhoods, although it had no specific development plan in mind. With just a few exceptions, Harvard said further, no tenants would be displaced in the short term. These mostly noncontiguous properties were a long-term investment.

Secrecy is often necessary in land assembly. Without secrecy, you can wind up with holdouts. It's fairly easy (and entertaining) to spot holdouts in Manhattan. These are the tiny little two- or three-story buildings that are surrounded on almost all sides by towering skyscrapers. The owners of these buildings either refused to sell at any price, or demanded prices that were so outlandish that "building around" the properties was more feasible economically. In Zeckendorf's case, he didn't have bottomless pockets, and the City Within a City (and later, the United Nations complex) could have been stalled by a few well-placed holdouts. Fortunately for his purposes, the slaughterhouses themselves constituted the bulk and the core of the property. Land assemblers aren't always so lucky.

Harvard's case was somewhat different. The properties weren't all contiguous, and no grand scheme would have been defeated if Harvard's intentions had become known, and if, as a result, one or more of the properties that Harvard was interested in had become unaffordable. In one sense, I suppose, this is an argument for a more thoroughgoing disclosure. On the other hand—as I've often said in conversations with my colleagues at Harvard and elsewhere—I don't see any compelling reason why a purchaser should have to pay a premium for a given property, just because the purchaser happens to be Harvard. Harvard was not planning to convert any of the properties to an institutional (read "tax-exempt") use; instead, it intended to keep the properties more or less as they were, and keep paying taxes on them. Every individual or institution that sold to Harvard's intermediaries presumably did so only after getting a satisfactory price. Harvard wasn't under any special obligation to make them happier.

What are the alternatives to secrecy, in the process of land assembly? One is to make purchase of a given parcel conditional upon certain other things happening. Through negotiations with the seller, the would-be purchaser secures an option on the property, which may or may not lead to money changing hands. The longer the option, the more likely it is that the seller will demand a big deposit, which may have to get bigger over time.

For example: Suppose a buyer is only interested in a given property if the property's zoning gets changed to allow a more intensive use. He or she may secure an option on the property to explore whether such a change can be effected. In many cases, the buyer goes this route knowing that the purchase price may go up (or fail to go down) as a result. In effect, the seller is being asked to assume some of the risk inherent in the development process. Logically, the buyer should be prepared to share some of the upside potential, along with the risk.

One problem with the option is that the time line for securing the needed approvals is almost always longer than the seller is willing to wait. This presents a difficult dilemma for the buyer, who in many cases is forced to take an option for a shorter period and hope to extend, when the time comes. Obtaining the initial option, and then receiving extensions of that option from a skeptical seller, takes time and money. And, of course, there's always the risk that the seller will run out of patience, and *won't* extend.

Why would the seller not extend? More often than not, the seller does not want to get back the property. (That's why he or she is selling.) The seller may have a real concern about the buyer's ability to obtain financing, or perceive changes in market conditions, or realize that costs have become higher than anticipated. If another potential buyer doesn't have these problems, then the seller has every reason to refuse to extend.

It may sound painfully obvious, but, if your land-assembly effort involves options to purchase one or more properties based on contingencies, keep a close eye on the expiration dates of those options. If you're in a competitive situation—and most of us are, one way or another—your competitors are probably keeping tabs on your options.

In the late 1990s, one of the largest supermarket chains in the Boston area foolishly and prematurely announced plans to build a giant store just down the street from one of the stores operated by its arch-rival. Almost all of the parcels needed for the new development were optioned, the chain's press release said, and progress was being made on the last outlying parcels. By going public, the acquiring supermarket's spokespeople were signaling that there were no serious obstacles to the proposed development. Imagine their surprise when the rival chain announced that it had purchased a key property almost dead-center in the middle of the proposed site. How was this possible? It turned out that one of the options had expired, and the owners of the long-established supermarket, intent on defending their turf, pounced on the parcel to kill the larger deal.

Another approach is to share the problem of land assembly with the potentially interested parties. In the last chapter, I mentioned the Chattanooga-based REIT on whose board I sit: CBL Properties. When CBL decided that they wanted to build an extension on one of their shopping centers, they did a preliminary investigation and discovered that this would require the acquisition of some twenty parcels adjacent to the existing center. They contacted all twenty owners, announced their intentions, but said that they wouldn't acquire *any* of the parcels unless they could get them all. This put a very different face on the negotiations that followed, because CBL acquired allies—landowners eager to sell—who helped make CBL's case for them. It took a long time, CBL probably wound up paying a premium for the properties, and the company definitely incurred some costs (such as the expense of moving homes and businesses). But the process was ultimately successful, and CBL was seen by most parties as a "good neighbor." This can be extremely important when the approval process, described below, gets underway.

For large-scale developers, land assembly involves not only the price of the land, but also the *time frame* for payment. The longer the time frame allowed by the seller, the bigger the deposit and the higher the overall price the buyer is likely to be willing to pay. In some cases, a large tract of land can be set aside and "released" to the purchaser as the progress of the project warrants it. The seller often receives a monthly fee to compensate for this willingness to stage payments, as well as a higher overall fee. Release clauses are another way that developers manage risk, especially in single-family-home projects. The developer "takes down" a portion of the "banked" site for a roughly proportionate piece of the overall price, digests that piece, and—when circumstances permit—comes back for more. The danger for the seller, of course, is that only the best lots may be taken down. This potential problem can be headed off by differential pricing of the lots.

There are rare cases in which a municipality gets involved in land assembly through the process of eminent domain, a legal term referring to the rights of a public entity to seize a property for a public purpose in exchange for fair compensation. Most often, this occurs when a few holdouts are threatening the viability of a large-scale project that is perceived to hold great value for a community—for example, a civic center comprising a hotel, convention facilities, and a sports arena. If the holdout controls a vital parcel (perhaps needed to close a gap in the local transportation network), the city may decide that it can't afford to let the whole project collapse, and take the property by eminent domain.

During the 1950s and 1960s, eminent domain was used as a tool to assist master planning for large chunks of areas in many of our older cities. This process, called *urban renewal,* accomplished a lot of good in renovating downtowns, but also forced relocation of many neighborhoods, which was not so good. The federal government paid for much of the writedown and clearing of the land.

In the process of land assembly, don't forget that there is more than one way to "acquire" land. When I first started building in Harvard Square, I set my sights on a particular parcel, which turned out to be not for sale. Its owners, a Greek-American family, had an aversion to selling land under any circumstances. I was delighted to discover that I could *lease* the land, which I probably didn't have the resources to buy anyway. I received a long-term lease on the land, which commits me to paying an annual rent; then I went ahead and built my building. The lease agreement allowed me to subordinate my payments to them to a new first mortgage that was limited to the costs of development. In essence, their land lease became a second mortgage until the first mortgage was repaid. Otherwise, it would have been difficult to obtain financing. Eventually, the land and the building on it will revert to the owners of the land, but the long-term nature of the lease made the present value of that reversion—far off in the future as it was—insignificant.

There are some complications inherent in leasing land, of course. Much of the land under what is today Rockefeller Center in New York City was leased from Columbia University. Columbia was given the land (much of which originally had been an herb garden, and was in default on its taxes) by the New York state legislature. At the time of the transfer from the state to Columbia, the parcel was valued at $5,000 (!).

Enter John D. Rockefeller, Jr., who leased the land in 1928 from the university in order to assist the Metropolitan Opera in its plan to build a new opera house on the site. When that plan fell through in 1931, he decided to clear off the 229 deteriorating brownstones then occupying the land, and develop the (leased) land himself. Given the deteriorating economic conditions at that time, this was a courageous decision, indeed. The result was the magnificent Rockefeller Center, which became a commercial and architectural landmark.

By the 1980s, however, the astronomic appreciation of land values in midtown Manhattan had created a pleasant problem for Columbia. The leased parcel came to be valued at more than $400 million, which represented roughly 40 percent of the university's entire endowment—far too large a percentage to be tied up in one asset. Claude Ballard, whom we met in Chapter 3, arranged the sale of the land from Columbia to the Rockefellers.

So a piece of leased land can "outgrow" its owner. It can also outgrow its tenant—a peril that can be minimized by a formal (and fair) rent-review process. If a regular review of the rents (based on cost of living measures, land valuation, or some other measure) is not built into the lease agreement, the lessor may be hurt. On the other hand, if such a review *is* built in and rents skyrocket, a long-time lessor can be put in a tough spot.

The Graybar Building—a major office building on New York's Lexington Avenue—was built on the air rights over the old New York Central Railroad's tracks. The lessee built the building based on an agreement to pay $390,000 per year in rent to the railroad. Then land prices in Manhattan began to soar. At the first rent review, prompted by an adjustment-to-market clause in the lease, the successor to the railroad (long since bankrupt) raised the rent to *$5 million* a year, thereby taking most of the profit out of the building for its developers.

Here are the three basic approaches to the valuation of leased land, arranged in decreasingly attractive order from the lessee's point of view:

- valuation based on current use (lessee's best case)
- valuation based on the higher of the value of its current use or the value of the raw land in its "highest and best" use (which might involve tearing down the existing structure and reusing the land)
- valuation based on the overall value of the land and buildings upgraded to their highest and best use (lessee's worst case)

Even the best case above can be unattractive (as it was for the lessees of the Graybar building). So far, this hasn't happened to me. (My land lease contains a clause that guarantees a certain percentage of the revenue generated by the property to the landowners.) If you and the seller structure a lease agreement with regular rent reviews and reasonable caps on year-to-year increases, then subsequent generations on both sides should be able to handle further eventualities.

THE APPROVAL PROCESS

Having a town or city tripping over itself to simplify your life as a developer is an unusual luxury. Far more often, local governments perceive the developer as an unwelcome threat to the status quo. Even in cases when town or city officials are inclined to be supportive, they may find it politically impossible to help a given project succeed.

Many years ago, when I was working in the office of another developer, we came across a beautiful sixty-acre wooded parcel in a suburb of Boston. Although in a surprisingly pristine state, the land was already zoned residential, and was therefore ripe for single-family-home development: one house for every two acres, as I recall it. Mostly for environmental and aesthetic reasons, we decided to take a different approach. With the help of an architect, we sketched out a wonderful plan for the site, which involved clustering the allowable units to leave a considerable percentage of the parcel untouched. We commissioned some elevations (or "head-on" architectural drawings) of what our development might look like, and how it might sit on the property. We asked for a meeting with the local zoning board to discuss our proposal.

When we arrived at the meeting, there were some two hundred *very angry* people prepared to argue against our plan. Many, it turned out, were abuttors or nearby neighbors, who enjoyed the use of the property and the scenic vistas and rural feel that it lent to the neighborhood. Tempers flared and the rhetoric escalated. We quickly gave up and went home. Our chances for success were minimal, and our personal appetites for controversy were low.

One point of this story is that we still had the luxury of being able to *go* home. We had an option on the property, but as of that hearing, no money had changed hands. The only costs we had incurred, other than our time, were some legal fees and the architect's fees associated with our short-lived presentation. If our costs had been greater, we probably would have been more reluctant to give up, but I'm convinced it still would have been the right decision.

There's no simple rule about when you should bail out of a deal. It depends not only on your likelihood for success, but also on the potential risk and reward, plus your personal situation and alternatives at the particular point in time.

Another point of this story is that neither reason nor fairness will necessarily prevail. I have no doubt that our plan for the site was a good one—far better, in fact, than the zoning code specified. I'm sure that today, that particular property has thirty single-family homes on it. The pressure to intensify the use of that parcel could only have grown, in the months and years following our quick exit. The neighbors could not have succeeded indefinitely in using someone else's property for free. And I'd be surprised if any developer arrived in our wake with a plan for a clustered-unit development.

A similar case a few years back received national attention. A Boston-area developer, Boston Properties, owned a large wooded parcel near Walden Pond, where Henry David Thoreau once lived in his isolated cabin and contemplated the vagaries of human existence. One day, Boston Properties announced its plans to build an office building on the site, which (at least in the eyes of the developer) seemed to be an allowable use under the applicable zoning code. There was some local opposition, but it seemed manageable.

What Boston Properties didn't anticipate was that in California, rock star and Thoreau aficionado Don Henley would see a brief report on the controversy on a cable news show and take up the cause. Henley joined forces with the local opponents, and together they mounted a strenuous effort to protect "Walden Woods" from development. (The former Eagle helped finance the campaign by holding benefit concerts and involving other prominent "glitterati.") Years of contentious and highly visible debate ensued, and Boston Properties eventually was forced to abandon the project.

Back on the other coast, Stanford University has been trying for more than a decade to extend Sand Hill Road, one of the most prestigious addresses for venture capitalists in the world, all the way to El Camino, a major north-south spine in the San Francisco Bay area. For years, the citizens of Palo Alto have successfully blocked what might appear to an outside observer to be a logical extension of an existing thoroughfare—but does not appear so to the neighbors.

By telling these stories, I don't mean to discourage people from looking for creative ways to make a particular project happen. The truth is that very few buildings are built entirely in conformance with local zoning and building codes (and very few locales have the cachet of Walden Pond). Sometimes all that's needed is a slight change in a setback regulation, or a compromise on the allowable building height, or a minor adjustment in parking requirements. If you are proposing a nonconforming use (that is, a use that doesn't conform to local codes) for a particular property, be prepared for a lot of interest from the abuttors at the first public hearing on the subject. (They'll be notified in advance by the relevant town board.) Be prepared to explain how the change you are preparing will make life better for people in the neighborhood. Be ready to sell your idea—and also to compromise. You have little choice, in most cases; it's far too easy for your potential opponents to tie you up in court.

Some things turn out to be more negotiable than others, and this has a lot to do with the *scale* of the exception that the landlord is seeking. If you ask for major increases in the floor-area ratio (FAR)—that is, the ratio of the square footage built on the site compared with the square footage of the land—you will almost certainly create a serious issue for your prospective host community, even though your development will contribute substantial property taxes to those communities. (How your building will "fit" when compared with others in the area, both in terms of size and use, is critical.) Looking at the same issue from the other direction: Reducing your proposed sixty-story building to fifty-eight stories (a loss of only 3 1/3 percent of billable floor area) might be acceptable, whereas reducing your six-story building to four probably wouldn't be.

For its part, your prospective host community probably won't be inclined to give you a break on school-impact fees—fees charged to a developer whose project is likely to add to the school-aged population—especially if the town has a long tradition of imposing these fees. (Remember that it's far easier for a town to impose fees on its future residents, which is the net effect of a school-impact tax, than to raise taxes on current residents.) Impact fees can be levied for many purposes, including subsidized housing, new roads and utilities, and preservation of open space. In fact, many communities have become dependent on such fees.

But the town may be willing to back off on aesthetic niceties, or on issues that are arguably not the town's business. I remember one project that was imperiled by the town's insistence that the developer put up a series of elaborate and expensive noise barriers, the purpose of which was to insulate the new development from highway noise. The developer made the argument that finding tenants who didn't mind a certain amount of highway noise was *his* problem—and the town ultimately agreed. I'm not sure whether those future tenants were happy with his victory, but he carried the day, nevertheless.

Negotiating skills are critical in this phase of development. The rules I presented in Chapter 3 are germane: Understand what the other side needs. Understand value. Be clear-eyed. Leave your ego at home. Do your homework. This involves, among other things, getting the best possible sense of how much (or how little) your proposed host community *wants* to be your host. Develop credible alternatives to this particular site, and discuss those alternatives in an appropriate public setting: "Well, of course, I'd prefer to locate my new regional mall in Town X, but if that doesn't work out, my friends in Town Y, just down Route 35, certainly are making all the right noises."

Be prepared to quantify the effect of your compromises on your pro forma. Know exactly what it means to reduce density, or to agree to build a parking deck versus on-grade parking. I've seen many cases of developers making statements in the heat of a public meeting that they've later come to regret. The simple rule is, *Anything you say may be held against you, and anything you offer may well be accepted—and enforced.*

Play to the strengths of your project. If you believe, for example, that the proposed development will provide a social good, be as articulate and passionate as possible in describing that good. There is some government support available to build affordable housing units, and many states require their communities to provide affordable housing. Most communities, however, associate affordable housing with urban problems, and as a result, turn away such developments. But I've seen skillful developers make the case that it's the town's residents themselves—the retired police officers, the school teachers, and the grandparents—who will benefit the most from a proposed affordable-housing complex, and thereby win the support of a formerly reluctant community.

One piece of negotiating advice from Chapter 3—"be patient"—may *not* be particularly helpful in the development phase. At this stage, you are likely to have a great many balls in the air. You simply don't have the luxury of letting negotiations creep along at their own pace. In most cases, you can't hold out for the best possible deal. In fact, because of time pressures, you may have to do things that you find personally offensive.

For example: I was once well into the process of buying a fairly decrepit building, which I intended to tear down, when a particular retail tenant declared that he had no intention of vacating the building. His lease had expired; he had been given due notice. But he let me know that he was more than willing to declare bankruptcy, to initiate legal proceedings, or whatever—anything to slow me down, and hold onto his space in the building. My lawyers assured me that I could almost certainly overcome all of these stalling tactics within 120 days. But I didn't *have* 120 days. Eventually, I had to buy the tenant out, which may have been what he had in mind all along.

I wrote at length in Chapters 3 and 4 about the environmental approval process, which generally involves at least the lending institution (which wants to know what it's buying into) and one or more levels of government. Most of what was presented in those chapters pertains equally to the from-the-ground-up development process. Be particularly wary if you're building near wetlands, or water, or in an industrial area where long-forgotten companies may have dumped industrial waste decades ago. (Think of the book and movie *A Civil Action* as a real estate developer's cautionary tale.) Try to imagine the site's possible prior uses, and then ask, *What could possibly be wrong with this picture?*

An acquaintance of mine lived through one of these nightmare scenarios. He bought a beautiful apple orchard that was zoned for residential use. All of the required local approvals came through quickly. Then, en route to financing the project, he commissioned an environmental study. Only then did he discover that the pesticides that had been used on the apple trees all those years had contaminated the land and rendered it useless for residential purposes. In this case, obtaining an option on the property—even one that involved interim payments to the owner—would have been a better move.

Take a hard look at your neighbors, and the kinds of liabilities they might represent. If your neighbor's problem spills over onto your property, it becomes your problem. Yes, you can sue your neighbor to rectify the problem. But it can take a long time to get to a judgment in the courts, and if your neighbor has no money, you may not collect in any case. Meanwhile, if you decide that you want to sell or refinance your property, you'll almost certainly wind up doing the remediation work yourself.

What you've seen in the previous two sections is that taken separately and together, the processes of land assembly and approvals can be complicated, messy, expensive, and frustrating. It's possible to gain expertise at this process, but like most complicated tasks, it takes a lot of practice, and practicing this trade costs lots of money.

Not surprisingly, there are companies that specialize in the land-development side of the real estate game. These companies secure the rights to land, get necessary zoning changes, put in some level of infrastructure (ranging from minimal to less minimal), and then sell the property (or lots therein) to developers. This goes on not only in residential developments, but also in industrial parks.

One of the biggest challenges inherent in this approach is figuring out how much infrastructure to put in up front, and how much to put in later. (This ties in with my earlier explanation of staged land acquisition and payments.) Because there are good reasons (e.g., marketing and cost efficiencies) to put everything in at once, and equally good reasons (e.g., flexibility and cash conservation) to "stage" investments in infrastructure, land-development specialists often wind up splitting the difference. They may put in all the major water and sewer pipes at once, but hold off on laying out roads or putting in the distribution systems on the back half of the property until the development "catches up" with them.

THINKING ABOUT PLANNING

Planning and design are two of the most important and visible processes that go on during the development phase. In most cases, it is good planning and design that makes a project feasible—by winning necessary approvals, and by defining a facility that can pay its way.

The first question to answer, early in the planning stage, is, "What's the bigger picture?" What's the *context* for this project? Let me make an exception to my anti-soapbox policy, and argue here for a *responsible* approach to planning and design on the part of the developer.

The developer—in my opinion—needs to work with the community to understand the real needs and opportunities of a given site. The failure to do so can result in suboptimal (or even extremely dumb) solutions. Instead of putting relatively short money into a "brownfield" on the tattered industrial edge of a city, for example, the developer spends many more dollars to put that same facility on a country road in Exurbia. The result? More sprawl, more cars on an inadequate suburban road network, more demands placed on aging sewage treatment facilities, and so on.

Without involving himself or herself in a dialogue with the community, the developer is very likely to commit what I call a "scale blunder." The best example I can think of is in Paris. For the most part, the city of Paris vigorously enforces its height restrictions. To make this work, the city also zones certain areas for high-rises and office complexes. You can see the reasons for this policy when you look at the exceptions. In the middle of the Montparnasse section, for example, there is a truly hideous high-rise—an immense tower that is the only high-rise inside the Boulevard Peripherique, and which blights the hapless neighborhood huddling beneath it. This was a scale blunder of the first order. I suspect that it led to tighter zoning regulations, after the city realized how big a mistake had been made. It also influenced the creation of the La Defense office district to the west of Paris, where many of the area's high-rise office buildings are clustered.

Closer to home, Harvard put up a high-rise (William James Hall) to accommodate its expansion-minded Government and Psychology departments. Evidently, Harvard's planners and architects felt that this would be only the first in a series of high-rises, which would eventually transform a predominantly residential neighborhood into a more intensively used Education Canyon. Instead, the community made sure it was the last such structure. The out-of-scale Harbor Towers complex on Boston's waterfront prompted the same kind of outrage, and the city has taken steps to make sure it doesn't happen again.

Why does it happen in the first place? One of the most common reasons is that the developer has tied up the land at an above-market price. He or she then argues strenuously that the site requires a greater density. Should the community pay for the developer's overpayment? I don't think so.

Another trap is what might be called the Edifice Complex. This arises when the developer or major tenant says, "Make a building that's as monumental as *me!*" (One recent fictional example is Charlie Croker in Tom Wolfe's *A Man in Full.*) Greed is another factor. So is the anti-zoning bias, and the tradition of what I'd call a "qualified rugged individualism" in the United States. ("Don't tell *me* what to do," says John Q. Public. "But please tell my neighbors what to do!") So, too, is the disconnected nature of planning, in this country and others. Zoning is local, and planning is (or ought to be) regional. This creates huge openings for thoughtless or unscrupulous developers. The developer who expands his mall at the expense of other nearby communities may create very real problems for *all* the communities involved.

I'm not arguing that the developer has to serve as the sole conscience of a region or a community, and thereby lose all competitive advantages. Houston, Texas, has developed without any zoning controls at all, and some argue that the result is no different from other rapidly growing metropolitan areas. I'm arguing, nevertheless, that the developer should see his or her responsibilities as broadly as possible. I'm convinced that this is good business, as well—especially if you intend to do business in this particular community again in the future. There's no reason why a new or expanded regional mall can't become an exciting new "downtown" for its region. Why shouldn't the host community or communities be able to require the creation of public spaces in the mall as part of the approval process?

Going a step further, why shouldn't the developer propose something like this, and get credit for taking the initiative? Many of our urban waterfronts are enjoying a new vitality because far-sighted developers planned and carried out the reuse of many outmoded structures. It's hard to believe today that Boston once contemplated knocking down the beautiful old granite structures that make up Quincy Market. The Rouse Corporation, in collaboration with architect Ben Thompson, saved the market for future generations.

How does a developer think in broad terms, and for the long term, about context? Who else has already done good thinking along those lines? Zoning is only one possible answer to this question. Does your parcel sit in the middle of a designated development zone, or a historic neighborhood? If so, is there a master plan for the area? Is compliance with that plan optional, or mandatory?

Master plans range from very tight to very loose. In New York's Battery Park City, for example, the quasi-public authority that planned this large-scale mixed-use development did all the planning for the site. They said to potential developers, in effect, "You can build in this particular location to this specific height, creating this many units, using these kinds of materials." The South Beach District in Miami, by contrast, is less tightly controlled. There, civic leaders have designated a historic district, and help developers go in and make changes that conform to an overall "template" for the neighborhood. This template preserves the Art Deco feel of the neighborhood, while recognizing that a mix of colors and shapes was a key part of the Art Deco movement.

If there is no master plan, maybe there *should* be one. (Think broadly.) If you conclude that this is the case, you should think seriously about whether you're the individual or company that can make this happen. (In most cases, considerable clout is needed in a given community to develop an area-wide master plan.)

Even if there's no prospect of a master plan in your neighborhood, there may be other effective ways to place your project in a context. Are you putting up a building on a downtown street in a small-to-moderate-sized community? The National Trust for Historic Preservation's "Main Street" program serves as a clearinghouse for ideas about how to attract smaller stores to downtown areas—for example, by improving parking, planting trees, widening sidewalks, and so on. Should you (and maybe one or two other like-minded developers) embrace a program like this in a visible way?

Maybe there's a master plan in place that doesn't conform to your vision of the future for a given site or neighborhood. Or maybe the existing plan just doesn't get down to a fine enough grain of detail for your purposes. If you're someone who moves adeptly in political circles—or if you have a partner or a lawyer who does—you may be able to bend an existing plan with contributions of your own.

When my home institution, the Harvard Business School, started thinking in the mid 1980s about the future of its surroundings, it retained the renowned architect and planner Moshe Safdie to think Big Thoughts about the half-mile of riverfront that includes the Business School campus. Safdie's subsequent studies—which were publicly announced and reported upon—were used in part to stimulate conversations with the City of Boston (and more specifically, the Boston Redevelopment Authority), Conrail, the Massachusetts Turnpike Authority, various neighborhood groups, and Mother Harvard herself. There was never any real chance that all of these groups would wholeheartedly embrace a plan put forth by Safdie or the Harvard Business School. But the *dialogue* greatly increased the chances of finding solutions that were good for all parties. It also minimized the chances that the first mover would act in a way that hurt other parties unnecessarily.

In other words, *listen hard* to the people you run into during the planning process. Many of the people who serve on zoning boards and historic commissions are bright people with good taste. If you show them the respect they deserve, they may make a vital contribution (for free) to your project.

And this suggestion extends more generally throughout the development phase: Give people every kind of nonfinancial incentive you can think of to help you do your job well. You're neither a beggar nor a field marshal. Working collaboratively with people will serve you well, and is good practice for the later phases of development.

Train yourself to pay attention to the bigger picture. When you drive around a given city or region, think about what makes that area appealing. Is it easy to get to? Is it fun to walk around in? What things do you use there? If you can answer these questions brilliantly, your development business is sure to succeed. In my experience, cities with a great sense of scale, with a reasonably diverse economic base, and with safe, nearby residential and shopping neighborhoods, tend to grow and prosper; while those with only nine-to-five office buildings steadily lose market share to the suburbs.

Planning, you'll discover, is a process that doesn't ever really "stop"—even if you want it to stop. It is a way to rationalize the use of natural resources and our man-made infrastructure, reduce congestion and sprawl, and ensure a better living enviornment. But it is also a highly political process, in which short-term considerations often predominate. My advice is, Learn to enjoy it. Read Kevin Lynch's *The Image of the City.* Take a course in urban planning at your local university. Look at photographs from the last century of your neighborhood, and think about what that neighborhood looks like today. Are the changes mostly for the better? What should the neighborhood look like a hundred years from now, and how will it get there? This can be one of the most rewarding aspects of being a developer—sometimes even financially, as well as physically.

THINKING ABOUT DESIGN

The architectural design process is not well understood by people who are outside that process. Many people picture an architect standing at a drafting table—or nowadays, sitting in front of a computer screen—and coming up with a design for how a building will look. The architect delivers his or her floor plans and renderings, collects a fee, and goes home.

There's one specific circumstance, described below, in which that conception is more or less true. But most of the time, architectural design is a far more complicated process, involving numerous players. Depending on the scale and scope of the project, the architect goes through a more or less intensive process of investigation aimed at determining your needs, the opportunities and challenges presented by the site, and the range of possible solutions that might work for you. The architect takes these investigations through several distinct stages, using input from many sources (especially you) and gradually arriving at an increasingly specific solution.

Programming is the first stage in this process. It defines the purposes that the facility is supposed to serve. Some firms have very formalized approaches to programming; others are more ad hoc. In some cases, programming is performed by specialists, working either directly for the developer or as a subcontractor to the architect.

Schematic design takes the information gathered in the programming and lays out a preliminary plan for the facility. What goes next to what? If there's a specific "flow" that's needed through the building—of people, materials, or whatever—what comes first and what comes last? Rough square footages are assigned in schematic design (or, if you're starting with an allowable square footage, they are allocated).

Design development is the phase in which the facility takes a definite shape. If trade-offs have to be made, this is when they start to be made. What can you afford to spend—and based on market conditions, what *should* you spend—to accomplish your most important goals? The product of this phase is a set of drawings that are a fairly complete depiction of how the facility will work.

Construction documents (or working drawings) translate the design into the kinds of documents that a contractor needs in order to price and build the facility. Until contractors see the actual details, pricing is only an estimate, albeit a more or less educated estimate. Then, as the building gets built, any deviations from the plan are noted on the construction documents—or should be!—and these revised or annotated documents become the "as-built drawings."

It's also in the working-drawing phase that architecture gets most complicated and most expensive. The architect calls upon the skills of a large number of subcontractors, who do the civil engineering, the soil engineering, the mechanical and HVAC (heating, ventilating, and air conditioning) drawings, the electrical drawings, the plumbing drawings, and the structural drawings for the building itself.

In other words, all of the engineering functions associated with the project are performed by subcontractors, who have to be paid by the architect. The architect, in turn, has to be paid by you. This is where most of the real money goes when you're paying those daunting architectural fees.

Not surprisingly, developers try very hard to avoid paying these kinds of fees until they're sure that their projects are going to move forward. Sometimes, therefore, a developer hires an architect to serve as the "artist at the drawing board," as described above. In that circumstance, the architect does some quick studies, and produces a possible site plan and a highly speculative "picture" of what the facility might wind up looking like.

This is what we did when we proposed the cluster-housing development described earlier in this chapter. We took our handsome elevations and site plans, went to the hearing, got blown out of the water, and went home. We paid the modest architectural fee and moved on to the next project.

So it's smart to hold off on final designs and drawings as long as possible. Even after the facility gets its preliminary approvals and tentative financing, the developer may defer key decisions until fairly late in the process, in order to make alterations to suit late-arriving tenants. The risk in keeping your options open this way is that some potentially hostile constituency (such as a neighborhood group) may think that you're deliberately concealing some vital information from them. Keeping all important constituencies informed about your evolving plans is usually the best approach.

Remember that your *real* risk is that your construction estimates are too low, most likely because your drawings weren't detailed enough to develop firm quotes. (And in remodeling, this risk may be compounded by the Disaster Behind the Plaster.) To a certain extent, this is why developers go for conventional designs that have been built many times before. It also explains the love-hate relationship that exists between many contractors and architects. Contractors are more or less dependent on architects for their livelihood; at the same time, they are deeply suspicious that some detail in the architect's designs will prove to be unbuildable, and will come out of the contractor's hide.

In the *construction* (or *supervision*) phase, the architect visits the site periodically, explains drawings to the contractor, makes (and documents) field changes, approves contractor requisitions, and eventually makes "punch lists" (of remaining unfinished items) to ensure that the building is completed in accordance with the plans.

As for the design of your project, I can only offer some general suggestions. The first and most important of these is to *understand thoroughly the market you're designing for.* What does the customer *want,* and how are you going to provide it in an affordable way?

Homebuilders often make the mistake of building houses that they would design and build for themselves. In other words, they put all the features into a spec house that they'd put into their own home, instead of aiming to get to market at a particular price point. Is the potential homebuyer in this neighborhood likely to pay for the second bathroom you're building? Probably. Are they likely to pay for the third bathroom, or for that top-of-the-line skylight in the attic room? Maybe not—and if they don't pay for it, you will.

Many years ago, I was working for an apartment developer who retained a group of famous interior designers to design his model apartments. Each was more stunning than the next. Foot traffic was extremely heavy through these spectacular spaces, but almost no rentals resulted. It turned out that people were afraid that if they moved into this complex, they'd have to furnish their units to the standards (and prices!) implied by the showcase models.

What will people *buy?* Currently, there's a widespread trend toward something called "new urbanism" among developers and designers. This means that large residential developments attempt to create villages, rather than aggregations of unrelated houses plunked down on one-acre lots. Streets are narrower, houses are set closer to the streets, and all the houses have front porches. Seaside in Florida (where *The Truman Story* was filmed) is one example; Disney's Celebration is another. But do people really *want* this stuff, and will they pay a premium for it? What if they decide that these approaches are too restrictive, and stifling?

As an essentially urban creature, I like the idea of a village. But I also like the messiness, the variety of shapes and styles, that characterize some of my favorite places. I like neighborhoods that can adapt over the decades, accommodating different cultures, age groups, and income brackets. I can remember when Bill Levitt's huge housing developments—immodestly named "Levittowns"—were roundly criticized as being monotonous, boxlike, and boring. They inspired Pete Seeger's "Little Boxes" song, in which he complained about the "little boxes . . . made out of ticky tacky [that] all look just the same." But Levitt's genius was in realizing that what people needed above all was affordability. Veterans returning from World War II didn't want to live with their in-laws while they saved up for that dream house in an established suburb. They wanted less house, if necessary, but they wanted it *now.* So he designed cheap, modular, box-like units that could be built quickly, in large numbers, and sell for rock-bottom prices.

He also left enough space around them so that people could put on additions, as their young families grew. People added on, landscaped, and otherwise took advantage of the flexibility that Levitt had built into his towns. And today, a half-century later, the first Levittown—on New York's Long Island—has a lot of the texture and character that it lacked originally.

I recently visited some expensive condominiums in Mexico City designed by a famous international architect. From the outside, the curved, multicolored facade was spectacular. On the inside, it was clearly a challenge to make the units livable. Sales were slow as a result.

What will people buy? The same question ought to govern office design. What is the functional and price difference between the absolute *best* air conditioning system, and the one that works perfectly well on all but the hottest two or three days of the summer? Even if the tenants say they need it, are they willing to pay for it? Developers of office space sometimes assume that they can earn downtown rents for suburban spaces (just as suburban tenants sometimes decide they should receive downtown office space, fitted out, at suburban prices). When cost per square foot gets disconnected from potential income per square foot, trouble may be brewing.

Remember, too, that consumer tastes can shift over time, both for economic reasons and in response to other pressures. Don't assume that what's attractive today will be attractive tomorrow. During the boom years of the 1980s, for example, corporate clients wanted "signature" buildings, with fancy lobbies, lots of marble and glitz, and so on. Today, with hostile takeover artists possibly lurking in the wings, corporate executives don't want to be accused of living too lavishly.

The design of regional shopping centers has changed. With new delivery systems, individual stores need less storage space, outmoding many layouts. Changes in shopping habits have led to more food courts and entertainment-related uses being included. And who knows how Internet shopping will affect what is sold and where.

So bad design—design that isn't responsive to market needs—is bad business. But the converse is also true, and it is my second general design suggestion: *good design is good business.* I substantially renovated a building in Wakefield, Massachusetts, on a prime site overlooking some beautiful wetlands. I spent a lot of "extra" money opening up windows on the side of the building that faced the wetlands, and also included a very generous budget for landscaping. I did so in part because I felt some obligation to respect the beauty of the site, but also because I was convinced that the building would rent more quickly, and at higher prices, if our redesign made the building as special as the site.

Another example from my own experience: I own an industrial complex near Boston. Three of the buildings are in close proximity to one another. Working with a very skillful architect, we figured out a way to create a new entrance to the property that would be shared by all three buildings. The new entrance transformed the look and feel of the complex, by making it seem more vital and contemporary. It also gave me a whole new range of options for leasing the buildings in creative ways. The design definitely cost me more than either leaving the buildings alone or using a more mundane approach to the entry problem, but it turned out to be a great investment.

And creativity doesn't even have to be that expensive. I remember the public accolades when an office building on State Street in downtown Boston unveiled its refurbished lobby, full of gleaming marble. Few knew that the marble was recycled bathroom partitions, polished, cut, and rehung in a new setting.

Here's a third suggestion I'll offer, although with a qualification attached: *Don't innovate for the sake of innovation.* Because every building is virtually custom-designed, it's very tempting for an architect to try to do a "better" job every time out. Sometimes this takes the form of trying a relatively new and untested technology. This can be expensive both in the short term (the new thing costs more) and the long term (the new thing gets old fast and breaks in an unexpected way).

At the Harvard Business School, we used to teach a case about a developer who was building garden apartments in Savannah, Georgia. The architect proposed to design the complex following an open, "California-style" plan. The neighbors were grumbling about this departure from the typical architecture of Savannah, and the developer was anxious about his ability to rent the apartments once they were completed. Our class discussions usually came down on the side of conservatism. This reflected both an aesthetic judgment and a verdict on the developer's motives. Once they looked closely at the design, the students realized that the open-plan approach in this case was a way for the developer to cut down on the overall square footage of the units—in other words, not a "design solution" at all.

In some settings, conservatism can be smart. Most people who've managed buildings in New England will tell you that a pitched roof is good, and a flat roof is bad—period. (Three feet of wet snow on a flat roof represents a lot of weight, and almost always finds a way to melt into the building.) But conservatism can also be boring, and this brings me to the qualification I mentioned above. Does every building built in California have to be "Spanish-style"? I hope not!

One role of a good developer/architect team is to decide when *not* to be slaves to convention, acknowledging that any departure from the tried and true may increase both market risks and operational risks. The city of Bilbao, Spain, took a huge risk when it hired Frank Gehry to design the new museum in that city. Gehry's previous work had refused to settle into any particular idiom. (I can almost imagine the look on the contractor's face as he reviewed a portfolio of Gehry's previous work!) But I recently spent three days delighting in that museum and its collection. If the city fathers of Bilbao were betting that unconventionality would pay off, in terms of increased tourist revenues, they bet right!

Remember, too, that *planning never stops.* It continues before, during, and after the design stage. As you design today's building, what are you aiming for next? In and around my home base in Harvard Square, I spent the better part of two decades trying to get my fellow adjacent property-owners to go along with creating a public walkway between two streets. I had a perfectly selfish motivation: If I could bring the public halfway down the length of my long and skinny building, it would make the property more accessible and attractive. But I also had a bigger picture in mind. If our little commercial neighborhood could create a new "sidewalk" almost in the heart of bustling Harvard Square, that would have to be a good thing. Gradually, I worked our walkway from historic Brattle Street almost to Mt. Auburn Street, until the last segment came into place a few years ago. Today, we have a wonderful little pedestrian street that is good for everybody's business, adds some texture to the neighborhood, and helps people get from here to there faster.

Keep thinking, reading, and talking about context, as you refine your designs. One thing that makes Washington, D.C. work pretty well is its rigorously enforced height limit. One interesting result is that even undistinguished buildings tend to work out O.K., when they stand shoulder-to-shoulder with their neighbors.

Finally, keep in mind that it never hurts to *go back and reexamine all of your initial premises,* as well. Why are we doing what we're doing? Is there a smarter way to do it?

An example that's further removed from development, but makes the point: Once, in the days when I was involved with a local Boston television station, we were wrestling with the problem of storing stage sets, backdrops, and props that weren't in current use. We got very far down the road toward designing a new storage building, which would have cost hundreds of thousands of dollars had we gone ahead with it. Then one day, we started thinking about the unused railroad spur that snaked up behind the station. After a little more thought, we bought a boxcar for $5,000, parked it on the spur, filled it full of sets, and forgot about our storage building.

The developer who is likely to be most successful in the design phase is the one who can *think qualitatively, quantitatively, nonlinearly,* and *visually,* all at the same time. Suppose a question of fenestration (windows!) comes up. You need to be able to make decisions about how the windows should work (qualitative), how much they can be allowed to cost, both short-term and longer-term (quantitative), and how they might look (visual). If you feel yourself coming up short on one or more of these criteria, find a way to get a quick tutorial, or sign up some complementary helpers.

This raises the issue of selecting an architect, which is almost never easy. You wish that you didn't have to choose between creativity and practicality—and yet in my experience, that's often the case. Almost as tough is choosing between passion and experience. Do you pick that young architect who is obviously talented, has the time, and is motivated to kill himself or herself for you? Or do you go with the firm more experienced in doing buildings such as yours, whose senior partners made a superb presentation to you and almost certainly won't be directly involved with the job?

This is a constant refrain in these pages: Assess the work of the person who's likely to be directly performing your work. I admired the previous projects of a particular architectural practice, and was inclined to hire them for a substantial project. When I looked a little deeper, I found that *all* of the buildings I liked in this firm's portfolio had been designed by a single architect who had recently left the company.

Other, less concrete issues have to be considered, as well. *Aesthetics* is one of the most important of them. Here we're in very subjective territory. What makes for successful architecture? It's not simply expense; we've all seen expensive buildings that are aesthetic disasters. And by the way: Who gets to vote, and when should the vote be taken? People's views as to what's attractive, or what's worth preserving, evolve. What's the *time frame* within which we call a building successful? The corporate headquarters of the Cummins Engine Company in Columbus, Indiana, strikes most first-time visitors as a rabbit's warren of cut-ins and cut-outs, oddly placed mirrors, and other disorienting features. But for those who work there for months and years, the building refuses to get stale. That's "successful," right?

It's tempting to say that since there are no hard-and-fast rules, one can simply sidestep aesthetics. I disagree, strongly. Develop your own point of view, test it, and revise it as necessary. Once again, *do your homework.* Figure out why you like what you like. Read a positive review of a building you hate.

Meanwhile, of course, take care of business. Conduct interviews and site visits; follow up on *every* reference. Look carefully at the materials that are provided to you by your would-be designers. Many times, you'll find references to a project that seems to have fallen off the table. Ask what happened in that case. Ask about projects that didn't go well, and why.

After you hire your architects, build your relationship with them. Get to know their strengths, weaknesses, and prejudices, and let them get to know yours. Be open to challenges from them—especially challenges about your assumptions. They'll do much better work for you as a result.

BIDDING AND CONSTRUCTION

At the end of the design process, with the help of numerous experts you've probably never met, you finally have a set of what are called "bid documents." These include both drawings and specifications, precisely defining how your facility is supposed to turn out. These documents are used first to select a contractor, then to put a final price on things, and finally to get the project built.

One general rule to guide this phase of the process: *Understand the construction process yourself, or involve somebody who does.* If you can't read plans, for example, find someone you trust who does read plans, and has some experience in making estimates based on "take-offs" (i.e., detailed estimates of materials and quantities derived from the drawings). This may be someone on your payroll, or it may be another partner who is willing to play a relatively active role in the construction process. But never put yourself in a position where you're bluffing your way through technical issues you don't understand. No one will be fooled, and your credibility will be undercut.

Another general rule is, *Work with good people with whom you've worked well in the past.* This is true for both architects and contractors. They know you, and you know them. You can communicate easily, and effectively. But don't fail to scrutinize their bids carefully. If they're not hungry for work, they may not bid the job competitively. Maybe the second-lowest bidder will do the best job for you, this time out. Avoid picking a contractor who lost money with you in the past—especially if the job is likely to require extras!

A general caution about costs: Remember that in development, project costs are not limited to land and buildings. In addition to site acquisition and actual construction-related costs, there are also significant fees (architectural, legal, etc.), leasing commissions, marketing costs, and a host of other soft costs. The temptation is to think of a contractor's bid as "most" of your obligation—and in some ways, that's true. (Buildings cost more than lawyers.) But when the dollars get tight, the soft costs somehow loom a lot larger. Another way of saying this is that when you buy an existing building, the price of that building has all kinds of costs included in it. When you're building a building, each of those costs gets a chance to stand up and be recognized.

Sometimes there is a link between hard costs and soft costs. For example, the longer the construction period, the higher the overall interest costs will be, since you will be paying on your construction loan for a longer period. By controlling your hard costs, you can (to some extent) control your soft costs, as well. Remember that the longer a building takes to rent up, the greater the carrying costs. Such costs can be an important component of your soft costs.

When it comes to controlling your hard costs, hiring the right contractor is critical, and there are several ways to approach this challenge. One is the traditional route: Ask several contractors to bid on the job, and hire the cheapest on a fixed-price basis. It may be that the contractor will also design the project for you, and enter into a fixed-price design-build contract. A second, very different approach is to hire a construction manager and pay that person either a fixed fee for managing the job or—more commonly—a percentage of the overall construction costs, which will vary from 3 percent (on a very large contract) to 10 percent (for a small "rehab" job). This, in a sense, is a "cost-plus" job.

A third approach that I like is a hybrid of these first two. Suppose the bids come in and a contractor with whom you've had success in the past comes in as the second-lowest bidder. You can go to that contractor and say, "Look—I like your work, and I want to like your price. Let's consider that bid an 'upset' price, and sit down together to get the overall costs lower. If we find a way to save money—by renegotiating with subcontractors, choosing different materials, and so on—you can keep half of the savings."

Let's look at the bid process from the contractor's point of view. They get your bid documents (either from you or your architect) and go to work trying to come up with a bid that's both low enough to get the job and high enough to yield a fair (or unfair) return. This means that they have to bid it out to a large group of independent subcontractors. To this extent, the construction field is a lot like the architecture field: The person who gets the job (the "architect" or the "builder") is likely to be little more than the process manager. He or she is critically dependent on the interest, commitment, competence, and sharp pencils of those subcontractors.

Stay in the contractors' heads for another paragraph. As they go out looking for carpenters, electricians, plasterers, painters, and so on, they need to keep a lid on all these prices. But Acme Carpenters (for example) knows that the contractor is only one of several construction firms bidding on the job in question, and that each construction firm that's bidding is probably getting three or four carpenter's bids. So Acme Carpenters is only one of nine, or twelve, or fifteen carpentry outfits that's bidding on this job—and Acme knows that. Unless Acme's desperate for work, or is confident that their overall contractor has a good shot at the job, they won't put a lot of time into their bid, and they won't risk coming in on the low side.

For structural reasons, therefore, your contractors' bids may have more than a little padding in them, and this will necessitate some negotiations. Approach these negotiations in a constructive spirit: "I need your help finding cost-effective solutions." Don't overnegotiate. You'll lose time and credibility.

Make sure to give yourself enough time for the contractors to bid the job, especially in light of the calendar. If you send it out for bid on December 20th, not much will happen until the first week in January (if then). After the bids come in, you will need lots more time—to review the bids, to get feedback from the contractors, do some redesign, and get revised bids based on that redesign. Each step requires time, and probably more than you anticipate.

When you're reviewing bids, break them out into their component parts. It may be that the next-to-lowest bidder would really be the lowest, were it not for a high electrical bid. By substituting a different electrician, you may be able to lower the overall bid. Similarly, if all of the carpenters' bids seem outlandishly high, this is a good clue that there is something in your architect's detailing that's creating a lot of concern over at the contractors' offices. Find out what it is, and decide if you can live without it.

So let's assume that the bids come in, and you like the low bidder, and you've agreed on a reasonable time frame for completion. The downside is that you've never worked with him or her before. There are two absolutely critical processes that you need to set in motion: (1) checking references, and (2) visiting buildings the contractor has previously worked on. I'm always amazed at how much I learn from my fellow developers about their contractors—both favorites and least favorites. Sometimes people don't like to admit they've made mistakes, but other times, they're eager to set the record straight.

I'm also amazed at how well buildings tell their own stories. Walk around in them, look at how things fit together (or don't fit together), and talk to the people who work there. If possible, speak to the people who maintain the building. What's good about the building, and what's bad? Try to differentiate between a design mistake and a construction mistake. (Don't blame the contractor if the architect or owner should have done a better job.) Were the buildings finished on time?

Use an experienced lawyer, as well as your architect, to review the construction contract. Remember that the contractor's bid can (and usually should) serve as the starting point for a very important round of negotiations and ground-rule setting. What kind of warranties, on which goods and services, is the contractor proposing to provide? Does the plan involve the use of union tradespeople? (This question is usually answered by the prevailing community norms, but there are cases in which trade unions do some parts, but not all parts, of a job.) Where can costs be reduced? Who is going to be the superintendent on the job? And not least important: Who decides when the scope of work has expanded, which in turn means that the contractor is entitled to more pay?

During these negotiations, be prepared to give up some things that you really like about your plan. The mahogany baseboards may have to go when you see the cost of providing even "just O.K." lighting. On the other hand, you should have two kinds of expenses in your mind—structural costs and nonstructural costs—and fight hard against deep cuts on the structural side.

Why? Because these are the elements which can be costly, and for which you'll be responsible until you sell the building. To put it bluntly, don't scrimp on roofs, HVAC, elevators, and so on. When these elements fail, your tenants won't be obligated to help you out. ("Hey, it's not *my* fault the heating system fell apart a month after I moved in. *You* fix it.")

There is a risk, however, that in adopting this mindset, you'll make cuts in what look like "extras"—for example, an expensive landscaping solution. Keep in mind that compromising in these kinds of "extras" can easily hurt the marketability of your building. Try to draw up an initial budget that is realistic, and with a big enough contingency reserve, so that "extras" can be protected except in dire circumstances.

Once the bid is awarded and the job begins, remember that this is an incredibly detailed process, and that you (as the overall job captain) are responsible for every single detail. Obviously, you can't watch every nail get driven, every wire get pulled, and every brick get laid. But it's absolutely critical that you demonstrate a high level of interest in every aspect of the project. This is a business of details. You are creating an environment that you'll spend many future hours trying to rent or sell, and in which people will have to work or live. Doing it right the first time is much better than redoing it now or later.

Attend (or ask a key member of your staff to attend) the weekly job meetings at which the architect, contractor, and subcontractors discuss their problems and progress. I often encourage a tenant to send a representative, too, so that they have the benefit of hearing any bad news as soon as possible.

When something goes obviously wrong during construction, don't squint at it—*fix it.* In a major remodeling that I recently supervised, we cut a stairway from one floor of our building to another to allow our second-floor tenant to expand onto the first floor. When I went over to inspect the work, I found a large red sprinkler supply pipe snaking across the ceiling of the new stairwell. Nobody had called me up and asked me about rerouting it; they had simply gone ahead and built the new stairwell around a truly hideous pipe. I told my on-site supervisor to move it and send me the bill. I didn't want to spend the next twenty years hating that pipe, or apologizing about it to prospective tenants.

One major wrinkle in the construction process is that the contracting industry is highly fragmented, and the contractor rarely "controls" the subcontractors. At the beginning of the job, contractors set up a critical-path schedule for getting the job done by a specific date. They then call up all of their subs and tell them when they should plan on arriving at the job site: carpenters on day 32, dry-wallers on day 57, painters on day 63, and so on.

But these subs know that something is sure to go wrong before their appointed day—it always does!—and they adopt a more ad hoc approach to the schedule. They keep an eye on the job, and when it looks like the sub ahead of them is wrapping up, they start scrambling to find people to do your work. This is less true for a big job, where the contractor (and you) have more leverage, and where it's likely that the drywall tapers can get to work on the forty-first floor even though the carpenters are still framing out the forty-second floor.

There's not much you can do about this, beyond monitoring the progress of the job against the stated schedule and bugging your contractor about the implications of any delays. Will there be a domino effect? If so, can we get two subs working concurrently to get us back on schedule? Again, by paying attention to detail and demonstrating that you understand the small brush strokes that are adding up to the Big Picture, you'll increase your chances of getting a well-made and affordable building.

An aside that I've been avoiding: There is a good chance that someday in the not-too-distant future, your contractor will arrive on your doorstep looking guilty and ashen-faced. He or she will announce to you that he or she is "getting *killed* on this job," can't survive on the fixed-fee contract you've both signed, and needs more money.

At this point, you'll have an important decision to make: fight, or pay. In my experience, you should certainly deliver a lot of symbolic fussing and fuming—and then start figuring out the necessary compromise. At this point, for reasons we're about to discuss, you probably are under *intense* pressures to get tenants into the building (or homeowners into the homes) and make some money from your investment. In fact, you are over a barrel, and you don't want to stay there.

I'm often asked an interesting question: "When should I act as my own contractor?" My answer is, "Rarely." Most homeowners who've tried it would probably agree: Unless you have the time and the experience, you're probably setting yourself up for disappointment. Charlie Leonard, our small-scale developer on Beacon Hill, undertook the rehabbing of his small apartment building himself, and the results were mixed. He got it done on time—a real accomplishment!—but at a higher cost than anticipated, including damage to his personal relationships, as we'll see in later chapters.

In some cases, there are pieces of the job that you can do yourself. Many years ago I purchased a complex of buildings from Raytheon. The price had been heavily discounted because of the tremendous amount of interior and exterior demolition that would be required: hundreds of partitions in each building. But it was wintertime, and I had an idea. I put up a notice in the Boston College gymnasium, advertising for workers. The response was gratifying. I wound up hiring most of the college's football team for several weekends in a row (along with several experienced construction supervisors, of course, to keep an eye on things and make sure no one got hurt). One unexpected side benefit: I became fast friends with the proprietors of the local donut store and hamburger joint.

If you can do it yourself, safely and economically, and if doing so won't wreak havoc in other corners of your life, give it a try. Otherwise, hire professionals. As I've said in earlier chapters, good professionals are well worth what they cost.

GETTING AND USING MONEY

Let me stress that all of this activity is going on more or less at once. In the development phase, you are constantly juggling. There's no way around it. The approval process and the design process pretty much *have* to be concurrent, in order to be sufficiently interactive. The design process *has* to flow into the bidding process; otherwise, you can't adjust your design to reflect financial realities.

As suggested above, lots of projects wind up being badly compromised because the reserve for contingencies was unrealistically low, or because the owner came up short on cash when it came time to pay for the "extras." I'll say it again: Trying to redesign the project to reflect your deteriorating financial circumstances is tempting, but it can destroy the project's marketability. Don't put yourself in a situation where you have to forego large long-term profits for small short-term benefits.

The financing end of the venture begins early, and (in some form or another) continues until you finally sell the facility. In Chapters 3 and 4, you got some sense of the complexity of financing the purchase of an existing building. Now take that same level of complexity, and square or cube it. In development, you're trying to finance a building that doesn't exist yet. (In fact, you may not have permission to build it, and everybody around you knows you may *never* get the necessary permissions.) Perhaps there is organized opposition, coming from quarters you hadn't anticipated. You can't really say with confidence *when* you're going to build this thing, and every delay increases your costs in a number of directions. If the approval process takes two months, your legal fees may be $20,000. If it takes two years, they may be $200,000.

In Chapters 3 and 4, we looked at the pressures that arise when you want to close on an existing building and *get on with it.* (These pressures are also fueled by legions of professionals and consultants who won't get paid unless the deal goes through.) Now, in a starting-from-scratch development project, you may have *really* significant sums of money advanced, especially for design and legal services, and perhaps for options to tie up one or more parcels of land. Now you *really* have an incentive to blast ahead, even if the market isn't particularly friendly to your project at this point in time. Momentum can be your friend, but it can also work against you.

If you're a wealthy developer, willing and able to up-front this kind of high-risk money, you've got a leg up. But most developers have their cash tied up in one or more other projects. They simply don't have the money available when it's needed. So as you set out to fund an individual project—and remember that these are *all* individual projects—you'll almost certainly have to find a person (or better, a bunch of people) who likes this project and has faith in you. This is true both on the equity and the debt sides, but is particularly important on the equity side. When you bring other people into a development project, you're asking them to take really significant risks. They'll ask for, and they deserve, a major interest in the property. If you can live without them and keep control, great; if you can't, pick your partners wisely.

Much of what I've written about partnership agreements in previous chapters also pertains here—but again, the stakes are higher, and should be recognized as such. Your partnership agreement *has* to address the issue of how more money will be raised if it's needed. Will the current partners "pony up" more money? In equal amounts? Or does the general partner have the right to issue more equity, and thereby dilute the interest of the existing partners? Does everyone get diluted equally? Can the general partner make these decisions unilaterally? If so, are his or her interests sufficiently aligned with those of the equity partners to ensure that their interest will be protected? Is the general partner also the contractor, and therefore responsible for all cost overruns?

How much is the developer going to get paid for what he or she is doing, and when? Will the developer get compensated (perhaps retroactively) for having assembled the land successfully? For a successful leasing-up of the building? In many development deals, the developer's back-end fee is higher than in a straight investment project. Is that the model for this development?

What happens if somebody can't fulfill his or her function? What happens if the developer runs into trouble on other projects, and can't provide the services that this project needs? What happens if the project runs too long? Is the money behind the project committed indefinitely, or does the developer have a fixed amount of time within which to complete the project?

For all of these reasons and others, I usually include provisions in my partnership agreements for arbitration of every legal point of dispute. No arbitrator can be depended upon to take your side of an issue, of course. But disputes are time-killers, and therefore can put your whole project at risk. Find a way to end the dispute, *quickly,* and pay whatever it takes to get the project back on the rails.

Obviously, the complexities of development make their ways into the partnership agreements that make these new buildings possible. Risks are much greater. Cash flows are much more uncertain. Problems become acute *quickly.* So this is another juncture where hiring the best lawyer you can find is a smart idea—even if that lawyer (because of his or her relevant experience) costs much more per hour than the second-best lawyer.

On the debt side, you'll go through the same gyrations already described in Chapters 3 and 4. Again, however, this debt is scarier to financial institutions. You may have a proven track record, but this new facility doesn't. The banks will charge you accordingly. Permanent mortgage money tends to be ten-year commitments with twenty-to-thirty-year amortization schedules for a fixed amount. Construction money tends to be interest-only, short-term financing with floating rates, which is good news for capable operators and bad news for poor operators—unless, of course, interest rates in general rise, which is bad news for everyone.

One key difference in financing the development phase is that banks have more latitude in handling construction loans than in handling straight mortgages. Unlike mortgages, construction loans are likely to stay with the banks that make them. (They are too short-term and heterogeneous to be repackaged and shipped off to the debt markets.) Your word and reputation are likely to be more valuable in this particular stage of the game than in other phases. At the same time, the bank is likely to claim that they're taking greater risks, and charge you accordingly—and try to extract some sort of personal guarantee from you.

Banks have reason to be wary, because they usually have the deepest pockets. When project costs exceed the budget, it is a lot easier to go to the bank for more money than to put up your own money—especially if that resource is in short supply—or to go back and explain this bad situation to your equity partners. The bank's reaction to your unwelcome request is likely to depend on a whole variety of factors: whether the additional money will increase the pro forma cash flow, whether the loan-to-value ratio is low, whether you are providing a personal guarantee, whether the bank officer has been delegated the authority to change the deal, and whether the bank thinks highly of you.

In other words, getting more money can be a crapshoot. This means that money management is absolutely critical. Spreadsheets are indispensable tools for watching the project eat up the available dollars. Far too often, developers say, "O.K., I've got $1 million to work with." Then, after spending $900,000, they discover that they've got a $1.1 million project on their hands—and all of the remaining $200,000 is nondiscretionary spending. It's absolutely vital to manage the individual parts of your project so that you can see where you're running over, and see it early enough to take appropriate steps. Will you: (1) get more money, (2) cut back in other areas, (3) cut deals with certain tenants to do their own lease improvements, or (4) do something else?

In the development field, you need *contingencies.* My father's cousin Sam Poorvu was a very successful developer. When I was first starting out, he was kind enough to go over my numbers with me. We'd be extremely conservative with every line in the budget—by which I mean that we'd estimate high, including more time to finish and lease up than I anticipated. We'd finish with a bottom line that felt very bloated to me. Then on his way out the door, Sam would always sing out, "And Bill—don't forget to add 10 percent." And he was never wrong, except that sometimes it should have been "15 percent" or "20 percent."

As big sums of money flow in and out of your project, you should find yourself becoming intensely focused on what you're doing. Using other people's money tends to create and maintain this focus. (If it doesn't, look again!) Even if you have the right to issue more equity or incur more debt, there's only so much income that this property will ever produce. So every dollar counts. And all kinds of things translate directly into dollars saved, or dollars wasted. If you develop and maintain excellent relationships with your architect, contractor, and subs, you will save dollars. If you annoy or offend somebody gratuitously, you will probably waste dollars.

Let the flows of money, in and out, remind you that *this is the crucial time frame.* This is where you make money—or you get killed, and provide an excellent opportunity for the *next* owner.

MARKETING YOUR CREATION

And with that happy thought in mind, don't forget to market this property. While you're building good relationships in every direction, and chasing and conserving dollars, you are also either leasing your future space, or (in the case of a residential subdivision) selling pieces of it. Yes, you're likely to have a leasing broker working for you if the project is above a certain scale, but once again, *you're* the project manager, and you're the one who has to guarantee the success of the marketing effort.

As any self-respecting leasing broker will tell you, leasing is complicated. In some cases, you may succeed in preleasing space. (In some cases, your financing institution will require a certain amount of preleasing.) Perhaps during the land-assembly process, for example, you've cut a deal with existing property owners to accommodate them in the new facility. If you're building a shopping center, you've surely gotten commitments from the necessary "anchor" stores well in advance. But unless you're one lucky developer, leasing (or selling) is likely to continue all the way through the construction phase, and even afterwards.

Your marketing strategy should be derived from (1) your understanding of the current market, and (2) your willingness to invest resources in specific directions that are mainly dictated by that market. Is there a "high end" of this market—and if so, do you want to position your property there? If you've determined that you absolutely need to keep this residential development at the low end of the single-family housing market, how will you control costs tightly enough to achieve that goal? Standardization will help your budget, but may hurt your efforts to sell those houses. If the solution lies somewhere in the middle, how will you link the marketing, design, and bidding functions effectively enough to protect everyone's interests?

How is your marketing strategy tied to the larger real estate cycle? If the bottom falls out, will your current market disappear? If you've designed the project well, you've built a certain amount of flexibility into it. What marketing opportunities arise out of that flexibility?

This is a point worth stressing: *The leasing function is intimately connected with both the design and financing of your project.* Potential tenants are looking for the deal that will best meet their functional needs and reflect their aesthetic preferences. In most cases, you'll have to compete to win their business. This means working with them to customize their space, while staying within your larger budget constraints.

This may sound simple, but consider a specific example. Suppose a potential tenant looks at your standard light fixtures, and decides that they want something better (read "more expensive"). The first question is, who'll pay the difference? Even if you assume that they'll pay the difference, a lot of work is being created for people involved in the construction process. Someone has to locate the new fixtures, and obtain assurances that they can be delivered on time. Someone has to determine that the fixtures fit in the already-designed ceiling grid. (I wince painfully, reflecting on recent experience, as I write that last sentence!) Someone has to find out whether your electrical contractor will charge you a premium to install what may turn out to be more complicated fixtures. Someone has to cut back on the order for the standard fixtures, and then make sure that (1) the reduction actually happens, and (2) your bill for that purchase actually goes down.

What happens when the changes come from the other direction? If your project is running over budget, you'll either have to obtain more money or cut back. If you cut back on the levels of finish that you've promised to your prospective tenants—and especially if those higher levels of finish are implied in your rents—then you have a second-round marketing problem on your hands.

O.K. I've made my market-driven pitch. Now I want to adjust the balance a bit by emphasizing *salesmanship.* If you're not a salesman, this is the time to learn to be one. When you're leasing your building or selling your new homes, you are selling dreams—your dreams, and their dreams. You're doing more than finding occupants of space. You're matching other people's visions with your own vision. To some extent, you're building a vision together.

Here's where your architect can be extremely helpful. I've never met the head of a successful architectural firm who wasn't a superb salesman. (In fact, that's what they spend most of their time doing, if you define "sales" broadly enough.) You'll probably have to use this resource sparingly, but you'll know when the time is right. If an important prospective tenant is having trouble visualizing something, get your architect to help that tenant. (Prospective tenants tend to be nonvisual types, in my experience.) You may pay extra for some additional drawings or renderings, or for some extra dog-and-pony shows, but these will be dollars well invested.

Make sure you've got the best leasing agent for the job. Ask who in the firm will actually be doing the work, and ask to see that person's work and credentials. Once that person is signed up, work with him or her to develop an appropriate advertising campaign. Set a budget and stick to it. Once again, *listen* to that person, and get access to his or her expertise! If you start hearing bad noises about how this project isn't quite reaching its market, figure out what's really being said.

Your leasing agent should have a feel for what kind of handout or brochure is appropriate, and where to send it when it's available. Keep your eye on the marketing effort, and ask for specific progress reports at regular intervals: number of contacts made, number of responses to specific advertising or other outreach efforts, number of on-site tours, and other measures that you trust. It may feel like a waste of your time to be on-site when the broker is doing a first showing to a prospective tenant; however, I've found this to be an invaluable way to learn about how your building and its location are perceived.

In budgeting for your marketing program, don't make the mistake of spending too much of your marketing money up front for elaborate brochures or models, for elaborate ground-breaking parties, or for expensive advertising buys in national media. Instead, determine the most economical ways to reach your target market, and retain contingency funds in case your time frame stretches out or you need to redesign (and therefore remarket) your project.

ON THE INTERNATIONAL FRONT

Most of the challenges outlined in this chapter only intensify when you move into the international arena. Now you're juggling dozens of people and processes simultaneously against what may be a totally unfamiliar and culturally different backdrop. Once again, the watchword is *caution.* Identify the risks in front of you, and find a way to manage them.

For example, the approval process in many countries is, well, *individualized.* I read recently in the paper about a bold new initiative by the mayor of Mexico City. He announced that going forward, all fees related to planning, design, and construction would go into the city's coffers—rather than into the pockets of city inspectors. This simple change, he said, would move the city from a deficit position to a positive operating balance. That story implied a great deal about the realities of putting up a building in Mexico City, at least until the mayor took his stand (and perhaps even afterward).

In going overseas, you should ask yourself what particular attributes you bring to the party. There are essentially three good answers to that question. If you don't have any of these attributes, you may want to rethink the move.

The first attribute is *skills in planning, design, or construction* that the local community doesn't possess. It may be that a certain kind of office tower hasn't ever been built in Berlin, and you know how to build it. Maybe the suburbs of Madrid are still awaiting their first outlet mall, and you know best how to put one together.

The second attribute is *marketing skills.* In a community where a large percentage of the tenants are expected to come from other countries, especially your own, you may have an advantage over the locals in reaching these tenants. For example: The American community in China might respond better to the work of an American developer than a Chinese developer. Perhaps you understand better the kinds of amenities or services these Americans want, and you may therefore have an advantage over the locals. (Or maybe not.)

And finally, you may have *money.* In developing countries, there often isn't the capital that's needed to build large projects. This is especially true in countries that recently have been bedeviled by hyperinflation. Long-term mortgage money is either unavailable, or it's so expensive that no one can afford it.

Let's look at three examples of developers going overseas, and how they prospered (or didn't prosper). The first of these is the true story of the Houston-based Hines company going into Mexico City. Hines is one of the largest office developers in the United States, with lots of blue-chip corporate connections. (For many years, Hines was IBM's principal partner in providing office space to the computer giant.) Several local developers in Mexico City knew Gerald Hines from various industry association meetings, and invited him to visit. They hoped that Hines would bring both marketing contacts and credibility—which would translate into capital that the local partners could raise in Mexico. Hines agreed, did his due diligence, and eventually committed himself to co-developing an 800,000-square-foot complex in Mexico City. Local partners took on the approval and permitting process, and Hines retained famed architect Cesar Pelli, and lined up corporate tenants. Construction began.

Hines soon found that development in Mexico City was very different from development in Houston. In the United States, there is plenty of heavy equipment and relatively few construction workers; in Mexico, the opposite is true. This reflects the relative cost of labor in the two countries, as well as the cost of capital. (Cranes are expensive.) Hines soon found itself putting up somewhat shaky scaffolding at dizzying heights.

Hines also was faced with a devaluation of the peso in the middle of the construction phase. This changed all of the immediate calculations dramatically, but also had unpleasant longer-term implications. For example: Most of the people who were supposed to buy the expensive condominiums in the residential condo part of the project were suddenly too poor to afford them. The volatility of local currencies is something that a U.S.-based firm must come to grips with. Either the profit margin must be huge or the budget adequate to allow for the periodic and unpredictable devaluations that take place and/or currency-hedging costs—which can be considerable.

When Dan Dubrowski, Hines's Mexico City project manager, asked Gerald Hines what he needed in order to succeed at his new job, Hines thought for a minute and replied, "The ability to take bad news really well." This turned out to be wise counsel.

The second example of an international development project comes from China, where the Singaporean government is playing an interesting role as a quasi-developer. Technically, the developer is not the government itself, but rather a consortium of businesses, most of which are Singaporean-owned. Nevertheless, the consortium has the clout that one normally associates with a national government. A similar consortium was first organized to build an industrial park in Jurong, one of Singapore's major industrial areas. The project was highly successful, and attracted numerous Western tenants. Expanding on this successful model, members of the consortium developed a series of industrial parks in Indonesia, India, and the smaller islands around Singapore.

At the request of Western companies, and with the tacit consent of the Chinese government, the consortium agreed to build the Suzhou Industrial Park near Shanghai. The consortium contributed skills, connections, and capital to the effort. U.S. companies—worried about the Foreign Corrupt Practices Act, among other things—welcomed an intermediary that could obtain the necessary approvals in China. Chinese officials appreciated an intermediary that could figure out appropriate ways to provide help to Westerners needing a whole range of services, including shipping, recruitment of employees, job training, security, and so on. The consortium's Suzhou Park began its operations in 1996, and got off to a good start.

Then something interesting happened. The Chinese government had taken accurate notes, as it did business with the Singaporeans. The Chinese realized that Suzhou was a high-priced venture, and that a stripped-down version could compete effectively with the Singaporean venture. Within a short time span, a second industrial park opened up in Suzhou—this time run by another local quasi-governmental consortium. Not surprisingly, the higher-priced industrial park is suffering as a result, although it may still turn out that there's a market for both.

Our third example is a more individual one. You'll recall the case of Cameron Sawyer, introduced in Chapter 1. He left his legal practice in Atlanta, moved to Russia in search of real estate opportunities, learned Russian, and began making contacts there. When he entered into his first land deal, he did so in partnership with a Moscow agency that was willing to go into a joint venture, but only if they could lease their land to the venture. (Selling land, for many Russians, is anathema.) Sawyer, conserving his limited capital, readily agreed.

To Sawyer, the agency represented a critical point of entry into a restricted market. To the Russians, Sawyer was someone who knew how to build a building, find capital, and attract Western tenants.

As it turned out, Sawyer found that securing the necessary capital was more difficult than expected. He had planned to raise money in the United States, but found investors there leery about putting their money into Russia. On the other hand, U.S. companies were so interested in finding acceptable space in Russia that they agreed to an unusual structure: They would pay their rents in U.S. dollars regardless of what happened to the (volatile) dollar/ruble exchange rate.

But this would only be helpful *after* the property was built. Somebody still had to incur the political risk and put up the money to get the building built. It took a great deal of leg work to find investors who were willing to contribute the up-front money, which Sawyer ultimately succeeded in doing.

The collective point of these three stories, again, is that operating internationally makes a tough process (development) even tougher. It introduces currency risks, political risks, cultural and language barriers, and other legal and tax complexities usually not found at home. If your skills don't match these additional challenges, then international development may not be appropriate for you. Think of the odds, too: Despite the globalization of many industries, there are *very few* examples of firms that have developed successfully on an international basis.

THE FOUR PITFALLS, AND HOW TO STAY OUT OF THEM

It is more than a little difficult to summarize the planning, design, construction, financing, and marketing of a new building in a small amount of space. These are all complicated processes in and of themselves. They tend to overlap significantly, and vary according to location, type of project, timing in the market cycle, and a variety of other factors.

I'd like to suggest, however, that as you approach a development project—for the first time or the fiftieth time—you keep in mind what I'll call the "four pitfalls," and try your best to avoid them.

The first pitfall is *inexperience.* This isn't simply a trait of a newcomer to the development field. The minute you step sideways in the real estate industry—say, from being a developer of warehouse space to a developer of office space, or even building a known product in a new market—you are inexperienced. Even for developers who are "sticking to their knitting," and staying in their own established realm of expertise, the sheer variability of buildings can present surprises. Every building is custom-designed, more or less. Almost every project team is new. Every new community in which you ply your trade presents different challenges.

The way to overcome inexperience is to identify and manage the risks inherent in each phase of the game, and that is what this chapter has been about. Do your homework. Check references. If you can't read a blueprint, get someone on board who does. Know your market, and cater to it. Never stop thinking and planning. Understand what the guy on the other side of the table is thinking, and anticipate his next move.

The second pitfall is *undercapitalization.* In fact, many successful people in the real estate game are both wealthy *and* undercapitalized. Their wealth is in the equity of the illiquid real estate projects they have developed in the past. Their incentive is to leverage projects. If you can put half as much money in Deal 1, that means that you can launch Deal 2 simultaneously. And if you make your money by making projects happen, then you'll try hard to make as many projects happen as possible. Putting up one building where you'll get an override of 20 to 50 percent of the back-end profits is good. Putting up *three* buildings on the same terms, through higher leverage, is three times as good—until the next downturn. Large multinational companies are nearly as prone to this pitfall as local entrepreneurs.

Promoters may also receive fees for construction or project supervision or as leasing commissions. These fees are often essential to cover their overhead, both in the field and in the central office. There is an incentive to keep these fees coming.

During the construction period, there's much more pressure put on you to personally guarantee what you're creating. Your lenders, whoever they are, are conservative. They don't have the reassurance of a proven cash flow, which is always the best evidence that their money will be repaid.

They are almost entirely dependent on your ability to pull the deal off, and get the job done. They want to make sure that you won't back out of the deal casually, For all these reasons, they are likely to demand a personal guarantee from you (or your company, if it's big enough) on some aspect of the job, and you (or your company) will probably have to provide one.

And this exacerbates the problem of undercapitalization, especially if the developer doesn't really understand the nature of his or her "wealth." It's not uncommon for a successful developer to be "worth" $5 million or $50 million—and for most of that money to be tied up in (illiquid) real estate. Many of my colleagues with substantial net worth never have more than, say, $15,000 that they can lay their hands on quickly (or, say, $115,000, if they sold all their stocks and bonds). Suffice it to say that $100 million in real estate is not the same as $100 million in municipal bonds. If you're illiquid, you're not well capitalized.

Beware of the trap of assigning as collateral another specific asset you own when a bank asks for a personal guarantee. When one of your lenders gets such a plum, they'll all want one—and soon, most or all of your assets will be pledged. These pledges probably won't get called unless there's a collapse in market values, which will be the worst time to unload these assets. If you're not careful, this could quickly cut through your net worth.

Real estate deals *always* cost more than you anticipate. Few contingency funds turn out to be adequate. I've never seen a spreadsheet that goes out longer than ten years, but I've seen lots of projects that take longer then ten years to develop and rent up fully. So the question you have to ask yourself, as you go into your project, is, *Do I have adequate reserves?* Let's say you're building a $1 million project with $800,000 in debt financing and $200,000 in equity. Halfway through the project, you discover that your costs have gone up 10 percent—not unusual! This brings you to $1.1 million, which requires a 50 percent increase above your original $200,000 equity.

Understanding the arithmetic of undercapitalization is the first step toward avoiding it. Other steps may sound obvious, but are worth repeating: Pick partners with deep pockets. In your partnership agreements, give yourself the authority to issue more equity, in case it's needed to finish the job. (If your partners squawk, ask them how *they* would propose to deal with this still hypothetical turn of events.) Stage your deployment of resources. If you don't need to build everything at once, don't. Consider leasing the land, perhaps with an option to purchase it later. If you leave the second floors in the residences unfinished, make that a selling point

("Yes—you can design the baths and bedrooms according to *your* tastes!"). Watch your declining cash balances like a hawk.

The third pitfall is *ignoring changes in the external context.* As I've emphasized in previous chapters, these changes can come in many forms. If the real estate market tanks, of course, most of your projections can be tossed out the window. It took twenty years for New York's Battery Park to be designed, approved, and built. Boston's ambitious Fan Pier development was conceived in a great rental market, and was destroyed when that market disappeared. Now the area is going through its umpteenth master planning exercise.

But things can go wrong in the other direction, as well. If you get early cost estimates in the down side of the cycle but don't build until the upswing, you may find that your actual construction costs far exceed your earlier estimates. Also, interest rates tend to rise during an economic upturn. Meanwhile, your own financial circumstances may change. In the bad times, you had no projects calling on your money. Now you've got five or six—and this particular project is getting harder and harder to finance. Or maybe your longtime, most stalwart investor falls upon hard times. Or maybe he or she looks you in the eye and says, "Bill, I've been doing some thinking. Why should I make 10 percent on your real estate deal, and tie up my money pretty tightly, when I could be making 20 percent in the stock market and stay reasonably liquid?"

Sometimes it's enough to say, "Because you get to work with *me.*" More often, you'll be off in search of a new investor.

The last pitfall is *ego.* (Recall the Edifice Complex, mentioned earlier!) Real estate developers—both those who build new structures and those who creatively recycle old buildings—are *builders,* in every sense of the word. *They* know why 10 percent free and clear in real estate is "as good as" 20 percent somewhere else. (They *like* leverage!) Real estate people like to feel that squirt of adrenalin hit their heart. They like a good challenge (or a whole hive full of challenges). Conversely, they hate to shut things down. They hate to be bored. They believe in their heart that they have the skills to manage (or at least negotiate their way through) whatever comes up. They are convinced that negative market changes will hurt their competitors' projects more than their own. Doing the deal can become an end in itself.

These are all great traits to have during the upside of the cycle. (Surely nothing would get built without them.) But they can be *terrible* traits during the downside. Ego, drive, energy, the need to push into something new—all well and good at the right juncture, and all terrible when the real estate market is poised at the top of a cliff.

There are no known remedies for this affliction. Cultivate some good hobbies to fall back on. Take good care of your spouse, family, and friends during the up cycle, so that there's some chance they'll want to see more of you during the down cycle. Get a partner or advisor who is as much like Eeyore (from Winnie the Pooh) as possible—gloomy, slow-moving, even dour. And *listen* to that person, at least some of the time, when he or she launches into a pessimistic analysis of the state of the world.

Try to achieve a balance in your real estate portfolio, and refrain from putting all of your eggs in the development basket. There is no easy answer as to how much leverage is right, but owning income-producing properties with stable cash flows may cover not only your company's overhead, but also your personal expenses. Diversifying your net worth—in the sense that it's not all in real estate—may set you up to disprove the old adage that you can't both sleep well and eat well.

BEFORE THE NEXT PHASE

I've tried to keep this development chapter reasonably generic, blurring or ignoring the real distinctions among property types, in order to keep the chapter to a manageable size. Obviously, you'll need to know a lot more about the particular property type you're interested in developing, and a good place to start is the Note on Property types in the back of this book.

Moving on: Once you build it, somebody has to operate it. Operations—the blocking and tackling phase of the real estate game—is the subject of the next chapter.

CHAPTER 7

OPERATIONS

In this chapter, the activities of our two groups of active players of the real estate game—the buyers and builders—converge again. Whether you wind up with the building by buying it or creating it from the ground up, there will most likely come a time when you have to *operate* it.

This is the unsexy part of the real estate business. As you've probably observed in your own experience, real estate war stories tend to focus on the dramatic buying and selling of properties, the against-the-odds creation of new buildings, or the inspired reuse of old ones. The reason for this bias, as explained in previous chapters, is that rewards in the real estate game (as in other games) come from *creating value.* In most cases, creating value involves change.

Operations aren't quite the opposite of change, but they're close. Operations involve growing or defending your margins (or in the worst case, minimizing the shrinkage of your margins).

Operations are rarely heroic. Few real estate moguls find convincing ways to brag about how they fixed a leaky roof, placated an impossible tenant, or restriped the parking lot to accommodate four more cars. But even though discussing operating issues is unlikely to make you the center of attention at a real estate cocktail party, your ability to manage properties effectively will have major impact on your short- and long-term cash flow.

WHY WORRY ABOUT OPERATIONS?

In Chapter 2, we saw how small swings in the cash flow from operations in a leveraged property can affect your return on investment. This is illustrated in the accompanying example of operating leverage.

	Base Case	+20%	–20%
Cash flow from operations	$100	120	80
Financing charge	70	70	70
Cash flow after financing	30	50	10
Net change		+67%	–67%

Revenues consist primarily of rental income. Changes in revenues are dependent upon (1) local conditions, especially in terms of demographic changes and improvement or deterioration of the location, and (2) the supply of available space that competes with yours, as compared with the aggregate demand for that space. The condition of the economy and consumer expectations are areas over which we have little control. But it is important to remember that even in a weak market—in which, say, the average vacancy rate is 20 percent—80 percent of the available space is still occupied. (The glass is not one-fifth empty, but four-fifths full.) In such circumstances, keeping your building 90 percent occupied (or better!) at reasonable rents should be your goal—even though the rental rate for the most recent leases may be less than anticipated in your budget.

For all the reasons outlined in the previous chapters, real estate people start out seeing their prospective tenants as numbers to be plugged into a formula. (Banks and partners demand to see these formulas working out the right ways.) When they're showing the space, these prospective tenants are treated as customers. Then, when lease negotiations begin, landlords see them as bargainers across the table—not necessarily adversaries, but certainly not allies. It is only later that the landlord and the tenant begin to see themselves as allies. Some people never get to this point. Many landlords persist in viewing tenants as a necessary evil, and many tenants persist in perceiving landlords as the Bad Guys.

I maintain that tenants and landlords *are* allies. Each provides an indispensable resource to the other. In a very real sense, each is the other's customer, because they are mutually dependent. Of course, it's not unusual for things to go awry in landlord-tenant relationships. But speaking personally, those are the times when I try to remind myself that I'm speaking to a *client.* When times are good—I try to tell myself—this is an important client. When times are bad, this is an *extremely important* client. This is one of the customers who will help me lift my occupancy rates above those of my competitors, and help keep my ship afloat.

In Chapter 6, we considered issues related to the marketing of your property. But attracting and retaining tenants is not simply a matter of a good marketing campaign, or skillful negotiations when you're trying to lease up this new (or newly acquired) property. It also requires careful planning to ensure that you've (1) spent your money in appropriate ways, in advance, to position your property; and (2) held enough in reserve to make the tenant improvements needed to clinch the deal. So in the operations phase of the real estate game, as much as in the development phase, cash management is a key success factor.

WHO SHOULD WORRY ABOUT OPERATIONS—AND HOW?

Is there anyone in the real estate game who *doesn't* have to worry about these issues? For the active player, the answer is an emphatic *no.* If you think you can simply sign on a management firm to take all the problems of operations off your hands, you are in for a rude awakening. In my experience, there are many decisions that only the owner can make.

As for passive investors, I'd say that the Boston-based investor in a California-focused REIT probably can't concern himself or herself much with operational issues (although if on a trip to California you discovered that some of the underlying properties were noticeably dirty or rundown, I'd say it was time to worry!). But passive investors in, say, a syndicate—investors who are largely betting on the skills of a few individuals—should definitely worry about the ability of those individuals to operate a property. And I maintain that it's useful for all sorts of investors in real estate to understand the differences between good and bad management practices. "Know what you're investing in, and why," as investment guru Peter Lynch puts it.

Our appendix on property types presents a number of different types of developments, and implicitly shows how different they are. Building an office park is very different from building a residential complex. Unfortunately—for the purposes of this chapter—the same holds true for operations. There's no one comprehensive way to talk about "operations" across the incredibly broad range of properties in which you might become involved.

So I'll adopt a simplified framework and encourage you to apply its basic principles to the specifics of your particular situation. That simplified framework is the *tenant lease,* which we will work our way through, clause by typical clause.

In Chapter 4, we scrutinized the purchase and sale agreement because it provided a useful way to think about the complex decisions that lie behind the sale and purchase of a property. In this chapter, I want to use the tenant lease in the same general way. *Leases are legal documents—and therefore give us a toehold on the legal aspects of operating a property—but they also implicitly capture the principles that underlie the successful operation of a property.* I derive some confidence in this approach from the fact that even though property types differ dramatically, the headings in most leases are remarkably consistent. The clauses are there for a good reason: They solve a problem.

For example: Every lease includes a specified rent, and almost every lease provides a description of the services that will be provided by the landlord in return for that rent. Similarly, almost every lease spells out the additional obligations assumed by the tenant in addition to paying the stated rent on time. And finally, most leases include a more or less comprehensive group of clauses that talk about what will happen when and if things go wrong.

As I make my way through the component parts of the tenant lease, I will try to present each point from both the tenant's and the landlord's points of view. I will try to describe both the differences that arise between those points of view, and also the types of compromises that are usually arrived at to resolve these differences.

Finally, after looking at operational issues at the level of the individual property, I will step back, go up one level, and look at the management of the *business of the property,* especially in terms of lender and investor relationships. Many building managers make the mistake of getting caught up in the thousands of details of operating a property at the expense of the business. I will argue that attention to all of these details is critically important—and just as important is keeping a close eye on the big picture. This property is a *business.* Is it making money? Why or why not? This approach is often referred to as "asset management," which can be thought of as one level up from property management.

Before we start, one major caveat, which I've already implied in the preceding paragraphs. By adopting a legal document (a lease) as our roadmap for navigating the terrain of operations, I don't mean to imply that all problems between landlords and tenants can or should be solved through a rigid adherence to a lease. Westerners—and particularly Americans—are inclined to think of legal agreements as cast in stone, and to think of renegotiations as somehow dishonorable. I suggest that we take a more Japanese approach to leases and other contracts. Legal documents place bounds on our behaviors, but that's only a small part of doing busi-

ness. In many cases, personal relationships are far more important in determining how people will behave, especially if they hope to do business together over the long run.

WALKING THROUGH THE LEASE

Using our lease structure, I have more than two dozen subjects to present in the following pages. This is a long list, but each separate subject comprises one or more issues that you should understand for the effective operation of your property. Again, none of the following discussions attempts to be comprehensive, but all are intended to point you toward key related concerns.

The subjects (defined by the headings of a standard lease) are:

The parties
The commencement date
Building and premises
Use of the premises
Term: original and extended
Base and additional rent
Parking
Tenant's obligations
Landlord's obligations
Compliance with laws
Environment
Insurance
Damage to premises
Eminent domain
Default by tenant
Default by landlord
Security deposit
Subordination, estoppel certificates, and nondisturbance
Subletting and assignment
Consents
Condition of premises
Tenant improvements
Landlord's work
Broker
Miscellaneous

Looking at this list, which necessarily implies a sequence, underscore basic challenge in thinking about "operations." The processes or events c ered by many of these clauses are interrelated. They may be concurrent may be mutually contingent. As an example, it's not sensible to settle u a rent without knowing which specific tenant improvements will have t carried out (and by whom), or without defining precisely who is goin provide which services. For the moment, you'll have to keep in mind premise that real estate is an exercise in general management, and you the ultimate general manager—are responsible for keeping everythir sequence and closely coordinated. And by the time we're through wit list of several dozen topics, you should have a sense of how the opera phase of the real estate game fits together.

THE PARTIES

Much of the time, tenants are dependent solely on the owner of a property to meet obligations under their lease. Since the landlord may well sell the property (or change the managing agent) before the expiration of the lease, the tenant has no security regarding who will be responsible for operating a property throughout the course of a lease. As a tenant, therefore, you should check out the reputation and history of the landlord in advance. Does that history suggest that this landlord is likely to sell? If so, is the property one that's likely to go to a responsible institutional purchaser? (The answer depends on several factors: the landlord's track record, the quality of the building, the state of the local market, etc.)

And perhaps most important, from the tenant's perspective: Is the property leveraged to the point where there will be inadequate cash to provide the agreed-upon services in an acceptable manner, take care of routine maintenance, and make capital improvements that will maintain not only the physical structure but also the image of the building? If the answer is "yes," your life as a tenant may be uncomfortable or unpleasant.

From the landlord's perspective, it is equally important to get financial statements from (or on) the tenant. An illustration from personal experience: Just as I was writing this paragraph, my son Jonathan came to see me about a prospective tenant who wanted to lease some of our office space. This would-be tenant was a high-tech subsidiary of a larger firm. The subsidiary had a $150,000 net worth and was carrying a $1.4 million loan from the parent company on its books. Obviously, we wouldn't go ahead without a guaranty from the parent, especially in light of the fact that the tenant wanted us to make expensive improvements.

Reviving one of our earlier characters, Ben Alexander (who inherited the frame apartment house in Collegetown) was renting his apartments to students. After personally experiencing the problem of tracking down students who had left town with overdue rent, he required either a large security deposit from his prospective tenants or a personal guarantee from the students' parents.

It's useful to look at this case from the other side of the fence. If you're a student rooming with others and you have all signed the lease, remember that the landlord can go after any one of you for all overdue rent and/or damages. In other words, a clause that may look like "boilerplate" if you only review your lease casually may take on real meaning somewhere down the road. If you don't understand what you're reading, get advice from someone who does.

THE COMMENCEMENT DATE

From the landlord's standpoint, downtime between tenants—vacancy—is poison. But either the landlord or the tenant (or both) may find advantage in having the space empty for a short period of time. The landlord may need time to make repairs and spruce up the space. The tenant, too, may want to make changes in the space, or may have an existing lease and want to delay the start date to minimize paying double rent.

There is no one standard practice to follow in setting the commencement date. This is a negotiation that normally ends in compromise. The landlord, commonly optimistic about getting his or her own work done on or ahead of schedule, will make the case that the tenant's work should be done on the tenant's nickel. The tenant, of course, wants the space to be usable from Day One and doesn't want to agree to move out of existing space until that happens. Usually the phrase "substantial completion" or "operable completion" is used, with the landlord's architect as the arbiter. In short, both sides should be prepared for some give-and-take even after they have signed the lease.

Put less positively, don't do what *I* did recently, which was to agree on a date for a restaurant to commence paying rent a specified number of days after its liquor license transfer was approved. I had been told that forty-five days was enough to effect the transfer—but in fact, the wheels of government turned slowly, the transfer took ninety days, and I lost forty-five *additional* days of rent. In fairness, the tenant did not want to start renovations until they were positive they had their all-important license, and then they needed time to complete a significant renovation. So their premise was logical, but the outcome wasn't what I had expected.

As a landlord, your ability to finish renovations quickly is critically important. The better you are at what you do, the more tightly you'll want to schedule your renovations. Then you run directly into the reality of the contractors, most of whom "work to their deadlines." This means they put out the hottest fires first, and as a result, most of their work takes place during the last two available weeks. This can be frustrating and nerve-wracking for landlord and tenant alike.

In short, settling on the commencement date is only the first challenge on the road to occupancy. Hitting the commencement date, in many cases, is even tougher. And deciding what constitutes "substantial completion" ends up being a matter of mutual goodwill—a commodity that can sometimes be in short supply during the chaos and anxiety of a move. Building enough goodwill to get both parties over the bumps in the road is essential.

BUILDING AND PREMISES

Many leases include an attachment showing the outline of the premises to be occupied under the lease. Agreeing upon the size of the space to be leased might seem to be simple enough, but in fact, the calculation of the square footage involved can be dicey. There is no problem in the case of, say, a residential rental, where the rent is calculated on a per-unit basis. Similarly, condominium sales don't usually present a problem, because the square footage is defined by the space actually occupied.

But in the case of most commercial uses, space measurement is more of an art than a science. The Building Owners and Managers Association (BOMA) distinguishes among "gross," "rentable," and "usable" space, and those differences are spelled out in detail in the Property Types appendix. But to give a quick example of how this works in practice: I was recently in a meeting with representatives of a large bank that was contemplating leasing out some valuable retail space in its building. They talked about leasing out 20,000 square feet, which was a number calculated by their architect. I pointed out that six months earlier, they had been negotiating with a user for the same space—but at that time, they had been defining the space as consisting of 22,500 square feet. No big deal, right? Wrong! At $70 per square foot, that was a difference of $175,000 per year! Measurement (in most cases) is money. The landlord who doesn't get this fundamental piece of his or her act together will give away money.

The space efficiency of your building is also a critical concern. The ratio of public areas to rentable space depends in large part on the type of building you're operating. (A tall, slender tower tends to be much less efficient than a one-story building.) The percentage of public space to total space in the building is sometimes referred to as the "load." A 12 percent load is reasonably efficient, whereas an 18 percent load would in most cases be considered inefficient. If your building is "inefficient," then "market rates" may not be sufficient. The first challenge, again, is to figure out exactly what you've got, normally with the assistance of an architect. Your next challenge may be either to convert some public space to rentable space, or to position your building so that it commands higher-than-market rents: "The way office buildings *used* to be built!" or whatever. This will make it easier for you to add a "load factor" to your rental rates.

Load factors are relatively arcane, and most prospective tenants won't get into a discussion with you on this level of detail. But keep your measurements and calculations handy, and be prepared to share them with that unusual tenant who wants to understand exactly how you've priced the space in the building.

On the subject of public or common areas: Make sure, also, that *access to* and the *extent of* the common areas is defined. This means not only vis-à-vis your tenants, but also vis-à-vis your fellow landlords. Access is all-important, and can't always be taken for granted. A friend of mine was forced to walk away from his equity and give back a building to his lender because he lost the legal right of access to what he thought was a shared elevator bank with an adjacent building.

USE OF PREMISES

Both the landlord and tenant share a fundamental objective—to guarantee a safe and productive environment for working or living. Translating that objective into allowable uses of the premises, however, is not always easy. Under certain circumstances, either side may want to push for a broader or narrower definition.

In the retail area, for example, tenants often try to limit the ability of their competitors to lease space in the same complex, while landlords often want the continuance of particular retail uses that are synergistic with other retail uses in the property. Residential condominium purchasers may try to limit the ability of other unit owners to rent out their condos. Office tenants may or may not want a day-care center on the site, and they may resist (or welcome) medical facilities in the building.

Landlords, of course, want to retain maximum flexibility to fill their own space, while also preventing tenants from subletting to "undesirable" users. In a manufacturing context, environmental and noise issues are important. (The landlord can't allow Tenant A's noxious by-products to make life unbearable for Tenant B.) On the retail side, some potential uses need lots of parking, while others are far less parking-intensive. Again, common sense has to be invoked to head off these kinds of problems, and to resolve them when they do arise. Neither the landlord nor the tenant should give in to the temptation to throw their weight around, nor should they tolerate the intolerable. If you're a tenant, stick up for your rights as you see them. (Remember that if you ever sublet your space, you may find it helpful to have a lease with more leeway, accommodating additional kinds of business uses.) If you're a landlord with tenants who are getting too specific in trying to restrict you, remind them that what you give them, you will *certainly* have to give to others. They don't want other tenants restricting their rights.

The "use of premises" clause speaks to the short term. But it also has very real consequences for the long-term health of your building. From an operating standpoint, the landlord always has to keep in mind the image and reputation of his or her building—both to protect his or her investment, and also to protect the rights of both present and future tenants.

TERM: ORIGINAL AND EXTENDED

From a management standpoint, one of the trickiest issues is deciding how long a lease you want to write. Residential leases generally run from one to three years; other leases longer. Some of the factors to take into account are:

- Is this a landlord's or a tenant's market? Are rental rates currently above or below historic averages? How much other space do you have vacant?
- How much work has to be done and by whom? How expensive would it be for the tenant to move in the future?
- Do your lenders to the property want longer leases, especially from larger tenants, to secure their cash flow?
- Are lease expirations in this particular case running in parallel with those of other tenants—and in particular, adjacent tenants? You want to provide future leasing flexibility for others as well.

Price is probably the most important factor, for most tenants; but as a landlord, you never underestimate how much value a tenant may see in an option to extend. From a tenant's standpoint, in fact, the ideal would be a one-year lease with 100 one-year options to extend.

In practice, it is not uncommon to sign a three-, five-, or ten-year lease with one or two options, and with one year's notice to exercise that option. The logic for granting such extensions is based upon bargaining power, improvements made to the space, and need for flexibility with regard to other tenants. Retail tenants may place a special interest in the right to stay put, on the assumption that their sales are driven in part by the specific location.

Tenants also may request options to expand into particular spaces, or ask for rights of first refusal on specific adjacent spaces. This is a difficult and critically important juggling act for the landlord. You need to accommodate the legitimate needs of your ongoing or new tenants; at the same time, you need to retain enough flexibility to be able to make attractive deals for future tenants.

Fast-growing firms sometimes want special considerations. For example, they may want a cancellation clause linked to the landlord's ability to provide expansion space when it's needed. (In other words, if you can't provide more space, they have the right to bail out of their lease.) Up to twelve months' notice is common. Many leases are written to award the landlord a cash penalty if the cancellation clause is exercised, especially if special tenant improvements were made to the space.

In negotiating with tenants, remember that tenants generally retain the right to sublet if they want to leave early. This sounds ominous, but it is bounded by some practical realities. For example: There may not be enough time left on the lease to appeal to a sublessee. In such a case, you should work with the departing tenant and a potential successor to write a new and longer lease. (This may generate profits—a topic discussed below.) Remember: Your goal is to keep your building occupied.

BASE AND ADDITIONAL RENT

First-time renters are often surprised that the rent isn't listed first on a lease. After all (they reason), it's the first question you ask, and—if wrangling is appropriate—the issue you wrangle the most over.

In one sense, the initial rent is market-driven, and reflects both the quality of the space and the range and quality of services provided by the landlord. In another sense, "rent" is in a sense an aggregate figure, combining the answer to five questions which may or may not be the subject of negotiations:

- Who performs and pays for improvements to the premises?
- What additional charges (and increases in charges) for services should be paid for by the tenant?
- What step-ups in rent should occur over the course of the lease?
- Should existing tenants get special treatment?
- How will real estate taxes be handled?

Who should pay for tenant improvements? Unfortunately, there's no simple answer. In some cases, the tenants are entirely on their own. Again, some measure of common sense has to prevail. The condition of the building and its systems will influence whether the landlord should absorb certain costs that will bring the property to a certain level. (I'll return to this issue under the "landlord's work" clause.)

In other cases, the landlord gives a specific per-square-foot or dollar allowance to a tenant. Any costs above that amount are either paid for directly by the tenant, or are paid for by the landlord and amortized over the term of the lease.

In this scenario, the landlord may ask for interest on the balance of the amount being amortized. It's important for both parties to realize, however, that for tax purposes, these improvements normally have to be amortized over a longer time frame (27.5 years for residential and 39 years for commercial property) than the term of the lease. In other words, it's very likely that the landlord will have to pay taxes on the income received as reimbursement, and these will more than offset the depreciation deduction. As an example: payments to amortize a $100,000 improvement on a ten-year office lease would result in $10,000 of income with an offsetting depreciation deduction of only $2,640.

Multiple factors go into the determination of "base rent" versus "additional charges." There is no simple rule that determines what should be included in which category. In apartments and office buildings, most services except electricity are included (although tenants may be responsible for costs above a certain dollar-per-square-foot level, especially in office buildings with longer lease terms). Shopping center tenants are accustomed to being charged a common-area maintenance fee encompassing all operating costs. Many warehouse leases are net, with the tenant paying all operating costs. In buildings where there are multiple tenants, certain costs may be allocated.

Landlords want to keep their own costs under control, especially over the longer term, and therefore are inclined to charge everything possible to their tenants. Tenants, of course, want both fairness and predictability when it comes to charges. Both sides want the property properly and efficiently run; the question is, who pays for the component parts of a good operation? Some issues are more debatable than others. Can management costs be considered a billable item? (If so, what percentage?) Landlords and tenants may disagree on this one. On the other hand, most tenants agree that increases in real estate taxes—over which the landlord has no control—should be picked up proportionately by the tenants. The overall goal is for both parties to agree upon a clear definition of who pays for what and when.

Rent step-ups (that is, rent increases not tied to increased operating expenses) involve different kinds of calculations. The tenant would like a fixed rent over the entire lease period, while the landlord would like an ever-larger return on the asset itself. (The landlord's logic is that the asset is increasing in value over time, and the landlord is entitled to a return on that increase.) But again, this is the stuff of negotiation. Tenants may agree to significant step-ups in later years of the lease in order to keep rents low in the first year. In the case of retail tenants, it's common to link rent increases to growth in the tenant's sales above a certain level. This is known as a "percentage rent" clause. In theory, it's a sensible approach; in practice, such clauses are easier to enforce with large, national tenants than with the corner grocery store.

As for setting rent during option periods, the norm is to pay the higher of two figures: the rent in the last year of the current lease, or some percentage (often 90 percent) of current market rates for similar space elsewhere. This can present some difficulties: Even though there is often good rental information available for a given locale from local brokers, each rental is a custom transaction, and defining an "average" current market rate may be problematic. An alternative is to tie rent increases to a larger index, such as a national (or regional) cost-of-living index.

This is a good time to reinvoke the idea that the tenant is the landlord's *customer.* Landlords should not let themselves lose a good tenant. The cost of replacing a good tenant can be high, in terms of time and money. (If you're a good tenant, this is your leverage.) Even for apartment or warehouse tenants, where a change in tenants may necessitate only cosmetic improvements, there are often leasing costs or downtime between tenants. Other uses—retail, restaurants, and so on—create much larger exposures. There can be considerable downtime between occupancies, since specialized uses (such as the restaurant in my building, mentioned earlier) require special "fit-out." Turnover is inevitable, and from a landlord's perspective, turnover is only good if (1) you have a bad tenant, and (2) the tenant has locked in below-market rates. Even in the latter case, however, my inclination is almost always to try to keep good tenants, even if their rent is somewhat below market. No matter how logical an existing tenant's layout may appear to be, somehow it is never quite right for the next tenant.

So rent is important. But what's *more* important (within the bounds of reasonable compensation) is a good working relationship with your tenants. Negotiate fairly at the outset, and stay fair. In some cases, tenants will need to expand or contract during the course of their lease. The way in which they perceive you and your building will affect their decision making, and give you the chance to renegotiate, if necessary.

Collaboration can be a lifesaver, and this can go both ways. When a good tenant hits short-term cash-flow problems, I sometimes defer rent, at least the first time. Am I crazy? Not really. I will never forget the dark days of the 1970s when the oil crisis resulted in a tripling of energy costs almost overnight. I was then (and am still) the co-owner of a 250,000-square-foot, multitenant industrial complex, and I was stuck with long-term, fixed-rate leases that included all electricity costs. I was getting killed, to put it mildly. I went to each tenant individually to explain my predicament. Something like 95 percent of my tenants agreed to pick up the added costs voluntarily—concessions that saved the building for us. Many of those tenants are still with us today. I continue to be grateful for their cooperation, and I know I think about tenants differently as a result of that experience.

I mentioned real estate taxes earlier, and noted that landlords can generally pass these costs along to tenants. An alternative is for the landlord to seek a tax abatement, if he or she thinks the property has been overassessed. But this is not without risk. Most landlords see a long-term advantage in maintaining good relations with the local assessors, and challenging their conclusions through the abatement process on every possible occasion may work against that long-term goal.

Most assessors require annual operating statements from property owners, and will perform an overall reassessment of properties every three years. It's important to remember that in the current economic environment, communities are caught in a bind. Municipal expenses keep going up, in part as a result of federal and state government cutbacks in more or less important services. Many of these services are being picked up by local governments—but local voters, whose property taxes pay for this "expanded government," have become increasingly unhappy with their residential property-tax burden. Few officials want to run for office after a major increase in residential property taxes—and yet, they need more money. The trend, therefore, has been to tax commercial property at a higher rate than residential property, and to push aggressively for higher commercial assessments.

Obviously, if your tenants are picking up all or most of these increases, you won't experience any cash-flow discomfort. But in most cases, your tenants also expect *you* to be aggressive, when it comes to controlling their costs. Just sitting back and passing big tax increases along may not be an adequate response. And remember that when your current leases roll over, market conditions may be such that *you* will wind up eating some or all of these costs.

So what can you, as a commercial property owner, do to minimize the impact on yourself and your tenants? First, work as closely as possible with the assessors when they make their periodic reassessments. That is the best time to make the case that either your income is below what they are projecting, or that you are being taxed to a disproportionate degree vis-à-vis your neighbors. Whether you do this yourself, or hire a local attorney to do it for you, depends upon your level of familiarity with the process and with the local community. If you are an outsider, it's almost certainly better to hire a local attorney to represent you in this process.

Determining a "fair" assessment is as difficult as putting the "right" price on a property that's coming up for sale. The problem is greatly compounded by the political pressures that can be brought to bear on the assessor's decision. And governments are prone to adopt a short-term fix by overassessing, even in the knowledge that they'll have to pay later. Delaying abatements in practice makes it easier to balance the local budget, at least in the short run. My experience, though, is that in most communities, especially in the suburbs, assessors try to be fair and if you cooperate with them and furnish good information, they will be forthright in dealing with you. Generally, they will explain what rental and expense assumptions are built into their calculations. Don't forget that they are entitled to use *current* rental rates—not those in your leases, which may be above or below market.

If the assessors turn you down, you can always appeal to the courts. Up until the point when your case gets to court, the cost of such an appeal to each side is minimal. Don't be surprised, however, if your case isn't heard for years. (It will not be a priority in a clogged judicial system.) I've also discovered that it is usually just when the case is about to go to trial that settlement talks begin to get productive. Meanwhile, it may be a good idea to keep your tenants informed of your progress. If you're looking out for their interests, they should know about it.

PARKING

The two main negotiable issues covered by the parking clause are (1) the number of spaces allocated, and (2) whether or not these spaces are assigned (and if so, where). Depending upon the type of property and its use, zoning regulations commonly require a landlord to have a certain number of spaces per residential unit or a certain number per 1,000 square feet of floor area for other uses. (Residential may require 1.5 to 2 spaces per unit, depending upon the location and size of the units.) A regional shopping center, for example, may require 4.5 to 5 spaces per thousand, an office building in the suburbs may need three to four, and a warehouse or a downtown office building near good public transportation may call for only one space for each thousand square feet.

The easiest approach is for a landlord to allocate spaces proportionately among tenants. This is "fair," but it may not solve all of your problems. For example, in the case of older properties where parking isn't up to current codes, there is likely to be a shortage. Some tenants are likely to have an above-average number of workers per square foot, and may therefore request more spaces. In a downtown building, a strong tenant may make its lease conditional on the provision of extra spaces for key executives.

As a rule, my preference is not to assign specific spaces to specific tenants. Not everyone will be using all their spaces all the time anyway, and in my experience, keeping spaces unassigned "creates" about 20 percent more spaces. Second, declining to assign spaces dodges the issue of who gets the spaces closest to the building. (The early bird gets them.) Third, the lack of assigned spaces frees you from the operational headache of policing the lot—for example, when Tenant A grabs a space in Tenant B's section. Take it from me: Without fail, the first car you tow will belong to the CEO of your biggest tenant. You will wind up paying the tow charges, and also for that mysterious dent in the hood.

More efficient striping of the lots, and especially the creation of compact-car sized spaces, can add to your overall total. More spaces is better, of course; but for those of us living in the north, it's important to make sure that we have enough space for piling up the aftermath of the occasional blizzard.

TENANT'S AND LANDLORD'S OBLIGATIONS

These clauses get us back to what is required, according to the terms of the lease. In the context of rent, I've already discussed the issue of who pays for what services. The next related question—who provides the services?—depends in large part upon the nature of the tenant's business. In manufacturing, retail, and residential uses, the landlord is rarely responsible for cleaning or repairing anything other than common areas, while many office tenants don't want (or expect) to have to worry about cleaning and repairs.

As explained in Chapter 6, the landlord almost always is responsible for structural repairs, generally including roofs. In some cases, however, roof repairs can be included under "general maintenance," and therefore can be charged back to the tenant. How that clause is worded, in fact, may help you decide whether to patch that roof or put on a new one.

Lots of potential improvements to a property sit in the grey area between structural repairs and tenant improvements. Yes, the landlord has some obligations to provide handicapped access and life-safety equipment—but those requirements may stop short of the tenant's expectations. Depending upon the age and condition of the building and the negotiating powers of the parties, the landlord may be able to include in "expenses" an amortization of some of these capital improvements, as well as capital expenditures that result in lower operating costs. The landlord will push to define marginal expenses as operating expenses, and the tenant will push to define them as capital expenditures. And like many other things, this becomes the stuff of negotiations.

Next question: What happens if the parties do not meet their obligations? Suppose some more or less vital building system fails. The tenant understandably wants his or her leak fixed, the HVAC system working, the space cleaned properly and promptly, and so on. Tenants may become impatient enough with a slow-moving landlord to want to bring in their own carpenters, HVAC specialists, or whomever to solve the problem—and then attempt to bill the cost to the landlord. Obviously, landlords don't want expenses generated over which they have no control; equally important, they don't want outsiders who are unfamiliar with the property mucking about in the building's innards. For these reasons and others, "self-help" clauses for tenants are generally resisted by landlords.

Again, if relationships are good, both sides will work together to help meet each other's needs. For their part, tenants have to recognize that solving the problem at hand may not be a simple task. Like the construction industry, the "repair industry" (in which I'll include all the tradespeople listed just above, and many others) is highly fragmented. It consists of a number of small, generally underfinanced firms that for the most part have very limited capacities. In the wake of a major rainstorm, a roofer (even a *bad* roofer!) may be hard to find. The day after an arctic cold front moves in, a heating specialist may be the scarcest commodity in town. Yes, an established owner who does a lot of business with a given subcontractor probably has a better chance of getting results than an individual tenant. But as anybody who owns a house knows, repairmen work on *their* schedule, not yours. Tenants have to be patient—up to a point.

Tenants should also understand that how their landlord behaves may be a direct result of that landlord's available cash. The first day into a crisis is far too late for the tenant to be discovering that their building is "broke" (in the financial sense of the word). If the tenant suspects that this is the case, he or she should push hard to get the landlord to commit to a satisfactory schedule for resolving the crisis—and make it clear that failure to deliver according to this schedule may lead directly to an illegal withholding of rent, which neither party can afford. The tenant may be forced to pay the rent, but the landlord will still have to solve the problem.

Tenants, too, have to look to the kinds of problems that *they* cause. Because they send in a single rent check—and not forty, or four hundred—a given tenant tends to see itself as a single entity, rather than a collection of forty or four hundred employees. From the landlord's perspective, however, a tenant can have many heads. Some like it hot, and some like it cold—and the landlord may spend a great deal of time solving "problems" that amount to differences in personal tastes. One solution is for the tenant to name one individual as a liaison with the landlord, who has responsibility—among other things—for picking and choosing among the kinds of issues that will be brought to the landlord's attention.

And tenants have to play it straight, refraining from kidding either themselves or their landlords. Recently, we had a major fight with a small, two-year-old high-tech tenant. This company's research director insisted on smoking in our smoke-free lobby, which irritated other tenants in the building. Meanwhile, this same character regularly abused our cleaning people, and once called our maintenance supervisor at home at midnight because a fluorescent bulb was out. Despite our regular (and intensifying) complaints, our tenant simply refused to rein in this obnoxious person. When I read one morning in the paper that the company was being sold to a French firm for more than $300 million, I understood what had really been going on: This R&D guy was simply too important to risk irritating, and so his employers had let him run wild at our expense.

COMPLIANCE WITH LAWS

In the previous section, I introduced the question of who pays to redress a violation of an existing code or law, or to meet the standards imposed by a new code or law. One sensible approach would be to agree that if the problem existed before the tenant's occupancy, it is the landlord's problem; if the problem arises while the tenant is in the building, the problem belongs to the tenant, especially if the problem is created (or exacerbated) by the tenant's use of the premises. For example, suppose a tenant remodels the premises to an extent which "triggers" the installation of new handicapped-accessible bathrooms, or requires a new (or larger) sprinkler system—situations that were "grandfathered" until the new building permit was filed.

My general rule is that tenants are responsible for meeting all obligations caused by their own use, and I write that into my leases. On the other hand, if the tenant makes capital improvements that stand to benefit me over a period longer than the lease—such as these new bathrooms—I might share in the cost, regardless of what the lease says. An improved space will make this tenant more likely to renew, and will make the next tenant more likely to sign up. This is a good investment.

ENVIRONMENTAL

It was not many years ago that landlords were required to begin meeting new and tougher environmental standards, which comprised not only preventive measures but also remediation of existing environmental problems. For the most part, these standards were set by regulators with good intentions, and with only a secondary concern about the perspective of the property owner. This led to well-founded grumbling from the real estate community. The grumbling got louder when it became clear that the diffuseness of these standards meant that the bulk of the money expended by landlords would be spent on lawyers and engineers, rather than the cleanups themselves.

That having been said, many existing environmental problems pose real hazards, and must be cleaned up—which means that someone has to pay the piper. For the regulators to identify the relative responsibilities of past and current landlords would be unworkable, and would further delay the necessary cleanup. From the standpoint of the lease, we again can conclude that continuing problems from an earlier day are the landlord's responsibility, and that new problems caused by the tenant belong to that tenant.

The best way to avoid a new problem is to avoid signing up the kind of tenant who is likely to create such a problem. The relevant laws are complex, and I for one have never understood all the legal references to specific statutes in the lease document. (My lawyer assures me that they are all important.) But based on unpleasant personal experiences, I'd have two suggestions for landlords looking at potentially toxic tenants. First, go see the tenant's current space. Get a clear sense of what this business is about, what risks are involved, and what steps the tenant is currently taking to mitigate those risks. Second, make sure that your lease specifies that if your tenants create environmental problems, they will be responsible not only for the cleanup of those problems, but also for any legal, engineering, or other costs incurred by you not only in the process of the cleanup, but in the investigation of the problem. Remember: In many cases, these fees can cost more than the cleanup itself.

Remember, too, that environmental violations affect not only relations between you and your tenant and you and the regulatory community—but also between you and your lenders, current and future. To put it simply, no lender will touch you if you have a serious environmental problem. And the relevant laws are so complex, and so unevenly enforced, that lenders will almost always err on the side of caution. (These laws are so complex, in fact, that your own lawyer may not want to talk to you without first consulting a specialist in environmental law.)

In short, when it comes to environmental issues, a landlord can't be too careful. Think of all kinds of ways to be careful.

INSURANCE

This clause defines who is responsible for what when there's a fire or other extraordinary damage to the building, and also who is responsible for what's known as "public liability" (for example, when someone slips and falls on the sidewalk leading up to the building). In terms of fire and similar kinds of damage, the lease generally distinguishes between the building (which is covered by the landlord's insurance) and the tenant's personal property (which is not covered by the landlord's policies). When tenant-funded improvements to the premises are damaged or destroyed, insurance payments for that damage generally go the landlord if the landlord retains the improvements at the expiration of the lease. (It would be a foolish landlord, however, who failed to apply that money toward restoring the damaged improvements.) In most insurance clauses, both sides agree not to sue the other for damages—except, of course, in the case of gross negligence—if covered by their own insurance.

If your tenant leases, your policy with your insurer, or your agreement with your lender requires the space to be restored to its precasualty condition, make sure there is a waiver of depreciation by your insurer in determining how much you are reimbursed. Replacing space after a few years of use could cost a multiple of your original cost.

It's especially important (for both parties) for the agreement to stipulate explicitly that *no matter what the problem,* neither party can seek what are called "consequential damages" (such as loss of business or profits) from the other. Think hard about defining what kinds of damages will be covered by your respective insurance policies. For example, is water a problem if you don't live in hurricane country? Answer: absolutely, even if you live in the desert! Sprinkler pipes that burst, or are activated by smoke or heat, can cause as much damage as they prevent.

Speed may be of the essence, especially from the tenant's point of view. The tenant probably carries some sort of insurance against interruption of business—just as the landlord is probably insured against an interruption of rents—but these policies are mainly designed to minimize short-term losses. Looking longer term, most tenants can't afford to lose customers or employees, and therefore want to get back in business just as quickly as possible. Some businesses can relocate temporarily more easily than others, and some real estate markets provide interim spaces more readily than others. But most tenants would prefer not to vacate in the first place, and want to get back into their space quickly.

Lease negotiations should focus, among other things, on how much of the space has to be damaged or taken by eminent domain for the tenant to be off the rental hook. Similarly, they should define the circumstances under which the landlord can demolish (or elect not to repair) the property. Think broadly about these issues, at least the first time you think them through. Think simply, too: At what point does the property become unusable, from the tenant's point of view? Think about partial catastrophes and reversals: What happens if the damage (or the necessary repair) results in a taking of some or all of the parking lot or common areas?

Often, a threshold of 25 percent of the space being damaged makes a lease cancelable, unless the damage is repaired within an allowed timeline, say, between four and six months. The problem is that both sides need a concrete set of numbers to sign on to—but the reality, in the wake of a major disruption, is rarely so cut and dried. More often, defining when "25 percent of a space" is damaged is a judgment call, and requires outside consultations. In such situations (often exacerbated by emotion and very real financial pressures), the tenant should remember that the landlord's actions may be governed wholly or in part by the demands of the insurance companies and the lenders involved. The landlord, in effect, may wind up taking orders from these outside parties.

And it needs to be said: Aggressive landlords and tenants sometimes use these unhappy circumstances to get out of, or at least renegotiate, an above- or below-market rental lease. My advice would be that the day after lightning has struck is not the time to go down this difficult road.

The best way to resolve these kinds of catastrophes is to do everything in your power to prevent them. If you're a landlord, check your buildings to make sure that they meet current fire safety codes. Visit your tenants in person to see if any obvious hazards are brewing. If there's a good potential that nonobvious hazards are brewing, bring in an expert. (Are electrical systems

"Negligence" is a grey area, as indicated above. If either party is willfu or grossly negligent and thereby damages the other party, they should p That's easy enough to say, and agree to. But I've never understood how o defines the various levels of negligence, so let's hope that none of us is e involved in such a suit. If it comes to that, get out your insurance policy a call your insurance agent and your lawyer.

Landlords should carry, and should require their tenants to carry, l bility and business-interruption insurance, although the amount is up negotiation. (As a landlord, make sure that you review the tenant's ins ance policies to ensure that they conform to the lease, and make sure keep a copy of these policies.) Similarly, the landlord may want the right require tenants to increase their liability coverage under certain circu stances over time. Again, this is grounds for negotiation.

A word about insurance agents: A good insurance agent not only can h you obtain good prices, but can also advise you about what coverages should have. Review your policies periodically. Property owners and manag often spend considerable time working out initial coverages, and then fo about their policies and let them get out of date. Here's one measure of y insurance agent: Does he or she call *you* and suggest it's time for a review?

DAMAGE TO PREMISES AND EMINENT DOMAIN

First, an old story about a serious topic: Two relatively young guys strike a conversation at an exclusive yacht club in South Florida. It turns out they're both retired, and they both keep their yachts at this particular c Eventually, the conversation gets around to how they wound up there. first says he had a fire in his building, collected the insurance, and reti The second guy says he had a flood, collected the insurance, and retired.

The first guy looks puzzled, thinks for a minute or two, and then a "But how do you make a *flood?*"

You obviously can't make a flood, and I'm certainly not advocating you set a fire (!). But you must be protected against potentially catastro scenarios. What happens if all hell breaks loose, and there's an earthqu and the building is so badly damaged that people have to evacuate, t porarily or permanently? What happens if the local government dec that your property must be taken by eminent domain? In case of fire, repairs something that is damaged, how long do they have to comp their work, and at what point does the landlord or tenant have the rig cancel the lease?

overloaded? What's that whiff of a burning smell in the air?) This is one of the few rules that I don't have to qualify: *Prevention is best.* If you do have a loss, get a good fire adjuster. They know more than you do about what the insurance company will and won't agree to cover, and the insurance company will usually cover the expense of that adjuster in making the final settlement.

In the case of eminent domain, be prepared for the public authority to take forever to decide whether or not to condemn. (Meanwhile, of course, your property is depreciating rapidly and your tenants are heading for the hills.) Even after the seizure—if it comes—the government will be slow in proposing a reasonable settlement; when the first offer comes, it will be too low; and a final settlement may be delayed for years. In short, eminent domain is a rat hole and a time sink, out of which few landlords emerge whole. Fortunately, it's an extremely rare event.

Have I persuaded you that prevention is the best policy?

DEFAULT BY TENANT OR LANDLORD

There are basically two kinds of default: monetary and nonmonetary. The more important of these is monetary default. The lease generally calls for the rent to be paid on the first of the month in advance. (Certain charges for additional rent may be billed monthly or quarterly.) But what happens if the rent isn't paid on time? In theory, the landlord usually has the right to cancel the lease upon ten days' notice, and may also have the right to charge interest or a penalty.

In practice, few landlords will be that draconian. Very likely, there will be no consequences if the rent occasionally comes in late in the first week, and into the second week of the month. But in my experience, the occasional late payment has a habit of becoming a routine. Meanwhile, you (as the landlord) most likely need this money to meet your own monthly obligations. I therefore keep an eye on payment patterns, and try to "train" tenants to pay their rent promptly. The best training is to set a good example: When it comes time to crack the whip, call quickly about an overdue rent payment. ("It's the fifth of the month. Can I expect the rent check today?") Calculating and sending out your bills for additional rents promptly, and following up on them, has the same general effect.

Keep in mind that you may be looking at the first crack in the dam. For a tenant in financial difficulty, as more and more months of rent become past due, the less and less likely it is that this tenant ever will be able to climb back out of this financial hole.

This leads naturally (and unfortunately) to the question of enforcing the landlord's rights in the case of a bankruptcy. As a landlord, don't take much comfort from the fact that your lease seems to have lots of sentences in it giving you rights in the event of a bankruptcy. Bankruptcy, by and large, protects the tenant. The law tends to favor the "little guy" over the "big guy," in cases like this. Eventually, you probably will regain control of your space, but in most cases judges will give tenants ample time to reorganize their affairs, and continue or reject your lease, even if the rent is below market. Meanwhile, during this process, the value of your property is impacted, and the process can run from six to twelve months or longer.

The brightest spot in this generally bleak picture is that your monthly rent must be paid during the period post-bankruptcy, up until the point when the tenant decides whether or not to continue the lease. In the case of residential tenants in default but not yet in bankruptcy, those tenants whom you sue are generally allowed to "cure" (or correct the default) by the act of paying their back rent. This is often true for commercial tenants, as well.

One moral of this story, as you might expect, is not to let your tenants get behind. Collections are time consuming, expensive to prosecute, and rarely make you whole—no matter *what* it says in the lease. I have even seen cases where landlords have ended up paying tenants who are in default to leave. It's easy to exaggerate the scope of this problem, however. The overwhelming majority of tenants pay their rent promptly. (After all, rent is just one of their expenses—usually no more than 4 to 6 percent of total costs.) Most have no more interest than you do in getting into legal squabbles. And as I confessed earlier, on very rare occasions, I've been known to cut a tenant some slack under adverse circumstances—especially if they're brave enough to advise me in advance about some impending problem they're facing, and it's the first time. As I tell my students, Aunt Agatha's untimely death can be used only once a term to excuse a late paper.

The other type of default, nonmonetary default, pertains to other obligations in the lease, particularly the obligation of the landlord to provide certain services, on the one hand; and the obligation of the tenant to keep up the space and behave properly, on the other. Usually, either party will have twenty to thirty days after being notified of a problem to remedy it. (There are numerous circumstances, however, under which the cure requires more time, and if the offending party can demonstrate that it is doing its best to resolve the problem, more time is generally granted.) Generally speaking, these kinds of problems almost always get solved a little slower than either side would like, but almost always *do* get resolved amicably, in less than twenty to thirty days. In fact, I can't remember a single instance in which I've gone to court over a nonmonetary issue.

Sometimes the clause will state that if one party does something wrong, the other can take steps to cure the default. As explained above, landlords have real concerns about "self-help" clauses in a lease, because the tenant may not be cost-conscious, may not worry adequately about the quality of a repair, and may not be realistic about the time needed to fix a given problem. Lenders definitely do not approve of clauses that impact payment of the rent. Keep this in mind: Regardless of what the lease says, if tenants are *really* frustrated with your apparent inaction, they will make the repairs themselves, they will deduct the costs of those repairs from their rent, and you will wind up paying for it in one way or another. So don't get into this situation, if you can possibly avoid it.

And finally, keep in mind that all bets are off if there are (1) strikes or (2) "acts of God." This is another phrase that gives some potential tenants pause, but floods, hurricanes, and blizzards do happen, even in idyllic eastern Massachusetts.

SECURITY DEPOSITS

The amount of the security deposit should depend on the credit of the tenant, the ease of rental of the space, and the nature and extent of any special work paid for by the landlord. The knowledge that a security deposit may hang in the balance also encourages departing tenants to clean up their premises at the end of their leases.

In the case of commercial leases, a guarantee based on a letter of credit—which is generally for one year, with provisions for forfeiture if not renewed prior to the expiration date—may be an acceptable substitute for a deposit. Residential properties often have a standard deposit of one month's rent. There are rarely legal limits on what you can demand for security, and you should ask for what's actually needed. (The tighter the rental market, of course, the more leverage the landlord has, but "gouging" is silly in any case.) A startup bio-tech company with special plumbing requirements, for example, may really have to put down six months' rent in order to give you the security you feel you need, while one month may be sufficient for a triple-A credit risk.

From a tenant's standpoint, keep in mind that it is likely that the landlord will commingle your security deposit with other funds, unless of course your state requires that residential deposits be segregated. If these funds are indeed commingled, make sure that the landlord is creditworthy, and also verify that future owners would be obligated to return your deposit. You may or may not be paid interest on your deposit, so be prepared to negotiate this point.

SUBORDINATION, ESTOPPEL CERTIFICATES, NONDISTURBANCE

We discussed these items in earlier chapters, in the context of closing a sale. Both present and future landlords, as well as the participating lenders, have a right to know of any unmet obligations on the part of any participants in the deal.

From the tenant's vantage point, it's a very good idea to get a nondisturbance agreement from the *lender.* Such an agreement says that the tenant's lease will not be canceled without cause if a foreclosure occurs, although the lender may not agree to make good any prior landlord defaults. Usually if a property is in trouble and the lender takes over, the overall market will be weak, and the lender will be happy to continue a tenant's lease. It never hurts to have this kind of thing in writing, though. Your landlord may be surprised, but may also respect your thoroughness. The lender will determine the legal form of the agreement.

There should be no problem getting this agreement from new lenders. For existing lenders, the landlord's commitment to "using best efforts" is the norm.

SUBLETTING AND ASSIGNMENT

In renting space for longer time periods, the landlord will often agree that if the tenant's needs change or the company is sold, the tenant retains the right to sublet part or all of the space. But at the same time, the landlord does not want to relieve tenants of their obligations—especially if the subtenant or purchaser is of inferior credit. The landlord must also be concerned about the use of the space and the reputation of the proposed subtenants. Finally, the landlord needs assurances in writing that the subtenant can and will honor the lease provisions.

What a landlord can *really* lose sleep over is the situation in which a tenant makes money off a sublet because the market has improved, especially if the lease has options to extend at favorable prices. Some leases give the landlord the right to take back the space, or to share in the profit, if the tenant vacates. For their part, tenants should ensure that if they have to pay for improvements—or if they have to pay a commission to get a new tenant—those costs are reimbursed before the landlord shares in the profit. Also, if a space is being sublet only until the tenant itself needs it, the tenant does not want to lose the space to the landlord.

How this clause plays out in practice depends on the particular circumstances at hand: the condition of the market, the needs of the tenant, and so on. In any case, there is a need for a formal consent by the landlord to a sublease or assignment: the subject of the next clause.

CONSENTS

As the preceding pages have demonstrated, the landlord/tenant relationship is a complex one. Not surprisingly, there are many circumstances that call for written consents (almost always from the landlord to the tenant). The only leverage that the tenant usually holds (but only if it's written into the lease) is that this consent can not be unreasonably withheld or delayed. Landlords sometimes try to write leases that permit certain consents to be withheld from the tenant without any reason; I personally have found that a difficult position to defend, and I therefore agree in almost all cases to mutuality. The definition of "reasonable" is likely to evolve as the landlord/tenant relationship evolves.

This is a good point to emphasize once again that this relationship is all-important. Without a good landlord/tenant relationship, everything is more difficult. With one, most things are easier.

CONDITION OF PREMISES

As a landlord, you don't want arguments as to what the tenant expected the condition of the space to be like. It is important that the tenant acknowledge that they have inspected the space and have found it acceptable "as is," except as defined differently under "Landlord's work" (below) or elsewhere in the lease.

Since the burden is then on the tenant, the tenant may want the space to be inspected professionally. He or she should make sure that the landlord's responsibilities to maintain and repair the building structure and common areas, as well as the specific premises, are clearly defined in the lease, especially if the building is an old one.

TENANT IMPROVEMENTS AND LANDLORD'S WORK

These clauses often involve big money, and are integral to the rental rate. Tenants don't like to be responsible for doing construction work. (That isn't their business, in most cases.) Very few like to give a blank check to someone else to do construction work for them. But landlords, who better than anyone else know the uncertainties of operation, usually prefer to avoid these kinds of risks and headaches. Somewhere in between, the parties have to make a deal.

One question that almost always arises is the rental value of the improvements made for Tenant 1 the day after Tenant 1 vacates the premises. New tenants generally want customized layouts. Meanwhile, building codes and regulations continue to change. My back-of-the-envelope analysis always assumes that whatever Tenant 1's layout, it won't work for Tenant 2.

On the other hand, new elevators, handicapped bathrooms, new roofs, and updated lobbies do have longer lives, which neither side should be expected to pay for in their entirety. Recently, I made a deal with a tenant for a seven-year lease with a ten-year amortization of improvements. In effect, I picked up 30 percent of the costs, which struck both parties as fair.

These clauses underscore once again a key point about the real estate game: It's very important to be able to think visually, and to be able to make at least rough translations from a tenant's wish list to the realities of a tight budget. Stated another way, in order to stay competitive, you need to be able to understand the needs of a tenant and to translate those needs to your property. A prospective tenant may be looking at several buildings simultaneously. If so, you don't have weeks to go out and get quotes. Even if you (as a landlord) are giving a specific dollar build-out allowance to the tenant, the tenant will most likely want to know what, if any, extra costs will be incurred for their particular layout.

As you are carving out space in your building to meet the specific needs of a particular tenant, keep the broader picture in mind. What's the next tenant to arrive on your doorstep likely to ask for? Will what you're doing with this tenant hurt your chances to satisfy a second tenant? For example: The fewer the fixed partitions, the more flexibility you have.

The property manager needs to have an overall view of what direction he or she wants this building to take. This should be considered a "rolling" plan, subject to revision as market conditions change. When I first built an office building on Brattle Street in Harvard Square, for example, I knew that my tenants were most likely to be architects and engineers who wanted open, very basic space. This direction worked well, for the time being. But as these design-oriented tenants moved to cheaper space near MIT, I had to scramble a bit to figure out a new direction. I decided to upgrade the building to accommodate consulting and financial-service firms that were (1) in need of higher-quality space, and (2) willing to pay higher rents to get that kind of space.

Of course, that involved spending money, capital which I had accumulated over the years as a reserve for just this kind of eventuality. But to reduce my outlay as I attracted new tenants, I offered to charge them lower rents if they agreed to pay directly for some of the improvements. You or your property manager may bring in rental brokers, architects, engineers, and contractors to help with these kinds of decisions, but in the last analysis, *you* will have to make these kinds of capital-management decisions.

In most cases, a series of exhibits—with plans and specifications or a description of the work to be done—is attached to the lease itself. Remember that the *timetable* is important to both sides, and should be clearly specified. Make sure that the tenant has designated someone who is able and willing to make key decisions along the way. (Invariably, there are "field decisions" that will need to be made, most often against some kind of pressing deadline.) Don't forget to leave a reserve for future changes. A 10 percent reserve is far more realistic than a 3 percent reserve. (Talk this out ahead of time, so that both sides are comfortable with either spending or not spending the reserve.)

At best, making improvements—pricing them, carrying them out—is an imperfect process. As the landlord, you must balance the amount of rent, type and cost of improvements, length of lease, and the credit of the tenant against (1) your market options, and (2) your own cash situation.

What's the most important lesson to take away from this clause? Easy: *Hold on to your tenants!* The tenant who stays is almost never as demanding about redoing a space as the potential newcomer, especially in a weak rental market.

BROKER

Do any of the preceding pages seem at all confusing to you? If so, you can understand why the trend is not only for landlords to hire brokerage firms (to help fill their vacancies), but also for tenants to want their own representatives (to protect their interests). When both sides employ brokers, the commission is often split. If an existing tenant hires a broker to help in negotiating a lease renewal, on the other hand, that fee is often paid by the tenant.

Good brokers not only save time in finding both space and other brokers; they also help negotiate deals. Good brokers know their market, and are able to help the parties understand what's (1) important, and (2) customary.

As is true in all professions, there are good brokers and bad brokers. The bad ones, in my experience, tend to overnegotiate in order to justify their existence. The good ones just earn their fee by making things seem effortless. (They aren't.)

Brokers' fees are generally determined by practices in the area—although in a weak market, landlords may pay double commissions, just as they may bargain more in a strong market. Legally, brokers within a geographic area can't collude to set one commission rate. In practice, brokers' fees turn out to be relatively standardized within markets, although concessions are sometimes made in the case of larger deals. (This standardization is becoming more prevalent as the brokerage industry consolidates, because national firms don't want all their local brokers negotiating different arrangements.) The fee, especially on a long term lease, can be 15 to 30 percent of the first year's rent, and—although paid in cash up front—is capitalized and expensed for tax purposes over the term of the lease. The fee is only earned when the deal goes through. Many landlords pay their broker's fee upon occupancy by the tenant, although others pay it upon lease signing. The brokerage fees for renewals and option periods are often set at one-half the initial rate.

Larger property-management firms have a big enough staff to do their own rentals. Some use multiple brokerage firms; others give outside brokers an "exclusive" listing—generally for a limited time!—and let that one brokerage firm advertise and manage that account. Still others designate a lead broker, who then must sublist with others. Use whichever approach feels right in your particular situation; change approaches if it stops feeling right. Don't fall into the trap of many homeowners, who give the listing to the broker who proposes the highest selling price. (Watch how fast an unrealistically high price comes down when the actual offers come in!)

MISCELLANEOUS

At the tail end of most leases are a number of "boilerplate" clauses, such as where to send notices, details of any special arrangements between the parties, and so on. Tenants—who rarely find much to celebrate in a standard lease—should take some comfort from the fact that there is usually a "quiet enjoyment" clause back here, somewhere. This states that if the tenants do everything that is spelled out for them to do in this multipages document, they are entitled to occupy their premises in peace. "Quiet enjoyment" may be stretching it, in today's business world; but at least you'll be left alone to be busy.

THE ASSET MANAGEMENT FUNCTION

By following a sequence of standard lease clauses, we have thrown a spotlight on the individual property. This is the right power of magnification for most issues. But there are many circumstances—easily overlooked, in the crunch of owning and operating a property—in which the *business* of that property has to be carefully considered. Law firms have managing partners, whose main job it is to ensure that the *business* of their firm, as opposed to the individual cases, gets sufficient attention. As the operator of a property, you have to manage the entity that owns the property. Sometimes this is called the "asset management" function.

SELECTING A MANAGER

There are several concerns that necessarily sit outside the clauses of a lease. The first of these has to do with selecting a manager for the property. Some owners feel that self-management is the way to go, especially when it comes to smaller properties, or properties in smaller markets which might not get the necessary attention from outside managers.

When you go to outside management, the first question you're likely to encounter is that of *scale.* (We encountered this issue in Chapter 5, in our discussions of REITs.) For virtually all types of properties—office, retail, industrial, residential, and hotel—large management firms are promoting the virtues of being large when it comes to the bulk purchase of supplies, insurance, and services. These management firms also point out that there are national tenants who are inclined to deal with one agent. Finally, these management firms say, larger firms (just like themselves) often have more experience with adding services that provide extra revenue, and their reporting tends to be more timely and thorough.

The competition, which consists of smaller local management firms, claim that local firms try harder, that virtually all rentals are done at the local level, and that standardizing the purchase of supplies results in poor choices (the wrong material or equipment, or a steep price). Each side in this debate claims that they can attract more motivated managers.

Clearly, there are options here that the owner of the property has to sort out. This is done the old-fashioned way: through homework. Before you make your choice, meet not only the heads of the management firm, but also the person who will do the actual work on your building. Look at their reporting package to see if it meets your needs. Visit comparable properties that they manage for other owners, and call those owners. I've said it before, but it's amazing what you can find out simply by checking references.

When you have selected a manager, it's common to sign a contract that is generally cancelable by either party on thirty or sixty days' notice. The items covered by such a contract (see sidebar) are a good checklist for evaluating a potential or a current manager.

The two other keys to asset management are *lender relations* and *investor relations.* We will look at these separately.

DUTIES OF A PROPERTY MANAGEMENT FIRM

1. Bill and collect rent and other payments due landlord for deposit in separate account.
2. Enforce tenant obligations to landlord.
3. Operate and maintain property, including:
   - Hire, supervise, and pay employees, suppliers, and contractors.
   - Pay in a timely manner bills for utilities, insurance, real estate taxes, and services required for the property, including landlord's obligations to tenants under their leases.
   - Advise, contract for, and supervise capital expenditures agreed to by owner.
   - Comply with all codes and regulations.
   - Advise as to appropriate insurance coverage.
   - Supervise leasing of premises in cooperation with outside brokers.
   - Pay in timely manner any mortgage payments designated by owner.
   - Report any conditions requiring attention of owner.
4. Prepare and render to owner monthly, quarterly, and annual financial statements in a form agreed to by the parties. Prepare and discuss annual budgets with owner.

LENDER RELATIONS

Under the terms of the closing documents, you have almost certainly obligated yourself to make periodic payments of interest and principal plus (in some cases) a reserve for real estate taxes by a certain date (often by electronic transfer). You have also agreed to furnish annual, quarterly, and sometimes monthly reports, and meet a number of operating standards. Because your loan most likely has been (or soon will be) sold off as part of a larger package, you now have (or will soon have) a faceless individual who is responsible for answering your questions and providing you with the necessary consents. Keep in mind that this person has almost *no* authority to deviate from the loan documentation. Neither do you. File everything on time, with all the i's dotted and t's crossed. The bank might not notice an omitted report on your part when things are going well. But believe me: If times ever get dicey for you, the bank's lawyers will be quick to use any prior "default" against you, including "defaulted" reports. They will claim that they are only doing their job in asserting all of their rights—but in my experience, they seem to enjoy the process a little more than is absolutely necessary.

Your lender may have required you to establish reserves for the payment of real estate taxes, insurance, and capital expenditures. As I've said many times in the previous pages and chapters, I recommend setting aside ample reserves for capital expenditures—which leads naturally to the subject of investor relations.

INVESTOR RELATIONS

In managing a limited partnership with outside investors, there is one cardinal rule: *Do not put yourself in a position where you have to call for additional cash contributions from your partners.* How do you avoid that unholy situation? Simple: Don't distribute all your cash. Be careful what you project for future years, in terms of both looming expenditures and likely cash inflows. Many promoters and their clients get into trouble when rosy projections are made to attract investors, but such projections can only be hit in the short run by deferring maintenance.

I don't know how to make this point more forcefully, except to say it again. Limited partners may grudgingly accept a capital call in the development phase. Unless they're saints, and perhaps more than a little naive, they *won't* accept such a call in the operating stage. Although an increase in the regular cash distribution rate is positive, a decrease in the rate can be seen as signaling big trouble. Your partners don't like surprises. (If they did, they'd be in the stock market, or gold futures, or worse.) Many are accustomed to using your check to cover living expenses, or to meet their own capital obligations. If you can't perform according to your promises, you may be putting them in an untenable situation.

My suggestion is to *communicate regularly with your partners,* especially if you see significant changes or risks up ahead. Say, for example, that there are an unusually large number of leases expiring in the near future, or large and unbudgeted capital expenditures looming ahead. Call or write your partners, and tell them so. My experience is that knowledgeable partners tend to be more cooperative in a downturn. (Of course, it doesn't hurt if you have made money for them in the past.) In any case, you want to maintain a good reputation for future deals.

I'd also like to make a plea here for better year-end tax reporting at the partnership level. There is nothing more frustrating than waiting in early April for the receipt of the tax filing from a small investment that you made years ago. I have rarely seen a valid reason why a manager can't get the operating results to the accountant by early or mid February, or why the accountant can't issue the tax return by mid-March. In any case, the general partner should be able to provide a good estimate by that time.

FROM OPERATIONS TO HARVEST

In real estate, which appears to the outsider to be a solid, predictable game, the only real constant is *change.* Everything changes: the value of specific locations, tenant needs, the physical condition and functionality of a given property, the regulatory environment, and so on, and so on. Dealing with such changes over the long run—positioning and repositioning the property creatively and effectively—is probably the general partner's or asset manager's greatest operating challenge and responsibility.

And after you've wrapped yourself in glory as an operator of properties, you may well get the chance to move on to the next and final stage of the real estate game: harvesting. Refinancing and selling, and all of the colorful variations of these processes, are the topic of the next chapter. They are not easily done well. As George Bernard Shaw once said of another field of human endeavor, "Any fool can start a love affair; only a genius can end one."

CHAPTER 8

THE HARVEST

BUY low; sell high. Buy wholesale; sell retail. In both of these prescriptions for success, the real estate entrepreneur—like his or her counterpart in other entrepreneurial fields—is encouraged to think in advance about the "harvesting" phase of the business. Harvesting, which I'll define as gaining access to some of the value you've added through your successful participation in the real estate game, is the subject of this second-to-last chapter.

But harvesting is difficult. Why? In many cases, entrepreneurs go into their ventures without giving much thought to their exit strategies. In fact, many entrepreneurs (including some I've met) intend to live forever—a strategy that will enable them to keep creating value in their businesses indefinitely, and avoid any consideration of the "end game."

A second impediment to harvesting can be simple emotion (or at least inertia). People often don't want to sell the buildings into which they've poured so much of themselves. In addition, entrepreneurs are often *optimists* by nature, and nowhere is this more true than in real estate. They think that in good times, rents will continue to rise, and in bad times, rents will stabilize and rise again. Why sell a building that is only going to become more valuable and throw off more cash in the very near future?

And finally, it is often both difficult and expensive to sell a property. Capital gains taxes, for example, complicate an owner's calculations. Assume that you sold a building that proved to be a very profitable investment. After you paid the capital gains due on the property, you wouldn't have enough money to repurchase that same building. And even if you did have the resources to get back into the market, finding and buying the next good property can be a formidable challenge. Why sell Property X, and incur substantial transaction costs, when you're not totally confident that you'll be able to find anything better any time soon?

But the fact remains that in many cases, there are compelling reasons to sell. Underneath it all, real estate is a cyclical business. Locations and properties change in value. Individual circumstances of the owner may force a sale. On the positive side, better opportunities elsewhere may make an irresistible case for selling currently owned assets. Many people go into real estate in the first place in part because they don't need to start the game with much, in terms of net worth. They borrow and scrape to pull together the necessary resources to finance their first deal. Then comes the next and better opportunity—which they can't jump into without gaining access to some of the value they've already created. They can't buy "wholesale" again without first selling something else "retail."

Under certain circumstances, in other words, optimism, inertia, expense, uncertainty *should* be overcome, and a harvest *should* take place.

In this chapter, we'll look at those circumstances. I'll describe the harvesting process in real estate: why and how it's done, especially in the context of the larger economic cycle. I'll explain why real estate is a good industry for family businesses, how families in real estate sometimes get into trouble together, and how some of those problems can be headed off with good planning. Finally, I'll describe some of the ways in which real estate can be helpful in estate planning and wealth transfer.

HARVESTING: NO SIMPLE TASK

The accompanying diagram shows the real estate cycle over the past thirty years. At the risk of stating the obvious, it shows that the best buying opportunities were available when real estate markets were very bad, and that the best selling opportunities tended to arise when they were very good. This diagram might make it seem like playing the real estate game—and especially getting in and out of it—is pretty easy. Just figure out where you are in the cycle, and jump in (or out) nimbly at exactly the right moment.

One problem here, of course, is that in real life you never know exactly where you are in the cycle. Yes, there are times when supply and demand are clearly out of whack. There are times when properties are selling above replacement cost (bad time to buy!), and other times when assets are selling well below replacement costs (a good time to buy, if you have the capital). But because none of us has a crystal ball, it's easy to get your timing wrong.

REAL ESTATE CYCLES 1970–2000

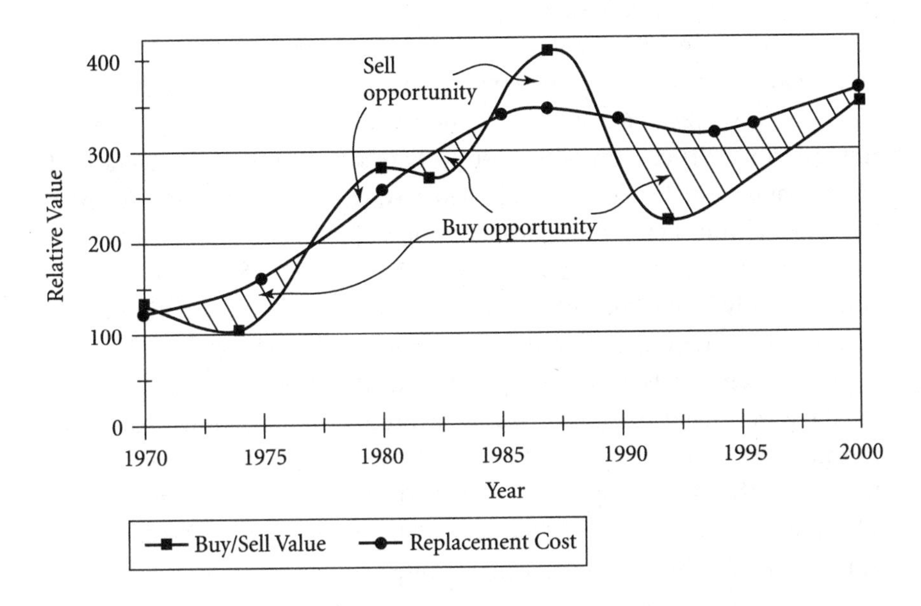

There are lots of other reasons besides greed and mistiming that can make people slow to sell their real estate. One is *transaction costs,* which we've looked at in earlier chapters. Competition has brought the cost of selling a stock way down in recent years; not so with real estate. The combination of legal costs, brokers' costs, the cost of transfer stamps (imposed at the state level), and other charges can add up to between 3 and 5 percent of the overall transaction cost. As noted earlier, transfer taxes alone in some countries outside the United States can amount to between 10 and 20 percent of the total sales price. The effective cost on your cash is even higher if you have, say, a 70 percent mortgage.

This doesn't take into account, moreover, other financing implications. Most commercial real estate loans written today have huge prepayment penalties built into them. (This is one unhappy outcome for the borrower of the trend toward securitization of real estate loans.) What it means for you is that your bank has protected itself against the loss of *any* interest spread—which means in turn that you'll most likely be required to pay any interest-rate differential if selling your property means prepaying your loan.

Another disincentive to sell, as noted above, is the *difficulty of finding your next investment.* This was an implicit message in Chapters 3 and 4: Finding and buying a good property is far from easy. Contrast this process with, for example, the process of buying a new stock. You can sell a stock on a given Tuesday morning, and buy a replacement stock almost instantaneously. Not so with real estate!

Another disincentive, and perhaps the major one for many in the real estate game over the long term, involves the *recapture of taxes on the depreciation you've already taken.* We've done this exercise before, but it's worth doing again in the context of harvesting. Let's say you buy a property for $1 million and hold for several years while your basis depreciates down to $700,000. If you then sell the property for $1.2 million, you pay a tax not only on the $200,000 of gain, but also on the $300,000 of depreciation that you've already deducted, and the tax on the recaptured depreciation is at a 25 percent rate (as opposed to the 20 percent capital gains rate).

This is a perfectly reasonable position for the government to take. After all, the government has given you the depreciation deduction at ordinary income rates—that is, up to 39 percent—over the period in question, on the theory that your property is actually depreciating. If it turns out that your property has indeed held its value, then they should be able to tax the amount previously deducted at a higher rate.

Another disincentive to sell is the frequently more attractive alternative of *recovering value through refinancing.* Going back to the example just cited: Let's assume that on the $1 million property, you had a mortgage of $600,000. Let's say further that during the time that you reduced your depreciated base from $1 million to $700,000, you also paid down your mortgage from $600,000 to $400,000. Meanwhile, your building has appreciated, and is now worth $1.2 million.

Finally, let's assume that instead of selling the property for $1.2 million, you are able to pay off your existing mortgage with no prepayment penalties and refinance it with an 80 percent loan-to-value mortgage, or $960,000. This gives you $560,000 of incremental cash ($960,000 minus the $400,000 balance on the previous mortgage). Obviously, you can use this $560,000 for any sort of investment that looks promising, including your next real estate deal.

By contrast, in the $1.2 million sale scenario, you would be required to pay a 25 percent tax on $300,000 (the depreciation) and a 20 percent capital gains tax on the remainder of the gain of $200,000, or $115,000 in overall taxes. You would walk away with $685,000 free and clear, and (for the moment at least) be out of the real estate game. By taking the refinancing route, you get access to somewhat less cash—but you avoid transaction costs (which would likely have eaten up most of the $125,000 difference). You don't need to find a new investment, and you continue to benefit from any additional increases in value that this property may experience.

So in summary: By accident and by design, the system is structured in ways that often encourage property-owners to hold on to their properties. This is distinctly different from the circumstance of individual homeowners, who are allowed to take up to $500,000 in tax-free gain on the sale of their residence. The policymakers have decided that homeowners, especially those in the later stages of life, should be allowed to escape from their now-oversized houses, and take some or all of their gains with them, thus freeing up homes for the next generation.

Not so with commercial real estate! And for the most part, there is no commercial equivalent of the "burning of the mortgage" celebration that middle-aged homeowners enjoy so much. Most commercial real estate is not debt-free—and if it is, it is likely to be viewed as an asset that is only awaiting the right moment to be releveraged. On the commercial side, that is how the real estate game is played.

Let me add one more disincentive to the sale of real estate: cultural tradition. In many European cultures, for example, land and buildings are seen as the one constant—the one thing that can survive even hyperinflation. In our country, we forget the possibility that inflation may heat up. Should it erupt, property owners would do relatively well in the longer term. Ask the Grosvenor family, whose estate owns a high percentage of the land that the city of London is built upon, and who have owned some of their English properties since 1066. The tradition of holding the land has served the Grosvenors well.

SO WHY HARVEST?

If the system (and in some cases, the culture) discourages sales, why do people sell? Again, there are several answers.

The most important of these has already been introduced: In the real estate game, you often need to free up capital to make your next deal possible. From buying wholesale to selling retail to buying wholesale again: This is a proven value-creation formula in real estate. A second reason to sell is an assessment that the market may be peaking. This was our impression in Groton, at the time we sold. Electric Boat, a leading employer in the area, was just starting to lay off people, and the long-term prospects of the defense industry seemed doubtful. It was this concern about the overall market—and the local market in particular—that led us to search for buyers.

Another pair of players from earlier chapters was Sam Plimpton and Dan Prigmore, who run the real estate assets in the strategic value fund that invested in the Lowell manufacturing facility. That facility was only one of a large number of properties that the pair had purchased for the fund in the early to mid 1990s. Plimpton had an interesting motto, that he invoked regularly in the mid 1990s: "If I'm not willing to buy at the price I can sell, I'm a seller." By 1997, they had sold many of these properties, and reinvested the proceeds in both U.S. and European properties. Their assessment was that some European markets were at their lows, even as the United States had strongly recovered. Through years of market research, cultivation of relationships, and some unsuccessful bids, they (along with a third partner) had identified several European assets that could be purchased at bargain prices. With the help of Tom Blumenthal, one of the fund's other partners, they were able to cope with currency-hedging challenges, cross-border financings, tax complications, and controlling and motivating their local partner.

I've also let the JBG Properties story unfold over several previous chapters. JBG was the redeveloper of Twinbrook Metro—a large, multibuilding complex they purchased from Equitable. After several years of profitable operation, JBG considered the state of the market and decided that the public companies (especially the REITs) were paying a premium for buildings. Beyond that, JBG realized that public companies would pay an ever greater premium for *groups* of buildings, because that would allow them to build asset size more quickly. Based on this analysis, JBG packaged Twinbrook Metro with some eighteen other properties and (with the help of an investment banker) put this entire package out to bid. A highly reputable company—Trizec-Hahn—came in with a bid that was even higher than JBG expected, and the deal was quickly consummated.

The same kinds of market signals can be heard in less grandiose settings. In the mid to late 1980s, as mentioned in a previous chapter, I found myself unable to bid successfully on almost *anything.* Each time I went to buy something, I was outbid by at least 20 percent. There were only two possible conclusions: Either my assessments of these properties was too low, or my competitors' assessments were too high. I decided that I either had to change my approach or sell—and sell I did.

Discretionary sales, based more on a view of the market than a need for cash, must overcome *inertia,* among other things. In many cases, it's easier to find reasons to sit tight than to find the will to entertain the idea of such a sale. But as a player of the real estate game, you have to be prepared to overcome your own inertia—and any other factors that argue against a sale—when the market *demands* that you sell.

There are many other circumstances that may necessitate a sale, including external forces. During the late 1980s and early 1990s, for example, overleveraged property owners were selling under duress. You'll recall that this was the period in which banks with extensive real estate exposures had gotten into deep trouble and were calling loans left and right. Many were forced to sell their properties at the worst possible point in the market cycle simply because the banks were unwilling or unable to roll over their mortgages.

In Chapter 5, I explained the origins of the most recent wave of REITs. In the 1990–92 period, a number of regional shopping center developers were determined to hold on to their malls in the face of the banks' urgent demands for repayment. In the regional mall business, the development and operational sides are most complex, and most tenants—who tend to be national—insist on experienced operators. In this corner of the real estate industry, *size* is important. One would not want to sell off a major percentage of one's portfolio. Thus, these mall owners went public, taking in additional equity capital that they then used to pay down their bank loans. In a sense, these REITs—adopting the UPREIT formula, which allowed them to continue to defer taxes—used a kind of refinancing gambit to *avoid* a premature harvest in which they didn't particularly want to participate.

Sometimes you sell because you've made a mistake, and it's time to pull the plug. When we discovered the duck manure in the river alongside our Long Island property—and also began having trouble with the local planning board—we decided that it was time to bail out. In that case, as noted, we got our money back, but we surely didn't recover anything for the many hours we had spent trying to make that project work. But when something can't be made to work, you really only have two choices: (1) waste more time and money, or (2) bail out. We bailed.

Sometimes you sell because differences have arisen among the partners in a deal. The more partners you have in your deal, the greater the chance that one of them will find himself or herself wanting to exit ahead of the others. Development takes a long time—sometimes longer than anticipated—and it's very possible that even before an extended development is completed, one or more of the partners' financial goals or needs may have changed. Or perhaps more money is needed for the project, and one partner is unwilling or unable to pony up for this next round of investment. This presents all kinds of interesting challenges for the other partners—not many of them welcome!

The biggest challenge, of course, is that it's not easy either to buy or sell a partial interest in a property. Many partnership agreements stipulate that a departing partner first has to offer his or her share to the other partners in the deal, on a time-limited basis. (In many cases, the "internal sale" effort is time-limited so that the continuing partners can't simply stall.) If no one expresses interest, then the would-be seller has the right to try to sell outside the existing group.

While expanding the circle of potential buyers might sound promising, the fact is that an outside buyer is likely to pay only a fraction of what that interest is worth. For one thing, the would-be seller is most likely asking the prospective buyer to tie up his or her money under the control of a general partner who has the right to make all operating decisions (and from whose authority the seller is attempting to escape). There may be adverse tax consequences, or limited financial information available about the property. This is generally a tough sell, and calls for a discount.

But the numbers also serve to force a discount. Let's assume that the property in question originally cost $1 million, and that it had an $800,000 mortgage on it. This means that the original partners put up $200,000 in equity. If you took 10 percent of the deal, you would have put up $20,000. Let's assume further that the mortgage has now been paid down from $800,000 to $400,000. Assume that your partners are unwilling to refinance the whole property, or incur substantial transaction costs, just to liberate your 10 percent share, and assume that the property is worth at least what it originally cost.

From your perspective as the would-be seller, you may feel that you're entitled to 10 percent of the $400,000 in additional equity that resulted from the pay-down of debt. So you expect to get a profit of $40,000 in addition to recovering your initial $20,000 investment, for a total of $60,000—and (as you surely see it) you're forgoing any claim on possible appreciation of the property. But any prospective buyer of your interest is likely to see it very differently. He or she may only be interested in the deal if it is a real bargain.

Venture capitalists often structure their deals on the assumption of a near-term "out." A venture capital deal may call for a public-market event within, say, five to ten years of the initial investment. Real estate, by contrast, generally calls for a "stay-put" structure. When a specific time horizon is defined, as in the case of the commingled funds described in Chapter 5, it tends to be closer to a ten-year "horizon to sale." Even then, as previously noted, the general partner may have the right to defer a sale.

Let's get back to some more positive reasons to sell. One of these is the opportunity to participate in a value-adding change of use. The farmer is highly unlikely to convert his cornfield into a minor-league ball park or a shopping center; this requires special skills. The owner of the low-rise structure in downtown Chicago can't build a skyscraper himself; he has to *sell* that asset in order to participate in a change of use. A sale to a specialized developer—which can be initiated by either side, by the way—is often the highest-value outcome.

I've discussed in previous chapters the characteristics of a typical player of the real estate game. One of them is that real estate people love to make *deals.* They love transactions. Once they're deeply into the day-to-day routine of managing properties, they lose interest in that routine. A sale at the right juncture can free people up to do what they like the best (which often overlaps with what they *do* best).

JBG's sale to Trizec-Hahn, described above, resulted in an interesting two-track employment path. Many of JBG's employees, especially those involved in the management and leasing sides of the business, happily went to work for Trizec-Hahn. Some of JBG's principals decided to follow their hearts and start a new firm, where they could make a new round of deals (when the time was right!). With several new partners, they took advantage of the fund-raising climate at that time period by starting a fund in which the general partners put up 5 percent of the money, and to which a single institution contributed 95 percent. They were once again in a good position to buy wholesale for eventual resale to institutional buyers, when the market next created attractive new opportunities.

HARVESTING, THE BUSINESS, AND THE FAMILY

The injection of one's family into a business context can exacerbate all kinds of business issues. The kinds of disputes that normally arise among business partners can be intensified if those partners are also siblings, spouses, or other relatives. At the same time, the family provides special opportunities for harvesting, which need to be explored and understood.

Real estate firms have very often been family-owned firms. I'd like to think that this is because the sons and daughters of real estate people know a good thing when they see it. More likely, it has to do with the unusual starting-from-scratch nature of a real estate company, as each new deal presents a new opportunity for investment at the wholesale level. Although my son Jonathan was too young to be involved in our deals decades ago, he has been able to enter the real estate game as a partner in new deals in recent years. As his own capital grows, he is able to participate in larger and more numerous deals. This is a kind of flexibility that isn't afforded by, say, a typical manufacturing company, in which the stock was issued years ago, and new shareholders have to pay a price-per-share that reflects the stock's current value.

Talking through the issues, and making sure the next generation gets adequate training, are two ways to improve the odds for family-business success. In Jonathan's case, we agreed that whatever happened in the business would not affect our friendship. It was also important that he had worked in real estate for other firms in Washington, D.C. before we tried (successfully, I think) to work together.

Another reason why family members often become involved in the family real estate firm is that the older generation can sell the younger generation limited partnership interests at some discount, make loans to them, or transfer properties at prices that allow the younger generation to take advantage of future growth in value.

Gifting is an important way to transfer assets to the next generation, and there are few contexts in which gifting is more advantageous than in real estate. If your son or daughter is married and your spouse is living, you can each give $10,000 per year tax free to each of your children and also to their spouses. This means that you can pass along a total of $40,000 in value every year. And if that $40,000 comes in the form of an asset that is valued at a discount to its true market value, this can be a very valuable tool for family estate planning. Obviously, this requires a good appraisal at the time of each gift. And this is not an area in which to cut corners: get the best legal and tax advice you can find.

What can you do beyond $40,000 per year? One possibility is to utilize the one-time $650,000 gift exemption—rising to $1 million by the year 2006—allowed by federal law. (Under the terms of this exemption, every adult can either make a tax-free gift during his or her lifetime, or exempt from tax the first $650,000 of his or her estate. The numbers double in the case of a couple.) For example, suppose you have a property in which the equity is worth $400,000. Suppose, too, that you think this property is undervalued, and will go up in value over time fairly dramatically, but at the current time, there is no large capital gain. Under the guidelines of the one-time exemption, you could make a gift of 25 percent of that equity, or $100,000, using about 15 percent of the lifetime exemption, and then take back a loan at a relatively favorable interest rate for the other $300,000. Then you can forgive that loan in $40,000 "chunks" over the next seven and a half years.

Alternatively, you can gift the whole $400,000 property at once and use up more of the one-time exemption. If you are gifting partial ownership in an entity, as described earlier, 20 to 30 percent discounts may be permissible to compensate for illiquidity. Meanwhile, of course, the property may appreciate over time, making your $400,000 gift an even more generous one. For those with grandchildren, there is a $1 million per donor generation-skipping transfer tax exemption. This exemption can be used in connection with overall gifting allowances, and is not an additional allowance. Again, you should get the best advice available; but many in the real estate field find that this is a valuable way to handle inheritance issues.

In some cases, it makes the most sense to sit tight. As in the case of many appreciated capital assets, holding real estate until "estate time" avoids the capital gains tax that would be due if the property were sold prior to death. The heirs receive a step-up in basis to the value of the property in the estate.

Another approach involves mixing a gift with a "good." I've talked about my friend Ava Bergman in previous chapters. (Bergman moved from Philadelphia to New York after buying a co-op from a prominent society figure who was moving to California.) At the time Bergman moved into her co-op, she gave a major interest in it to her children, with the stipulation that she would be able to live there for a certain number of years and pay all expenses related to the co-op. This is known as a "qualified personal residence trust," also called a "grantor retained income trust" (GRIT).

If Bergman dies before the specified time period elapses, then the co-op becomes part of her estate. But if she lives beyond that time, the entire property is technically owned by the children (or by a trust that she may have set up for them). The advantage is that the government considers only part of this transfer a "gift." Assume it's a $1 million co-op. The IRS might rule that only $400,000 of the transfer was a gift, whereas the other $600,000 was a "good"—that is, the value of living in the residence for that certain number of years.

In Bergman's case, she was able to use the purchase price of the unit as the appraised value. In the absence of a recent sale, a fair appraisal would be necessary. This, too, can be managed to good effect. A parent or other family member looking to make this kind of gift would naturally be advised to make the transfer and obtain the appraisal at a time when the market is in a down cycle, thereby establishing a relatively low value on the property.

Even family businesses that aren't real estate businesses can use real estate to solve knotty problems. Take the classic case in which the daughter goes into the family business, and the son doesn't. How do the parents divide up their estate in a way that is fair to all? One way I've run across is to give the real estate "under" the business to the nonparticipating sibling, and to leave the operating business to the sibling who is actually operating it. This way, the business pays rent to the nonoperating son—providing a dependable cash flow—while giving full operating control to the daughter who's actually running the business. This also works when you give the business to the siblings, while allocating the rental cash flow to the aging parents.

We have one more character from earlier chapters to bring back on the stage. That character is Charlie Leonard, who—with limited capital, and as a new entrant to the real estate game—bought a small apartment building on Boston's Beacon Hill. Leonard and his wife fixed up one apartment and moved into it; then, over the course of a year, they gradually transformed the whole building, serving more or less as their own contractors.

The property progressed more or less according to plan, but unfortunately, the Leonards' young marriage couldn't stand up under the collective strain of tight money, missed deadlines, and a twenty-four-hour-a-day commitment to (hard) work. Shortly after the building was completed, the Leonards' divorce was finalized. Because they had almost no assets beyond the building, they agreed to sell it to allow them to separate their finances. This, again, was a harvest precipitated by an outside force—and one which no one would have predicted even a year earlier.

From a personal standpoint, this was a very unhappy outcome. (I won't argue that couples or siblings shouldn't work together, but I will argue that couples should make sure to take time *away* from work together, and that siblings should take some time apart!) There was a small silver lining to this cloud, however. As a result of (1) the Leonards' added value, and (2) a sharp increase in the value of rental properties in the Boston area, both Charlie Leonard and his former wife wound up with a good nest egg with which to start their individual lives over again.

WRAPPING UP THE GAME

Novelists often report that their characters get away from them—that they refuse to stay within the roles set out for them in the plot outline. I confess that Charlie Leonard got away from me. I didn't expect that we'd have a divorce at the end of our harvesting chapter. But the Leonards seemed determined to make the point that despite hard work and the best of plans, things rarely turn out as they're supposed to—and so I let them make that point. I'm reminded of a play I saw recently, in which one of the characters asks the others what makes the gods laugh.

"People who make plans," came the response.

Our next and last chapter summarizes some of the larger lessons I've tried to capture in this book. It reinvokes the "game diamond" metaphor, and refocuses us on the importance of bringing together the four kinds of cards—properties, players, capital markets, and external forces—in a productive balance, as you play the real estate game.

CHAPTER 9

BACK TO THE GAME

THIS book was written almost entirely within calendar year 1998, which turned out to be an interesting year for real estate. It was also a year that illustrated many of the important themes that I've introduced throughout the previous chapters.

The year started out on a very positive note. REITs had just come off a 30 percent average share-price increase in 1997. U.S. property rents were up almost everywhere, in almost every property type. A tremendous amount of capital was flowing into real estate projects of all shapes and sizes. The real estate game was being played at a fevered pitch.

By October, only nine months later, it was a very different environment. REIT stocks were off an average of 20 percent. Capital was drying up and projects were being put on hold. Developers were walking away from deposits and pulling out of deals. Sellers were bid 10 to 20 percent less than they thought they'd receive. In the United Kingdom, real estate stocks were off 50 percent from their highs only a few months earlier. In Hong Kong—where the turbulence of the larger Asian markets was accentuated by the uncertainties of coming under Beijing's direct control—the average property stock was off more than 75 percent from its high of two years earlier.

To some extent, real estate was the victim of larger trends. The near collapse of the highly visible Long Term Capital fund and other hedge funds, as well as the "Asian flu" that lurked in the background of all economic transactions in this period, put all kinds of deals (including all kinds of real estate deals) in jeopardy. When business gets the jitters, the airlines and hotel chains—the proverbial canaries in the coal mine—are the first to suffer. When hotels suffer, hotel-based REITs suffer accordingly, and confidence in all types of real estate begins to plummet.

Meanwhile, a liquidity squeeze emerged, as the interest-rate spread between mortgages and Treasuries widened. Lenders who had committed to mortgages at a fixed rate relative to Treasuries (such as the Treasury rate for ten-year bonds plus 1 percent) found they could resell these mortgages only at a loss, because the actual spread in the market for Treasuries was 1.5 percent. New funds were withheld from the market because of uncertainties about the level at which prices would stabilize.

By the fall of 1998, real estate as an asset class was not the darling it was less than a year earlier. In fact, for many people, real estate had become the game *not* to play.

The end of the story? Not quite. By the end of the year, liquidity was beginning to reappear. Both the private and public markets in the United States and Europe (although not Asia) had recovered about half of their earlier losses. Looking forward into 1999, forecasts varied widely. It was hard to know where you were in the cycle; indeed, it was certainly not a typical cycle. Property values declined without rents declining; mortgage securities slipped without a pickup in defaults; and development activity was reduced despite relatively low interest rates. The difference between what the public and the private market were willing to pay for properties began to narrow.

How did the seasoned players respond to this see-sawing reality? Did they bail out in anticipation of a large-scale collapse? Or did they go the other way, and take advantage of reduced prices? Let's revisit some of the characters who have popped up several times in the pages of this book, and find out what they were doing in this time of turbulence and uncertainty. At the same time, I'll introduce a few new players—including one whose famous grandfather we've met earlier—to help make some useful points.

STILL IN THE GAME

You'll recall that Trizec-Hahn purchased the large Twinbrook Metro complex (and other properties) from JBG Properties, and that the former JBG staff went off in two directions. The JBG partners who went out on their own were convinced that the market would soon be turning up again, and were judiciously purchasing properties in the Washington, D.C., area, despite the overall anxieties about real estate.

The Trizec-Hahn people, for their part, were quite pleased with the deal they had struck for Twinbrook Metro. Their prime tenants, the federal government and various quasi-governmental outfits, were not cutting back on their demands for good office space. In fact, Trizec-Hahn became convinced that the market for research and office space in the health-care field would only grow; as a result, they began remodeling additional buildings in the Twinbrook complex for federally funded researchers. Meanwhile, they were offered the opportunity to negotiate for a redevelopment of land next to the metro stop for their property, which—if done well—held the potential to enhance the desirability and value of the larger property considerably.

CBL, the Chattanooga-based shopping-center REIT on whose board I sit, continued to build throughout 1998. This may surprise readers who are aware of the travails of the retail trade in recent years. But CBL saw several factors as arguing strongly for selective new investment in regional shopping centers, especially those in subareas of growing communities without an already established mall. And moving up one level: Every mall in the country was getting older. Sooner or later, all of those malls would need updating or replacing. CBL had the necessary resources to update their existing centers, which included expanding and upgrading the entertainment components of those centers (which more and more shoppers were beginning to demand).

CBL also involved itself increasingly in so-called "power centers," which featured big-box stores like Home Depot, Wal-Mart, Borders Books, and so on. These "category killers" were grabbing an ever-larger share of their respective retail trades, and CBL was quick to move in their direction, even though there was some concern that even this fast-growing retail sector was at risk of being overbuilt.

Finally, CBL took advantage of their access to lower interest rates to increase their leverage and acquire some underperforming shopping centers. They used their management skills to improve the operating performance of these retail centers, and initial results were very promising. Still, the public markets did not treat retail REIT stocks kindly, fearful of the long-term impact of the Internet on shopping habits.

I can't revisit Bill Zeckendorf, Sr.—the impresario who helped transform a grim slaughterhouse on the East Side of Manhattan into the United Nations complex—because Zeckendorf has long since left the real estate game (and this mortal coil). But I have an interesting stand-in: Bill's grandson Will Zeckendorf, a former student of mine, who also deals in real estate in New York City. That's where the resemblance to his grandfather ends, however. Will, along with his brother and two other partners, buys smaller projects. They use investor money, for the most part, which means that they are properly capitalized (and aren't required to give personal guarantees on their deals). As a base for their New York operations, they use Brown, Harris & Stevens, a major New York leasing and brokerage firm, which they bought in part to give them a leg up in their local investing. The project that Zeckendorf and his brother launched in 1998, the 515 Park Avenue Condominium, established the highest average sales price in Manhattan at $1,700 psf, and the building is well on its way to being sold out.

Sam Plimpton and Dan Prigmore, the real estate heads of the investment group that purchased the undervalued Lowell manufacturing facility that we visited in earlier chapters, continued to sell U.S. properties throughout 1998, reflecting their belief that the potential for growth presented by these properties was limited. At the same time, Plimpton and Prigmore continued to develop in two major European cities. The office buildings that they are renovating there were on schedule, and rents had increased to well above forecast.

Other international investors were beginning to bet heavily on properties in Poland, on the theory that the lingering perception of Poland as an Eastern bloc backwater was obscuring that country's true potential for doing business with the European Community. Cameron Sawyer, meanwhile, is trying to interest investors in shopping malls in the suburbs of Moscow. He hopes to provide more accessible shopping for those middle- and upper-middle income Muscovites who now have to go all the way into the center city to make their purchases.

Closer to home, I received an interesting call last week from a former student who heads one of this country's biggest residential REITs. Let's call him Brian Walsh. Walsh more or less shrugged off the turbulence of 1998, telling me that the industry's recent ups and downs weren't of particular concern to him. His existing apartment complexes were doing well. Of great interest to him at that moment, he told me, were his company's plans to begin building a new kind of housing at selected sites across the United States. For the first time in years, he said, the twenty-to-thirty-year-old age cohort would be growing. Graduate students and young adults taking their first jobs would welcome new housing choices, Walsh told me with obvious excitement, and his company intended to provide those choices. His bet is that young people in this age group are interested in having less private space and more communal space than is afforded by the traditional apartment. Given that Walsh is a smart guy and that his REIT is amply capitalized, I wouldn't bet against him.

So what do these stories tell us, collectively? I think they tell us two things. First, at least as seen in some lights, the problems in the capital markets in 1998 were very beneficial to the real estate industry. It appears that to some extent, they choked off speculative building, which meant that supply and demand were kept in better balance than would otherwise have been the case. Of course, further external shocks could change the equation by affecting the demand side, but for the moment, the supply side—the excesses of which caused the downfall of high-riding real estate markets of the past—was under control.

And second, these stories make a key point in different ways: that although we are prepared to hold for the long-term play, external factors are able to inflict lumps and bruises on individual projects, and these can't be ignored. And yes—as Plimpton and Prigmore would be quick to point out—there are investment strategies that call for hard-nosed exits from properties that have achieved their financial targets and have little upside potential. But when your overall calculation argues for persistence (and your bankroll allows it!), then staying the course is often the best way to play the real estate game.

THE PHASES OF THE GAME

Let's look at a very elementary visual aid to review some of the key lessons that I've tried to present in previous chapters. It's a simple matrix, with the phases of the real estate game along the vertical axis, and the four corners of our game diamond along the horizontal axis.

	Properties	Players	Capital markets	External factors
Concept to commitment				
Commitment to closing				
Development				
Operations				
Harvest				

As you follow the vertical axis from top to bottom, you find the phases of the real estate game that have served as the focus of five of our chapters. (We'll return to that empty box at the bottom, under "harvest," shortly.) Remember that these are the phases that *direct* players of the real estate game go through. Remember, too, that many real estate transactions involve existing properties; and these transactions would not include a development phase.

In the *concept to commitment* phase (Chapter 3), I focused on the importance of spotting opportunity, getting good information, managing money, and managing time. The judicious use of time and money, especially before you know for sure whether a particular property deserves much of your attention, is critically important. Finding opportunity grows out of working with people and property types that you know intimately. This is a *hands-on* business, which requires intimate knowledge of a property's locational, physical, and regulatory characteristics. If there is an opportunity involving an existing property, where does it fit into its local market? What do the leases look like? Is the property in good physical condition and up to date, or will it require extensive capital expenditures?

In many cases, distinguishing between good and bad opportunities is accomplished by back-of-the-envelope (BOE) analysis, which can be used to examine and understand the valuation of key drivers in potential real estate deals. (For a summary of the key criteria that need to be considered for pro formas for each of the six major property types, see Appendix A: Note on Property Types.) Being prepared—and understanding both your own point of view and the viewpoint of the seller—is the best way to set up productive negotiations for the purchase of a property.

Building good relationships with banks (or other sources of mortgage money) is important as the deal approaches the commitment stage. (Changes in the world of banking have diminished the latitude of bankers, but in many cases, they're still your point of access to money.) So is building good relationships with potential partners. Real estate is a field in which it is fairly easy to split the returns among the parties. The key is to be able to "follow the cash." The fact that most properties are owned by separate entities makes it easy for both new and old partners to share in the equity.

During *commitment to closing*, described in Chapter 4, the challenge is to tie up a project while minimizing your personal financial stake. After completing the purchase-and-sale (P&S) agreement, the typical real estate buyer must perform due diligence—which can be very expensive—while also putting together both the necessary debt and equity financing. (In most cases, both of these "money negotiations" must succeed if the deal is to go forward, and rarely is this an easy task.) Unfortunately, the due-diligence and financing processes are at the same time unrelated and intimately intertwined. It takes both skill and luck to get everything done that needs to be done, on time—and not wind up paying for anything twice.

Due diligence is a huge subject in and of itself. It comprises environmental, code, structural, mechanical systems, legal, zoning, and tenant-related issues. This can be a daunting list—but all participants in the deal (especially you and your fellow investors) need adequate assurances that all the bases are being touched. This is the point, well before the big money is put down, that you want to discover any ticking time bombs associated with the property. This is also the stage in which your attorneys—if they are good—can help you understand what's essential from a legal standpoint. They can help you distinguish between what's negotiable and nonnegotiable in the various legal documents that come your way.

At the same time that due diligence and the hunt for financing are consuming large amounts of time, the buyer in most cases is also negotiating with potential tenants. Understanding the needs and desires of future tenants is crucial to putting the right price on the project, which in turn has important implications for the "money hunt."

This is also the beginning of the option phase, in which the developer of new buildings uses conditional agreements to purchase a property at the same time that he or she is attempting to secure the local approvals that will be needed before the project can move ahead. It's hard work to bind a property far in advance of (for example) a rezoning. On the other hand, it's dangerous to start the rezoning process prior to obtaining a binding commitment from the seller, because it's too easy for someone to take the deal away from you if the rezoning is successful, and you don't have the property locked up.

Closings—the end of the commitment-to-closing phase—can be gratifying. They can represent the successful conclusion to many months (or even years) of hard work. But it's important to remember that there is no dishonor in abandoning a deal that can't be made to work. Some of the more successful players of the real estate game have been those who are willing to drop out of the game during this phase, rather than pushing ahead with an untenable project. Better to lose a deposit than to lose far more money by carrying an ill-conceived plan through to completion.

Easy to say; hard to do. As you approach a closing, all the incentives and momentum are pushing for the deal to go through. Lawyers, brokers, engineers, architects, and others want the money they're already owed. (And they may see the prospect of more work from you in the very near future if the closing proceeds.) You, too, have reason to keep moving forward. You've put up your own money, which your investors and lenders will allow you to recoup (only) if the deal goes ahead. And besides, you and your staff may have an emotional commitment to making this exciting project—in which you've invested so much time, money, and love—come to fruition.

So O.K.; I have to say it again. Resist the rush into a bad deal. Remember the old real estate maxim that warns that there are many more happy *third* owners of buildings than happy *first* owners of buildings. This is the phase in which you need to discover whether this project will create happiness or unhappiness. As my HBS colleague Howard Stevenson likes to say, "Watch out what you negotiate for; you may get it!"

In *development,* described in Chapter 6, both the risks and the rewards increase exponentially. Development is the process whereby the player of the real estate game adds significant value—or, if things don't go well, incurs significant losses. Development means "buying wholesale and selling retail," which necessarily focuses the developer on issues of the larger cycle. In a perfect universe, you'd buy wholesale at the bottom of the cycle, and sell retail at the peak of the cycle. Few people are so lucky on a regular basis—especially if they engage in large, long-term projects that are extended over several cycles. External conditions change. Your contractor gets into trouble on two other projects. Your financial partners become unable to fulfill their obligations. Things *change.*

Meanwhile, the developer—while coping with changes from on high—gets rewarded for effecting beneficial change. This may mean upgrading an underutilized property, or changing either the nature or intensity of use of a property. Indirectly, the developer gets rewarded for assembling and successfully managing a team of more or less disparate contributors. It's this ability—to motivate and direct multiple groups and individuals who may never have worked together before—that makes the real estate game fun, challenging, unpredictable, and sometimes very profitable.

Development means forging into new activities. Land acquisition, for example, requires patience, empathy, negotiating skills, and political savvy. The relative success of the entire project may hinge on appropriate deals being made during the approval process.

Managing the planning and design of a project is sometimes exhilarating, and sometimes intensely frustrating. It requires an understanding of context, and of the range of options that are available to you as you set out to make changes in the physical environment. Master planning, site planning, and creative problem solving through architecture—in consultation with planners, architects, and other experts—can be among the most rewarding aspects of real estate development. Three axioms that often prove useful in this phase of the real estate game are: (1) *Good design is good business; (2) don't innovate for innovation's sake;* and (3) *planning never stops.*

The developer has ongoing practical responsibilities, even as he or she is enjoying the resolution of aesthetic and other contextual issues. Chief among these is the *marketability* of the product that is coming off the drawing board. Does anybody want this thing you're cooking up, and will they be able to afford it at the price you're paying to build it?

Sometimes this latter question gets answered when the first construction bids come in. Construction is almost always extremely capital intensive, and therefore deserves as much of your attention as you can possibly give it. Bidding requires that either you or someone you trust understands the construction process intimately. It requires an understanding of how a highly fragmented "industry"—actually a loose confederation of trades that are only sequentially related—comes together to build an intensely complicated product. Unfortunately, the system does not lend itself to cost efficiency.

Remember that architectural working drawings cost a great deal of money to generate, and that in most cases, you can't get real construction quotes without them. The architect has to bring in numerous engineering subcontractors, and commission all kinds of specialized tests, just to design something as relatively straightforward as (for example) a foundation. But at the point when the bids come, if they are higher than your budget or pro forma allow, it can be very difficult indeed to cut costs sufficiently without hurting the marketability of the overall project. The intimate interrelations between design, budget, marketability, and the realities of construction dramatically raise the stakes for the developer (and argue, again, for getting it right the first time!).

Managing construction is inextricably related to the challenge of managing money. This is the phase in which the relationships among the investors—and the adequacy of the partnership agreement—may get tested by unexpected circumstances. If more money is needed, where will it come from? If disputes arise among the partners, how will they be resolved? And although banks have more latitude in lending short-term money for construction than in lending long-term or permanent mortgage money—which is most often part of a larger securitized package—they will still stick their noses squarely into your business. This may well be the phase in which you (reluctantly) offer your first personal guarantee on a loan, in order to keep the project adequately capitalized.

As if all of this were not enough, this is also the phase when salesmanship becomes critically important. Although your architect and other experts may be helpful in the preleasing effort, it is ultimately you and your building that have to make a successful pitch. And it is you who has to decide how much to alter your designs and finishes in order to win over a key tenant.

Development becomes immensely more complicated when it takes place outside of your home region or country. By and large, there are only three ways that developers working far from home have an advantage over the locals: (1) specialized expertise in planning, design, or construction; (2) marketing skills vis-à-vis a specific tenant or class of tenant; (3) access to capital. If one or more of these resources is not available locally, and can be integrated with local opportunities and partners, then international development can make sense. If they can't, the developer is probably wise to stay home.

This raises the issue of what I call the Four Pitfalls of development: inexperience, undercapitalization, changes over time in the external context or the circumstances of the players, and hubris: thinking you can create something that's never been created before. It's worth remembering that almost all projects take longer and cost more than expected. This puts more pressure on a deal's capital structure, and also exposes the project to more external risks. Over time, the odds can shift against you: More things can go wrong than can go right.

The *operations* phase, described in Chapter 7, is the unsexy, "three yards and a cloud of dust" phase of real estate, in which careful and relentless attention to detail often makes the difference between success and failure. The vacancy rate is to some extent an indicator of overall market conditions, but it is also the single best and most important indicator of your skills as an operator. (A skilled operator can always beat the average vacancy rate, even in a moribund market.) The cheapest tenant, in almost all cases, is the *continuing* tenant; therefore, the smart landlord does what it takes to keep good tenants happy and in place.

So one key aspect of operations involves relations between, and the respective responsibilities of, landlords and tenants. These relations and responsibilities are to a large extent (but not exclusively) governed by a contract: the lease. Almost everything in a lease is negotiable, and—as is the case with most negotiations—both parties may find ways to trade unimportant things for important things. But there are other elements of the landlord-tenant relationship that exist outside of the formal lease agreement.

There are circumstances (many of them dire!) in which a landlord and a tenant have to make up the rules as they go along. In such cases, it's extremely helpful to have an effective, mutually beneficial relationship already in place.

A second key aspect of operations—and one that is often underemphasized—is the asset management function. This is the "business of the business," and it includes such vital concerns as selecting a manager and promoting strong relationships with both lenders and investors. Property management firms can assume many of these responsibilities, but you—as the player of the real estate game who stands behind this property—also need to be involved in the critical decisions.

Most pro formas assume only minimal capital expenditures, in part to win over potential investors and lenders. And when this kind of head-in-the-sand wooing is successful, the natural tendency then is to try to avoid or delay such expenditures, since in an undercapitalized deal they will compel you to reduce the cash distribution rate to yourself and to your partners. But the failure to spend this money leads, over the long term, to the deterioration and obsolescence of your property. In some cases—for example, shopping centers—this kind of deterioration gains such momentum that it becomes almost irreversible.

In the relatively recent past—for example, the 1970s—the assumption was that ever-higher rents, resulting from high levels of inflation, would bail out undercapitalized projects and cover such capital expenditures. But when inflation became a nonissue in recent years, this back-door approach to funding capital expenditures stopped working. The moral? Operate profitably, build bigger reserves than you think you'll need, and have a plan in mind for where you'll go next for money.

I've already explained "buy wholesale/sell retail" (which under ideal circumstances is dovetailed with "buy low/sell high"). This axiom becomes of even greater interest during the *harvest* phase. Harvesting represents the end of the real estate game—and in many cases, sets the stage for the beginning of a new real estate game.

Harvesting is always unappealing to some players (e.g., those from cultures who consider real estate to be the best safe harbor from inflation). It is sometimes unappealing to *all* players (e.g., at the bottom of the down cycle). The difficulties of reentry into the real estate game (e.g., the difficulty of finding a property as good as the one you're selling), high transaction costs, and tax recapture all add up to effective disincentives to selling. And not to be overlooked is simple inertia: If it ain't broke, and if it's generating a respectable operating profit, why sell it, and pay a lot of taxes on it?

But "harvesting" doesn't necessarily mean "selling." As many homeowners know, refinancing is another way of taking value out of an appreciated or upgraded property, and it can be a particularly attractive option for the property owner who sees opportunities (either in real estate or elsewhere) that can beat the cost of releveraging an existing property. Just remember that at some point, you have to be prepared to pay this money back.

On the other side of the ledger, there are many circumstances in which the advantages of harvesting outweigh the disadvantages. The most obvious of these is making possible a whole new buying-wholesale/selling-retail cycle. This is the underlying value-creation formula in real estate, and it depends upon the infusion of large amounts of cash at the beginning of the game.

Sometimes the souring of a deal forces a sale. Sometimes the disintegration of a partnership—whether for personal or financial reasons—mandates a sale. Sometimes an owner of a property can properly exit only by selling to someone with grand plans for redevelopment or upgrade.

A major subset of harvesting issues concerns wealth management, especially between and across the generations of a family. Real estate has long been dominated by families and family firms, in part because the nature of the business over time—a succession of more or less unrelated deals, with new equity opportunities with the acquisition of each new property—is far more welcoming to the next generation than, say, founder's stock in a long-established company. And although the tax laws change regularly, it's fair to say that the rules governing gifts across generations can be used to advantage when it comes to transferring wealth.

REVISITING THE GAME DIAMOND

The other axis of my matrix consists of the four corners of the "game diamond" that I introduced in Chapter 1: players, properties, capital markets, and external forces. I asked you to imagine that at each corner of the game diamond was a deck of cards. You get into the real estate game by pulling (or having pulled for you) a card from one of these four "decks."

Each of these cards, when pulled, influences the other three. If you draw a "property, large" card, for example, you have to approach the "players" and "capital markets" decks much differently than if you pull a "property, small" card. And if you draw a "property, large" card, you're very likely to have to deal with an array of external factors—both because you'll be showing up on everybody's radar, and because your project will simply take longer to get done. See the chart for an updated version of the diamond.

THE REAL ESTATE GAME: AN INDUSTRY PERSPECTIVE

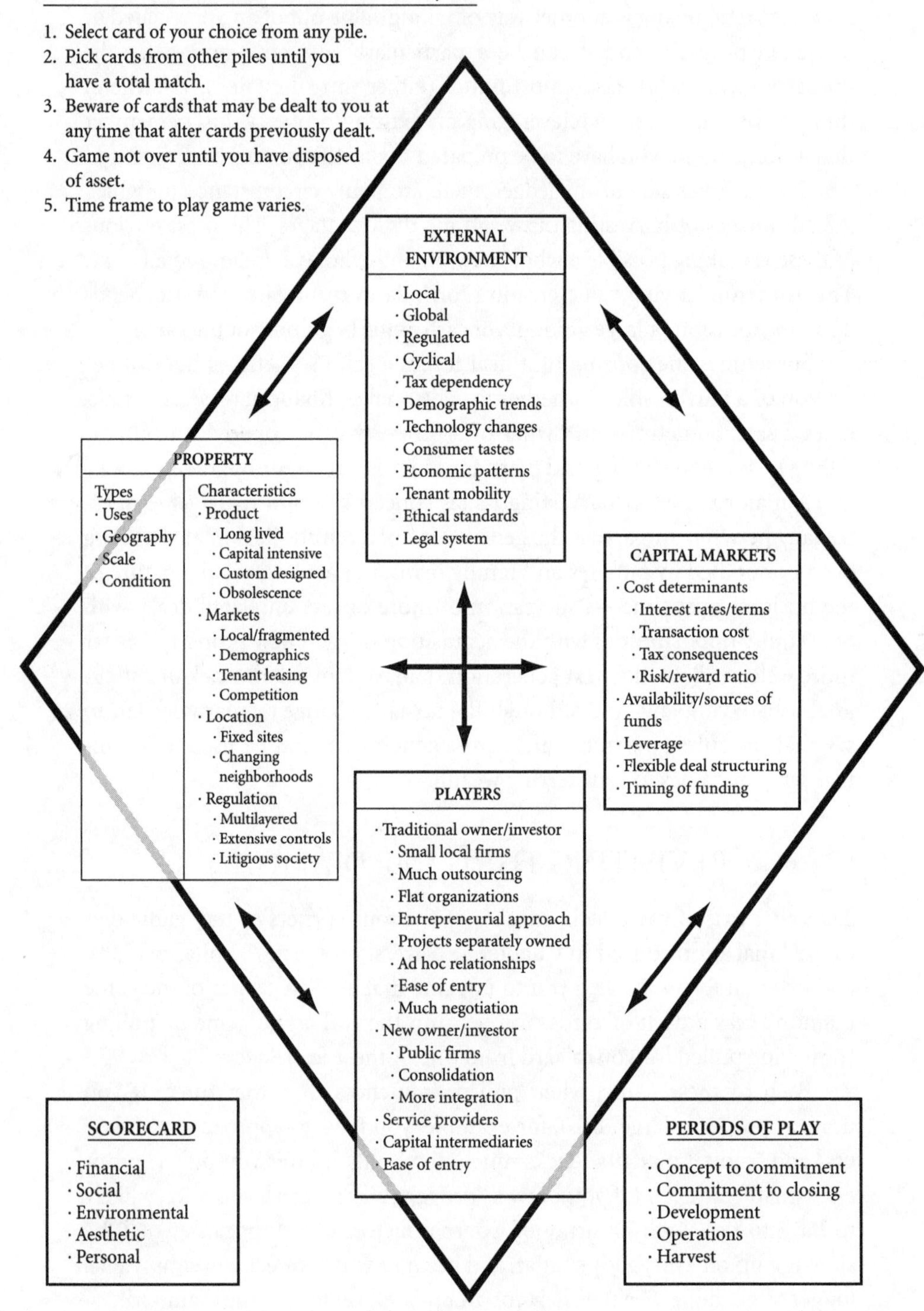
Rules of the Game (Unlimited Number of Players)
1. Select card of your choice from any pile.
2. Pick cards from other piles until you have a total match.
3. Beware of cards that may be dealt to you at any time that alter cards previously dealt.
4. Game not over until you have disposed of asset.
5. Time frame to play game varies.
EXTERNAL ENVIRONMENT
· Local
· Global
· Regulated
· Cyclical
· Tax dependency
· Demographic trends
· Technology changes
· Consumer tastes
· Economic patterns
· Tenant mobility
· Ethical standards
· Legal system
PROPERTY
Types
· Uses
· Geography
· Scale
· Condition
Characteristics
· Product
· Long lived
· Capital intensive
· Custom designed
· Obsolescence
· Markets
· Local/fragmented
· Demographics
· Tenant leasing
· Competition
· Location
· Fixed sites
· Changing neighborhoods
· Regulation
· Multilayered
· Extensive controls
· Litigious society
CAPITAL MARKETS
· Cost determinants
· Interest rates/terms
· Transaction cost
· Tax consequences
· Risk/reward ratio
· Availability/sources of funds
· Leverage
· Flexible deal structuring
· Timing of funding
PLAYERS
· Traditional owner/investor
· Small local firms
· Much outsourcing
· Flat organizations
· Entrepreneurial approach
· Projects separately owned
· Ad hoc relationships
· Ease of entry
· Much negotiation
· New owner/investor
· Public firms
· Consolidation
· More integration
· Service providers
· Capital intermediaries
· Ease of entry
SCORECARD
· Financial
· Social
· Environmental
· Aesthetic
· Personal
PERIODS OF PLAY
· Concept to commitment
· Commitment to closing
· Development
· Operations
· Harvest

If you perceive compelling long-term opportunity in Chinese real estate, for example, you're in good company. But if you get involved in properties in China, you'll have to learn new ways to deal with people, you'll have to learn exotic new ways to interact with the capital markets, and you'll have to be *very* comfortable with exposure to external factors over the long term. In my mind, the real question is, "Is there *anybody* out there who can stick it out long enough to benefit from China's potential?" The people who get that one right will do very well for themselves and their investors—but they'll only do so if they put together the right combinations of cards in the right sequence.

Now that you've been through all the y-axis phases (concept to commitment, etc.), you've learned for yourself that these four decks of cards change their stripes in the different phases of the game. They vary in importance from phase to phase, or within phases. Let's examine each of them in turn.

PLAYERS

In the introduction, I suggested that people were as important to the real estate game as properties. Now I'll amend that assertion. I think people are *more* important than properties. A property is, in one sense, the lump of clay on the potter's wheel. It's people who take that lump of clay and, through skilled and hard work, add value to it. Remember that in my definition, "players" include not only the owners and managers of properties, but also the whole firmament of people who work in and around the industry: the service providers, lenders, intermediaries, regulators, competitors, and so on. And yes: tenants, too, are players.

The skilled player of the real estate game takes a fragmented field and builds relationships within it. Think about the wide range of more or less specialized professionals we've encountered in the previous chapters, including:

- brokers (who are often loosely organized by locale, and who include such disparate groups as leasing brokers and mortgage brokers)
- architects (often focused on specific building types, and usually with a local or regional client base)
- lawyers (either generalists or specialists, often with a substantive or geographic focus)
- engineers (with very specific, even rarified, skill bases)
- contractors (often skilled at running specific kinds of projects)

- subcontractors (usually with a deep and narrow expertise in a particular building function)

The skilled player of the real estate game also works with a wide range of partners and other kinds of investors. Here, the scale of the proposed project can be key. For a small project, you can call on your friends, your accountant's references, or whomever. But for a large project, you'll have to work effectively with local banks (who are more or less in thrall to aggregators of loans), investment bankers, or other institutional investors.

And it's not just a case of working with a wide variety of actors. It's also a case of dealing with different kinds of "lawyers" (for example) depending on which phase of the game you're in, and what kind of property you're dealing with. Early in the game, you'll most likely be dealing with someone else's broker; in development and operations, you'll most likely be dealing with other rental brokers. And in between, of course, you'll be dealing with architects, bankers, engineers, general contractors, politicians, activists, and all sorts of other people.

Meanwhile, the rules of the game are changing. Several decades ago, the real estate business consisted almost entirely of small firms with no vertical integration and limited horizontal integration. Almost all functions were outsourced, and risks were externalized whenever possible. Although these kinds of firms still make up the bulk of the industry, new players have entered the scene. These tend to be larger companies with more vertical integration, which in many cases have a large regional (or even national) presence. With the ongoing centralization of capital markets, these larger firms are better able to compete for funding, and some are taking advantage of marketing and operating efficiencies. Remember our game diamond: as the capital markets evolve, the types of players who can connect individual properties to the capital markets must also change.

Both pension funds and public companies, especially REITs, now own much of the institutional-investment real estate in the United States. They have been the prime beneficiaries of the flow of capital in the past decade. They also have been the prime beneficiaries of federal tax laws that benefit tax-exempt investors.

Behind even these larger, seemingly faceless institutions, however, are real people making real deals. I talked at length in Chapter 5 about syndicates and REITs, which in the financial pages of the newspaper look like so many bloodless abstractions. Far from it! In fact, a REIT is nothing more or less than a collection of individual real estate deals, brought to a successful completion by individuals. Yes, these deals are financed differently, and their rewards are doled out in distinctive ways, and the people behind these organizations have different incentives—but they're still players, operating according to the rules of the game.

Real estate is about people. It's about the complex, varied, unpredictable challenge of managing large numbers of more or less unruly people, all with their own agendas, skills sets, resource bases, and timetables. For me, this is one of the great joys of the real estate game.

PROPERTIES

Properties also are "all over the map"—literally and figuratively. Successful players of the real estate game figure out which property types they work with most effectively, and stick with those types (sometimes increasing the scale of their operations over time). And sometimes, after taking plenty of precautions and spreading as many risks as possible, they venture out into new property types, and thereby find new ways to succeed (or fail!).

No book—or even a series of books—could hope to present a comprehensive look at the universe of properties that exist out there. In this book, for reasons of space, I've stayed at a fairly general level when describing particular types of properties. But in part to compensate for this necessarily general treatment of properties, I've included at the end of this book the appendix to which I've already referred (A Note on Property Types). In it, I describe five large groups of properties: apartments, offices, hotels, industrial buildings, and retail facilities. For each of those property types, I review six key variables:

- quality
- structure
- location
- target tenants
- ownership
- valuation

Please consult this appendix (which also includes definitions of key terms pertaining to each of these property types) for specific ideas about how these six variables affect, and are affected by, the real estate game. But remember that these are necessarily only short summaries. Each of these property types is the subject of many books, the best of which the specialized investor or developer should become familiar with. The Urban Land

Institute (on the Web at www.uli.org/homepage.htm) can steer you toward these kinds of resources.

CAPITAL MARKETS

In earlier drafts of this manuscript, I was less than charitable toward some of the gyrations and manipulations of Wall Street. This grows out of my personal experiences, particularly in the realm of REITs, which (at least until their most recent reincarnation) seemed like a good idea that was doomed to failure, mostly as a result of the way incentives were structured to benefit financial institutions and promoters.

This draft is more even-handed. The capital markets, fickle and unpredictable as they are, serve a necessary function. And truth be told, they are no more at fault for the wild swings of the real estate cycle than are real estate moguls themselves. It takes two both to tango and to overbuild.

The capital markets are an essential, unavoidable backdrop to the real estate game. They greatly influence (and are marginally influenced by) the real estate industry. Stock prices and real estate prices are often related. Both are greatly influenced by the level of interest rates. When the demand for stocks is high, price-earnings multiples will rise, which should also lower the expected returns for real estate and simultaneously raise prices for real estate as an investment option. The problem for real estate, as well as for stocks, is when growth expectations of investors exceed reality.

As I implied at the outset of this chapter, the recent resurgence of REITs has at least one salutary subplot. To the extent that the recent (1998) fall in REIT prices chases capital away from the real estate industry, we may avoid the kinds of overbuilding that have led to crashes in the past. Wall Street may do a better job of rationing capital—through its control of the sale of securitized mortgages and REIT shares—than the thousands of S&Ls that previously dominated the game. If this turns out to be true, this will be a very good outcome, indeed.

Throughout history, players of the real estate game have responded quickly—some might say slavishly—to changes in the capital markets. Bluntly stated, we follow the cash. If Wall Street is willing to put money into REITs, fine; we can do that! If Wall Street finds it easier to invest in larger REITs, fine; we'll assemble properties and merge them; and keep merging larger and larger assemblages of projects (and even companies) if that's what's required. And if Wall Street concludes that it's time for the pendulum to swing back, the private buyers will again step forward.

Players in the real estate game have to be respectful and wary of the capital markets, and also realistic about their agendas. The capital markets, as noted at the beginning of this chapter, are like the ancient gods of Olympus: They can either shower riches on players of the real estate game, or hurl deadly thunderbolts at them. We mortals need to act accordingly.

EXTERNAL FORCES

In this same realm, but more so, is the aggregation of variables that I've called the *external environment*, or external forces—collectively, all of those larger economic, regulatory, social, demographic, and environmental trends that define our human existence, and incidentally make and remake the real estate landscape.

In real life, the capital markets and external forces are mostly inseparable. The flow of money between public and private markets swings back and forth with changes in the capital markets, government policies, and the preferences of Wall Street investors.

But as suggested in the list just above, all kinds of other external forces have an impact on real estate. For example:

- The twentieth century may well be remembered as the one in which mankind made its greatest strides toward reducing both the incidence and the morbidity of diseases. Is this far removed from the mundane walks of real estate? No, because longevity has a profound impact (more than any other single factor) on residential housing, work, and recreational patterns.
- The decision to build the vast interstate highway system was originally driven by concerns about national defense. That network had an incalculable impact on urban, suburban, and even rural real estate in the United States, as well as on shopping and work habits.
- The return of waves of G.I.s after World War II led directly to the Baby Boom, which at the turn of the subsequent century is leading many to investigate housing opportunities for aging Baby Boomers.
- The growth of office and service jobs filled by women entering the work force helped fuel a boom in office construction. Meanwhile, companies' ability to outsource or move manufacturing to other parts of the world has led to dislocations in many of the older U.S. industrial areas.
- The increase in two-wage-earner families has raised the level of consumer expenditures. It also has altered the makeup and needs of individual families.

- The European Economic Community was not created to benefit the international real estate community. But it appears to be providing numerous and exciting cross-border opportunities in an area that—due to demographics—otherwise had limited potential for growth.
- I mentioned China earlier. The emergence of China as a (or the) economic powerhouse in the twenty-first century will create as yet unforeseeable opportunities for players of the real estate game. Yes, China's unique economic system calls for new approaches to the game; but the game will be played there in *some* way, by somebody, for very high stakes.

Some of the most dynamic and "successful" real estate entrepreneurs have been those who have been able to figure out how one of these large external forces will affect the real estate game in the years and decades ahead. But note that I have to put the word "successful" in quotes. The ability to look too far ahead—even correctly—doesn't always translate into profits. Ask Bill Zeckendorf, Sr., who transformed cities (and how we think about them), and never benefited financially from his own inventiveness. And yet, it's fair to conclude that Zeckendorf achieved his real objective, which was to make his visions a reality. If we did a long-term IRR on his developments, we would probably find that they *did* succeed in making money—for subsequent owners.

THE SCORECARD

Zeckendorf's example brings me back to a point I made at the very outset of this book. Let me bring back my modest matrix for one amendment. I want to add a line at the bottom. In Chapter 1, I introduced the idea of a "scorecard," which has great value at both the beginning and the end of the real estate game. At the beginning of the game—I argued—it's helpful to really think through what is important to *you,* personally, as you enter into this game.

Why? For one thing, getting into real estate is probably a little too easy. All you have to do is "pull a property card"—or form a company aimed at providing one of the many services that tend to be outsourced by owners—and you're in. (Whether you'll be able to *stay* in is, of course, another matter entirely.) But for many people, real estate is different from widget making. One way or another, it's more than just a way to make a living. For many people, real estate is also a way to express one's most personal convictions—social, environmental, aesthetic, and otherwise. In my HBS class on

	Properties	Players	Capital markets	External factors
Concept to commitment				
Commitment to closing				
Development				
Operations				
Harvest				
Scorecard				

assisted living developments, I try to get my students to realize that the potential tenants for these projects may be their own grandparents. How do they want their grandparents to live, and how do they see their own responsibilities, and their parents' responsibilities? What should be the role of government, and who should pay?

So why do *you* want to play the real estate game? As you look ahead from the beginning of the game to the end, what do you think will make you happy when it comes time to cash out?

The scorecard, as I see it, has another important purpose. Most of us want to do well financially, but at what expense to ourselves, our families, and our communities? At the *end* of the game, I think, we need to look back and ask ourselves honestly how we did.

One way to do so is by looking again across the x-axis. What did I do with my properties? Is the physical infrastructure better or worse because I got my hands on it? Did I design a building I can be proud of? How well did I treat the people I came across? Have I built long-term relationships, or have I mostly engaged in one-time, transactional experiences? (Is one better than the other, from my own point of view?) If trust is a sort of bank account between people, am I cash-rich or am I overdrawn? When I do my next deal, whom can I count on? Of whom should I be wary?

And by the way, did I make money? Did I work effectively in and around the cycle, balancing the debt and equity ratios, using other people's money whenever possible, investing and harvesting at smart times? Did I make money through a short-term play? Did I make good operating profits? As I harvested, did I leave the property, or recommit myself (and possibly my family) to it?

By definition, "external factors" don't get shaped by too many people.

But external factors all too often come to bear on the real estate industry precisely because that industry—*my* industry—fails to take care of its broader responsibilities. So as a particular real estate game comes to an end, I try to run through those Big Trends out there, and ask what my efforts have done to push in the right direction by these measures. Have I housed anybody better? Have I, through better planning and design, reduced congestion in a beleaguered neighborhood, or improved the quality of the architecture? Have I reduced, avoided, or at least minimized various kinds of pollution?

What I've tried to convey in this book is a *value-investing strategy* for real estate. The best opportunities come from buying at a discount to replacement cost, seeing catalysts such as having tenants for vacant space, discerning the possibility of converting spaces to a higher-value use, or obtaining better sources of financing. A key piece of this strategy is being prepared to sell at the right juncture, as difficult as that may be (for any of a number of reasons). You have to be willing to be patient, and not feel compelled to be in the game when you think current conditions make the game not worth playing.

I'll end this book where I started it: Real estate is the best game around. There is no more exciting or rewarding field in which to make a living. There is no field that presents more opportunities to make things "better," in all the ways that word applies to the built environment. And there is no field that is more *fun.*

I hope this book serves to make you at least a little bit more informed and more skilled. For those of you already experienced in the field, I hope you have learned enough to warrant the time you've put into reading these chapters. For those of you who have just pulled your first card, I hope I've provided some good guidance as to how to fill out the rest of your hand. I hope, too, that you possess the two indispensable complements to smarts and skills: good luck, and great timing. May you move from having smarts to having wisdom, and acquiring it at an affordable price! And for those of you who haven't yet gotten your feet wet, I hope I've encouraged you to jump in.

Welcome to the real estate game!

APPENDIX A

NOTE ON PROPERTY TYPES

With a total estimated worth of $4 trillion in the United States alone, commercial real estate is a major vehicle for investment. Within this field, there are five distinct property types, each with important characteristics that must be understood to determine how value is created:

- apartment
- office
- hotel
- industrial
- retail

First, some general observations: Within each of the five property types listed above, there is obviously a wide variety of buildings. For example, the category "office" comprises a huge array of disparate buildings, ranging from an older, 20,000-square-foot medical office building in a midwestern suburb to a brand-new, 2-million-square-foot tower complex in downtown Los Angeles.

The first step in analyzing each property type, therefore, is to discuss the various ways the real estate industry classifies properties within that property type. In real life, the industry would put the two office buildings in the preceding example into different subclasses: the first in "Class B, suburban medical office," and the second in "Class A, central business district office." On the surface, they would seem to have little in common. Yet they both are affected by the market forces of supply and demand in similar ways, and for the purposes of this note will be left grouped together. Land is not considered as a separate class, but incorporated within the individual property types, since it is the use that determines its value.

The approach in this note will be to use roughly the same methodology that is used by investors to analyze market fundamentals for a particular investment opportunity. The analysis centers on six characteristics:

- quality
- structure
- location
- target tenants
- type of ownership
- pricing variables

Each of these characteristics is examined from both a "macro" and "micro" standpoint. On the macro level, this note highlights the economic, demographic, and sociological trends that affect aggregate demand for a given property type, as well as the factors that influence supply. At the micro level, the key issues are what makes one particular property more likely to generate tenant demand than another, and what factors at the local level (such as zoning laws) can affect supply. Again, this is the same path that many investors tend to follow when they examine an investment opportunity.

For each property type, there is included a table summarizing the essential "building blocks" that an investor should understand and use when preparing pro forma projections of property performance. The real estate investment world is undergoing substantial change with REITs owning almost one-half and pension funds almost one-third of many types of institutional-quality real estate in the United States.

APARTMENT PROPERTIES

The aggregate value of all apartment properties is almost $1 trillion, or roughly 25 percent of the total commercial real estate market. Especially in comparison to other property types, apartment properties provide a relatively stable income stream, their capital requirements are easy to forecast, and they present a relatively low risk of product obsolescence. With the exception of niche apartment communities that attract a narrowly defined type of tenant, well-kept-up apartments properties as a whole have lower downside risk for investors than most other property types.

QUALITY

The investment community classifies apartment properties according to several criteria, the most important of which is quality. Each property is assigned a quality rating (either Class A, Class B, or Class C), depending on both the property's characteristics and the prevailing local market definition of the classes. As seen with other types of property, it is impossible to arrive at a universally accepted definition of these classes. (The elusiveness of these distinctions is sometimes strategic. The apartment building may well be rated "Class A" by the seller and "Class B" by the potential buyer.) This classification scheme is further complicated by rehabilitation, which might or might not warrant an "upgrade" from one class to another.

In general, Class A refers to newer buildings that offer luxury amenities in prime locations. Class B may be used to describe somewhat older buildings (ten to thirty years, depending on the market), or newer properties in a mediocre location or suburban properties missing certain amenities such as a clubhouse, while Class C is reserved for much older buildings often in less-than-prime neighborhoods, serving low- or middle-income tenant populations. These distinctions, although fuzzy at times, shed at least some light on the term "investment-grade property," which is generally reserved for Class A properties. Most institutional investors are willing to invest only in Class A properties, although in overheated investment markets, standards tend to slide.

STRUCTURE

Another obvious (but sometimes useful) way to distinguish among apartment properties is according to their size and layout. Generally speaking, apartment buildings are labeled as either high-rise, mid-rise, or low-rise. This distinction, too, can be affected by contextual considerations. The same twelve-story building that would be considered a "high rise" in Cambridge, Massachusetts, would be considered a mid-rise—or perhaps even a low-rise—in Manhattan.

Height is an important consideration, because taller buildings generally present a significantly higher cost structure to their owners, due both to the higher initial cost of development as well as the continuing relatively high cost of more complex operating systems in the building. In nearly every market, moreover, developers' activities are restricted by zoning laws, which specify the maximum heights and densities that are allowed on a given piece of land.

SUPPLY AND DEMAND

For both urban and suburban locations, demographic trends drive demand growth for apartment properties. A key indicator is household formation, which is strongly correlated with the number of people in the prime renter age group of twenty-five to thirty-four. Another important indicator is trends in household composition. In particular, the recent increase in single-person households (singles tend to be renters) offsets the downward demand effects of the numerical decline in the twenty-five-to-thirty-four age group since 1990. Moreover, the average renter moves every two or three years, while the homeowner average is closer to eight years.

The main competition for rental apartment properties is home ownership: nearly two-thirds of Americans live in single-family homes. The attractiveness of home ownership at any given time—as determined by economic conditions, mortgage interest rates, and the affordability of homes—is referred to as the "substitution effect," and is often an accurate predictor of demand for apartments.

Economic growth can be a multiedged sword when it comes to demand for apartments. On the one hand, prosperity generally leads to rising incomes which favors home ownership. Lower interest rates also increase affordability. On the other hand, economic growth encourages increased immigration (at least into certain cities), and immigrants typically rent their first residence.

Prosperity also increases the likelihood that grown children will move out of their parents' houses and into their own apartments. A less than healthy economy encourages young people to room together under more crowded conditions. A healthier economy makes it possible for people to take apartments with fewer roommates, which drives up demand for space even further.

Changing consumer preferences also can affect demand. Traditionally, the over-fifty age group has had the highest percentage of home ownership. There is some preliminary evidence, however, that this could be changing, as more and more "empty-nesters" opt for smaller and more manageable homes. In many cases, this means trading high-maintenance houses for no-maintenance apartments or condominiums. As the Baby Boom cohort moves en masse into the over-fifty age group, any changes in their lifestyle preferences that amount to a verifiable trend will have enormous impacts on housing demand, including demand for apartments.

The supply of apartment properties is driven both by vacancy rates and absorption rates (i.e., the rate at which new apartment units are leased). In addition, supply is affected by other planned apartment developments (direct competition) and planned new home developments (indirect competition). Supply can be constricted in some locales by zoning laws, difficult approval processes, and high land costs. The actual construction of rental apartments, however, tends to be a relatively simple task, with little or no customization offered to tenants (except at higher income levels). The short cycle for apartment construction has the predictable (and perverse) effect of increasing the risk of overbuilding, especially in places with loose zoning and easy approval processes. As one industry observer has commented, "There is great development risk in apartments, mainly because they can be put up so damned quickly!"

Tax laws affect the demand and supply of apartments in several ways. First, U.S. tax law explicitly encourages single-family home ownership by allowing deductions for mortgage interest and real estate taxes. Second, the recent change to capital gains tax laws eliminated the tax on the first $500,000 of gains on homes sold. This has the potential, in effect, to free a generation of middle-aged Americans from their homes (although it is far from certain that they will cash out and move to apartments). Third, depreciation schedules for apartment buildings have been tinkered with over time, as Congress has attempted to advance one housing policy or another. Recently, when the schedule for commercial properties was increased from 27.5 to 39 years, residential was left at 27.5. Fourth, the subsidized housing industry is entirely dependent on financial commitments from the U.S. and state governments, in the form of rental vouchers (given to tenants) and tax credits and favorable mortgage rates (given to developers).*

LOCATION

Like all of our criteria, location has to be understood on several levels. At the regional level, the same dynamics of population growth, economic growth, and the relative attractiveness of home ownership are used to assess the aggregate demand for apartments. When combined with a review of local supply forces, such an analysis reveals significant variation from region to region. For example, despite population growth and a strong economy, the U.S. South has a soft market for apartments, in part because home prices are so relatively low. The U.S. West—and especially California—has roughly the same population growth and a comparably strong economy; yet astronomical home prices keep the demand for apartments strong.

*Local authorities using federal subsidies have also been developers of apartment buildings primarily for public housing. State housing authorities again using federal and state subsidies created a substantial amount of mixed income housing However, government involvement in apartment construction peaked in the 1960s and '70s, and has been drastically reduced by now.

At the local level, most communities have neighborhoods with distinctive physical, social, and economic characteristics. This is inextricably linked to a consideration of location at the property level. Here is where the old real estate adage ("location, location, location") is relevant. Both demand for and supply of apartments in specific locations is related to the proximity to jobs, schools, and support services (e.g., dry cleaning, groceries, etc.). Demand at the property level is also related to the physical appearance of the property, the size and layout of the units, availability of parking, and any on-site amenities.

Apartment buildings have traditionally been designed and built to suit broadly defined groups, such as "low-income," "middle-class," or "luxury" renters. Increasingly, developers are targeting smaller niches, through specialized unit designs and carefully packaged amenities. For example, in an effort to appeal to the expanding numbers of "lifestyle" renters—that is, people who can afford homes but prefer the hassle-free lifestyle available to renters—developers are putting an increased emphasis on amenities such as a clubhouse, meeting rooms, pool, fitness center, and even the kinds of concierge services normally found at luxury hotels. Deals have been made for the delivery of pizzas. National hotel developers such as Hyatt and Marriott have made huge commitments to senior housing, applying a niche strategy to attract tenants in different segments of the assisted living market. Privatization of prisons has been another rapidly growing area. Others are funding housing projects for a student population that is projected to grow substantially in the coming decade. As niche strategies proliferate, owners will be increasingly vulnerable to changing tenant preferences.

OWNERSHIP

The commercial real estate universe includes investor-owned apartment buildings. Like single-family home ownership, the option to own an apartment unit (in a condominium or cooperative building) provides renters with a competitive alternative to renting.

Much of the recent flurry of REIT activity has been focused on public-market ownership of apartment properties. One measure of the maturity (or saturation) of the apartment REITs is their newly emerging willingness to invest in Class B properties. Nevertheless, public-company ownership of apartments is still dwarfed by private ownership.

Local and regional firms have long dominated the real estate industry. Recently, such firms as Insignia, Apartment Investment Management Company, and Equity Residential have implemented aggressive national strategies designed to bring economies of scale to bear on their apartment operations. Office tenants operating on a national scale sometimes provide the opportunity to achieve scale economies, and these tenants often prefer to deal with national office property owners. In apartments, however, all tenants are local, and it is unclear how substantive the benefits that come from economies of scale will be as a percentage of gross revenues. In the purchase of some individual items such as insurance or purchase of kitchen equipment there will be definite benefits.

VALUATION

Apartment properties are associated with relatively stable returns. In the last ten years, apartments have provided an 8.4 percent annual return, with a standard deviation of 4.8 percent. As noted above, this low volatility results from the stable nature of the apartment income stream, relatively predictable capital expenditure requirements, and a limited risk of obsolescence. Leases are drawn up for relatively short time periods; except where rent-control laws apply, this assures that apartment rents rarely lag behind market rents for long.

For all of these reasons, commercial and savings banks, insurance companies, and investment banks traditionally have been willing to lend on apartment properties. The typical leverage is 60 to 80 percent of value, but in times of easy credit, leverage can go as high as 100 percent.

Market conditions dictate whether debt on apartment properties will require personal guarantees. In the early 1990s, at the bottom of the market cycle, personal guarantees were standard. By the mid 1990s, however, most lending was nonrecourse. Capitalization rates for apartment properties generally range between 8 and 9.5 percent. Investment-grade properties usually trade at the low end of this range, while smaller and older buildings often trade at the high end.

PRO FORMA BUILDING BLOCKS

TERM	KEY CONCEPTS
Per unit	The most common measurement for description and comparison of apartment properties. Less frequently, apartment financial results may be analyzed on a per-square-foot basis.

TERM	KEY CONCEPTS
Lease	Lease terms in most markets are for one year. In softer markets, six-month leases are common. In vacation markets, leases can be for as short as one or two weeks.
Rent	Varies significantly by region and location. Rent is the key assumption in any pro forma; it is essential to understand local market conditions, and to understand how the subject property fits into the market.
Rent-up	The amount of time it takes to lease up a new building usually ranges from six to twelve months. To re-rent vacancies in an existing property ranges from one to four months assuming a reasonably strong market.
Vacancy	Expressed as a percentage of gross potential income. Requires analysis of local market conditions. Ranges of 3 to 7 percent are common.
Operating expenses	The owner generally pays for insurance, on-site payroll, real estate taxes, cleaning, painting, water, and repair of common areas; security; removal of garbage and snow; and all routine maintenance inside of apartments. Owners generally pay for heat, unless electric; tenants almost always pay for telephone service and electricity. The payment of utilities is negotiable, and depends on local market conditions and whether units can be independently metered.
Capital expenditures	Major expenditures in apartment properties are generally more predictable than in other property types. Hot water heaters, refrigerators, and stoves, for example, generally have a ten-year life span; carpets will usually last for five years. For pro formas, a per-unit, per-year figure is used to account for expected costs of roof replacements, parking lot repavings, and any other major expense items.

OFFICE PROPERTIES

The value of all U.S. office properties, including corporate owned assets, is more than $800 billion, or roughly 20 percent of the total commercial real estate market. Office properties present a set of unique challenges to developers, investors, lenders, and tenants. For the developer, the challenge is to juggle fluctuating economic and capital market trends with the ever-changing space and balance sheet needs of tenants and with tenant preferences to lease or own their buildings. Investors and lenders share the challenge of profiting from office properties, which historically have been the most volatile sector of the cyclical real estate industry. Large tenants have to predict space needs several years in advance, and then maneuver effectively through the complex processes of negotiation, leasing, and development. Small tenants (particularly growing companies) face the challenge of managing quickly changing space needs.

QUALITY

Just as in the case of apartment properties, office buildings tend to be labeled with somewhat mysterious quality rankings (Class A, Class B, and Class C). Again, these quality ratings are far from precise, and vary depending on local market standards. For example, in Baltimore, "Class A" space refers to large buildings that are less than twenty-five years old, in prime locations, and with first-class tenants. In Cincinnati, by contrast, Class A means less than ten years old. (The other criteria are the same as in Baltimore.) Rehabilitations, again, confuse the issue. (Some investors would consider a rehabilitated building Class A, but many would continue to call it Class B.) The extent and quality of tenant improvements may also affect a building's classification.

STRUCTURE

Office buildings are either high-, mid-, or low-rise structures. Naturally, central business district settings are more likely to have high rises, while suburban (and sometimes even rural) areas are more likely to have corporate campus and office park settings with several two- to ten-story buildings. Taller buildings generally have higher per square foot development costs, as well as higher levels of tenant improvements.

Many suburban office parks have additional land available for expansion. This means that projects can be built in phases, to make sure supply and demand stay in balance. (In dense central business districts, this kind of flexibility is rarely available.) The size and nature of the target tenants often affects the configuration of these kinds of projects such as whether the tenant is willing to accept an open plan with considerable interior space in a roughly square building or requires many private offices in a more rectangular structure.

SUPPLY AND DEMAND

Returns on office properties are particularly volatile. This volatility can be attributed to a combination of macroeconomic, supply and demand factors, and firm and property-specific factors.

On the supply side, key drivers are vacancy rates; absorption rates (the amount of space newly leased in a given market during a given period of time); the effects of other planned development in the same market; barriers to entry, such as zoning and regulatory approvals; and the effects of potential and existing competition from other, nearby markets (for example, when suburban properties become expensive, investors and tenants often move back to central business districts, or CBDs, for better deals; this has obvious impact on new supply in the suburban market).

The demand for office space is correlated most closely to job growth—or more accurately, projected job growth. In addition, demographic, societal, and technological trends can affect both the amount of space firms need (square feet per employee) and the type of space. Changes in standard working conditions, for example, dictated that more space be allocated per employee in 1975 than in 1945; but in the late 1990s the pendulum swung back, as companies put employees into (relatively dense) open offices. The square footage allocated per person dropped from a range of 250 to 350 square feet to 200 to 250 square feet. Increasingly, tenants want open and flexible floor plates to accommodate the increased density.

While it is unclear if technological advances have reduced the need for space, they have undoubtedly affected the types of space tenants need. Some accounting firms have eliminated private offices for employees who spend most of their time on the road. The ever-increasing use of personal computers by attorneys has reduced the need for administrative assistants (and therefore for the space they formerly occupied). At the same time, increased computer usage (and videoconferencing, and other higher-tech office functions) creates a demand for ever more complex telephone and computer systems.

Vacancy and absorption, the two key indicators of demand and supply, are measured at local and regional levels, due to wide variations between regions.

LOCATION

At a local or regional level, both demand and supply can be impacted by tenants' needs for access to:

- customers and suppliers
- skilled labor
- support services for employees
- highways, airports, and reliable public transportation
- parking (four or five spaces per 1,000 square feet of office space, up from 3.5 a few years ago, is standard in the suburbs where most new building occurs).

TARGET TENANTS

Office properties are often designed and marketed to fit a particular type of tenant, based on a very localized market need. For example, an owner of a medical office building next to a hospital targets medical practices and labs, and therefore has to provide sufficient customer parking as well as other amenities. "Standard" office buildings in suburban settings may attract a broader range of tenants, but owners must nevertheless stay in tune with local needs. Some office buildings focus on R&D users, some of whom may do some production on site; nevertheless, these buildings are generally put in the office (rather than the industrial) category.

The average office tenant tends to occupy a far larger proportion of space in a building than, say, the average apartment tenant occupies in a fifty-unit building. Therefore, if one large office tenant moves out, often because of changing space needs, the immediate impact on the overall vacancy rate may be substantial. Moreover the customized design of the space may make tenant replacement more costly.

The ability and willingness of tenants to pay varying levels of rent has a major impact on what gets built. Because of the variety of spaces available to a given user, commercial brokers are often used to facilitate the leasing process. These brokers will have local offices. Some are also affiliated or part of regional or national firms.

OWNERSHIP

Institutional investors have long buoyed the private market for office properties, both through direct investments and investments in funds focused on office properties. This trend has intensified, with the occasional cooling-off during market dips. Public market ownership of office property tripled in 1997. Many of the acquisitions by office REITs were of high-grade, "trophy" properties. As larger tenants consolidate and spread their operations, there is more willingness to lease, foregoing the ego gratification often associated with ownership. Besides, there is often pressure to minimize the property account on the balance sheet by leasing.

Unlike apartment REITs, it doesn't appear that office REITs are quite ready to plunge into the Class B and Class C markets. Some firms seem intent on both achieving scale economies and on cornering the supply of Class A offices in certain markets. In effect, through concentration, they hope to drive down costs and raise revenues, a strategy that is, as yet, essentially untested.

VALUATION

As I noted above, office-property returns are volatile. (Returns over the ten-year period starting at the height of the market in 1988 were only 3.1 percent with a standard deviation of 9.6 percent.) This volatility creates significant valuation problems. Not only macroeconomic but also other factors affect the ability to value office buildings accurately. Due to the long length of most leases, for example, the current rent paid is usually different from market rent. A prospective lender or buyer is forced to predict the market rent at lease expirations several years out. Tenant improvements and leasing costs tend to be extremely "lumpy," which in turn leads to uneven cash flows. Changing the assumptions behind either one or both of these factors significantly changes the valuation.

Lenders generally are willing to lend between 60 and 70 percent on office properties. Capitalization rates range from 8 to 12 percent, and there tends to be an enormous difference in rates between investment-grade properties and smaller, older properties owned by local players.

PRO FORMA BUILDING BLOCKS

TERM	KEY CONCEPTS
Per square foot (psf)	Other property types may use "per unit" (apartment) or "per room" (hotel) as standard measures, but psf is used in office properties as the most relevant measure. Development costs, sales price, rents, expenses are all calculated in psf. Each local market measures space differently; increasingly, however, most markets use common definitions such as gross, rentable, and usable square footage.
Gross area	The entire physical area of all floor space in a building, measured in square feet.
Rentable area	The area for which rent can be charged. Generally it is the gross area of the full floor, less the area of all vertical penetrations (elevator shafts, stairwells, mechanical shafts, etc.). Rentable area includes the tenant's premises plus an allocation of the common area directly benefiting the tenant, such as restrooms, first floor lobby, common corridors, mechanical and janitor's rooms, and the elevator lobby on the tenant's floor.
Usable area	The secured area occupied exclusively by the tenant within the tenant's leased space. The usable area, plus the tenant proportionate share of common areas, results in rentable area on which rent is charged.
Leases	Lease terms vary by market and by building, but typically most leases are "gross leases" whereby the owner pays operating costs and real estate taxes up to a specific amount or "stop" (which is usually equal to expenses incurred in the year the space was leased). In the United States leases are typically for five years with renewals at market rates or a predetermined percentage of market rates. The length of the lease is often positively correlated to the amount of tenant improvements paid by the owner.

TERM	KEY CONCEPTS
Tenant improvements (TIs)	A tenant improvement allowance is the amount of money, usually measured psf, that the owner will pay for customizing and preparing the tenant space at time of lease or re-lease. It is analogous in some respects to "capital expenditures," and must be amortized as such for tax purposes. However, for pro forma purposes, TIs are much harder to accurately predict than regular capital expenditures. This is because TI amounts are subject to negotiations, which are affected by market conditions as well as by rapidly changing consumer preferences.
Lease commissions	Another significant expense is commissions paid to a leasing broker. Generally the owner (but sometimes the tenant) pays a negotiated fixed fee or percentage of the entire lease amount to the broker. Longer leases tend to generate lower-percentage commissions. For pro forma purposes, lease commissions can also be reduced to psf. The broker, however, tends to think of commissions in dollars.
Operating expenses	Typical operating expenses include cleaning service, routine repairs, security, snow removal, common area maintenance, management, real estate taxes, and insurance. Utilities may be included, or may be metered separately and billed directly to the tenant.
Parking	A standard tenant request is three to five parking spaces per 1,000 square feet of office space. Urban areas with access to mass transit may have only one space per 1,000 square feet. Local zoning ordinances may require more or less spaces.
Turnover	In addition to assumed vacancy rates, several assumptions about turnover are required for pro forma projections. How many lease expirations will result in renewals? How long will it take to re-lease the space? Will the owner have to give free rent for several months to attract a new tenant? Of course, all of these assumptions impact the projected bottom line, and they all will be affected by market conditions in the future.

TERM	KEY CONCEPTS
Floor area ratio (FAR)	The ratio obtained by dividing the gross floor area of all buildings located upon a lot or parcel of land by the total area of such lot or parcel. Zoning ordinances regularly prescribe maximum allowable FARs, as well as height and setback restrictions and parking requirements.

INDUSTRIAL PROPERTIES

Industrial properties, which have an aggregate value of $570 billion, or 14 percent of all commercial real estate, historically have been the least volatile of all property types. Because the estimated $1.2 trillion of company-owned real estate assets are not part of the commercial real estate universe, this segment of the note discusses primarily rental warehouse properties and other types of rental industrial properties.

The term *industrial property* covers a diverse set of real estate needs related to both production and distribution of products. Most manufacturing facilities are company owned: The large, specialized investments required to set up a manufacturing facility encourage asset ownership, to avoid unnecessary dependence on renewal of leases. Warehouse space, used to store inventories and facilitate distribution, is most often occupied on a rental basis. As the accompanying chart shows, warehouse space is the most common form of industrial property. The other industrial property types—R&D space and office showroom/flex space—make up a smaller portion of the industrial property universe.

		U.S. Total Sq. Ft. (000's)	Rental Sq. Ft. (000's)	% Rental
Warehouse	<15% office with 18–30 ft. ceilings and dock height loading	5,390,009	3,686,766	68
R&D	10–15 ft. ceilings with dock and floor-height loading	810,848	654,354	81
Office showroom/Flex	Varied office space with finished exterior on building front	831,759	478,068	57
Manufacturing	Special use with 10–16 ft. ceilings supporting overhead cranes	2,961,074	1,376,899	46
Total industrial		9,993,690	6,196,088	62

Due to several factors unique to industrial properties, they are likely to be in demand/supply equilibrium, less susceptible to high turnover, and less likely (at least in recent years) to require "lumpy" capital investments. Solid investment returns over the past fifteen years have led to a favorable comparison with other property types, especially retail and office. Yet challenges remain for industrial property developers and investors, especially those with older properties at risk of product obsolescence or deteriorating locations.

QUALITY

Industrial properties are less likely to be categorized according to the "class" system (A, B, and C) used for apartments and offices. Instead, they are referred to as either "obsolete," "older," or "newer" space. (In many markets, this system corresponds closely to the class system.) Warehouses may also be described in terms of their use, such as bulk or self-storage warehouses. Self-storage warehouses depending upon their size and location may cater to a variety of residential and commercial users.

STRUCTURE

Industrial buildings used to be considered simply "roofs and parking lots." In recent years, however, the design of new buildings has evolved in response to changing user requirements. Users and investors often prefer to be in established industrial parks with specific covenants and restrictions with regard to access, site coverage, green space, signage, parking, and—in many cases—design and materials used in construction. Parking is increasingly a critical concern. Historically, properties required one space per 1,000 square feet. As buildings gain more cubic capacity, however, more parking is needed, in order to accommodate the trucks that move a larger volume of goods into and out of the facilities.

Property obsolescence remains one of the biggest challenges facing industrial investors, especially as firms consolidate into fewer locations with larger buildings. In many cases, older buildings are so far beyond rehabilitation that they are converted to other uses. Such uses, if there is ample parking, include office space, which is an inexpensive alternative for firms that can't afford Class A or Class B space.

In some cases where the location is suitable and parking plentiful, industrial properties may be converted to retail use. In still other cases, the land that the property sits upon is valuable enough to warrant the demolition of the building to make way for an upgraded use.

SUPPLY AND DEMAND

Demand for industrial space is closely correlated to the strength of the economy. Demand for industrial space increases in periods of economic expansion, and contracts during economic slowdowns. The GDP growth rate alone, however, is an incomplete proxy for warehouse demand. Just as telling are the structural trends that underlie changes in GDP. In the 1990s, for example, the erosion of the U.S. manufacturing base—as well as a sharper focus on reducing inventory levels through more efficient operations—threatened to reduce demand relative to the level of economic output. But an expansion in international trade, concurrent with the strong economy in this period, led to an increase in absolute inventory levels.

Because of a very short development cycle, the supply of industrial space is extremely responsive to demand shifts. A developer seeking to build a warehouse can generally obtain permits within three months, build within six months, and—in a sufficiently strong market—lease-up in an additional three to six months. The same cycle for an office building, in sharp contrast, may take several years. Because of this short lag time in warehouse development, any mismatches between warehouse construction starts and demand for those properties will be corrected quickly. For example: while national suburban office vacancy rates soared to more than 20 percent in the early 1990s, national industrial vacancy rates never exceeded 12 percent—and 12 percent was still very high relative to the historic average of around 5 percent. A reinforcing factor is that warehouse owners tend to write shorter leases during downturns when rental rates are under pressure.

As noted, new supply of warehouse buildings is relatively easy to put on the market. Rising vacancy rates in a particular market will lead to a reduction in new supply. High vacancy also increases the risks associated with speculative building (that is, building with no particular tenants under contract), and reduces its use by developers. As an alternative, developers in down markets may resort exclusively to "build to suit." The converse, of course, is equally true.

High land costs and environmental issues are the two main impediments to new supply. In the major warehouse markets, such as Los Angeles, land prices can serve as an effective barrier to entry to new supply. Environmental problems can have the same effect almost anywhere in the country.

LOCATION

All industrial tenants share a critical need for access to transportation. In the United States, due to the overwhelming dominance of trucking, access to rail service is only critical in certain markets. All other things being equal, locations with the easiest access to the most extensive transportation systems are likely to enjoy the strongest demand. Another key driver of demand is access to an adequate pool of cheap, skilled labor. And if sales operations are conducted from the industrial site, proximity to customers may be important.

Many new warehouses are being built to accommodate tenants who have made commitments to just-in-time inventory systems. These new warehouses are run with fewer personnel and more inventory-management technologies, such as bar-code scanning devices. The increased use of robots has created a demand for "super-flat" floors. Other features, such as energy-efficient heating, cooling, and lighting systems; high-capacity electrical systems; high-volume sprinkler systems; and high floor-load capacities, bear on the desirability of these newer facilities.

The new "cube" warehouses, which are characterized by highly flexible floor plans, can be used by one or more tenants. Demand for these more flexible spaces is threatening to obsolete many older, plain-vanilla warehouses, despite the higher rents associated with the newer facilities. But there are some markets in which older facilities are more than adequate for many users, especially due to their prime locations. In markets (such as Boston) with a high proportion of small tenants, conventional spaces may be sufficient for years to come.

OWNERSHIP

Public-company ownership of industrial assets has grown in tandem with the rise of the overall REIT market. Pension fund advisors have aggregated pools of properties into commingled funds. Because of the relatively small size of individual investments it is possible to put together diversified portfolios. As is the case with office and retail properties, newly national firms expect to take advantage of scale economies, especially in negotiations with national tenants. But regional companies (and a few private national companies) still maintain control over the vast majority of industrial properties; and a well established network of regional rental brokers permits smaller, local owners to survive and compete, as well.

Obsolescence is the key challenge facing industrial investors today. In addition, they will continue to feel the effects of a dwindling manufacturing base. They have fared well in recent years, due to the vibrant economy, the increase in imports and the introduction of new product types. It remains to be seen, however, how long industrial properties can provide competitive and stable returns.

VALUATION

Industrial property has provided a 6.3 percent annual return for the last ten years, with a standard deviation of 7.6 percent. The performance in this sector, therefore, is not quite as stable as that of apartments, but is less volatile than the performance of office properties. Tenant improvements—the biggest unknown expenditure for office properties—are generally far less of a burden to industrial property owners. Industrial tenants tend to stay longer than office tenants, and even upon turnover, the dollar amount of tenant improvements per square foot is much lower in industrial buildings than in office properties. Other capital expenditures, such as roof replacements, tend to be predictable over the longer term, if not on a year-to-year basis.

Along with offices, industrial properties have long been a favorite of institutional investors looking for direct investments. Strong and stable performance in this sector, as well as the interest of public companies, has steadily reduced capitalization rates to between 8.5 percent and 10.5 percent. As is true for apartments and offices, investment-grade industrial properties—especially the new "cubes" with triple-A-credit-rated tenants—trade at lower cap rates than smaller and older properties. Financing ranges between 60 and 80 percent, again depending on the relative competitiveness of the property.

PRO FORMA BUILDING BLOCKS

TERM	KEY CONCEPTS
Per square foot (psf)	Standard measure for development costs, rents, expenses, sales price, etc.

TERM	KEY CONCEPTS
Lease length	Varies by market. In most cases, warehouse leases are for five years, with renewal options and rent increases written into the original lease. Warehouse tenants tend to stay in their space longer than office, apartment, or retail tenants.
Triple net lease	In a triple net lease, the tenant pays (1) operating costs, (2) real estate taxes, and (3) utilities in place of the owner. In addition, of course, the tenant pays rent to the owner. The use of triple net leases is common in warehouse leasing, although lease terms vary by market.
Industrial gross lease	An alternative to the triple net lease in some markets, the industrial gross lease is one in which the landlord pays real estate taxes, insurance fees, and the cost of structural and roof repairs.
Tenant improvements (TIs)	TI costs are low relative to office properties (generally $1 to $2 per square foot). Typical TIs include replacing loading dock doors, fixing cracks in floors, adding or removing office space, and upgrading (e.g., making handicapped-accessible) rest rooms.
Operating expenses	Typical expenses include snow removal, landscaping, painting and striping of parking lots, real estate taxes, and insurance. (See "triple net lease," above.)
Capital expenditures	Any major expenses for common areas that will usually not be passed through to the tenants. For example, repaving a parking lot or replacing a roof usually qualifies as a capital expenditure.
Vacancy/turnover	Assumptions about vacancy are not as critical in modern warehouse property pro formas, because tenants tend to stay longer, and the cost of TIs necessary to attract a new tenant is generally not a significant burden. Obsolete properties in less desirable locations, on the other hand, may stay unrented for considerable periods.

HOTELS

Hotels, with an aggregate worth of nearly $185 billion in 1996, or 5 percent of all commercial real estate, historically have been the most volatile sector of the commercial real estate universe. Despite demand that is easy to predict—it correlates on a macro basis almost exactly to gross domestic product—supply has long been prone to cyclical overbuilding.

Hotels obviously have a real estate component that contributes significantly to their performance. Mastering the *operating* business of a hotel, however, is of paramount importance. More than other sectors of the larger real estate industry, operational skills provide a real opportunity for an owner to add value. But this cuts both ways. Excellent operational skills, for example, create and reinforce a hotel's "brand"; while poor operations can quickly undercut that brand. For these and other reasons—including the high financial and operating leverages typical of this sector—hotels present a significant challenge to real estate investors.

Because both property companies and hotel companies invest in hotel properties, there is almost an unlimited variety of deal structures. A local real estate investor, for example, may build and own the hotel, and then contract with a national hotel company for management services. In other cases, the investor and the hotel company form a joint venture to share in the equity investment. In another common format pioneered in the 1980s by Marriott, the hotel company develops the property, and then spins off the real estate in a syndication while retaining the management contract. "Dumping" the real estate on limited partners is, of course, a way of reducing the amount of capital needed to expand a hotel empire. The management company in turn creates a more predictable earnings stream, which makes it more attractive to Wall Street.

This strategy allows Marriott to maintain unusually low debt-to-capital ratios. Most property companies can manage the enormous capital requirements of the hotel business only through high financial leverage. Loan-to-value ratios of 60 to 80 percent are common for privately owned hotels.

But the major challenge for hotel owners and operators is their near-total dependence on the economy to provide demand for their rooms. A secondary, but very real, threat is overbuilding.

QUALITY

Hotels are not assigned class rankings like apartment and office properties. A proxy for quality in this industry is the particular price segment that the hotel tries to target: budget, economy, mid-price, upscale, or full-service/luxury.

STRUCTURE

Based on the price segment, the target tenants (business, convention, or leisure travelers), and the location (urban, suburban, highway, airport, or resort), hotels come in a wide variety of shapes and sizes. In general, the design of a hotel, together with its package of amenities, is its most important marketing tool. One look at a hotel's lobby—whether the Plaza in midtown Manhattan or the Motel 6 in Kalamazoo—tells the user what to expect. America's highways are cluttered with prefabricated, look-alike motels and hotels; but the ambitious hotels of Las Vegas provide ample evidence that bold design can play an essential role in resort hotel marketing.

SUPPLY AND DEMAND

Assessing aggregate demand characteristics for hotel rooms in the United States is uncomplicated. Basically, there are three types of travelers who use hotels: business, convention, and leisure. For each, demand is directly related to the state of the economy. A healthier economy leads to more business travel and more leisure travel, resulting in higher demand for hotel rooms. The nearly perfect correlation between GDP and hotel room demand can be disrupted by large price swings in oil (which usually affect transportation prices), the value of the dollar (a strong dollar discourages foreign tourism), bad weather, and political unrest. Industry observers have long predicted that improving technologies, such as videoconferencing, would have negative impacts on the hotel trade; so far, though, this has not come to pass.

The *supply* of hotel rooms is also determined by multiple factors. Some markets—for example, crowded urban areas—have little available land, which constrains new supply even in periods of strong economic growth and high hotel profitability. Sometimes these two converging factors lead to the conversion of downtown office buildings into hotels, but these kinds of conversions rarely alter the fundamentals of supply and demand. In short, high barriers to entry (such as the lack of buildable land and the high per room cost) lead to higher profitability in a strong economy, and mitigate overcapacity in a down economy.

This is less true in nonurban areas. Hotels in the mid, economy, and budget price ranges are quick and easy to build, especially in the suburbs. Assuming there are no effective barriers to entry (e.g., restrictive zoning, high land prices), hotel construction starts can quickly respond to high industry profitability. Of course, new supply can quickly erode profits (in a strong economy) or create oversupply (in a down economy). A 75 percent occupancy rate for a hotel is considered very good. Few hotels are strong both in weekdays and weekends. There are often seasonal differences in occupancy.

LOCATION

At the local level, demand for a particular hotel is linked to its proximity to either local attractions or businesses that generate travel. Airport hotels, for example, provide convenience to business travelers. Being next to (or part of) a convention center can be a major plus. Resort hotels, of course, depend heavily on their natural (or man-made) attractions, and also on relative ease of access.

As long as there have been commercial lodging places, these businesses have tried to segment the market based on the profile of a target user. But this segmentation is far from complete, and the creation of new segments is considered a key activity for national hotel companies that want to maintain growth. In the fall of 1998, for example, Marriott launched a new line of hotels with "roomy and practical" accommodations, aimed at middle-class families and business travelers. The addition of this new "product line" meant that Marriott was now operating in eight distinct segments. They (and their competitors) will no doubt continue to look for more such segments.

OWNERSHIP: OPERATIONS

As noted, the operating component is more critical in the hotel business than in any other category in real estate. The benefits of economies of scale have been well tested and proven, with all of the leading hotel companies having had national portfolios well before the recent industry consolidation. Size and national scope, of course, creates buying power; but the real key to economies of scale in hotels is the recognizable brand name. Branding gives operators leverage in booking reservations, attracting top management, and building relationships with large numbers of customers. These factors, in turn, provide real advantages when the hotel company goes after new market niches (essentially brand extensions). The presence of strong brands in a particular market niche often serves as an effective barrier to entry to would-be competitors.

The similarities between hotel companies and airlines are numerous. They both require huge capital investments, and both involve large and fixed operating expenses. In the simplest sense, both airlines and hotels have to "fill the seats." The more complex target for the operators of both airlines and hotels is "yield management," which means finding the right combination of prices and occupancy levels to maximize profits (or minimize losses). Airlines pioneered the practice of charging dozens of different prices for the same class of seat on the same flight. This practice has more recently been adopted by national hotel owners, and will no doubt intensify in the future.

The savvy investor or developer who surveys the hotel industry quickly concludes that this is not a business for the inexperienced. He or she usually concludes that the best way to get into the hotel business as a property owner is to team up with a national hotel company. This often means awarding a management contract to the experienced partner. In most such cases, the developer (or investor) owns the real estate, and pays an annual fee plus a share of the profits to the hotel company, which has full operational control. Because the hotel company usually has a strong bargaining position, it is usually able to extract a long-term (often twenty-year) contract, with numerous provisions restricting the owner, including limits on the amount of cash the owner can take out of the property or requirements as to the size of a reserve for replacement.

One of the hardest-fought issues between owners and managers, in these cases, is the extent to which the hotel company agrees not to compete within the given market area. For obvious reasons, the owner argues that he or she doesn't want another Hilton next door to this one; while Hilton argues that it should be left entirely to the market to determine where Hiltons can be located.

OWNERSHIP: PUBLIC AND PRIVATE

Publicly traded companies have dominated the hotel business for many years. Until recently, however, the form of public ownership for industry leaders—such as Marriott, ITT-Sheraton, Hilton, and the Four Seasons—was through standard corporations, rather than REITs.

There was a good historical reason for this. REIT law allows for no corporate-level tax on income, provided (among other things) that (1) the bulk of income is *not* earned from operating businesses such as hotels, and (2) 95 percent of net income is paid out in dividends. In the 1990s, however, several "paired-share" REITs discovered a loophole in the law, which essentially allowed them to include hotel income as REIT income—and therefore shield that income from taxation at the corporate level. Companies such as Starwood Capital and Patriot American quickly used the loophole to vault into the upper reaches of the hotel business—and in Starwood's case, to bypass the "old guard" and emerge as the largest operator of hotel rooms in the world.

This story, though, is still being written. Hotel REITs have never operated in a hotel-industry down cycle. Hotel REITs must distribute 95 percent of their net income, and are therefore effectively prohibited from accumulating significant retained earnings. Hotel REITs rely heavily on continued equity and debt offerings to provide their capital, and a downturn in either the hotel business or the REIT stock market would quickly test the ability of hotel REITs to meet the enormous capital needs of their industry.

Recognizing the potential pitfalls of a hotel REIT, in fact, Starwood converted from a REIT to a standard C-corporation, which pays income taxes at the corporate level, shortly after Congress eliminated the tax advantage of the paired-share format. Observers expected the other paired-share REITs to follow suit, leaving the hotel industry once again dominated by publicly held C-corporations. Both these and other operators will likely still attempt to finance building costs through spinoffs of their real estate into new REITs or other off–balance sheet financing mechanisms.

VALUATION

Hotel performance far surpassed every property type in the last five years, posting an annual return of 19.1 percent. But we should assume that the recent upswing is only the latest in a long history of turbulent cycles. Even with stellar five-year returns, hotels over the last ten years returned only 10.1 percent annually, with a huge standard deviation of 11.4 percent. "Profits" in the hotel business are frustratingly elusive; there is a continual need to plow back profits into the enterprise to refurbish and upgrade the facilities.

Volatility of returns is due to the unhealthy but necessary combination of high operating leverage and high financial leverage. The significant fixed costs of operating a hotel, as well as a typical leverage of 80 percent, make hotel owners extremely vulnerable to both competition (oversupply) and economic downturns (lack of demand). Hotel financing is generally a more specialized form of lending, which means that fewer lenders are willing to become involved and the interest rate is normally higher.

PRO FORMA BUILDING BLOCKS

TERM	KEY CONCEPTS
Per room	A widely used standard of measure for every aspect of development, sales, revenues, and expenses.
Occupancy	One of two key assumptions (along with ADR, below). National occupancy rates are tracked by groups such as Smith Travel Service, and have hovered at around 65 percent for several years. A closer look into distinct segments and local markets, however, reveals wide variations in occupancy rates. When making assumptions about both occupancy and ADR, consider the operator's skills, the niche, the fundamentals of supply and demand on the local level, and the relative power of the hotel "brand."
Average daily rate (ADR)	The average daily price for all occupied rooms over a given period of time (usually one year).
Room revenues	To derive total room revenues for the year, multiply occupancy percentage times ADR, times the number of rentable rooms, times 365.
Other revenues	Food and beverage are generally the largest generators of ancillary revenues although the profit margins are generally lower than other segments Other sources include rental of meeting and conference rooms, health clubs, telephones, and business services. In many cases, as you would expect, there is a correlation between these revenues and occupancy rates.
Expenses	Some expenses are fixed, such as property taxes and insurance. Others are mostly fixed, but have some variable components (e.g., marketing, property operations and maintenance, energy, and general/administrative). The remainder of expenses

TERM	KEY CONCEPTS
	(e.g., food, beverage, telephone, room cleaning, supplies) are variable.
Reserve for replacement of furniture, fixtures, and equipment	Depreciation of hotel assets is real. Capital expenditures, usually in the form of room and lobby makeovers, are required at regular intervals to keep a property attractive and competitive. Even for newer hotels in the upscale segment, the annual budgeted reserve can exceed $1,000 per room. The actual amount of reserves for pro forma purposes depends on the market segment, location, age, and condition of the property, as well as any requirements set forth in the management contract.

RETAIL

Retail property comprises roughly $1.2 trillion, or some 30 percent of all commercial real estate. In the United States in 1997, there were more than 42,000 shopping centers, comprising more than 5 billion square feet of leasable retail area—by far the highest amount of retail space per person in any country.

While owning retail property doesn't necessitate an operating expertise to the same extent as the hotel trade, it does require a sophisticated understanding of the retail business. More than is true for any other property type, investor returns are tied to tenant business performance—as well as to the rate of inflation, which affects price levels and consequently rents. Developers and owners must contend with powerful national tenants, who have long approval processes and who are able to negotiate hard for large spaces in exactly the right locations.

In comparison with every other property type, retail property performance was weak throughout the 1990s, despite the sustained economic boom during that decade. This fact, along with several characteristics of retail supply-and-demand dynamics, makes owning most retail properties a risky venture. The investor faces many challenges, including the threat of obsolescence due to changing tenant needs, the threat of oversupply (which exacerbates the obsolescence problem), the "downward spiral" phenomenon of a declining property, and the great difficulties and expense associated with returning a deteriorated property to financial viability. On the other hand, dominant malls have shown an adaptability to market trends and often are priced at a favorable capitalization rate.

With the growth of public REITs, there has been considerable consolidation of companies. They hope to have more clout with potential tenants and obtain better financing terms. By also using the corporate name for all their centers, some hope to establish standards in shoppers' minds equivalent to the standards created by marketers of consumer products, in essence a form of branding.

QUALITY

More than for any other property type, the quality of a retail project is judged by the quality and viability of the tenants. Why? For one, retail tenants are visible in a way that apartment tenants or hotel guests are not. Second, large retail tenants (and especially national tenants) do enormous amounts of market research on the trade area and the exact location before they commit to renting a site. Their willingness to commit to a particular location is a powerful endorsement of that site's quality. The endorsement of one large tenant can have a positive effect on the leasing of the rest of the property.

The reverse is also true. Older, run-down malls that lose prime tenants to newer competitors find it increasingly difficult (if not impossible) to attract new tenants. This is the downward spiral: As the obsolete mall is slowly abandoned, that decline scares off both investors and prospective tenants, and thereby feeds upon itself.

On a monthly basis, nearly 190 million shoppers visit a U.S. shopping center. The landscape in America is dotted with various sizes and types of centers, and it is very difficult to locate many of these properties in a neat subclassification. The International Council of Shopping Centers identifies eight dominant types of centers (see table).

SUPPLY AND DEMAND

Demand for retail property correlates to demand for retail goods. Both are affected by: household income; the distribution of wealth (people with lower income levels spend more with every marginal increase in income than people with higher income levels); the growth or decline in population of the fifteen-to-twenty-four-year-old and over-fifty groups (the big spenders, at the time of this writing); and consumer spending habits (*how much* will be spent, and *how* it will be spent).

Type of Center	Concern	Sq. Ft.	Acres
Neighborhood	Convenience	30,000–150,000	3–15
Community	General merchandise; convenience	100,000–350,000	10–40
Regional	General merchandise; fashion; some entertainment (mall, typically enclosed)	400,000–800,000	40–100
Superregional	Similar to regional but has more variety and assortment	800,000+	60–120
Fashion/Specialty	Higher end, fashion oriented	80,000–250,000	5–25
Power	Category-dominant anchors; few small tenants	250,000–600,000	25–80
Theme/Festival	Leisure; tourist-oriented; retail and service	80,000–250,000	5–20
Outlet	Manufacturers' outlet stores	50,000–400,000	10–50

Trends in spending patterns are particularly important to the highly fragmented retail industry, because they affect how much and what type of space will be needed. In the 1990s, consumers displayed a growing desire to do all of their shopping in one place. For working women, shopping was no longer viewed as a leisure activity. Instead, power centers—tenanted by "category killers" such as BJ's Wholesale Club and Home Depot—gained popularity in part by satisfying this desire for one-stop convenience. At the high end, new fashion malls cater to the disproportionate wealth of upper-income families.

Evolving business practices also affect demand for certain kinds of spaces. Many regional malls were built with 150-foot-deep floor plans, which allowed tenants ample room for back-area inventory storage. When just-in-time delivery became standard operating procedure, many retailers needed only 75-foot depths. The combination of this newly "useless" space and changing consumer habits was enough to drive many older regional malls out of business, even in the midst of a sustained economic boom. And as noted above, the "downward spiral" phenomenon drives existing tenants out of failing malls, and deters new ones from signing on.

As anchor tenants move more extensively into areas traditionally served by mall stores (such as women's apparel) and as existing mall stores with lower storage requirements downsize, food courts, multiplex cinemas, and other entertainment uses are being added to attract new customers.

The Internet presents yet another trend that seems certain to alter the face of retail shopping and associated space needs. Every on-line purchase of a good or service that was formerly purchased at a retail location reduces the aggregate need for retail space. Shopping centers managed to grow both in terms of number and sales-dollars-captured despite the rapid rise of mail-order businesses in the 1980s and 1990s. It remains to be seen whether in the long term, traditional retail approaches can survive the assault of the Internet. Many established retailers will expand into multiple distribution channels, with some Internet operators opening small stores as well. Price competition is likely to increase, putting pressure on rents.

One ray of hope lies in the fact that regional malls have become the new "Main Street." They not only provide convenient and (in many cases) economical ways to shop, but also entertainment, restaurants, and many other ways to socialize in an increasingly isolated and atomistic society. It seems clear that the successful malls of the future will be those that understand and take full advantage of this fact.

The supply of retail property seems endless—even overwhelming. Even the casual observer wonders how so much new retail construction can be undertaken as older malls are failing left and right. The fact is that America is "over-stored," and that each new center that comes on line is replacing an older one. New centers are often built to suit a credit-worthy national retailer that is expanding into a new market, and—due to their preleasing—these centers are virtually assured of profitability in the short run. But owners of older centers are victims of a "double whammy": The new building in town highlights the fact that your own facility is aging, and your tenants begin to lose customers to the new store.

In this cutthroat environment, developers have every incentive to add new supply that meets a market demand, despite declines in certain segments of retailing. Oversupply is held in check only by some centers going out of business or being converted to other uses.

LOCATION

In addition to highly trafficked locations with good visibility, retail developers look closely at population density (current and projected), household income levels, buying habits and other demographic data for a profile of the trading area. Naturally, an analysis of the trading area includes a review of existing competitive retail centers, as well as a survey of land available for possible future competition.

	Typical Anchor(s) (or large tenant where no anchor)			
Type of Center	Number	Type	Anchor Ratio (% of total leasable area taken by anchor)	Primary Trade Area (miles)
Neighborhood	1 or more	Supermarket	30–50	3
Community	2 or more	Discount dept. store; drug; home improvement; large specialty/discount apparel	40–60	3–6
Regional	2 or more	Full-line dept. store; jr. dept. store; mass merchant; discount dept. store; fashion apparel	50–70	5–15
Superregional	3 or more	Full-line dept. store; jr. dept. store; mass merchant; fashion apparel	50–70	5–25
Fashion/Specialty	None	Fashion	NA	5–15
Power	3 or more	Category killer; home improve.; discount dept. store; warehouse club; off-price	75–90	5–10
Theme/Festival	None	Restaurants; entertainment	NA	NA
Outlet	None	Manufacturers' outlet stores; off-price retailers	NA	25–75

TARGET TENANTS

The retail property owner must have a marketing plan for the whole property, as well as for the individual spaces, and that plan must be compelling to prospective tenants. Typically, such plans center on one or more anchor tenants that are compatible with the location, size, and classification of the shopping center. The table above, also from the International Council of Shopping Centers, groups these considerations by each of the eight types of shopping centers.

OWNERSHIP: OPERATIONS

Anchor tenants usually pay little or no rent, preferring to own their own store built on a site or *pad* provided by the mall owner. The mall owner's revenue is generated, therefore, almost entirely by *in-line* or mall space, occupied by smaller tenants. In a way, for the developer it is an advantage for the anchors to own their own stores since as "loss leaders" their leases would not generate much profit. Anchors do pay their share of common-area maintenance.

Leasing and negotiations in retail properties require special mention, because among all the property types, retail and office are the most likely to generate tense negotiations prior to a lease signing. In hotels, a tenant (i.e., a guest) almost always accepts the room and rate without discussion, and there is little else to discuss. In the case of apartments, there may be minor issues to negotiate—such as the installation of a new appliance—but by and large, lease terms are standard. Retail and office leases, however, hold the potential for multiple conflicts, no matter who the party on the other side of the table is. The small, local mom-and-pop retailer knows that every penny he or she can squeeze out of an owner goes directly to the bottom line. The national retailer can retain a battery of experienced negotiators who are prepared to argue over the implications of every word in a lease. In either case, the retail property owner can expect a long negotiation. Rental brokers are generally used in smaller centers while the major developers often have direct relationships with the national or regional retailers.

OWNERSHIP: PUBLIC AND PRIVATE

Public-company ownership of retail centers has increased recently, especially in the regional mall arena, in which there had already been considerable consolidation. The complexities inherent in building such centers—and the unwillingness of national tenants or lenders to do business with amateurs—restricts the number of competitors in the field. At the same time, generally limited sales growth and a bleak outlook (caused by oversupply) have, for some retailers, dampened investor interest.

It is not uncommon for a national tenant to bundle lease negotiations with one owner for several different retail centers. In this and similar circumstances, experienced management has been shown to add value.

VALUATION

Ten-year performance in the retail sector shows an annual return of 5.7 percent with a standard deviation of only 5.4 percent. Because of this unspectacular although stable return, retail property has been falling out of favor in the past several years, as investors revise their perspective on the entire retailing industry. For all except the best malls, the stagnating sales that characterized the recent economic boom years have fundamentally changed the perception that continued retail sales growth was inevitable.

Some economic trends that are welcomed by other industries hurt the retail property sector. Most retail leases have a clause stating that the tenant will pay the higher of two sums: 1) a base rent, or (2) a percentage of sales, fixed in advance and reflecting the nature of the tenant's business. The relative lack of inflation in recent years has hurt landlords who anticipated inflation-fueled growth in sales.

Retail is the only property type in which capitalization rates rose during the tremendous real estate up-cycle in the 1990s. The disparities between values for specific properties are even more pronounced than is true for office properties. Well established regional malls in markets with high barriers to entry command premium prices, with cap rates averaging nearly 8 percent. Older regional malls that have new competition—either on the ground or on the drawing boards—are sold at steep discounts, with cap rates averaging more than 11 percent. Strip or neighborhood centers sell in the 9 to 10 percent range. There is considerable lender interest in well located, well anchored centers, and very little interest in troubled centers. The ability to find replacement tenants is less certain in retailing than in other property types. Strong tenants such as Wal-Mart that cannibalize sales throughout a market may force many existing tenants out of business.

PRO FORMA BUILDING BLOCKS

TERM	KEY CONCEPTS
Per square foot	Standard measure for development costs, rents, expenses, sales price, etc.
Lease length	Varies by market. In most cases, leases for national retailers are for ten years (longer for anchors; five years for local retailers), with renewal options and rent increases written into the original lease.
Triple net lease	In a triple net lease, the tenant pays (1) operating costs, (2) real estate taxes, and (3) utilities. In addition, the tenant pays rent to the owner. The use of triple net leases is prevalent in retail leasing, although lease terms vary by market. Included in operating costs are a pro rata share of the costs of maintaining common areas.
Sales per square foot	Because of percentage rent terms (see below), tenants are usually required to report their sales figures to owners on a monthly or quarterly basis.

TERM	KEY CONCEPTS
Common area maintenance (CAM)	Tenants collectively pay for routine maintenance of the property. Each tenant pays a pro rata share of cleaning, trash removal, landscaping, maintenance of parking lots and the exterior of the building, utility costs, and other costs related to common areas. In larger centers, the cost of management and promotion of the center are also included.
Percentage rent	Typical leases have three components: base rent, CAM charges, and percentage rent. If the tenant's sales go over a predetermined threshold, the owner is entitled to a percentage of the excess. This provision allows the owner to share in the tenant's success, on the theory that the owner contributed to that success by properly managing the center. Negotiating an appropriate threshold is a skill of critical importance to both the tenant and the owner.
Tenant improvements	TI costs depend very heavily on local market conditions. Sometimes they can be quite high, relative to office properties. But in other cases there will be no TI, because tenants pay the entire cost of fixing up their space. In such situations, an owner may finance the tenant fix-up by providing credit to the tenant.
Capital expenditures	Any major outlay for a common area or for the base building that may or may not be passed through to the tenants (e.g., repaving a parking lot, replacing a roof, etc.).
Vacancy/turnover	Power centers with national tenants may experience little or no turnover. In weak regional malls or strip centers, however, empty space can take months (or even years) to rent. Even in the better centers, 10 to 15 percent vacancy is not uncommon for mall stores. Because of changes in the fortunes of individual retailers, a poor-performing store can affect others around it. Assumptions must therefore be tailored carefully to reflect these and other differences among property types.

APPENDIX B

COMMERCIAL REAL ESTATE DUE-DILIGENCE CHECKLIST

START-UP

1. Preliminary inquiries
   - Flood zone
   - Environmental issues/asbestos
   - Physical issues/roof/seismic
   - Lease rollovers
2. Prepare preliminary financial spreadsheet
3. Obtain written proposals from third-party consultants
   - Environmental
   - Structural
   - Seismic
   - ADA
   - Roof
   - Floor
   - Market studies
   - HVAC/mechanical systems
   - Landscape
   - Elevator
   - Sprinkler
   - Traffic/parking
   - Tenant credit
   - Appraisal (if required)
4. Obtain certificates of insurance from all third-party consultants
5. Obtain written confirmation of transaction; determine due-diligence fees w/consultants
6. Prepare due-diligence team roster
7. Prepare due-diligence budget
8. Prepare schedule of key dates
9. Obtain summary information—brochures, photos, maps
10. Check with insurance advisor

LEGAL, TITLE AND SURVEY

1. Letter of Intent
2. Purchase and Sale Agreement
3. Exhibits to Purchase and Sale Agreement
4. Posting of Deposit
5. Assignment of Purchase and Sale Agreement
6. Assignment of Leases and Rents
7. Bill of Sale
8. Deed
9. Preliminary Title Report
10. Review Title Exceptions
11. Final Title Policy
12. Review existing surveys
13. Review updated survey with certification
14. Review reciprocal-use easements and restriction agreements
15. Review owner's association documents
16. Review zoning
17. Obtain zoning opinion from local counsel if deemed necessary
18. Review financing documents if any
19. Review seller financial statements
20. Review ground lease documents if any

PHYSICAL

1. Obtain complete plans and specifications
2. Obtain tenant improvement plans
3. Verify ceiling height, floor slab, number/types of loading docks, turning radius, lighting
4. Verify number of parking spaces
5. Verify rentable/leasable square footage (architect's certificate); reconcile to rent roll

6. Obtain draft third-party reports
7. Review any guarantees or warranties for building or systems
8. Review any construction documents, inspection reports
9. Prepare list of deferred maintenance items
10. Prepare list of capital expenditures required
11. Prepare memo re deferred maintenance and capital items
12. Code compliance, notices of violations, possible code changes
13. Replacement cost analysis

TENANCY AND LEASES

1. Review all leases
2. Review all tenant correspondence and files
3. Compare leases to seller rent roll/financial projections
4. Review schedule of concessions—tenant improvements, free rent, lease buyouts, other
5. Examine tenant options—termination, renewal, rights of first refusal, expansion
6. Review historical accounts receivable information
7. Conduct tenant interviews
8. Review tenant interview notes in file
9. Review tenant complaint file
10. Obtain insurance certificates for all tenants
11. Review Certificate of Occupancy for all tenants
12. Review tenant sales information (retail)
13. Review historical percentage rents, percentage rent billings (retail)
14. Review leasing status report form listing broker
15. Review standard lease form
16. Review estoppels; match to rent roll and financial projections
17. Review list of security deposits and match to rent roll and estoppels
    - Check interest required on security deposits?

18. Review parking requirements/reserved parking in leases
19. Review operating covenants, recapture, co-tenancy clauses in lease (retail)
20. Review scope of standard tenant improvements

FINANCIAL AND OPERATIONAL

1. Review seller's current year operating budget
2. Review prior years' operating statement
3. Review year-to-date operating statement
4. Review common area maintenance (CAM)/other reimbursable expense billings
5. Review prior years' capital expenditures
   - Review real estate taxes
   - Assess impact of sale on real estate taxes
   - Engage consultant for real estate tax review
   - Review current and prior years' real estate tax assessment notices
   - Review bonds/special assessments (if any)
6. Review utility invoices and utility reimbursements
7. Review personal property information
8. Review service contracts
9. Review any permits or licenses required to operate property
10. Review parking agreement
11. Verify parking income
12. Review antenna, cable, or other special agreements
13. Review owners' association documents, by-laws
14. Review union contracts
15. Review appraisal (if required)

MARKET

1. Tour competing properties
2. Perform study of competition and market rent comparables
3. Review competitive vacancy, market vacancy

4. Obtain general background information on market
5. Perform demographic analysis (retail)
6. Obtain traffic counts (retail)
7. Analyze sales potential analysis (retail)
8. Analyze merchandising/strategic plan (retail)
9. Analyze potential competition—planned/entitled projects
10. Analyze building and land sale comps

PRE-CLOSING

1. Notify accounting of capital call at least 30 days prior to close (assumes no outside financing)
2. Prepare final investment brief
3. Due-diligence materials for review
   - Final purchase and sales agreement
   - Environmental
   - All engineering reports
   - Projections
4. Management agreement
5. Leasing agreement
6. Notices to tenants re change in ownership, management
7. Terminate/transfer service contracts
8. Utility cutoff
9. Transfer of warranties
10. Obtain final versions of third-party reports
11. Review settlement statements
    - Security deposits (plus interest if any)
    - Prorating of rents, service contracts
    - Proper treatment of reimbursements
    - Verify real estate taxes; tax period
    - Return of deposit (plus interest)
    - Proper allocation of closing costs
    - Define rights to receivables or payables due to seller

12. Review accounts receivable as of closing date
13. Review estoppels

POST-CLOSING

1. Prepare post-closing transition memo
2. Check insurance sheet
3. Send closing/settlement to accounting
4. Send leases to asset management
5. Pay all due-diligence/closing bills
6. Finalize adjustments based on bills to be received post-closing
7. Coordinate delivery of seller information to property manager

A BACK-OF-THE-ENVELOPE GLOSSARY

abatement. (1) A reduction in the property tax bill, usually as a result of successfully contesting the assessed valuation. (2) A reduction of environmental contamination. (3) A reduction in rent.

absorption rate. The rate at which vacant space is filled, or units in a building or lots in a subdivision are sold. This is a way of calculating demand.

acceleration clause. Clause used in a note and mortgage (or deed of trust) which gives the lender the right to demand payment in full after a default by the borrower.

accessibility. The ease of access to a site by customers, employees, carriers, and others necessary to the intended use of the property. To be "handicapped-accessible" involves compliance with various federal, state, and local codes.

accrued interest. Interest on a debt instrument which has been earned but not yet paid. Since interest is usually paid in arrears, accrued interest may not necessarily indicate a delinquency in payment.

acquisition costs. Total costs of acquiring a property, including amounts paid to seller and other related costs and fees.

acre. A measure equal to 43,560 square feet or 160 square rods configured in any shape. It usually refers to land.

ad valorem. "According to value." A method of taxation using the value of the item taxed to determine the amount of tax. Taxes can be either "ad valorem" or "specific." Example: A tax of $5.00 per $10,000.00 of value per house is "ad valorem." A tax of $5.00 per house (irrespective of value) is "specific."

addition. A portion of a building added to the original structure.

adjustable mortgage loans (AMLs). Mortgage loans under which the interest rate is recalculated periodically based on a predetermined formula—such as in relation to changes in the Treasury rate for 30-year bonds—to more closely coincide with current rates. AMLs are also called adjustable rate loans, adjustable rate mortgages (ARMs), flexible rate loans, or variable rate loans.

adjusted funds from operations (AFFO). A performance measure used to analyze **REITs** (see below). AFFO is intended to provide a better approximation of REIT cash flow than funds from operations (**FFO,** see below). AFFO is a refinement of FFO that is calculated by starting at FFO and subtracting a reserve for normal capital expenditures as well as leasing and tenant-improvement expenses.

agent. One who is authorized to act for or represent another, usually in business matters. The agent's authority may be express or implied.

air rights. The right to the use of the air space above property without the right to use the surface of the property. Such air rights may restrict the surface rights of the owner of the land.

amortization of loan. Repayment of debt through installments of principal payments.

amortization schedule. A schedule specifying loan payments to be applied to reduction of the principal balance. Most loans call for a constant monthly payment of interest and principal where the portion allocable to principal increases as the balance of the loan and the interest needed to service the loan decreases.

amortization term. The time period over which the principal amount would be retired on the basis of periodic installments specified to be paid. Not to be confused with the **mortgage term** (see below).

anchor tenants. The largest tenants in a shopping center, usually the department stores. The strength of the anchor tenants greatly affects the rentability of the smaller stores and the availability of financing for the shopping center. The term may also be used to describe a major tenant in an office building, industrial park, etc.

appraisal. An opinion of value based upon a factual analysis by a disinterested person of suitable qualifications.

appraisal methods. In an appraisal, the valuation is usually based on three major methods: cost approach, income approach, market value (comparables) approach.

appraiser. An individual who has the experience, training, and legal qualifications to appraise or value real or personal property. Appraisers must be certified or licensed by the state in order to appraise property involving a federally insured or regulated agency.

"as is" condition. The condition of a property existing at the time of the sale or the signing of a lease for occupancy of a particular space. An "as is" clause is used to limit the warranty of the lessor or seller. Also referred to as an "as is, where is" clause.

assemblage. The acquisition of contiguous properties into one ownership for a specific use.

assessed value. Value placed upon a property for real estate tax purposes by the local tax assessors, generally broken down between land and building values.

assignment of lease. The transfer by a lessee to a third party of the exact interest of said lessee. It differs from and should not be confused with a sublease. Assignment and/or subleasing may be restricted in the lease.

assumption of mortgage. Agreement by a buyer to assume the liability under an existing note secured by a mortgage or deed of trust. The lender usually must approve the new buyer. The existing debtors may or may not be released from their liability.

basis for depreciation. The value of property for purposes of depreciation. Generally, the property's basis is calculated by adding the total costs of acquisition and the costs of capital improvements less the value of the land.

blanket mortgage. (1) A mortgage covering more than one property of the mortgagor, such as a mortgage covering all the lots of a builder in a subdivision. (2) A mortgage covering all real property of the mortgagor.

blueprint. A plan of a building in such detail as to enable contractors to build or remodel space. The name comes from the photographic process that produces the plan in white on a blue background.

bridge or gap financing. A form of interim loan made to cover a temporary cash shortfall.

build to suit. A method of constructing property whereby the contractor customizes the building to the user's specifications, often at a previously agreed-to price or rental.

building code. A comprehensive set of state or municipal laws that control the construction or remodeling of buildings, including design, materials used, and construction methods.

capitalization rate. Also known as "cap rate." A rate of return used to calculate the capital value of an unlevered income stream. In a way, it is the inverse of a price/earnings ratio. The formula is *value equals the net operating income divided by the cap* rate. Because the cap rate is applied to only one year of income, it is often referred to as the "current expected yield before capital expenditures." The income stream may be based on the current, prior, or stabilized year.

carrying charges. (1) The costs of owning a property that has not yet reached positive cash flow. (2) The financing costs of a property.

cash flow after financing. Equal to **cash flow from operations** (see below) less any financing charges such as interest and principal payments or any ground lease payments.

cash flow from operations. Net operating income (see below) less an allowance for normal capital expenditures and leasing costs.

C-corporation. The standard legal form of corporate entity, in which all shareholders own stock in the company and have liability limited to their invested capital. Profits in a C-corporation are taxed at the corporate level, which is not the case with profits in a Subchapter S corporation (see below). In addition, shareholders are subject to taxation on dividends from the corporation.

certificate of occupancy. A certificate issued by a local building department stating that the building has met all applicable codes and is in proper condition to be occupied.

closed-end fund. A fund (sometimes dealing in real estate or mortgages) that does not accept new investors. The shares generally are not sold and redeemed through the fund but on the open market. The fund may have a limited offering time frame and a predetermined life span.

closing statement. The statement that lists details of the financial settlement between buyer and seller (and sometimes lender). Costs include not only the transfer price of the property, but also such items as transfer taxes, recording costs, title insurance, allocated operating expenses including property taxes, and other payments or fees due at the closing such as to third-party brokers.

cluster zoning. Zoning allowing the construction of buildings closer together than otherwise permitted under the zoning code. As compensation the balance of the property is kept as open space, often under common ownership.

commercial mortgage-backed securities (CMBS). A group of mortgages that are packaged together and sold as bonds. The mortgage packages may be broken up into tranches of varying durations and risks. Investors are able to diversify the geographic and property-type risk as well as obtain greater liquidity.

commingled fund. Also known as "pooled fund." A real estate mutual fund in which the investments of multiple investors are lumped together and generally invested in a variety of properties, in either **open-end funds** (see below) or **closed-end funds** (see above).

common area. For lease purposes, the areas of land and building that are available for the nonexclusive use of all its tenants, e.g., lobbies, corridors, parking lots.

common area maintenance (CAM). Office, retail, and warehouse tenants and condominium owners often pay, on a proportionate basis, CAM charges, through which they collectively reimburse the landlord for certain agreed-upon expenses that relate to such items as maintenance, servicing of common areas, management, and in the case of retail centers, advertising and promotion.

condominium property. A structure of two or more units in which the interior space of each unit is individually owned and the balance of the property (both land and buildings) is owned in common by the owners of the individual units. The size of each unit is measured from the interior surfaces (exclusive of paint or other finishes) of the exterior walls, floors, and ceiling. The balance of the property is called the common area, and generally is collectively maintained through CAM charges assessed to unit owners.

cooperative property. A structure of two or more spaces in which the right to occupy a defined space is given in return for the purchase of stock in a corporation that owns the property. Shareholders also agree to pay their share of the common expenses of the property.

cost of occupancy. The total cost (usually paid monthly) to occupy a property. Such costs include not only basic rent, but additional charges paid to the landlord or paid directly by the tenant for such items as utilities, property taxes, insurance, cleaning, and maintenance including real estate taxes.

cost-plus contract. A building contract setting the builder's profit at a set percentage of the actual cost of labor, materials, and an agreed-upon overhead.

current yield. A measurement of investment returns based on the percentage relationship of current, annual cash income to the actual cost or the current value of the property.

custom builder. One who builds for a specific owner, designing the building in advance to suit said owner's need, rather than building for outside sale.

dark store clause. A clause usually found in retail store leases stating that the tenant must stay open for business, i.e., the lights cannot go out.

debt or loan constant. The percentage relationship of the annual financing payments of interest and principal to the initial face amount of the loan. For example, a $1,000 loan at 9% interest repaid over a 20-year period has a constant payment of 10.8%.

deed in lieu of foreclosure. A deed given by an owner/borrower to a lender to prevent the lender from bringing foreclosure proceedings on the property being held as security.

depreciable life. The number of years over which an asset is depreciated, either for income tax purposes (as determined by federal IRS regulation) or for financial reporting purposes (as determined by general accounting standards).

depreciable property. Property for which a useful life can be determined for depreciation purposes. For example: a building and its improvements are depreciable, but the land under it is not, as it is deemed to have an unlimited life.

depreciation. (1) Decrease in value to real property improvements caused by physical, economic, or functional deterioration or obsolescence. (2) A loss in value expressed as a deduction for income tax or financial statement purposes.

direct reduction mortgage. A mortgage on which the level of principal payments stays constant, with interest being computed on the remaining balance. The amount of the total payment declines as the principal balance of the mortgage is reduced.

due diligence. The process of underwriting a property by a prospective buyer or lender prior to the legal closing of a transaction. It encompasses a wide range of activities ranging from physical and environmental inspections, to verifying the validity of leases, to examining the legal title to the property.

easement. The right, privilege, or interest that one party has in the land of another, such as for a utility line to pass through a property.

EBITDA. Earnings before interest, taxes, depreciation, and amortization. It is often used in measuring the performance of a public company.

eminent domain. The right of the government or a public utility to acquire property for necessary public use by condemnation. The owner must be fairly compensated.

enterprise or franchise value. The perceived ability of a management team to add value and generate growth in **funds from operations** (see below). Used often in valuing **real estate investment trusts** (see below).

environmental impact report (EIR). A report of the probable environmental effects of a development on the site and its surrounding area, looking at such features as air quality, traffic, volume, and soil erosion. It also evaluates the proposed building's compliance with certain environmental standards and regulations as well as the existing soil and building conditions. The report is prepared by an independent company to guidelines set by regulators, lenders, or potential purchasers. A Phase I report primarily reviews the history of and title to the site and involves a visual inspection whereas a Phase II assessment involves more physical testing of the soil.

equity. (1) Any ownership investment (stocks, real estate, etc.) as opposed to an investment in a debt instrument. (2) The market value of real property, less the amount of existing liens. (3) A legal doctrine based on fairness, rather than strict interpretation of the letter of the law.

ERISA. The Employee Retirement Income Security Act is a law that governs the operation of most private pension and benefit plans. The act established guidelines for the management of pension fund assets and stimulated investment in areas such as real estate for diversification purposes.

escalation clause. A clause in a lease providing for an increased rental at a future time based on (1) a predetermined amount, (2) a cost of living adjustment using a particular index, or (3) an increase in prescribed expenses.

estoppel. A doctrine of law that stops one from later denying facts that were once acknowledged to be true and others accepted on good faith. Estoppel agreements confirming existing lease terms and specifying any current defaults under the lease are often obtained from existing tenants prior to a new owner's taking possession of a property or prior to a new loan's being put on record. The procedure for obtaining the estoppel agreement is spelled out in the lease.

fair market value. The price that would likely be negotiated between a willing seller and a willing buyer in an arm's length or independent transaction over a reasonable time frame.

financial leverage. Given the use of debt in a capital structure, the resulting financial leverage can be either positive or negative. For example: If the cost of the debt, i.e., the principal and interest payment, is 8% and the **return on assets** is 10%, an increase in the amount of the loan will increase the return on assets. Conversely, if the debt constant is 11%, an increase in debt will result in negative leverage.

financing costs. Debt or mortgage payments of principal and interest, often in the form of a constant payment that amortizes the loan over a given time period.

first refusal right. The right to match an existing offer either to lease or to purchase an existing property usually within a specified time frame.

floor area ratio (FAR). The ratio obtained by dividing the gross floor area of all buildings located upon a lot or parcel of land by the total area of the lot or parcel. Zoning ordinances regularly prescribe maximum allowable floor area ratios, as well as height restrictions. Depending on local rules, some square footage—such as space used for underground parking—may be excluded in calculating floor area.

foreclosure sale. A sale of property used as security for a debt, to satisfy a default. Sale is often at public auction.

frontage. The linear measurement along the front of a parcel or space, or in some cases along the side abutting a waterway or walkway.

full disclosure. In real estate, revealing all the known facts that may affect the decision of a buyer or tenant.

funds from operations (FFO). A performance measure used to analyze REITs. FFO is determined by starting with net income, adding back real estate related–depreciation and amortization, and then deducting for nonrecurring items such as gains or losses on asset sales. REIT prices are often described and compared in terms of an FFO multiple, which is the ratio of price to FFO.

general partner. In a partnership, the partner who conducts the business and whose liability is not limited. All partners in an ordinary partnership are general partners. A limited partnership must have at least one general partner, which may be an individual or a corporation.

grandfather clause. The clause in a law permitting the continuation of a use, business, etc. that, when established, was permissible but, because of a change in the law, is now not permissible.

gross area. The entire physical area of all floor space in a parcel of land or in a building, often measured in square feet or square meters.

gross lease. A lease that obligates the lessor to pay all or part of the operating expenses of the leased property, such as real estate taxes, insurance, maintenance, and utilities as well as the base rent.

ground lease. A lease of vacant land, or land exclusive of the building on it, usually obtained so that the lessor can develop a building or otherwise generate cash from the site. It is usually written as a net lease with the lessee paying all expenses.

ground rent. Rent paid for vacant land. If the property is improved, ground rent is that portion attributable to the land only, although the amount of the payment may reflect the value of the building on it.

hard costs. Development costs for tangible improvements, such as roads and sidewalks, shell construction, finish-out of units, and landscaping.

highest and best use. The use of land under its current legal strictures that will produce the highest economic value, and which is legally, physically, and financially feasible.

holdover tenant. A tenant who retains possession after the expiration of a lease.

holdback. Portion of a loan or payment held back until a contingency is met.

housing starts. Number of houses or units on which construction has begun. The figures are used to determine the availability of housing, the need for real estate loans, the need for labor and materials, etc.

HVAC. Heating, ventilating, and air conditioning system.

institutional lenders. Banks, insurance companies, pension funds, and other similar businesses that make loans to the public in the ordinary course of business.

internal rate of return (IRR). The discount rate at which the present value of the future cash flows of an investment equals the cost of the investment. It is used to measure the annual return on a given investment and to compare different investment opportunities.

junior mortgage. Any mortgage secondary to or of lesser priority than a first mortgage.

land bank. An accumulation of land held for future use.

land grant. A gift of public land to a state or local government, corporation, or individual.

land residual valuation. An appraisal technique to determine land value by first calculating the value of a current or proposed development, and then deducting the total cost of the current or proposed improvements including a developer's profit. It attributes any additional value to the land itself.

landlord. An owner of leased real estate.

lease. An agreement by which an owner of real property (lessor) gives the right of possession to another (lessee), for a specified period of time (term), for a specified consideration (rent), and under certain conditions.

lease with option to purchase. A lease under which the lessee has the right to purchase the property. The price and terms of the purchase or the procedure for establishing the price must be set forth for the option to be valid. The option may run for the length of the lease or for only a portion of the lease period.

lessee. A party who is given use of an asset through a lease agreement in return for a consideration, generally rent.

lessor. A party who gives use of an asset through a lease agreement for a consideration, generally rent.

letter of commitment or letter of intent. When the **term sheet** (see below) is signed, it is called either a letter of commitment or a letter of intent. Such a letter may or may not have a penalty or damages for nonperformance.

letting. A synonym for leasing, often used in Great Britain.

lien. A voluntary or involuntary encumbrance against property to insure a monetary obligation. All liens are encumbrances but all encumbrances are not liens.

limited liability corporation (LLC). A type of company, authorized in most states, whose owners and managers receive the limited liability and (usually) the tax benefits of a Subchapter S corporation (see below) without having to conform to the Subchapter S restrictions. Many real estate investors who in the past faced a difficult choice between forming a general or limited partnership and a Subchapter S or C-corporation have chosen the LLC as a "bridge" between the two.

limited partner. Contributor of a capital to a limited partnership, who does not participate in running the business and is liable only up to the amount of his or her contributed capital.

listing. An agreement between an owner of real property and a real estate agent, whereby the agent agrees to attempt to secure a buyer or tenant for a specific property at a certain price and terms, in return for a fee or commission if the transaction is consummated.

listing agent. A real estate agent obtaining a **listing** (see above) from the seller, but who may or may not actually sell the property.

load factor. (1) The ratio of rentable to usable space in a building. It can serve as a measure of design efficiency. (2) The amount of weight per square foot that the floor can support.

loan coverage ratio. The ratio of the annual cash flow from operations to the carrying cost of the debt. Lenders use it as a measure of security for the loan.

loan origination fee. A one-time fee charged by the lender for making or committing to make a loan.

loan servicing. The bookkeeping, monitoring, and collection of a loan. It may be done by the lender or by a third party for the lender.

loan to value or cost ratio. A key underwriting ratio, expressed as a percentage, derived by taking the amount of a loan and dividing by the value or projected selling price or the cost of real property. Usually, the higher the ratio, the greater the interest charged, because of the perceived greater risk.

lot. Generally, any parcel of real property. Often refers to a portion in a subdivision.

lot line. The boundary line of a lot.

management fee. (1) The amount paid for property management calculated either as a percentage of collected revenues or as a fixed fee. (2) The amount paid for the overall management of an investment calculated as a percentage of value, cost, or income.

master lease. A lease for an entire or a portion of a property that may be subdivided into subsequent leases.

master plan. A zoning or development plan for an entire area.

maturity. The time when a note becomes due in its entirety.

mechanic's lien. A lien created by statute to secure priority of payment for the price or value of work performed and materials furnished in construction or repair of improvements to land, and which attaches to the land.

minimum lot size. The smallest allowable lot size for development of a particular use, as stipulated by local zoning laws.

minimum rental. A base rental in a lease. There may be additional charges for certain operating costs, a rise in the cost of living, or in the case of a lease for a retail store, a percentage of sales over a certain level.

mini perm. A loan generally of 5 years to cover not only the construction period but also the initial years of rent-up and operation.

month to month tenancy. A tenancy where tenant's occupancy can be terminated by either party on 1 month's notice, sometimes referred to as a "tenant at will." There may or may not be a written lease between the parties. Some jurisdictions may have additional restrictions on termination by a **landlord.**

mortgage. (1) To hypothecate, or pledge as security, real property for the payment of a debt. The borrower (mortgagor) retains possession and use of the property. (2) The instrument by which real estate is hypothecated as security for the repayment of a loan.

mortgage or loan broker. One who, for a fee, brings together a borrower and a lender and handles the necessary applications for the borrower to obtain a loan against real property.

mortgage constant. The percentage relationship between the total of monthly principal and interest payments on a loan and the original face amount of the loan.

mortgage term. The original or remaining number of years to maturity of a mortgage loan. If the mortgage term is less than the **amortization term** (see above), there will be some principal still outstanding at the loan's maturity. All such principal is due upon maturity in a lump-sum payment known as a "balloon payment."

mortgagee. The party making a loan and receiving the mortgage payments. The loan is secured by a lien on the property.

mortgagor. The party who borrows the money and grants the mortgage lien.

negative cash flow. When the income from an investment property does not equal its expenses. The owner may have to come up with cash from other asset sources to meet these expenses.

net lease. A lease requiring the tenant to pay, in addition to a fixed rental, certain specified expenses of the property leased, such as real estate taxes, insurance, or maintenance. Some refer to this arrangement as a "triple net lease."

net operating income. Income from property after operating expenses have been deducted, but before financing expenses (interest and principal payments), depreciation, capital expenditures, tenant improvements, leasing commissions, and income taxes have been deducted.

net present value. The calculation that discounts at a predescribed rate of return, generally on an annual basis, the net cash flows from operating and selling a property net of the discounted value of the original or future cash investments.

nonconforming use. A use that violates zoning regulations or codes but is allowed to continue because it began before the zoning restriction was enacted.

nonexclusive listing. A listing under which the real estate broker is given the right to sell a property, but the owner is not obligated to pay a commission if the property is sold directly or through another broker. Also called an "agency agreement."

nonrecourse loan. A loan in which the lender's only recourse in the event of default is the security (property) and the borrower is not personally liable.

notice to quit. A notice by a landlord to a tenant to vacate rented property for nonpayment of rent or another default. The notice for nonpayment may grant the borrower a specified time to cure the default.

occupancy rate. (1) The ratio of actual income to the income if the property were fully rented. (2) The ratio of square footage leased to total rentable square footage. (3) The ratio of units rented to total number of units.

open-space ratio. Ratio of space without buildings on a site to its total lot size. This ratio is often a zoning requirement.

open-end fund. A **commingled fund** (see above) in which investors can invest or divest at a specified time, much like a stock mutual fund albeit less liquid. Its value is usually based on an independent appraisal.

operating expenses. The costs of physically operating, managing, and providing services to an income-producing property. Such costs do not include any capital or financing expenditures.

operating leverage. The disproportionate effect of increasing or decreasing cash flow from operations on the cash flow after financing. The effect is disproportionate because of the fixed level of financing expenses.

opportunity fund. A pooled investment fund that buys distressed properties.

option. A right given for consideration, to purchase or lease property at an agreed-upon basis, within a specified time.

option for additional space. An option as defined above to rent additional space in a particular property.

origination fee. A fee paid to a lender for making a real estate loan, usually a percentage of the amount loaned.

overage income or rental. Rental that exceeds the base rent. May be from a percentage of the tenant's sales (see **percentage lease**) or some other agreed-upon formula.

overhang (for REITs). For **REITs** (see below), a large increase in the number of shares outstanding available for trading after an initial public offering, or an acquisition in which certain shareholders are precluded from selling stock until a certain date.

overhang (supply and demand). An oversupply of a particular property type in a particular market.

override. A disproportionate share of the profits of a partnership, given to the general partner or the promoter under the terms of the **partnership** or venture **agreement** (see below).

paper. A mortgage, deed of trust, or land contract, that is given instead of cash. A seller would take "paper" if he or she received a mortgage, deed of trust, or land contract as part of the purchase price.

parking ratio. The ratio of parking spaces to building area. For example: A rule of thumb for suburban office use may be 3 or 4 parking spaces per 1,000 square feet, and for apartment use, 1 to 2 parking spaces per unit.

partnership agreement. A legal document that spells out all of the relationships among the partners to a deal.

percentage lease. A lease, generally on a retail business property, using a percentage of the gross or net sales to determine the rent. There is usually a minimum or base rental.

permanent mortgage. A mortgage for a long period of time, usually at least ten years. The mortgage is normally obtained at the end of construction and lease-up or the acquisition or refinancing of a seasoned property.

PITI. Principal, Interest, Real Estate Taxes, and Insurance. The ratio of PITI to a buyer's total income is used by lenders as a test to determine a borrower's ability to repay a home loan.

planning commission. A board of a municipality that must approve or make recommendations in regard to proposed building projects, rezoning, or other related regulatory changes.

plans. Architectural drawings related to a construction project. Depending on the level of detail, the plans may be called preliminary or conceptual design drawings or, if more comprehensive, detailed plans and specifications or working drawings.

preliminary title report. A report showing the condition of legal title before a sale or loan transaction. At completion of the transaction, a title insurance policy or final report is issued.

prepayment penalty. A penalty under a note, mortgage, or deed of trust imposed if the loan is paid before it is due.

prime tenant. The major tenant in a building. It may be necessary to have a prime tenant in order to obtain financing. The tenant may be considered "prime" because of its financial strength and/or because of the amount of space it occupies. (See also **anchor tenant**).

principal. (1) A person who has, as a result of managing an investment or directed legal authority, the right to act for an entity. (2) Amount of a debt, not including interest.

profitability index. The ratio of the net present value of an investment to the total investment. It is sometimes a useful measure of comparison between various investment opportunities involving different capital contributions.

property management. The branch of the real estate business that involves the management of property. Tasks may include accounting, bill paying, tenant relations, physical operations, rent collection, construction management, and leasing activities.

property tax. Generally, a tax levied on either real or personal property. The amount of the tax is usually based on the assessed value for a particular property and the overall tax rate for similar properties in that community.

purchase and sale agreement. An agreement between a buyer and seller of real property, setting forth the price and terms of the sale. When signed by both parties it is a binding contract.

purchase money mortgage. A mortgage given from buyer to seller to secure all or a portion of the purchase price. It may or may not reflect the same terms that would be given by an independent lender.

real estate. Land and anything permanently affixed to that land, such as buildings. It also includes fences, and other attachments to the buildings, including light fixtures, plumbing and heating fixtures, and other items that would be personal property if not attached. The term is generally synonymous with "real property."

real estate investment trust (REIT). A real estate mutual fund that does not pay corporate-level tax on its income, provided (among other things) that 95% percent of net income is paid out in dividends. It sells shares of ownership and must invest primarily in real estate or mortgages. It must meet certain other requirements, including minimum number of shareholders, widely dispersed ownership, and asset and income tests.

real estate owned (R.E.O.). Most commonly refers to property owned by a lender, especially a commercial bank, as a result of foreclosure on a mortgage or trust deed. This property is usually being held for sale by banks, as they are prohibited from investing in speculative real estate as equity owners.

recourse. The right of the holder of a note secured by a mortgage or deed of trust to look not just to the property, but personally to other assets of the borrower or endorser for payment.

red-lining. The outlining on a map of alleged high-risk areas for real estate loan purposes. This means lenders will not extend credit in these areas for real property loans, regardless of the qualifications of the applicant. Some states have passed laws against this practice. The use of a red pen or pencil for the outlining gave rise to the term.

refinancing. Placing a new loan on a property to replace an existing loan without changing ownership.

renewal option. The right of a tenant upon notice to renew or extend the term of a lease for a stated period of time and consideration.

rent. Consideration paid for the occupancy and use of real property.

rent control. A legally mandated limit on rental payments and/or increases in rental payments. It usually applies only to residential property.

rentable area. The area for which rent can be charged. Generally it is the gross area of the full floor, less the area of all vertical penetrations (elevator shafts, stairwells, mechanical shafts, etc.). Rentable area includes the tenant's premises plus an allocation of the common areas directly benefiting the tenant, such as restrooms, first-floor lobby, common corridors, mechanical and janitor's rooms, and the elevator lobby on the tenant's floor.

replacement cost. The current total cost to construct a building having the same utility as the subject building but using modern techniques and materials.

reserve. A setting aside of funds, usually for indefinite contingencies such as future maintenance of structure or re-leasing costs, or for payment of certain operating costs such as insurance or real estate taxes.

return on assets. A performance measure obtained by dividing annual cash flow from operations by total property cost. Used most often by lenders to make certain there is sufficient cash flow to service the debt. It is a static measure that looks at only one year of performance, without considering tax effects or the effects of any future sale or refinancing.

return on equity. (1) A performance measure, also known as *cash on cash* return, derived by dividing the annual cash flow after financing (CFAF) by the initial equity. Because CFAF is a pretax measure, the return on equity calculation omits any tax effect. It also ignores the effect of any future sale or refinancing. The year used for measurement could be based on historical, current or projected results. (2) The total return on equity over the term of ownership of a property.

sale-leaseback. A sale and subsequent lease from the buyer back to the seller. Both transactions take place at the same time. It may be a way for the seller to obtain capital. The income tax consequences of such a transaction may be treated differently from its cash allocations.

second mortgage. A mortgage that ranks after a first mortgage in priority. (See also **junior mortgage.**) Properties may have two, three, or more mortgages, deeds of trust, or land contracts as liens at the same time. Legal priority would determine whether they are called a first, second, or third (etc.) lien.

security deposit. Commonly a deposit of money by a tenant to a landlord to secure performance of a written or oral agreement.

shared appreciation. The allocation of increases in cash flow among various parties.

site development. All improvements made to the land to enable construction of a building, such as grading, roads, and utilities.

soft costs. Development costs for all items other than tangible improvements. Typical soft costs include architectural, engineering, and legal fees, property taxes, marketing and leasing costs, and construction-period interest.

specifications. Detailed, written instructions, usually issued in conjunction with architectural drawings, defining how construction is to be performed.

Subchapter S corporation. A corporation that is allowed by the Internal Revenue Code to be taxed as if it were a partnership. It must have 35 or fewer shareholders and meet several other requirements of the code. Thus a small corporation can distribute its income directly to shareholders and avoid the corporate income tax while enjoying the other advantages of the corporate form, such as limited liability.

sublease. A lease under which the sublessor assumes the obligations of all or part of a prior lease of the same property. The sublease may be different in terms from the original lease but cannot be for a longer term.

syndication. An arrangement by which two or more people are assembled for the purpose of raising equity capital for purchasing real estate. Many properties are too expensive for an average investor to purchase alone. Therefore, in order to purchase such properties jointly, it is common for investors to combine their resources and establish a vehicle such as a corporation, cooperative, condominium, joint venture, or partnership.

takeout loan. The "permanent" financing of real estate after completion of construction, generally for a term of 10 years or longer. The loan replaces, or "takes out," the construction loan.

tenant. A holder of property under a lease or other rental agreement.

tenant improvement allowance (TIs). The amount of money, usually measured per square foot, that the owner will pay for customizing and preparing the tenant's space at time of initial or subsequent leasing. It is generally a capital expenditure and must be amortized as such for tax purposes. TIs are subject to negotiations that may be affected by changing market conditions as well as by changing consumer preferences.

term sheet. An outline of the conditions and arrangements to be specified in a formal contract, such as for a lease or loan.

title. The evidence one has of right to possession of land, subject to deeds and restrictions of record.

title insurance. Insurance against loss resulting from defects of title to a specifically described parcel of real property. Defects may relate to the fee (chain of title) or to encumbrances.

title search. A review of all recorded documents and regulations affecting a specific piece of property to determine the present condition of title.

transfer tax. An ad valorem tax on the transfer of real property based on the purchase price or amount of money changing hands. The amount of the tax varies by locality. Also called "documentary transfer tax."

underlying financing. A mortgage, trust deed, or land contract with priority over another mortgage, trust deed, or land contract.

unit. An individual apartment, condominium, or house in a larger property or subdivision, etc.

UPREIT. A type of **REIT** (see above) that does not own its properties directly but owns a controlling interest in a limited partnership that owns the REIT's real estate. If instead of receiving cash or REIT shares, property owners selling to the REIT take UPREIT "units," which are convertible into REIT shares, the sale is tax deferred until either the units are converted to REIT shares or the property is sold. Until converted, the shares are nonvoting.

upset price. A term signifying the minimum price at which a property may be sold.

usable area. The secured area occupied exclusively by the tenant within the tenant's leased space. The usable area, plus the tenant's proportionate share of common areas, results in rentable area upon which a per square foot rent is charged.

vacancy allowance or factor. On a pro forma income statement, the amount of income estimated to be lost as a result of space for which no rent is paid. It may be based on historical, projected, or comparable rentals.

variance. After a legal process, change of certain zoning requirements for a specific property without changing the overall zoning for other properties in that district.

working drawings. Drawing used to direct construction, and showing all details, such as for structure, mechanical systems, electric, HVAC, plumbing, partitions, and other materials to be installed.

zoning. The division of a city or county by legislative regulations into areas (*zones*), specifying the uses allowable for the real property in these areas, as well as height, setback, parking, and other restrictions.

zoning ordinance. A law (generally at the city or county level) controlling the use of land and construction of improvements in a given area (*zone*).

INDEX